Empowering Educational Development and Faculty Growth With AI

Nathan Pritts
https://orcid.org/0009-0000-7669-4721
University of Arizona Global Campus, USA

IGI Global
Scientific Publishing
Publishing Tomorrow's Research Today

Vice President of Editorial Melissa Wagner
Director of Acquisitions Mikaela Felty
Director of Book Development Jocelynn Hessler
Production Manager Mike Brehm
Cover Design Jose Rosado

Published in the United States of America by
IGI Global Scientific Publishing
701 East Chocolate Avenue
Hershey, PA, 17033, USA
Tel: 717-533-8845 | Fax: 717-533-7115
Website: https://www.igi-global.com E-mail: cust@igi-global.com

Library of Congress Cataloging-in-Publication Data

LCCN: (CIP Data Pending)
ISBN13: 9798337341293
Isbn13Softcover: 9798337341309
EISBN13: 9798337341316
British Cataloguing in Publication Data
A Cataloguing in Publication record for this book is available from the British Library.

Table of Contents

Preface xiii

Chapter 1
A Reflective Case Study on Course Creation: "AI, Power, and the Social Construction of Knowledge" 1
JoAnna Boudreaux, University of Memphis, USA

Chapter 2
Cultivating AI Literacies: A Taxonomy for Sociocultural Praxis and Academic Transformation 33
Angela Gunder, The University of Arizona, USA
Joshua Herron, Clemson University, USA
Nicole Weber, The University of Wisconsin, Whitewater, USA
Colette Anderson Chelf, Independent Researcher, USA

Chapter 3
Balancing AI-Driven Innovation With Authentic Learning in Higher Education 71
O. Bhaskaru, Vignan's Foundation for Science, Technology, and Research, India
K. Lalitha, Santhiram Engineering College, India

Chapter 4
AI-Enhanced Instructional Design and Curriculum Development for Next-Generation Learning Ecosystems in Higher Education 103
Aliye Saraç, Istanbul Topkapi University, Turkey

Chapter 5
The Role of AI in Reshaping Curriculum Structures for Future Learners 141
Punam Kumari, Amity University, India

Chapter 6
Artificial Intelligence as Faculty Development and Learning Innovation 173
Parveen Sharma, Lovely Professional University, India

Chapter 7
From Automation to Innovation: AI as a Catalyst for Faculty Growth.............. 203
Amrik Singh, Lovely Professional University, India

Chapter 8
Personalized Professional Growth: AI as a Mentor for Educators..................... 227
Arun Agrawal, Institute of Technology and Management, Gwalior, India
Dhanashri Rohidas Londhe, Zeal College of Engineering and Research, Pune, India
Komal Vikrant Rajgude, Nutan Maharashtra Institute of Engineering and Technology, India
Vaibhavi Avachat, Nutan Maharashtra Institute of Engineering and Technology, India
Mukesh Kumar Tripathi, KIET Group of Institutions, Delhi, India
Brijendra Gupta, Siddhant College of Engineering, Pune, India
Deepak Gupta, Institute of Technology and Management, Gwalior, India

Chapter 9
Co-Creating the Future: Collaborative Strategies for Integrating AI Into Faculty Development Initiatives 253
Pritesh Pradeep Somani, Balaji Institute of International Business, Sri Balaji University, Pune, India
Prachi Wani, Balaji Institute of Management and Human Resource Development, Sri Balaji University, Pune, India
Vishwanathan Hariharan Iyer, Balaji Institute of International Business, Sri Balaji University, Pune, India
Ushmita Gupta, Balaji Institute of International Business, Sri Balaji University, Pune, India

Chapter 10
Radical Transparency as an Antidote to Unclear Expectations for Generative AI Use 273
Jennifer C. Friberg-Fort, Illinois State University, USA
David Giovagnoli, Illinois State University, USA

Chapter 11
The Role of Educational Developers in AI Integration at Scale 289
R. N. Ravikumar, Marwadi University, Rajkot, India
S. Aarthi, Marwadi University, Rajkot, India

Chapter 12
Scaling Faculty AI Literacy: Strategic Models for Institutional Transformation and Sustainable Adoption 323
Ramadevi Vitthal Salunkhe, G.H. Raisoni College of Engineering, Nagpur, India
Chetan Arun Raut, St. Vincent Pallotti College of Engineering and Technology, Nagpur, India
Gunjan Chimote, Ramdeobaba University, Nagpur, India
Shruti Sarwate, Jain University, India
Roshan Ramesh Kolte, K.D.K. College of Engineering, Nagpur, India
Piyush K. Ingole, Yeshwantrao Chavan College of Engineering, Nagpur, India
Annaji Kuthe, K.D.K. College of Engineering, Nagpur, India

Compilation of References 369

About the Contributors 399

Index 405

Detailed Table of Contents

Preface xiii

Chapter 1
A Reflective Case Study on Course Creation: "AI, Power, and the Social Construction of Knowledge" 1
JoAnna Boudreaux, University of Memphis, USA

This chapter presents a case study on designing and implementing the undergraduate course AI and the Social Construction of Knowledge at a public university. The course was developed in response to students' growing reliance on AI-generated content and the rapid adoption of AI tools across disciplines, highlighting a cultural lag between technological innovation and institutional adaptation. By situating AI as a sociological object, the course emphasizes critical engagement, collaborative inquiry, and ethical knowledge production. The chapter details course rationale, learning objectives, assignments, and an Academic Integrity and AI Policy, while reflecting on key design decisions. It illustrates how social science educators can guide students in interrogating AI critically and ethically, positioning learners as active participants in the ongoing social construction of knowledge.

Chapter 2
Cultivating AI Literacies: A Taxonomy for Sociocultural Praxis and Academic Transformation 33
Angela Gunder, The University of Arizona, USA
Joshua Herron, Clemson University, USA
Nicole Weber, The University of Wisconsin, Whitewater, USA
Colette Anderson Chelf, Independent Researcher, USA

This chapter introduces The Dimensions of AI Literacies taxonomy (Gunder et al., 2024), a socioculturally grounded model for guiding ethical, accessible, and adaptable engagement with artificial intelligence (AI) in education. Building on literacy studies (Gee, 1999; Street, 1984), digital literacies (Belshaw, 2012), and open remix culture (Gunder, 2021), the authors frame AI literacies as plural, evolving combinations of skillsets and mindsets that differ across context, role, and community. Eight interwoven dimensions—cultural, cognitive, constructive, communicative, confident, creative, critical, and civic—are outlined to show how they emerge in practice and form "constellations of AI literacies" that strengthen institutional and community capacity. Using a culinary metaphor and a values-driven lens, the chapter reframes AI integration as a cultural and pedagogical opportunity, inviting educators, designers, and leaders to co-create AI-enabled ecosystems that are relational, reflective, resilient, and responsive to change.

Chapter 3
Balancing AI-Driven Innovation With Authentic Learning in Higher Education 71
O. Bhaskaru, Vignan's Foundation for Science, Technology, and Research, India
K. Lalitha, Santhiram Engineering College, India

Artificial Intelligence (AI) is increasingly shaping higher education by enhancing instructional design, assessments, and student engagement. While AI offers benefits like adaptive learning, predictive analytics, and smart feedback, it also challenges the preservation of authentic learning, which values real-world relevance, critical thinking, collaboration, and student agency. This chapter examines how educators and institutions can balance AI innovation with maintaining authentic pedagogy by proposing a framework that integrates AI tools while supporting core authentic learning principles. It draws on educational theory, case studies, and practical examples to show how AI can enhance teaching without undermining learning quality. Additionally, it addresses challenges such as faculty readiness, ethical issues, and policy gaps, offering recommendations for professional development, curriculum updates, and policy to ensure responsible AI use. The aim is to help educators and administrators foster environments where AI-driven innovation and authentic learning coexist effectively.

Chapter 4
AI-Enhanced Instructional Design and Curriculum Development for Next-Generation Learning Ecosystems in Higher Education 103
Aliye Saraç, Istanbul Topkapi University, Turkey

This chapter examines Artificial Intelligence (AI) as a transformative force in higher education, focusing on instructional design and curriculum development. AI is framed as a human-centered, ethical, and pedagogically aligned partner for creating flexible, inclusive, and future-ready ecosystems. Using models such as ADDIE, TPACK, and UDL, it highlights AI's role in learner analysis, adaptive content, real-time monitoring, and personalized evaluation. Applications include adaptive platforms, AI-driven feedback, and inclusive design, supported by LMS, LXP, analytics, and advising. Ethical issues like privacy, fairness, and accessibility are emphasized, presenting AI as a catalyst for adaptive and coherent education.

Chapter 5
The Role of AI in Reshaping Curriculum Structures for Future Learners 141
Punam Kumari, Amity University, India

This chapter will explore how Artificial Intelligence (AI) is fundamentally transforming curriculum design, development, and delivery in educational systems worldwide. Traditional curriculum structures often lack the flexibility to accommodate diverse learner needs, evolving job markets, and interdisciplinary knowledge demands. Through AI-driven insights, institutions can create dynamic, adaptive, and personalized curricula that continuously evolve based on learner performance data, emerging industry trends, and societal needs. The chapter highlights models of AI integration, ethical concerns, and future directions for curriculum innovation.

Chapter 6
Artificial Intelligence as Faculty Development and Learning Innovation 173
Parveen Sharma, Lovely Professional University, India

Artificial intelligence (AI) has been taking over the higher education sector and is likewise playing a role that defines the professional growth of faculty members. This chapter discusses how campus-wide AI based solutions can be used to enable faculty to grow through improved training, advanced learning analytics and to offer personalized professional learning at scale. A conceptual model is proposed to identify the 3 key pillars of AI in faculty development, including (i) AI in training and skill enhancement delivered via intelligent platforms, virtual simulations, etc; (ii) AI-based learning analytics to obtain actionable insights out of classroom interactions, with assessments, and predictive performance tools; and (iii) personalized professional learning driven by adaptive modules, AI tutors, and career pathway guidance. In addition, an AI benefits map is presented to show how these applications can be used to serve faculty responsibilities in the context of teaching, research, administration and mentoring.

Chapter 7
From Automation to Innovation: AI as a Catalyst for Faculty Growth.............. 203
Amrik Singh, Lovely Professional University, India

Artificial intelligence (AI) in higher education, moving beyond the automation of routine tasks to fostering genuine innovation in faculty roles and professional development. AI-driven tools ranging from automated grading systems to intelligent tutoring platforms are reshaping the responsibilities of educators, enabling them to focus on mentorship, critical thinking facilitation, and the ethical integration of technology in pedagogy.The discussion highlights the shift from traditional knowledge transmission to knowledge facilitation, emphasizing the importance of AI literacy and continuous professional development for faculty. By automating administrative and repetitive instructional tasks, AI empowers educators to dedicate more time to creative curriculum design, personalized student engagement, and collaborative learning environments. The chapter also addresses the challenges and opportunities presented by generative AI, including the need for ethical guidelines, the development of new assessment strategies, and the cultivation of a growth mindset among faculty.

Chapter 8
Personalized Professional Growth: AI as a Mentor for Educators 227
Arun Agrawal, Institute of Technology and Management, Gwalior, India
Dhanashri Rohidas Londhe, Zeal College of Engineering and Research, Pune, India
Komal Vikrant Rajgude, Nutan Maharashtra Institute of Engineering and Technology, India
Vaibhavi Avachat, Nutan Maharashtra Institute of Engineering and Technology, India
Mukesh Kumar Tripathi, KIET Group of Institutions, Delhi, India
Brijendra Gupta, Siddhant College of Engineering, Pune, India
Deepak Gupta, Institute of Technology and Management, Gwalior, India

Professional growth is essential for educators to keep pace with evolving teaching practices and learner needs. Traditional faculty development programs often lack personalization and flexibility. This chapter explores how Artificial Intelligence (AI) can act as a mentor, offering tailored support for continuous learning and improvement. It examines AI applications such as adaptive learning platforms, real-time teaching feedback, and predictive analytics that guide educators toward targeted skill enhancement. Real-world examples highlight how institutions are using AI tools for training, performance improvement, and research support. The chapter also discusses ethical considerations and the importance of balancing technology with human expertise. By embracing AI as a mentor, educators can build adaptive, future-ready skills that enhance both teaching quality and student outcomes.

Chapter 9
Co-Creating the Future: Collaborative Strategies for Integrating AI Into Faculty Development Initiatives 253
Pritesh Pradeep Somani, Balaji Institute of International Business, Sri Balaji University, Pune, India
Prachi Wani, Balaji Institute of Management and Human Resource Development, Sri Balaji University, Pune, India
Vishwanathan Hariharan Iyer, Balaji Institute of International Business, Sri Balaji University, Pune, India
Ushmita Gupta, Balaji Institute of International Business, Sri Balaji University, Pune, India

This chapter explores the collaborative integration of Artificial Intelligence (AI) into faculty development programs across higher education. Grounded in a conceptual framework supported by six interconnected variables—including technological readiness, pedagogical alignment, and institutional support—it highlights how AI can transform teaching, research, and learning environments when implemented through co-creative strategies. The chapter presents qualitative literature reviews and verified global and Indian case studies, demonstrating how institutions have effectively empowered educators to adopt AI tools in ways that are contextually relevant, ethical, and pedagogically sound. Emphasizing the importance of faculty-technologist collaboration, leadership engagement, and continuous learning ecosystems, this study contributes to both academic discourse and institutional practice. It holds relevance for policymakers, educators, and administrators seeking sustainable AI adoption in academia, with the broader goal of creating a digitally competent and innovative set-up ahead.

Chapter 10
Radical Transparency as an Antidote to Unclear Expectations for Generative AI Use 273
Jennifer C. Friberg-Fort, Illinois State University, USA
David Giovagnoli, Illinois State University, USA

This chapter shares our experiences as academic developers at a large, public, midwestern university as generative artificial intelligence (GenAI) exploded into the public consciousness in December of 2022. Needing to respond quickly to the issues that became evident with student and faculty use of GenAI, we looked at what we knew about evidence-informed pedagogy to develop resources and supports for our campus stakeholders – all focused on an adaptation of a popular pedagogical model: the Transparency in Learning and Teaching (TILT) framework. The chapter will present an adapted TILT framework for use in the age of GenAI and will share a model framework for how usage expectations can be clearly and consistently communicated to students across a course or a program of study. A case study will be presented to model the use of these models in an undergraduate writing course.

Chapter 11
The Role of Educational Developers in AI Integration at Scale 289
R. N. Ravikumar, Marwadi University, Rajkot, India
S. Aarthi, Marwadi University, Rajkot, India

This chapter highlights how AI is reshaping higher education, with educational developers playing a key role in guiding this transition. As AI transforms curriculum design and teaching methods, developers support faculty in adopting tools like personalized learning paths, intelligent tutoring, and automated assessments while ensuring alignment with learning outcomes. They bridge pedagogy and technology, lead institutional AI strategies, and promote inclusive, ethical practices. Developers also assist in shaping policies that address bias, privacy, and transparency in AI use. Through collaboration and innovation, they help institutions implement scalable, responsible AI solutions. This chapter showcases real-world examples and strategies for fostering resilient, AI-integrated education systems that empower both educators and students.

Chapter 12
Scaling Faculty AI Literacy: Strategic Models for Institutional Transformation and Sustainable Adoption.. 323
Ramadevi Vitthal Salunkhe, G.H. Raisoni College of Engineering, Nagpur, India
Chetan Arun Raut, St. Vincent Pallotti College of Engineering and Technology, Nagpur, India
Gunjan Chimote, Ramdeobaba University, Nagpur, India
Shruti Sarwate, Jain University, India
Roshan Ramesh Kolte, K.D.K. College of Engineering, Nagpur, India
Piyush K. Ingole, Yeshwantrao Chavan College of Engineering, Nagpur, India
Annaji Kuthe, K.D.K. College of Engineering, Nagpur, India

The accelerating integration of artificial intelligence (AI) in higher education is reshaping faculty roles and institutional strategies. Beyond basic tool use, faculty now require multidimensional competencies that include technical proficiency, pedagogical integration, ethical reasoning, and continuous professional growth. This chapter investigates how institutions can scale AI literacy effectively by addressing barriers such as lack of training, time constraints, infrastructural gaps, and policy ambiguity. Drawing on surveys, interviews, and policy analysis, it proposes sustainable models including progressive immersion, peer mentorship, and policy-driven innovation. International case studies demonstrate best practices in tiered learning, ethics integration, and community engagement. The chapter concludes with a phased roadmap and actionable recommendations for administrators, policymakers, and educators to foster systemic, equitable, and responsible AI literacy adoption.

Compilation of References 369

About the Contributors 399

Index 405

Preface

HUMAN-CENTERED, PRACTICE-DRIVEN, AI-ENGAGED: STRATEGIC PATHWAYS FOR FACULTY GROWTH AND EDUCATIONAL DEVELOPMENT

Artificial intelligence has moved swiftly from the margins of conversation to the center of concern in higher education. Now it's everywhere. What once seemed like a slow drift toward automation has become something more immediate, more pressing, and harder to ignore. Faculty are testing new tools. Committees are writing policies. Institutions are experimenting, often boldly, sometimes blindly, and always under pressure. There's a mix of energy and anxiety, a sense that something big is happening but without a clear consensus of what to do about it. And the implications, while still unfolding, are profound.

Across campuses and committees, the conversation around AI tends to orbit familiar poles. On one end, a fascination with the tools and trappings: which chatbot is most useful, which plugin saves the most time, which LMS integration promises the smoothest results. On the other end, a worry about students: their capacity to think critically, their willingness to engage authentically, their temptation to cut corners in a world full of shortcuts and hacks.

In between, there's an anxious middle ground where faculty and administrators are all just trying to keep pace with a technology that doesn't wait for consensus or best practices.

What's been most striking in these early waves of institutional response is how quickly the conversation narrows. Faculty development sessions turn into product demos. Brown bags become show-and-tell. There's value in exploring what's possible, of course. But when exploration becomes fixation, we lose the bigger picture of *why* we're teaching the way we are in the first place. Of course, running alongside this is a focus on students, often framed through worry. Will they cheat? Will they stop thinking for themselves? Can they tell what's real anymore? Policies emerge quickly, many punitive, some protective, but the tone is often the same: we need to act fast before students get away with something. I've been in too many rooms where generative tools are discussed not as something to be learned with, but as threats to be managed. And while that anxiety is understandable, it rarely opens space for more nuanced conversations about agency, transparency, or the learning process itself.

And alongside all of *that*, there's the quiet but constant undertow of fear. Fear of being replaced, of losing control, of falling behind. You see it in faculty who feel overwhelmed by yet another shift they didn't ask for. You hear it in the department meetings where someone mentions "the robots" only half-jokingly. You feel it in the pause before a colleague asks, "Are you using this stuff in your classes?" The uncertainty is real. But fear, when it becomes the dominant frame, rarely leads to thoughtful change. It rushes us toward decisions made in haste and policies crafted based on headlines, not developed through practice.

Within all of this activity, the hype and the hesitation, it feels like there's something missing. Where's the sustained attention to the infrastructure of growth that enables any meaningful change to take root? Or the systems that support faculty development, the professional learning opportunities that invite thoughtful exploration, and the people who do the often-invisible work of translating innovation into practice? This book offers one answer to the question of what's missing.

Educational developers, instructional designers, teaching center staff, and indeed classroom faculty—those of us committed to cultivating reflection, experimentation, and pedagogical care—have long worked in the spaces where change meets practice. We understand that innovation is not just about adopting a tool but reshaping the conditions under which learning occurs. We know that new possibilities only become sustainable realities when faculty feel confident, supported, and seen.

This book begins from the premise that AI, for all its technical prowess, will only matter if it connects to that human infrastructure, if it becomes a catalyst for professional growth rather than a pressure point of compliance or confusion. And right now, in the midst of disruption and ambiguity, we need frameworks and models that can guide our collective response.

I come to this work as someone who's always been drawn to the spaces between. Between teaching and design. Between vision and implementation. Between what faculty need today and what institutions will need tomorrow. It's in those spaces, often murky, just as often overlooked, where I've found the most potential for meaningful change. I've spent years working with educators across disciplines and contexts, not just helping them adapt to shifting technologies but asking deeper questions about *what kind of teaching futures we want to build*. And again and again, I've seen that change doesn't happen through tools alone. It happens through relationships. Through thoughtful questions. Through invitations to imagine differently.

That perspective shaped earlier work developing AI-powered assessments in first-year writing courses (Pritts, 2025), where I argued that teaching students to use generative tools like ChatGPT wasn't about chasing trends but should be about building confidence, developing process awareness, and positioning AI as a collaborator in learning rather than a replacement for it. That work deepened as I turned my attention to faculty practice. I started by asking how we, as educators, might become more conspicuously human in the online classroom as a counterpoint to AI (Pritts, 2023). And I have tried to identify ways that faculty can use AI to support student success, paired with practical strategies for doing so (Pritts, 2024). Throughout, my goal has been to find ways to scaffold faculty confidence and capacity at scale. That same lens now shapes my thinking about faculty development in how we design systems, structures, and supports that make space for curiosity, experimentation, and collective growth.

When AI began to reshape the landscape of higher education, I didn't see it as a disruption to manage, I saw it as a conversation we weren't quite ready for. A conversation that wasn't just about automation or efficiency, but about purpose, pedagogy, and professional identity. A conversation that needed translators and builders, those of us who could sit with complexity, guide reflective practice, and help turn uncertainty into growth.

This book is one way of holding space for that conversation. It's not a guidebook or a rulebook. It's a set of perspectives from people who, like me, believe that educational development isn't a side project in this moment. It's strategy. And the mindset I bring to this work, the one I know animates every chapter in this volume, is simple: curiosity over certainty. That's how we move forward.

REFRAMING THE RESPONSE: A HUMAN-CENTERED, DEVELOPMENTAL APPROACH

Across higher education, artificial intelligence is often framed as a technical advancement, another tool to be adopted, integrated, and managed. But this framing misses the deeper potential, and the deeper challenge. AI isn't simply a technology to implement; it's a cultural moment that demands we rethink how we teach, how we support faculty, and how we shape learning environments for the future. Increasingly, scholars and policy makers argue that effective AI integration must be approached not just as a matter of infrastructure or compliance, but as a catalyst for professional learning and pedagogical evolution (Baidoo-Anu & Owusu Ansah, 2023; U.S. Department of Education, 2023).

Rather than treating AI as an add-on or efficiency mechanism, a human-centered approach calls us to engage AI through faculty development, ethical reflection, and iterative pedagogical experimentation. Faculty need not only tools, but time, training, and trust to integrate those tools meaningfully. As the U.S. Department of Education's (2023) guidance makes clear, emerging technologies require "intense re-thinking" of professional learning models that are too often reactive or disconnected from the reality of teaching practice.

Recent studies reinforce this view. Instructors are experimenting with AI tools like ChatGPT, but many report limited familiarity and usage, often due to concerns about ethical implications, lack of institutional support, and uncertainty about effective integration into teaching practices. For instance, a survey conducted at a large public university in the United States found that both faculty and students exhibited regular use of generative AI tools, with faculty expressing significant ethical concerns and a need for clearer institutional guidance (Kim et al, 2025). Another survey found that over three-quarters of faculty expressed interest in learning how to integrate AI into their teaching, yet fewer than a quarter felt their institution had adequately prepared them to do so (Baidoo-Anu & Owusu Ansah, 2023).

Frameworks are beginning to emerge that position AI integration as a sustained developmental process rather than a one-time adoption. EDUCAUSE (2025) emphasizes that AI in education remains "at a developmental stage" and that institutions need "deeply probing, thoughtful conversations" grounded in shared pedagogical values. Similarly, a workforce development review cautions that "AI adoption isn't just a tech challenge—it's a people challenge," underscoring the need for support systems that engage faculty not just as end-users but as co-designers of the future (OECD, 2023).

Some institutions are modeling this approach by embedding AI into faculty development ecosystems. The University of Texas at Austin, for example, piloted an initiative in 2023 that introduced faculty to AI-supported writing tools through a structured series of workshops, guided by principles of ethical use and learning design (EDUCAUSE, 2025). We'll discover other programs and initiatives in the chapters that follow. When it works, the results aren't just familiarity with a new tool but deeper engagement with teaching goals, student needs, and reflective practice.

In short, institutions that frame AI as professional learning are beginning to build the kind of capacity that leads to lasting, meaningful change. These institutions understand that AI, when taken seriously, is less about automation and more about transformation. And that transformation must begin with the people doing the teaching.

THE CRUCIAL ROLE OF EDUCATIONAL DEVELOPERS IN AI INTEGRATION

Within this landscape, educational developers, including faculty development specialists, instructional designers, teaching and learning center leaders, occupy a uniquely strategic position. They are often the first to recognize pedagogical shifts on the horizon and the first to respond with frameworks, workshops, and critical conversations. But while their work is essential, it is also frequently under-leveraged in institutional strategy around AI.

Educational developers operate at the intersection of teaching and technology, content and instruction. They understand how new tools function, but more importantly, they understand how instructors think and how students learn. As EDUCAUSE (2025) notes, the professionals who bridge pedagogy and technology are best equipped to help institutions approach AI "in a meaningful and human-centered way."

In practical terms, this means educational developers are often the ones translating AI's potential into faculty development initiatives, ethical teaching guides, and learning design strategies. Their work was not a top-down mandate, but a collaborative, iterative process rooted in the values of shared governance and pedagogical integrity. For instance, the PIER framework—Permission, Integrity, Empowerment, and Reflection—serves as an ethical decision-making guide for AI use in educational settings. Developed to foster AI literacy and critical thinking among faculty and students, it encourages thoughtful engagement with AI tools and prompts users to consider the pedagogical and ethical implications of AI integration (Green et al., 2025). This framework exemplifies how educational developers can scaffold AI adoption in ways that are reflective and aligned with educational values. Similarly, the ETHICAL Principles AI Framework, developed at California State University, Fullerton, provides a comprehensive model for ethical AI adoption in higher education. It emphasizes continuous learning, inclusivity, legal and ethical compliance, and critical evaluation of AI tools—supporting faculty in making informed, values-driven decisions (Faculty Development Center, 2025). By encouraging exploration and critical assessment, this framework supports faculty in making informed decisions about AI use, ensuring that integration efforts are both ethical and pedagogically sound.

These examples illustrate the role educational developers play in guiding institutions through the complexities of AI integration. Their efforts ensure that AI adoption is not merely about incorporating new technologies, but about enhancing teaching and learning in ways that are ethical, inclusive, and aligned with institutional missions.

Educational developers are key contributors to institutional sense-making. In moments of uncertainty, whether it was the (ongoing) shift to remote learning or the emergence of generative AI, they help campuses pause, reflect, and chart a path forward. Despite their impact, the role of educational developers is still too often reactive, confined to troubleshooting or optional workshops. What's needed now is a reframing, an acknowledgment that faculty development is not peripheral to AI integration but foundational to it. When developers are empowered to lead, to design structures of support, and to guide policy development, institutions are far more likely to implement AI in ways that are equitable, ethical, and enduring.

What this book attempts to offer, then, is that reframing. A way of seeing this moment and ourselves differently. The rise of generative AI in higher education has prompted urgent questions, but it also offers a rare opportunity: to rethink not only how we teach, but how we learn as professionals, how we design systems that support that learning, and how we build institutions that can adapt without abandoning their values. This book begins from the middle ground where educational developers already live and work. Not in the executive suite or the server room, but in the collaborative spaces where pedagogy is shaped, where faculty are coached and challenged, where ideas become experiments and experiments become practices.

To lead from the middle is to translate vision into action. To work shoulder-to-shoulder with faculty who are curious but unsure, overwhelmed but open. It's to sit at the intersection of policy and pedagogy, where decisions about technology aren't just technical but cultural. And it's to ask better questions—not just "what tool should we use," but "what kind of teaching do we want to make possible?" In that sense, this book isn't just about AI. It's about agency.

Because what's at stake here isn't just technical literacy. It's faculty confidence, the sense that educators can adapt without compromising their principles. It's equitable innovation, ensuring that AI doesn't widen gaps but helps us close them. It's student success, not measured only by outcomes, but by engagement, curiosity, and connection. And it's institutional agility, the ability to evolve intentionally, to respond without reacting, to grow without losing the thread of who we are.

This isn't a moment for shortcuts. It's a moment for reflection, for experimentation, for developmental work that is deliberate and sustained. And that's where educational developers come in, not just as support staff, but as strategic leaders. As the ones who help institutions change not in a rush, but with intention.

The objective of this edited collection is to explore the ways educational developers are strategically leveraging AI to enhance higher education. Framed through the lenses of faculty growth, instructional design, and institutional change, the chapters highlight both practical strategies and theoretical foundations for meaningful AI integration. Specifically, this book explores how AI can help to:

- Reimagine curriculum design and instructional strategies, fostering innovation across teaching and learning practices.

- Support faculty in adapting to technological change through professional development models and scalable practices.
- Guide institutional innovation by demonstrating the role of educational developers in embedding AI into planning and initiatives.

The contributors bring together research, case studies, and conceptual frameworks that offer readers concrete pathways for adopting and scaling AI-informed practices. It is my hope that this volume serves as both a practical guide and an inspirational resource, equipping educational developers, faculty, and institutional leaders with the insights needed to navigate—and thrive in—this era of rapid technological transformation.

I am deeply grateful to all the authors who have shared their expertise, experience, and vision. Their collective work underscores the central message of this book: when thoughtfully integrated, AI can empower educational development and faculty growth in ways that are both profound and enduring.

ORGANIZATION OF THE BOOK

Chapter 1: A Reflective Case Study on Course Creation: "AI, Power, and the Social Construction of Knowledge"

This chapter presents a detailed case study of an undergraduate course designed to explore the sociological dimensions of AI. Developed in response to students' growing reliance on AI-generated content, the course addresses the cultural lag between rapid technological innovation and institutional adaptation. By framing AI as a sociological object, the chapter emphasizes critical engagement, collaborative inquiry, and ethical knowledge production. It provides a comprehensive look at course rationale, learning objectives, assignments, and an Academic Integrity and AI Policy, illustrating how social science educators can guide students in critically and ethically interrogating AI while positioning learners as active participants in the social construction of knowledge.

Chapter 2: Cultivating AI Literacies: A Taxonomy for Sociocultural Praxis and Academic Transformation

In this chapter, the authors introduce *The Dimensions of AI Literacies*, a socioculturally grounded framework that reconceptualizes AI engagement as plural, context-dependent, and evolving. Drawing on literacy studies, digital literacies, and open remix culture, the chapter presents eight interwoven dimensions—cultural, cognitive, constructive, communicative, confident, creative, critical, and civic—that form dynamic "constellations of AI literacies." Using a culinary metaphor and values-driven approach, the authors argue that AI integration represents both a cultural and pedagogical opportunity, inviting educators, instructional designers, and leaders to co-create AI-enabled ecosystems that are relational, reflective, resilient, and responsive to change.

Chapter 3: Balancing AI-Driven Innovation with Authentic Learning in Higher Education

This chapter examines the dual role of AI in enhancing instructional design while preserving authentic learning experiences. While AI offers adaptive learning, predictive analytics, and personalized feedback, it also challenges principles such as critical thinking, real-world relevance, and student agency. The chapter proposes a framework for integrating AI tools that uphold authentic pedagogy and addresses practical concerns, including faculty readiness, ethical implications, and policy gaps. Drawing on theory, case studies, and applied examples, the authors provide actionable strategies for fostering learning environments where AI-driven innovation and authentic educational experiences coexist effectively.

Chapter 4: AI-Enhanced Instructional Design and Curriculum Development for Next-Generation Learning Ecosystems in Higher Education

This chapter positions AI as a transformative, human-centered partner in instructional design and curriculum development. Leveraging models like ADDIE, TPACK, and UDL, the authors illustrate how AI can support learner analysis, adaptive content, real-time monitoring, and personalized evaluation. Applications across adaptive platforms, AI-driven feedback systems, and inclusive design practices are discussed, emphasizing ethical considerations such as privacy, fairness, and accessibility. The chapter presents AI as a catalyst for flexible, inclusive, and coherent next-generation learning ecosystems.

Chapter 5: The Role of AI in Reshaping Curriculum Structures for Future Learners

Focusing on curriculum innovation, this chapter explores how AI enables dynamic, adaptive, and personalized learning pathways. By integrating learner performance data, industry trends, and societal needs, institutions can create curricula that continuously evolve and respond to diverse student populations. The chapter outlines models of AI integration, addresses ethical considerations, and offers a forward-looking perspective on curriculum development that prepares learners for an ever-changing professional landscape.

Chapter 6: Artificial Intelligence as Faculty Development and Learning Innovation: AI as Faculty Development

This chapter examines how AI can support faculty growth through scalable professional development. The authors propose a model built around three pillars: AI-enhanced training and skill development, AI-driven learning analytics for actionable insights, and personalized professional learning through adaptive modules and career guidance. An AI benefits map demonstrates how these approaches can enhance faculty responsibilities across teaching, research, administration, and mentoring, illustrating how technology can expand professional opportunities while aligning with institutional priorities.

Chapter 7: From Automation to Innovation: AI as a Catalyst for Faculty Growth

Here, the focus shifts to the transformative potential of AI in faculty roles, moving beyond automation toward fostering genuine innovation. AI tools—from automated grading to intelligent tutoring systems—allow educators to focus on mentorship, critical thinking facilitation, and ethical pedagogy. The chapter emphasizes the shift from knowledge transmission to knowledge facilitation, highlighting AI literacy, continuous professional development, and creative curriculum design as central to cultivating faculty growth. Challenges and opportunities, particularly related to generative AI, are also explored.

Chapter 8: Personalized Professional Growth: AI as a Mentor for Educators

This chapter explores AI as a mentor for faculty, offering adaptive, personalized support to enhance professional growth. Through applications such as real-time teaching feedback, predictive analytics, and tailored learning pathways, educators can identify areas for skill development and improve teaching quality. Ethical considerations and the balance between technology and human expertise are emphasized, illustrating how AI can help educators cultivate adaptive, future-ready competencies while enriching student outcomes.

Chapter 9: Co-Creating the Future: Collaborative Strategies for Integrating AI into Faculty Development Initiatives

Focusing on co-creative strategies for AI integration, this chapter presents a conceptual framework for embedding AI in faculty development programs. Grounded in six interconnected variables—including technological readiness, pedagogical alignment, and institutional support—the chapter draws on global and Indian case studies to demonstrate how collaborative approaches can empower educators, ensure ethical and pedagogical alignment, and foster sustainable AI adoption. The work highlights faculty-technologist collaboration, leadership engagement, and continuous learning ecosystems as essential for institutional transformation.

Chapter 10: Radical Transparency as an Antidote to Unclear Expectations for Generative AI Use

This chapter reflects on experiences at a large public university navigating the rapid emergence of generative AI. Drawing on the Transparency in Learning and Teaching (TILT) framework, the authors present an adapted model for clearly communicating expectations around AI use in courses and programs. A case study of an undergraduate writing course illustrates how transparency can guide ethical and effective AI integration, offering practical strategies for supporting both students and faculty in navigating this evolving landscape.

Chapter 11: The Role of Educational Developers in AI Integration at Scale

Educational developers are positioned as central to scaling AI integration in this chapter. The authors explore how developers support faculty adoption of AI tools, bridge pedagogy and technology, guide institutional strategy, and promote ethical and inclusive practices. Real-world examples demonstrate strategies for fostering resilient, AI-integrated education systems that empower both educators and students while ensuring alignment with learning outcomes and policy frameworks.

Chapter 12: Scaling Faculty AI Literacy: Strategic Models for Institutional Transformation and Sustainable Adoption

The final chapter examines how institutions can cultivate comprehensive AI literacy among faculty to drive sustainable, systemic change. Addressing barriers such as time constraints, infrastructural gaps, and policy ambiguity, the authors propose strategic models including progressive immersion, peer mentorship, and policy-driven innovation. International case studies illustrate tiered learning, ethics integration, and community engagement, culminating in a phased roadmap with actionable recommendations for administrators, policymakers, and educators seeking equitable, responsible, and scalable AI literacy adoption.

This book is not meant to be a road map. It's meant to be a companion. A collection of vantage points from people who are already doing the cultural and pedagogical work of AI integration, whether quietly in a single course or loudly through large-scale faculty development initiatives. Reading their chapters is not a matter of adopting best practices; it's a matter of joining a larger conversation about where we want this moment to take us, and what kinds of educators we want to become along the way.

My hope is that you read these chapters with the mindset of a fellow builder. If you are a faculty member, I hope you find approaches you can adapt, questions you can bring to your next class, or even just reassurance that uncertainty is not a weakness but a starting point. If you are an instructional designer or educational developer, I hope you see echoes of your own work—and perhaps new ways to scaffold curiosity, build capacity, or create spaces where experimentation feels both safe and supported. If you are an administrator or academic leader, I hope these pages help you imagine structures that make development the center of AI integration rather than an afterthought.

REFERENCES

Baidoo-Anu, D., & Owusu Ansah, L. (2023). Education in the era of generative artificial intelligence (AI): Understanding the potential benefits of ChatGPT in promoting teaching and learning. *Journal of AI, 7*(1), 52–62. (dergipark.org.tr) , DOI: 10.61969/jai.1337500.

EDUCAUSE. (2024). *2024 EDUCAUSE Horizon Report: Teaching and Learning Edition*. EDUCAUSE. https://library.educause.edu/resources/2024/5/2024-educause-horizon-report-teaching-and-learning-edition(library.educause.edu)

Faculty Development Center. (2025). *ETHICAL Principles AI Framework for Higher Education*. California State University, Fullerton. https://fdc.fullerton.edu/_resources/pdfs/teaching/ethical-principles-ai-framework-for-higher-education-february-2025.pdf

Green, D., Leung, C., Francis, R., & Paul, R. (2025). PIER: A framework for ethical decision-making and AI literacy in higher education. *TechTrends*. Advance online publication. DOI: 10.1007/s11528-025-01084-y

Kim, J., Klopfer, M., & Grohs, J. R.. (2025). *Examining Faculty and Student Perceptions of Generative AI in University Courses*. Innov High Educ., DOI: 10.1007/s10755-024-09774-w

OECD. (2023). *Skill needs and policies in the age of artificial intelligence*. OECD Publishing. https://www.oecd.org/en/publications/oecd-employment-outlook-2023_08785bba-en/full-report/skill-needs-and-policies-in-the-age-of-artificial-intelligence_fe530fbf.html(oecd.org)

Pritts, N. (2023, September 6). How to be conspicuously human in the online classroom. *Faculty Focus*. https://www.facultyfocus.com/articles/online-education/online-course-delivery-and-instruction/how-to-be-conspicuously-human-in-the-online-classroom/

Pritts, N. (2024, April 8). Two ways AI can support student success in online courses. *The Teaching Professor*.

Pritts, N. (2025). Innovative Approaches to Writing Assessment: Developing AI-Powered Prompts for First-Year Writing Courses. In Wachira, P., Liu, X., & Koc, S. (Eds.), *Educational Assessments in the Age of Generative AI*. IGI Global.

U.S. Department of Education, Office of Educational Technology. (2023). *Artificial intelligence and the future of teaching and learning: Insights and recommendations*. https://files.eric.ed.gov/fulltext/ED631097.pdf(files.eric.ed.gov)

Chapter 1
A Reflective Case Study on Course Creation: "AI, Power, and the Social Construction of Knowledge"

JoAnna Boudreaux
https://orcid.org/0000-0001-6466-9801
University of Memphis, USA

ABSTRACT

This chapter presents a case study on designing and implementing the undergraduate course AI and the Social Construction of Knowledge at a public university. The course was developed in response to students' growing reliance on AI-generated content and the rapid adoption of AI tools across disciplines, highlighting a cultural lag between technological innovation and institutional adaptation. By situating AI as a sociological object, the course emphasizes critical engagement, collaborative inquiry, and ethical knowledge production. The chapter details course rationale, learning objectives, assignments, and an Academic Integrity and AI Policy, while reflecting on key design decisions. It illustrates how social science educators can guide students in interrogating AI critically and ethically, positioning learners as active participants in the ongoing social construction of knowledge.

INTRODUCTION

At the time of writing this chapter, I am working at a public university launching an interdisciplinary undergraduate minor titled *AI for All* in the Fall of 2025. This new course is meant to reflect the institution's commitment to preparing students for the labor force in an increasingly AI-mediated society. The program invites

DOI: 10.4018/979-8-3373-4129-3.ch001

contributions from multiple disciplines, recognizing the transformative role of artificial intelligence in public health, culture, economics, politics, education, and overall society. As part of this initiative, the Sociology Department will propose a new course titled: *AI, Power, and the Social Construction of Knowledge*.

This chapter documents that process as a reflective case study situated within the *Scholarship of Teaching and Learning* (SoTL) (Felten, 2013; Yin, 2018; Stake, 1995). Using my own course design decisions, classroom materials, and iterative reflections as qualitative data, I analyze how sociological theory can inform ethical, participatory, and critically engaged AI pedagogy. Consistent with Schön's (1983) notion of the *reflective practitioner* and Brookfield's (2017) framework for critical reflection, I treat course creation as both inquiry and practice. I want students to view AI technology as a social object: specifically, it is a product of human choices, human values, and human power relations. As I create *AI, Power, and the Social Construction of Knowledge*, I reflect on my decisions and challenges to explain how this course came to life. I share this process to provide practical insights for other educators while also demonstrating how the classroom becomes a living site of knowledge production.

Literature Review

The Social Construction of Knowledge

The idea of socially constructed knowledge originates with Karl Mannheim's *Ideology and Utopia* (1936). Mannheim argued that all knowledge is shaped by the historical context and ideological position of those who produce it. In other words, knowledge cannot be separated from the social location of the knower. His ideas laid the groundwork for Peter Berger and Thomas Luckmann's *The Social Construction of Reality* (1966), which formalized the notion that reality itself is created and maintained through human interaction, socialization, and institutionalization, (Berger & Luckmann, 1996).

Building on this foundation, later scholars such as Hacking (1999), Cetina (2007), and Latour and Woolgar (1979) extended the sociology of knowledge into the study of science and technology. What counts as "facts" and "knowledge" are always constructed through negotiations between human actors, technical tools, and institutional settings. For example, in *Laboratory Life*, Latour and Woolgar (1979) showed how credibility and "truth" are manufactured within the social practices of laboratories. Cetina (2007) later conceptualized *epistemic cultures* to explain the distinct ways that different communities generate and validate knowledge. Hacking

(1999) emphasized that social constructions become powerful when they shape the very categories through which people understand themselves and their world.

These perspectives underpin the present case: AI systems are not neutral repositories of information but socially embedded products. The knowledge they construct are shaped by the assumptions, biases, values, and contexts of their creators. Within the sociology of knowledge, this framing enables educators to move from asking *"What is true?"* to *"Who decides what counts as true?"*: This question is central to understanding algorithmic authority and the epistemic power of machine learning systems (Wacquant, 2015; Gillespie, 2014).

AI Literacies and Student Engagement

Emerging scholarship on AI literacy emphasizes that students need more than technical proficiency; they also need critical, ethical, and sociocultural awareness (Ng et al., 2021; Zawacki-Richter et al., 2019). This growing field defines AI literacy as the ability to use AI tools effectively while also understanding AI's limitations, biases, and social implications. For higher education, this means helping students see AI as both a *technological tool* and a *social object* that reflects human priorities and inequalities.

Recent studies show that college students already use AI for brainstorming, summarizing, and writing, but many over-trust its authority and rarely question how outputs are generated. . This overreliance can suppress skills essential for lifelong learning such as critical thinking, creativity, and self-efficacy. Overreliance on AI can also reinforce existing inequities, as students with greater digital literacy or confidence in using AI often gain disproportionate advantages (Veletsianos, 2020).

At the same time, student experiences with AI vary widely. van Niekerk, Delport, and Sutherland (2025) observed differing levels of acceptance and concern among learners when engaging with generative AI in academic writing. Using the Technology Acceptance Model (TAM), they found that while many students recognized the usefulness and efficiency of AI tools, others expressed apprehension about overreliance and potential breaches of academic integrity.

Recognizing this variation aligns with the sociological understanding of technology adoption as a social process influenced by culture, access, institutional policy, and peer norms.

As Selwyn (2022) argues, technologies are never adopted uniformly; they are negotiated within everyday practices, shaped by both opportunity and constraint.

Taken together, this body of work suggests that fostering AI literacy in higher education requires a sociological approach that examines how students are using AI and how their engagement reflects broader patterns of power, privilege, and meaning making.

Ethics, Culture, and Pedagogy

The ethical implications of AI are widely documented (Bender et al., 2021; Crawford, 2021; Selwyn, 2022). Critical digital pedagogy scholars argue that universities must move beyond policy enforcement to cultivate a type of epistemic vigilance, or rather, learners must develop the the ability to question how knowledge is produced, validated, and circulated. Ethics in AI education cannot be reduced to avoiding plagiarism or bias; it must involve preparing students to think critically about how technology itself participates in the construction of knowledge. These discussions parallel international frameworks such as UNESCO's (2023) *Guidance for Generative AI in Education and Research* and Jisc's (2024) principles for responsible AI use in UK higher education, both of which emphasize transparency, inclusion, and critical engagement rather than prohibition.

Another issue highlighting the urgency for this course is the phenomenon of *cultural lag* (Ogburn, 1922). The concept of cultural lag was first brought to my attention by my colleague, Dr. Kendra Murphy. She shared an anecdote from a historical account in which an educator "ranted" that a new technology would destroy students and education, only to discover that the "new technology" in question was paper and pencils. This story perfectly captures cultural lag. Societies often struggle to adapt their nonmaterial culture (beliefs, norms, policies etcetera) to keep pace with material innovation.

This idea resonates deeply in higher education today. While AI tools such as large language models, generative image platforms, predictive analytics, and adaptive learning system continue to advance rapidly, universities continue to grapple with the ethical, pedagogical, and policy implications of their use. Material culture has surged ahead, while nonmaterial culture lags behind.

Studies indicate there are variations in student experiences with AI. The Higher Education Policy Institute (HEPI) Student Generative AI Survey 2025 found that 92% of students report using generative AI tools, and 88% said they used them in assessments. This is an increase from 66% and 53% in 2024 (Higher Education Policy Institute, 2025). Meanwhile, a global survey of more than 1,600 university educators across 28 countries revealed that 82% of faculty members expressed concern that students are becoming overly dependent on AI tools, while 83% doubted students' ability to critically evaluate AI-generated output (Rowsell, 2025). Recognizing this variation aligns with the sociological understanding of technology adoption as a social process influenced by culture, access, institutional policy, and peer norms. As Selwyn (2022) argues, technologies are never adopted uniformly; they are negotiated within everyday practices, shaped by both opportunity and constraint.

Overall, *AI, Power and the Social Construction of Knowledge* is meant to respond to both the ethical and cultural dimensions of AI integration. Students are situated as co-researchers and active investigators. The course is meant to disrupt the idea that AI is a neutral authority of knowledge production and illuminate it as a socially created object within broader systems of power and knowledge.

Methodology and Case Context

This chapter employs a reflective case study approach (Yin, 2018; Stake, 1995) within the broader framework of the Scholarship of Teaching and Learning (SoTL). The "data" consist of the artifacts generated during the course-design process: syllabus drafts, reading selections, assignment rubrics, and an AI integrity policy. Of course, I also include my contemporaneous reflections as instructor-researcher.

Following Schön's (1983) model of the *reflective practitioner* and Felten's (2013) SoTL principles, I treat the act of course creation as a site of inquiry.

The guiding research questions were:

1. How can the social construction of knowledge framework inform the design of an AI-focused sociology course?
2. What pedagogical strategies help students critically engage with AI as a social phenomenon rather than a technical novelty?
3. How can the design process itself model responsible, transparent collaboration with AI tools?

Data were analyzed through iterative reflection. I coded my own journal notes for recurring themes of *agency*, *ethics*, and *collaboration* and triangulated my codes with relevant literature. This methodological framing legitimizes the use of first-person narrative as a scholarly tool (Brookfield, 2017; Loughran, 2002) and connects personal teaching practice to collective disciplinary knowledge. The findings below reflect my final design decisions as I completed the creation of the course.

FINDINGS /DESIGN DECISIONS

The process of developing *AI and the Social Construction of Knowledge* unfolded as both a pedagogical experiment and a sociological inquiry. The design decisions ranged from learning objectives to selecting readings, creating assignments, and developing an AI and Academic Misconduct Policy. The decisions were based on three recurring themes in my reflections: (1) centering theory as a critical lens for technology, (2) balancing creativity with ethical awareness, and (3) positioning students as co-researchers and co-constructors of knowledge.

The Course Concept

The first question I faced was how to distinguish this course from broader "AI and Society" offerings that already existed in other departments. Rather than duplicating a survey-style approach, I grounded the course explicitly in sociological theory. I specifically selected Berger and Luckmann's (1966) concept of the *social construction of knowledge*. This framing allowed students to investigate not only what AI produces, but how its knowledge is legitimized, circulated, and contested.

In this design, AI remains a sociological object rather than a purely technical one. It is treated as a social product that is created, maintained, and challenged through collective human processes. This framing invites students to examine how data are socially sourced, how algorithms reflect institutional priorities, and how authority becomes encoded in code. To study AI sociologically is to ask who defines truth in algorithmic systems, whose perspectives are excluded, and how these structures reproduce or resist social inequalities.

My reflections during syllabus development revealed a persistent tension between wanting students to gain hands-on experience with AI tools while also interrogating those tools critically. To resolve this, I paired theoretical readings with applied exercises that illustrate the recursive relationship between knowledge and technology to help illustrate how human choices, data structures, and institutional norms shape algorithmic output. In doing so, the course situates AI within the same sociological processes of meaning-making that govern all forms of knowledge production.

The Learning Objectives and Student Outcomes

The learning objectives for *AI, Power, and the Social Construction of Knowledge* were designed to integrate sociological theory, critical analysis, and practical application in ways that promote both intellectual rigor and accessibility. My goal was to ensure that students engage with foundational sociological theories and apply them to real-world issues surrounding AI technology and society. When I first conceptualized the course, I imagined it unfolding in a traditional, discussion-driven classroom setting that emphasized live peer facilitation. However, once I learned the course would be offered fully online and asynchronously, I needed to reconsider how to sustain active learning and collaboration in a more flexible environment.

Student-led discussions, while valuable in person, are often difficult to maintain equitably in asynchronous settings where students participate across varied schedules and time zones. To preserve student agency and interaction, I replaced the discussion model with a structured sequence of reflective writing, collaborative policy-building, and project-based learning. These elements still allow students to co-construct knowledge and exercise critical judgment, but in ways that better support inclusivity, accessibility, and sustained engagement.

The course's specific learning objectives and student outcomes are detailed in full in Appendix A. Collectively, they emphasize sociological approaches to AI literacy by guiding students to apply classic frameworks from Mannheim and Berger & Luckmann, evaluate bias and inequality in AI systems, use AI tools ethically and transparently, and translate sociological insights into public-facing research projects. Together, these objectives frame the study of AI as a sociological investigation into how knowledge, ethics, and power are produced and maintained in the digital age.

Selected Readings

Selecting readings for *AI and the Social Construction of Knowledge* proved a bit more complicated than I anticipated. I spent many hours reading articles and book chapters to curate the final reading list. My goal was to balance foundational sociological theory, ethical and philosophical analyses of AI, and accessible case studies on real-world issues surrounding AI.

The course begins with instructor-prepared notes and summaries of classic and technical readings to make complex texts approachable for undergraduate learners. I wanted students to engage directly with the core ideas of each work without being overwhelmed by disciplinary jargon. As Schön (1983) observes, reflective teaching requires adapting theory for the audience at hand, and my approach reflects that principle.

The first two readings include Berger and Luckmann's (1966) *The Social Construction of Reality* and Harry Collins' (2018) "Why Artificial Intelligence Needs Sociology of Knowledge." These two articles provide the theoretical foundation. These texts introduce students to the idea that knowledge is produced through social processes and that AI, as a knowledge-making tool, must be examined through that lens.

To build an ethical bridge between theory and application, students then read Iason Gabriel's (2020) "Artificial Intelligence, Values, and Alignment," which examines how human values are encoded into AI systems. This reading illustrates how moral and political assumptions are embedded in the algorithmic designs of modern technological tools. Next, we turn to Ruha Benjamin's (2019) *Race After Technology: Abolitionist Tools for the New Jim Code*, which connects technology to structural inequality. Benjamin's analysis encourages students to see how data, algorithms, and automation can reproduce systems of racial and economic hierarchy under the guise of neutrality. Her concept of the "New Jim Code" complements the sociological frameworks explored earlier in the course and pushes students to consider AI's role in maintaining or disrupting injustice. Madhumita Murgia's (2022) *Code*

Dependent: Living in the Shadow of AI provides two accessible case studies: one on healthcare and one on government surveillance. Both of these case studies illustrate how algorithmic bias operates in real-world contexts. These chapters help students connect abstract theory to the social consequences of AI in everyday life. Finally, the documentary *Coded Bias* (Kantayya, 2020) serves as a visual capstone to the reading sequence. The film brings together many of the semester's key themes such as bias, ethics, and public accountability. The film is meant to help students visualize how individual stories and lived experiences reflect broader sociological theories of knowledge and power. To ensure accessibility and comprehension, all readings and media are provided on Canvas. Instructor-prepared summaries accompany each assigned text, offering clear, student-friendly access to key ideas while preserving the rigor of the original works. This scaffolding reflects my broader pedagogical philosophy: challenging students with complex theory while providing the support needed to engage it critically and confidently.

Assignments

Designing assignments for AI and the Social Construction of Knowledge required balancing theoretical depth, student accessibility, and the unique challenges of an asynchronous format. I wanted students to encounter sociological theory as a living framework for interpreting technology, inequality, and society. My overarching goal was to create assignments that invited curiosity, critical analysis, and creative expression while maintaining consistent structure and transparency.

Because asynchronous courses rely heavily on self-paced engagement, each assignment was intentionally scaffolded to build cumulative understanding. Students begin with short weekly reflections to establish conceptual grounding, move into comparative and creative analysis, and conclude with applied research and public communication projects. This sequence ensures that learning unfolds progressively, mirroring the sociological process of constructing knowledge itself. Assignment descriptions and the point breakdown are listed below in Table 1.

Table 1. Assignment Descriptions and Point Breakdown

Assignment	Description	Points
Synthesis Journal (3 × 100)	Each Synthesis Journal invites students to bring together ideas from course readings, lecture notes, and personal experiences to develop a deeper sociological understanding of AI and society. Entries emphasize synthesis rather than summary and can integrate creative forms as long as they demonstrate clear sociological insight and reflective analysis.: written essays, multimedia narratives, or visual journals—	300
AI vs. Human Knowledge Comparison	Students design a set of original questions on a topic of interest, collecting responses from both a human expert and an AI tool. They analyze similarities, differences, and assumptions in each, producing a brief written analysis and visual comparison. This exercise deepens understanding of knowledge as socially constructed and reveals how bias operates differently in human and machine contexts.	100
Weekly Reflection Questions	Each week, students submit a 200–300-word reflection responding to a prompt tied to the week's readings and lecture notes. Reflections connect sociological ideas (e.g., Mannheim, Berger & Luckmann, Collins, Benjamin) to real-world issues surrounding AI and society. Students are encouraged to move beyond summary to interpretation and application. There are ten reflections total, each worth ten points (100 points overall). While peer replies are optional, exemplary insights are periodically shared in weekly wrap-ups.	100
AI Creative Assignment	Students use a generative AI tool to explore how machines represent or interpret creativity. They choose a prompt such as asking AI to generate an image of a "beautiful person" or to write a poem about a social issue. They will then analyze what the output reveals about culture, bias, and representation. A 300–400-word reflection links these findings to key course concepts, including the social construction of knowledge and cultural power.	100
AI Research Practicum	Serving as the foundation for the Final Project, this practicum teaches responsible and reflective AI use in research. Students refine a topic, generate two to three research questions, and gather preliminary data or sources using AI tools. They document their process in a research log (prompts, screenshots, and notes) and write a 500–750-word short paper summarizing early findings.	200
Final Project	The Final Project shifts focus from academic writing to public communication. Building on the practicum, students create a public-facing product such as an infographic, video, podcast, or multimedia essay, that translates their research into accessible knowledge for a general audience. The project incorporates peer and instructor feedback, and all final products are shared in a "Project Gallery" discussion forum for class-wide reflection. Note: Students creating visual or multimedia projects must ensure accessibility by providing captions for videos, transcripts for audio, and alternative text for images. These practices align with Universal Design for Learning (UDL) principles and reflect the course's broader commitment to inclusive and ethical communication.	200

Total: 1,000 points

Together, these assignments create a rhythm of reflection, analysis, and creation that mirrors the sociological process of knowledge construction. The Synthesis Journals encourage integrative thinking; the AI vs. Human Comparison and AI Creative Assignment cultivate critical and ethical awareness; and the Research Practicum and Final Project allow students to apply theory to public issues. The Final Project specifically shifts the focus from academic writing to public communication. To promote ethical and inclusive engagement, students producing visual or multimedia work are required to include captions, transcripts, and alternative text for all materials. This practice follows the principles of Universal Design for Learning (CAST, 2018), reinforcing the course's broader emphasis on accessibility, equity, and ethical communication as essential components of knowledge production.

This structure also operationalizes key SoTL principles: transparency, iterative learning, and reflective practice (Felten, 2013; Brookfield, 2017). Each assignment builds toward the next, allowing students to trace their intellectual development across the semester. Rather than positioning AI as a threat to traditional learning, the course transforms it into a site of inquiry, where both human and machine-generated knowledge become tools for sociological analysis and creative exploration.

The Course Schedule

After finalizing the readings and assignments, the next step was to develop the course schedule. I mapped out a 13-week course schedule designed to build logically and pedagogically from theory to application. The structure mirrors the sociological process of constructing knowledge: early weeks introduce foundational ideas about ideology, social construction, and expertise; mid-semester units emphasize applied analysis of bias, ethics, and creativity; and the final portion focuses on independent research and public communication. The pacing and workload were carefully calibrated for an asynchronous online environment to allow students to engage with materials, reflections, and projects at a flexible yet consistent rhythm.

All readings and media are provided on Canvas, with instructor-prepared notes accompanying complex theoretical texts to make them accessible while preserving intellectual rigor. The complete schedule, including weekly readings, activities, and due dates, is included in Appendix A.

The Academic Integrity and AI Policy

Developing the AI policy for *AI and the Social Construction of Knowledge* required careful reflection on both ethics and pedagogy. I did not want a policy that would simply regulate behavior: it needed to model the very sociological processes of negotiation, institutionalization, and collective meaning-making that students were studying in the course. Rather than imposing a fixed set of rules, I designed the policy as a collaborative and evolving document, inviting students to co-construct norms for responsible AI use.

This approach grew out of my belief that academic integrity in the age of AI cannot simply be enforced; it must be *understood*. Many students arrive in our classrooms already using generative AI, often without a clear sense of boundaries or ethical standards. A purely prohibitive stance, I found, risks creating confusion or alienation, while a participatory model helps students engage critically and responsibly.

In Week 1, students begin by participating in an online discussion about their existing experiences with AI. This initial dialogue serves as both an assessment of prior knowledge and an opportunity to surface diverse perspectives on technology use. In Week 2, I synthesize their contributions into a preliminary draft policy, which students then review and refine. By Week 3, the class collectively finalizes the policy, which becomes our shared framework for the semester.

This collaborative process is meant to transform policy formation into a pedagogical exercise in the sociology of knowledge. Students actively witness how institutional norms take shape through dialogue, negotiation, and shared understanding. They also practice epistemological vigilance by questioning how definitions of "responsible use" and "authorship" evolve in an AI-mediated learning environment.

The final policy is included as part of the syllabus in Appendix A. The policy outlines both procedural and ethical expectations. It asks students to document prompts, describe how they used AI in their work, and reflect on its impact on their reasoning or analysis. Violations of the final policy or the university's academic integrity code are treated seriously, but the emphasis remains on learning through transparency and reflection rather than fear of punishment.

DISCUSSION

Balancing Ambition and Feasibility

Throughout the design process, I wrestled with scope. My initial outline included six reflection journals, multiple discussion components, and two additional theoretical readings. However, I realize that these plans risked cognitive overload, particularly in an asynchronous format. Simplifying the structure reinforced depth over density, a lesson echoed in active-learning research showing that meaningful engagement often depends on reducing complexity rather than increasing volume (Kozanitis & Nenciovici, 2023).

The final course design represents a balance between aspiration and feasibility. Each component was examined and re-examined for alignment with learning objectives and workload realism. This process also modeled the iterative adaptation educators must embrace in a rapidly changing AI landscape. This embodies what Punziano (2025) calls *adaptive epistemology*: the continual negotiation between knowing, learning, and revising in response to new contexts. These design choices also prompt a broader question: how could sociological theory inform both the content of the course but also its very structure?

Situating AI Pedagogy within the Sociology of Knowledge

The course design also demonstrates how sociological theory can anchor pedagogical practice in an age of technological acceleration. By framing AI as a social object, the course transforms what might otherwise be a technical literacy module into an exercise in knowledge construction and epistemological awareness. Students are not merely learning how to use AI tools but are learning how to examine and critique those tools in defining what counts as valid knowledge, credible expertise, and legitimate authority.

This framework draws on Berger and Luckmann's (1966) proposition that knowledge becomes institutionalized through repeated human interactions. In the digital era, these interactions increasingly occur through engagement with algorithms, datasets, and coding programs. These are forms of mediation that reconfigure how information circulates and who is recognized as a "knower." Framing AI within this theoretical tradition enables students to interrogate the human choices embedded in seemingly neutral systems. They are guided toward asking questions about who designs the algorithm, who curates the data, and who benefits from the resulting knowledge outputs.

The course's design intentionally mirrors Berger and Luckmann's three-part process of *externalization, objectivation*, and *internalization*. Early activities will prompt students to externalize their assumptions about AI through discussion and reflection to reveal social meanings they already attach to the technology. As the semester progresses, comparative and creative assignments will position AI as an objectified product of social interactions. By the time students reach the final project, they will be prepared to internalize new understandings about AI as a socially embedded phenomenon that reflects human priorities and power dynamics.

This approach aligns with what scholars of digital culture have long emphasized: AI does not create knowledge but reorganizes existing social patterns (Latour & Woolgar, 1979; Crawford, 2021). In this way, the classroom becomes both the *subject* and the *site* of sociological inquiry: a space where students can observe, critique, and participate in the social construction of knowledge in real time.

Addressing Student Dependence on AI

Empirical research increasingly demonstrates that student dependence on AI is not anecdotal but systemic. Large-scale surveys across the United States and United Kingdom show that more than 90 percent of college students now use AI tools for academic work, often as default extensions of their study habits (Higher Education Policy Institute, 2025). There is an illusion of fluency. That can lead to dependence. AI-generated text often appears polished, cohesive, and authoritative.

This dependence illustrates how new forms of epistemic authority are emerging in digital culture. Historically, expertise has always been connected to individuals or institutions with recognized credentials. In contrast, AI systems distribute that authority to nonhuman agents. Students may internalize the notion that knowledge is objective simply because it is machine generated. This reconfiguration of epistemic trust underscores the urgency of teaching students to interrogate AI as a knowledge-producing institution, as opposed to a neutral machine.

This course is designed to address this dynamic directly by transforming AI from an unquestioned authority into an object of study. For example, assignments such as the AI vs. Human Knowledge Comparison encourage students to adopt the stance of investigators rather than consumers of knowledge. Students will ask the same set of questions to both an AI model and a human expert. They will then analyze factual discrepancies, assumptions, omissions, and social contexts of the responses. This exercise is intended to make visible how data, training sets, and cultural norms inform what machines "know" and how they represent that knowledge. Overall, the goal is to empower students in developing a sociological habit of questioning how systems of knowledge are built and whose interests they serve.

Cultural Lag and Institutional Adaptation

Ogburn's (1922) concept of cultural lag offers a useful sociological lens for understanding higher education's uneven response to artificial intelligence. The rapid evolution of generative models, machine learning, and adaptive analytics represents the *material* dimension of culture: technological innovations that transform how we produce and distribute knowledge. In contrast, the *nonmaterial* dimension, our norms, policies, pedagogies, and ethical frameworks, tends to change far more slowly. The resulting lag between these dimensions generates uncertainty, anxiety, and, paradoxically, fertile ground for innovation.

In higher education, this lag is palpable. Institutions have invested heavily in AI-powered administrative and instructional systems while leaving faculty and students to navigate this evolving landscape largely on our own. The acceleration of technology has outpaced the creation of meaningful guidance, leaving instructors to improvise in real time. Syllabi banning AI "in all forms" coexist with others that integrate AI without accountability or clear learning outcomes. This fragmentation mirrors the broader social negotiation Ogburn described: the struggle to align technological progress with human values and institutional coherence.

By documenting and sharing the design of *AI, Power, and the Social Construction of Knowledge*, I hoped to offer a third path: a deliberate, theory-informed integration of AI grounded in sociological analysis. The reflective methodology used in this chapter models how educators can act as cultural mediators, translating new technologies into meaningful academic practice. Rather than attempting to eliminate cultural lag, the course embraces it as a generative tension as a space where critical reflection and adaptive pedagogy can thrive. In this sense, the course itself becomes a living example of what adaptive institutions might look like: responsive, reflexive, and socially aware.

Ethical Pedagogy and Transparency

Integrating an explicit AI policy is designed as a form of ethical pedagogy in practice rather than a bureaucratic requirement. Scholars such as Bender et al. (2021)) emphasize that transparency about data sources, algorithms, and decision-making processes is essential for responsible AI development. Extending this principle to the classroom, I treat transparency as ethical literacy: it is a way to make knowledge production visible, contestable, and collaborative.

In *AI, Power, and the Social Construction of Knowledge*, students are asked to document the prompts they use, explain how they modify or interpret AI outputs, and reflect on the social, ethical, and epistemological implications of those choices. This process cultivates what I call *ethical literacy*: the capacity to question not only what information communicates but also how and why it comes to exist. In documenting their reasoning, students practice the sociological habit of reflexivity, learning to situate their own knowledge-making within larger social systems of technology, power, and representation.

This approach reframes academic integrity from punishment to participation. Rather than policing AI use, the course begins with a collaborative exercise in which students and I co-develop guidelines for responsible engagement. These early discussions about authorship, originality, and accountability become sociological lessons in themselves. They illustrate how collective norms are negotiated and institutionalized. The co-creation of policy transforms ethics from an abstract principle into a lived classroom practice.

By positioning transparency as both a value and a skill, the course models what ethical participation in an AI-mediated society can look like. The aim is to foster a learning community where disclosure, reflection, and accountability are normalized rather than exceptional. Additionally, I hope to reinforce the idea that ethical reasoning is inseparable from the act of knowledge production. In this way, the classroom becomes a microcosm of the broader societal dialogue about AI accountability.

Pedagogical Insights

Several insights emerged from the reflective design process that extend beyond this single course. Together, they illustrate how sociological theory can serve as both a guide and a mirror for pedagogical decision-making in a rapidly changing educational landscape. While these principles were developed in the context of *AI, Power, and the Social Construction of Knowledge*, they also offer a replicable framework for educators across disciplines seeking to integrate emerging technologies without compromising critical inquiry.

1. Theory as Scaffold, Not Supplement

This course is grounded in the sociological frameworks of Mannheim (1936) and Berger and Luckmann (1966). This grounding provides a conceptual through-line that shapes every pedagogical choice from reading selection to assignment design. Too often, theoretical content in undergraduate courses is treated as a supplement: a discrete unit or an abstract backdrop for "real-world" applications. In this course, theory is the scaffold. It is the foundation that students could return to repeatedly as they encountered new technologies and debates.

Mannheim's idea that all knowledge is socially conditioned offers an entry point for students to question the assumption that AI-generated information is neutral or objective. Berger and Luckmann's model of externalization, objectivation, and internalization provides language to trace how AI systems become institutionalized forms of knowledge. Each time students engage with a case study (such as r examining bias in image-generation tools or the ethical challenges of data collection) they will use these frameworks to decode the social processes underlying what initially appeared to be technical phenomena.

This recursive engagement helps prevent the fragmentation that often occurs in interdisciplinary courses. Rather than moving linearly from one topic to another, students build cumulative understanding by applying theoretical concepts in progressively complex ways. For example, early in the course, they might use Berger and Luckmann to analyze how an algorithm reflects human social values; later, the same framework could be applied to critique how institutional norms legitimize certain uses of AI while marginalizing others.

For instructors, this approach demonstrates the enduring relevance of theory in a time when many pedagogical discussions prioritize tools and skills over conceptual grounding. Sociology reminds us that theory is not an abstract luxury but a navigational device. Theory remains a way of making sense of our realities and remains relevant in a climate of rapid technological change.

2. Reflection as Assessment

I deliberately replaced quizzes with synthesis journals and weekly reflections because I wanted to shift product-based evaluation to process-based learning. This decision was grounded in the Scholarship of Teaching and Learning (SoTL) literature, which consistently shows that reflection deepens understanding by connecting cognitive and affective dimensions of learning (Brookfield, 2017; Schön, 1983).

In the context of AI education, reflection takes on heightened importance. Students are grappling with new technologies and questions of what those technologies mean for knowledge, creativity, and human life. Written and multimedia reflections create space for this kind of metacognitive work. They allow students to articulate uncertainty, confront bias, and document shifts in their thinking (Memarian & Doleck, 2023).

In designing reflective assessments, I also drew from Dewey (1981) understanding of reflection as disciplined inquiry. Reflection is not introspection; it is the systematic process of questioning one's assumptions and relating them to evidence and theory. In practice, this means that a student's journal entry might begin with a personal observation such as "I use AI to brainstorm ideas" but move toward sociological interpretation: "My reliance on AI mirrors the institutional dependence on algorithmic systems described by Ogburn's (1922) concept of cultural lag."

This structure reinforces the principle that reflection is itself a method of sociological analysis. It transforms students from passive receivers of knowledge into active theorists of their own experience. Moreover, in an asynchronous online setting, reflective writing provides an equitable mode of participation. It allows students to engage deeply with material on their own time, accommodating varied learning styles and access levels while maintaining intellectual rigor.

Reflection also serves as a diagnostic tool for instructors. Reviewing journal entries offers insight into how students are processing concepts, where misconceptions persist, and how pedagogical strategies might be adjusted in real time. In this sense, reflection becomes a two-way feedback system. In other words, students learn through writing, and educators learn through reading.

3. Transparency as Practice

The third principle guiding the course design is the treatment of transparency as a pedagogical practice. This idea emerged while drafting the collaborative AI policy. Rather than viewing integrity as a fixed rule, I approached it as a *dynamic social process* that evolves through collective interpretation. This process in consistent with sociological theories on norm formation. Transparency, in this sense, refers to making visible the human choices, assumptions, and negotiations that shape all forms of knowledge production.

Incorporating transparency into the learning process means building assignments that prompt students to document their use of AI in deliberate, reflexive ways. Each major project includes a space for students to describe what tools they used, how they framed prompts, what revisions they made, and how they evaluated the reliability of outputs. This process mirrors the methodological transparency valued in social research, where credibility and reproducibility depend on clear documentation of process.

The intent extends beyond compliance. When students narrate their interactions with AI, they are invited to treat those interactions as sociological data. They are to analyze what the machine's responses reveal about cultural values, linguistic framing, or institutional bias. For instance, a prompt asking a generative model to define "success" may yield answers that privilege individual achievement over collective or relational measures, exposing the system's embedded value assumptions.

Transparency also functions at the collective level. In the opening weeks of the course, students will collaborate to develop guidelines for responsible AI use, defining together what counts as ethical, appropriate, and scholarly engagement. This democratic exercise reflects how professional and academic communities establish standards through negotiation, demonstrating that ethics itself is socially constructed. Through this process, students learn that human ethics are co-created through dialogue and mutual accountability.

4. Toward a Framework for Adaptive Pedagogy

Collectively, a transferable model for what I call adaptive pedagogy in the age of AI. Adaptive pedagogy recognizes that both technology and society evolve faster than static curricula can accommodate. It requires instructors to treat their own teaching as an ongoing inquiry, or rather, an iterative process of design, reflection, and revision.

This framework also aligns with what Punziano (2025) describes as *adaptive epistemology*, the continuous negotiation between knowing and unknowing that defines life in a digital world. To teach AI sociologically is to acknowledge that our methods, institutions, and values must evolve alongside the technologies we critique. By foregrounding adaptability, this approach resists both technophobia and technological determinism. It neither rejects AI as a threat nor embraces it uncritically as progress. Instead, it treats AI as an evolving social phenomenon that requires constant questioning, contextualization, and reinterpretation.

Ultimately, the pedagogical insights developed through this course design extend beyond sociology or even AI education. They speak to a broader transformation in higher education that reflects a shift from transmitting information to cultivating reflexive, ethically grounded thinkers. In an era where knowledge is increasingly produced through collaboration between humans and machines, such an orientation is not optional; it is essential.

In short, theory anchors, reflection deepens, and transparency humanizes. Together, they provide a model for how educators can sustain intellectual rigor and ethical engagement in an environment where both the nature of knowledge and the means of producing it are rapidly changing.

Limitations and Future Directions

As with any single-semester case, this study has limits. The analysis draws primarily on design artifacts and instructor reflections rather than formal student outcome data. While qualitative insights can illuminate process, they cannot substitute for empirical evidence of learning gains. Future iterations will incorporate mixed-methods assessment, including pre- and post-course surveys on AI literacy, qualitative coding of reflection journals, and focus-group interviews to measure changes in ethical reasoning and epistemological awareness.

These assessments also represent a step toward contributing to the broader Scholarship of Teaching and Learning (SoTL) in the social sciences. Systematic evaluation of how students engage with theoretical frameworks like Berger and Luckmann in applied contexts could yield valuable insights for other instructors navigating AI integration.

The course additionally highlights the potential necessity of interdisciplinary collaboration. While the current version is rooted in sociological theory, future iterations could involve co-teaching with faculty in computer science, communication, and philosophy. Such collaboration would model the very process of knowledge construction the course examines by demonstrating how diverse epistemologies can challenge and enrich one another. Institutional support for this kind of experimentation is crucial, especially as educators face the dual pressures of technological change and limited professional development resources.

Finally, AI technologies themselves evolve rapidly. What feels innovative in 2025 may be commonplace by 2026. Sustaining curricular relevance will require continuous revision, flexible pedagogy, and the courage to engage uncertainty as an inherent condition of teaching in the digital age. In that sense, *AI, Power, and the Social Construction of Knowledge* exemplifies the ongoing, iterative nature of both pedagogy and sociology: a reminder that the social construction of knowledge is never static but always unfolding.

CONCLUSION

Designing this course revealed that course creation is itself an act of sociological inquiry. Every decision reflected negotiation among values, resources, and institutional expectations. Treating the course as a reflective case study made these negotiations visible as I connected my individual pedagogical choices to broader questions about how knowledge, ethics, and authority are produced in the age of artificial intelligence. Through this process, I came to see teaching as both scholarship and praxis, or rather, an evolving conversation between theory and lived educational practice.

Three overarching conclusions emerge:

1. Sociology offers indispensable tools for AI education. Concepts such as social construction, cultural lag, and institutionalization provide critical frameworks for understanding how technologies shape knowledge, inequality, and power. These theories allow students to move beyond using AI as a technical aid to seeing it as a cultural artifact that both reflects and redefines human values.
2. AI pedagogy must prioritize reflexivity. Encouraging students to examine their own relationships with AI cultivates ethical awareness, critical thinking, and what I call cognitive resilience, or rather, the ability to maintain independent judgment amid algorithmic influence.
3. Faculty are co-learners with students in this evolving landscape. The reflective process documented here illustrates how educators can model adaptive epistemology (Punziano, 2025), approaching AI not as a threat but as an evolving site of inquiry that challenges traditional notions of authorship, expertise, and truth.

Ultimately, teaching AI through the lens of sociology reaffirms education as a collective, meaning-making enterprise, as well as preparing students for the contemporary workforce. The classroom becomes a living demonstration of Berger and Luckmann's premise that reality is created and sustained through interaction. That interaction is now extended beyond humans to include our dialogues with machines. In this shared process of exploration, both students and educators participate in the ongoing construction of an ethical and intellectually vibrant future where curiosity, transparency, and critical reflection remain at the heart of learning.

REFERENCES

Bender, E. M., Gebru, T., McMillan-Major, A., & Shmitchell, S. (2021). On the dangers of stochastic parrots: Can language models be too big? *Proceedings of the 2021 ACM Conference on Fairness, Accountability, and Transparency,* 610-623. https://doi.org/DOI: 10.1145/3442188.3445922

Berger, P. L., & Luckmann, T. (1966). *The social construction of reality: A treatise in the sociology of knowledge.* Anchor Books.

Brookfield, S. (2017). *Becoming a critically reflective teacher* (2nd ed.). Jossey-Bass.

Cetina, K. K. (2007). Culture in global knowledge societies: Knowledge cultures and epistemic cultures. *Interdisciplinary Science Reviews, 32*(4), 361–375. DOI: 10.1179/030801807X163571

Collins, H. (2018). Why artificial intelligence needs sociology of knowledge. *Social Studies of Science, 48*(6), 813–831.

Crawford, K. (2021). *Atlas of AI: Power, politics, and the planetary costs of artificial intelligence.* Yale University Press.

Dewey, J. (1981). *The later works, 1925-1953* (Vol. 3). SIU Press.

Felten, P. (2013). Principles of good practice in SoTL. *Teaching & Learning Inquiry, 1*(1), 121–125.

Gabriel, I. (2020). Artificial Intelligence, Values, and Alignment. *Minds and Machines, 30,* 411–437.

Gillespie, T. (2014). The relevance of algorithms. In Gillespie, T., Boczkowski, P., & Foot, K. (Eds.), *Media technologies: Essays on communication, materiality, and society* (pp. 167–193). MIT Press.

Hacking, I. (1999). *The social construction of what?* Harvard University Press.

Higher Education Policy Institute. (2025, February 26). Student generative AI survey 2025. https://www.hepi.ac.uk/2025/02/26/student-generative-ai-survey-2025/

Jisc. (2024, March 8). *Principles for the use of AI in FE colleges.* Jisc. https://nationalcentreforai.jiscinvolve.org/wp/2024/03/08/principles-for-the-use-of-ai-in-fe-colleges/

Kantayya, S. (Director). (2020). *Coded bias* [Film]. 7th Empire Media.

Kozanitis, A., & Nenciovici, L. (2023). Effect of active learning versus traditional lecturing on learning achievement in the humanities and social sciences: A meta-analysis. *Higher Education*, *86*(6), 1377–1394.

Latour, B., & Woolgar, S. (1979). Laboratory life: The social construction of scientific facts. *Sage (Atlanta, Ga.)*.

Loughran, J. (2002). Effective reflective practice: In search of meaning in learning about teaching. *Journal of Teacher Education*, *53*(1), 33–43. DOI: 10.1177/0022487102053001004

Mannheim, K. (1936). *Ideology and Utopia: An Introduction to the Sociology of Knowledge*. Harcourt, Brace & Company.

Memarian, B., & Doleck, T. (2023). *Fairness, accountability, transparency, and ethics (FATE) in artificial intelligence (AI) and higher education: A systematic review*. Computers & Education. *Artificial Intelligence*, *5*, 100152. DOI: 10.1016/j.caeai.2023.100152

Murgia, M. (2022). *Code dependent: Living in the shadow of AI*. Henry Holt & Company.

Ng, D. T. K., Leung, J. K. L., Chu, S. K. W., & Qiao, M. S. (2021). Conceptualizing AI literacy: An exploratory review. *Computers and Education: Artificial Intelligence*, *2*, 100041. DOI: 10.1016/j.caeai.2021.100041

Ogburn, W. F. (1922). *Social change with respect to culture and original nature*. B. W. Huebsch.

Punziano, G. (2025). Adaptive Epistemology: Embracing Generative AI as a Paradigm Shift in Social Science. *Societies (Basel, Switzerland)*, *15*(7), 205. DOI: 10.3390/soc15070205

Rowsell, J. (2025, January 17). Academics fear students becoming too reliant on AI tools. *Times Higher Education*. https://www.timeshighereducation.com/news/academics-fear-students-becoming-too-reliant-ai-tools

Schön, D. A. (1983). *The reflective practitioner: How professionals think in action*. Basic Books.

Selwyn, N. (2022). *Education and technology: Key issues and debates* (3rd ed.). Bloomsbury.

Stake, R. E. (1995). The art of case study research. *Sage (Atlanta, Ga.)*.

United Nations Educational, Scientific and Cultural Organization. (2023). *Guidance for generative AI in education and research.* UNESCO. https://unesdoc.unesco.org/ark:/48223/pf0000386693

van Niekerk, J., Delport, P. M. J., & Sutherland, I. (2025). Addressing the use of generative AI in academic writing. *Computers and Education: Artificial Intelligence*, *8*, 100342. DOI: 10.1016/j.caeai.2025.100342

Veletsianos, G. (2020). *Learning online: The student experience.* Johns Hopkins University Press.

Wacquant, L. (2015). For a sociology of flesh and blood. *Qualitative Sociology*, *38*(1), 1–11. DOI: 10.1007/s11133-014-9291-y

Yin, R. K. (2018). *Case study research and applications: Design and methods* (6th ed.). Sage.

Zawacki-Richter, O., Marín, V. I., Bond, M., & Gouverneur, F. (2019). Systematic review of research on artificial intelligence applications in higher education-where are the educators. *International Journal of Educational Technology in Higher Education, 16*(1), 39. DOI: 10.1186/s41239-019-0171-0

APPENDIX

Course Syllabus

SOCI 4435: AI, Power, & the Sociology of Knowledge

Course Rationale & Overview

Artificial intelligence is rapidly reshaping higher education, the labor market, and the production of knowledge across disciplines. While many AI courses focus on technical development, there is a growing need for courses that interrogate the social construction of AI knowledge systems and their implications for society.

This course fills that gap by situating AI within sociological and interdisciplinary frameworks. It supports the goals of *AI for All Minor* by offering students conceptual and applied tools to evaluate AI technologies as cultural and institutional products. Students will leave the course with both theoretical grounding and transferable skills in ethical reasoning, critical analysis, and public communication.

The course also enhances the sociology curriculum by expanding methodological and theoretical offerings. Its student-centered, project-based design aligns with best practices in online learning and will appeal to students across majors, including sociology, communication, computer science, public health, and the arts.

Course Description:

This course explores artificial intelligence (AI) as a sociological object. We will critically investigate how AI is shaped by human decisions, human ethics, biases, social norms, and power structures. Drawing on Karl Mannheim's sociology of knowledge (1936) and Berger and Luckmann's (1966) theory of the social construction of reality, students will analyze questions such as: Who designs algorithms? Whose perspectives are amplified or marginalized? How do AI tools reflect broader worldviews, ideologies, and historical contexts?

This course will use a student-centered, project-based approach: learners will engage directly with AI technologies while observing, documenting, and reflecting on their societal implications. In addition to building theoretical knowledge, students will develop transferable skills in ethical reasoning, interdisciplinary collaboration, and critical communication. Such skills are increasingly valued in fields such as social research, public health, policy, media, education, and nonprofit work.

Prerequisites: None. Open to all majors. No prior technical experience required.

Course Modality

This is a fully asynchronous online course. Students will work through weekly modules on Canvas that include a mix of short readings, videos, interactive assignments, and peer engagement activities. Students are expected to meet all deadlines and actively participate in online forums and provide collaborative feedback to their peers.

Credits: 3

This course is a core offering in the University of Memphis AI for All Minor, providing foundational knowledge and skills to apply AI ethically and effectively across any field of study.

Learning Objectives

By the end of this course, students will:

1. Develop a sociological lens for analyzing artificial intelligence as a cultural and institutional product of human decision-making.
2. Critically engage with AI technologies to uncover how they reflect and reproduce power, ideology, and inequality.
3. Practice ethical and responsible knowledge production, both by using AI tools with integrity and by co-creating classroom norms for AI use.
4. Apply sociological thinking to public and professional contexts, connecting theory to civic life, career readiness, and interdisciplinary collaboration.

Student Learning Outcomes

By the end of this course, students will be able to:

1. **Apply theory:** Explain how AI technologies reflect Mannheim's sociology of knowledge and Berger & Luckmann's social construction of reality, using these frameworks to analyze examples of AI systems.
2. **Evaluate bias:** Critically evaluate AI-generated content for bias, assumptions, and omissions, and compare outputs across human and machine knowledge systems.
3. **Analyze inequality:** Examine how AI reinforces or disrupts social inequalities related to race, gender, health, and culture.
4. **Demonstrate ethical use:** Use AI tools responsibly in academic research by documenting prompts, reflecting on outputs, and applying ethical reasoning in analysis.

5. **Collaborate in policymaking:** Participate in co-creating a classroom AI policy that defines responsible use and academic integrity standards.
6. **Lead discussions:** Facilitate interdisciplinary dialogue by leading one online discussion and engaging in structured peer response.
7. **Conduct research:** Complete a research practicum that refines a topic, generates research questions, and collects preliminary data using AI tools.
8. **Communicate findings:** Develop a public-facing project (e.g., infographic, video, podcast, or essay) that translates research findings into accessible knowledge for broader audiences.
9. **Reflect on careers:** Articulate how course concepts and skills (critical thinking, ethical reasoning, public communication) apply to future professional, civic, or academic contexts.

Required Readings & Media

All Readings and Media will be Provided on Canvas.

Note About the Readings: Many of the Course readings will be provided in the form of instructor-prepared notes and summaries. Many of the original texts are written for advanced academic audiences, so my goal is to give you clear, student-friendly access to the key ideas without overwhelming detail. Full citations and links will be provided if you would like to explore the originals.

- Instructor prepared notes on: Berger, Peter L., and Thomas Luckmann. 1966. *The Social Construction of Reality: A Treatise in the Sociology of Knowledge*. Anchor Books. (Excerpt)
- Instructor prepared notes on: Collins, Harry. 2018. "Why Artificial Intelligence Needs Sociology of Knowledge." *Social Studies of Science* 48(6): 813–831.
- Instructor prepared notes on: Gabriel, Iason. 2020. Artificial Intelligence, Values, and Alignment. *Minds and Machines* 30: 411–437.
- Benjamin, Ruha. 2019. *Race After Technology: Abolitionist Tools for the New Jim Code*. Polity Press. Assigned Excerpts Introduction and Chapter 1: "Engineered Inequality"
- Murgia, Madhumita. 2022. *Code Dependent: Living in the Shadow of AI*. Henry Holt & Company. Assigned Chapters 3 & 4
- Coded Bias (2020, documentary directed by Shalini Kantayya)

Assessment Overview

Student learning will be evaluated through a combination of reflection journals, structured discussion leadership, applied research assignments using AI tools, and a final public-facing project. All assessments are designed to build cumulatively toward the final project while fostering critical engagement and transferable skills.

Assignment descriptions and the point breakdown are listed below in Table 2

Table 2. Assignment List & Point Breakdown

Assignment	Description	Points
Synthesis Journals (3 × 100)	Three formal entries synthesizing course readings, media, and personal experiences with AI, including sociological and ethical insights. Creative formats encouraged.	300
AI vs. Human Knowledge Comparison	Comparative analysis using student-generated questions answered by both AI and a human expert. Includes written analysis and a visual element.	100
Weekly Reflections	Each student will write a short reflection (200–300 words) responding to a prompt connected to the readings and lecture notes. These reflections will be posted on a designated discussion board and are designed to help students apply key sociological ideas. Reflection must be posted by Wednesdays at noon (11:59 am). Peers must respond by Sunday (11:59 pm).	100
AI Creative Assignment	Students will use a generative AI tool to explore how machines represent or explain creativity. Student will choose a prompt (e.g., asking AI to generate an image of a "beautiful person" or write a poem on a social issue) and reflect on what the output reveals about how AI interprets culture, knowledge, and identity. Your 300–400-word reflection should connect your observations to key course concepts such as bias, representation, and the social construction of knowledge.	100
AI Research Practicum	This project is the first step towards your Final Project. In this assignment, you will use AI tools to refine a research topic, generate 2–3 research questions, and gather preliminary data or sources. You will document your process in a research log (showing prompts, screenshots, and notes). Finally, you will write a short research paper (500- 750) on your findings.	200
Final Project	The Final Project requires the student to shift their focus from academic writing to public communication. The students will use their research to create a public-facing product (such as an infographic, video, podcast, or multimedia essay) designed to share findings with a broader audience. Based on peer & instructor feedback, students will refine their research question, extend their data collection or analysis, and apply applicable theory more fully. Possible formats include infographic, video, podcast, essay, or multimedia narrative. All final projects will be posted in a class discussion forum (the "project gallery") where students will give and receive final thoughts and feedback.	200
Total		1,000

Grading Scale
A: 900-1000 points
B: 800- 899 points
C: 700-799 points
D: 600-699 points
F: 599 points and below

Artificial Intelligence (AI) Policy

Generative artificial intelligence (genAI) is a rapidly evolving tool with significant implications for how we learn and produce knowledge. Rather than presenting a fixed policy on AI use, this course will take a collaborative and democratic approach. Together, we will develop a set of norms and guidelines for how AI tools can and cannot be used in our assignments.

The Process:

1. Discussion (Week 1): In our first week, you will participate in an online discussion about what genAI is, how it works, and its potential benefits and drawbacks. We will explore questions such as:
   - o In what ways do you currently use AI?
   - o What strengths and weaknesses have you experienced with AI?
   - o What kinds of uses should be acceptable for our assignments?
   - o What are the potential consequences if AI is not used responsibly?
2. Collaborative Drafting (Week 2): After the discussion, I will collect your insights and draft a preliminary policy. You will have an opportunity to review this draft and suggest changes in the discussion board.
3. Finalizing the Policy (Week 3): Once we reach a shared agreement, the final policy will be posted on our course page and will guide our use of AI for the semester.

Note: Our syllabus is a *Living Document*: This policy is not fixed. As new technologies emerge or our perspectives shift, we may revisit and revise it together.

Academic Integrity and AI Use

While this course encourages the ethical and creative use of generative AI tools, students are expected to maintain academic integrity. Any use of AI must be properly documented in your assignments (e.g., indicating prompts used, tools accessed, and how outputs were modified or incorporated). Submitting AI-generated content as your own original work without acknowledgment (especially in assignments where independent analysis or reflection is required) will be considered a violation of academic honesty.

As part of our Week 1–3 deliberations, we will define what “responsible AI use” looks like in different types of assignments and how to cite or disclose it. Violations of the final AI policy or the university’s code of academic conduct may result in disciplinary action.

Instructor Qualifications

Dr. JoAnna Boudreaux is an Assistant Professor of Teaching and the Internship Coordinator in the Department of Sociology at the University of Memphis. She holds a PhD in Communication Studies and a master's degree in Sociology. Her teaching and research focus on race, gender, and health inequities, with an emphasis on community-engaged learning and applied sociology.

Dr. Boudreaux is currently exploring innovative pedagogical methods, particularly in relation to emerging technologies and interdisciplinary teaching. Her courses are known for their student-centered, project-based design and their emphasis on real-world applications of sociological theory. She regularly mentors undergraduate students in independent research and internship experiences that bridge academic learning with professional development.

Course Schedule

Week 1: Foundations of Knowledge & Ideology

Readings

- Instructor notes on Berger & Luckmann (1966), *The Social Construction of Reality*, Introduction & Ch. 1
- Instructor notes on Mannheim (1936), *Ideology and Utopia*, Part I (excerpt)

Assignments

- Participate in AI Policy Discussion Forum (introductions + initial discussion)
- Post Weekly Reflection #1: "How do social factors shape what we call 'knowledge'?"

Week 2: The Sociology of AI and Knowledge Production

Readings

- Collins (2018), "Why Artificial Intelligence Needs Sociology of Knowledge"

Assignments

- Continue AI Policy Discussion: Collaborative Drafting
- Post Weekly Reflection #2: "Can machines 'know' things sociologically?"

Week 3: Ethics, Values, and Alignment

Readings

- Gabriel (2020), "Artificial Intelligence, Values, and Alignment"

Assignments

- Finalize AI Policy (collective review and approval)
- AI vs. Human Knowledge Comparison assigned (due Week 5)
- Post Weekly Reflection #3: "Where do we see human values shaping machine learning?"

Week 4: Power, Race, and Technology

Readings

- Benjamin (2019), *Race After Technology: Abolitionist Tools for the New Jim Code*, Introduction & Ch. 1, "Engineered Inequality"

Assignments

- Synthesis Journal #1 due
- Post Weekly Reflection #4: "What does Benjamin mean by the 'New Jim Code'?"

Week 5: AI, Authority, and Expertise

Readings

- Murgia (2022), *Code Dependent*, Chs. 3–4

Assignments

- AI vs. Human Knowledge Comparison due
- Post Weekly Reflection #5: "Who gets to define expertise in the age of AI?"

Week 6: Creativity and the Social Construction of Meaning

Readings

- TBD short case or media example on AI-generated art, writing, or design (provided on Canvas)

Assignments

- AI Creative Assignment due
- Post Weekly Reflection #6: "What does AI-generated creativity reveal about human culture?"

Week 7: Public Knowledge and Algorithmic Bias

Media

- *Coded Bias* (Kantayya, 2020 documentary)

Assignments

- Synthesis Journal #2 due
- Post Weekly Reflection #7: "What does *Coded Bias* teach us about social accountability?"

Week 8: Research Practicum Preparation

Readings

- Student-selected research sources (approved topics)

Assignments

- Draft Research Practicum Proposal (topic, 2–3 questions, initial AI searches)
- Post Weekly Reflection #8: "What does it mean to use AI as a research partner?"

Week 9: Applied Research & Ethical Reasoning

Readings

- Continue student-selected source

Assignments

- AI Research Practicum due
- Post Weekly Reflection #9: "How do we balance innovation and ethics in AI research?"

Week 10: Translating Research to Public Knowledge

Readings

- Instructor note on Public Sociology and Knowledge Dissemination (Canvas)

Assignments:

- Begin Final Project planning (choose medium and outline key findings)
- Post Weekly Reflection #10: "What makes knowledge accessible to the public?"

Week 11: Peer Feedback & Revision

Assignments

- Submit Draft of Final Project to class discussion board
- Provide Peer Feedback to at least two classmates
- No new reading

Week 12: Public Presentation & Reflection

Assignments

- Final Project due

- Synthesis Journal #3 due
- No new reading

Week 13: Looking Forward: AI, Society, and Careers

Assignments

- Course Reflection Discussion: "How will you use sociological thinking about AI in your future work or field?"
- Optional: Update professional or academic portfolio with final project artifact

Chapter 2
Cultivating AI Literacies: A Taxonomy for Sociocultural Praxis and Academic Transformation

Angela Gunder
https://orcid.org/0000-0003-4977-7737
The University of Arizona, USA

Joshua Herron
https://orcid.org/0000-0001-5354-6785
Clemson University, USA

Nicole Weber
https://orcid.org/0000-0001-8723-5686
The University of Wisconsin, Whitewater, USA

Colette Anderson Chelf
https://orcid.org/0009-0003-6253-4024
Independent Researcher, USA

ABSTRACT

This chapter introduces The Dimensions of AI Literacies taxonomy (Gunder et al., 2024), a socioculturally grounded model for guiding ethical, accessible, and adaptable engagement with artificial intelligence (AI) in education. Building on literacy studies (Gee, 1999; Street, 1984), digital literacies (Belshaw, 2012), and open remix culture (Gunder, 2021), the authors frame AI literacies as plural, evolving combinations of skillsets and mindsets that differ across context, role, and community. Eight interwoven dimensions—cultural, cognitive, constructive, communicative, confident, creative, critical, and civic—are outlined to show how they emerge in

DOI: 10.4018/979-8-3373-4129-3.ch002

practice and form "constellations of AI literacies" that strengthen institutional and community capacity. Using a culinary metaphor and a values-driven lens, the chapter reframes AI integration as a cultural and pedagogical opportunity, inviting educators, designers, and leaders to co-create AI-enabled ecosystems that are relational, reflective, resilient, and responsive to change.

INTRODUCTION

Amidst the rapid reshaping of the educational landscape through the onset of artificial intelligence (AI), institutions and educators are challenged to respond to AI's presence not only with technical adroitness but with strategic foresight, ethical care, and culturally affirming approaches. While many early institutional responses to AI have emphasized basic tool adoption or compliance checklists, such approaches risk reducing AI readiness to a singular threshold, reinforcing a binary of "AI literate" versus "AI illiterate." This chapter argues for a more expansive and socioculturally grounded model of engagement—one that treats AI literacies as plural, contextually situated, interconnected, and evolving.

Building on theoretical lineages from (Gee, 1999; Street, 1984), digital literacies (Belshaw, 2012), and open remix culture (Gunder, 2021), the authors introduce the *Dimensions of AI Literacies* taxonomy (Gunder et al., 2024): a collection of eight interwoven literacies that reflect the formation of "constellating AI literacies," or combinations of skillsets and mindsets expressed in AI-mediated educational practice (Gunder, 2024; Gunder et al., 2024). Remixed from Doug Belshaw's *The Essential Elements of Digital Literacies* (2012) and encompassing eight interconnected dimensions—cultural, cognitive, constructive, communicative, confident, creative, critical, and civic AI literacies—these literacies emerge not as discrete competencies to be mastered but as patterns of growth that shift in context, cohere through reflection, and adapt across roles and learning ecosystems (Gunder et al., 2024).

The taxonomy was informed by a qualitative study using the portraiture method (Lawrence-Lightfoot & Davis, 1997) that coalesced the perspectives, practices, and insights of 61 educators representing 23 countries across six continents. In parallel with this inquiry, professional-learning activities and community-engagement initiatives conducted from 2023 to 2025 reached more than 400 educators in 15 countries through workshops, open calls, and pilot implementations. The taxonomy helps educators synthesize recurring patterns in practice and has been iteratively refined through practitioner feedback and real-world application in diverse institutional contexts.

Drawing from collective experience as educational developers, designers, researchers, faculty, and leaders, the authors frame *AI literacies* not merely as technical proficiencies but as cultural practices embedded in values, power structures, and institutional histories. They examine how these literacies are cultivated through practice, enacted across stakeholder roles, and supported by institutional ecosystems committed to reflective, human-centered, and future-oriented educational development and learning design. Throughout the chapter, metaphors from culinary and hospitality practices illustrate how *AI literacies* function like techniques in a kitchen: cultivated over time, adapted to and personalized for specific individuals, and combined with care for those they serve. The authors invite readers to see AI not as an external disruption to be managed but as a site of relational, intentional design, one in which educators and learners co-create meaning, close educational gaps, and reimagine the possibilities of academic transformation.

BEYOND TECHNICAL PROFICIENCY

Reframing AI Literacies as Evolving Skillsets and Mindsets

As the authors reflect on their own AI use both in their individual institutional roles and in their collective work toward institutional strategy on AI literacies, it becomes clear that the field must move beyond a focus on monolithic technical proficiency with specific tools. In any rapidly evolving technological landscape, individual AI tools will come and go; what endures are the underlying skillsets and mindsets that enable people to navigate ongoing change, adapt to emerging practices, and make informed decisions as new tools, processes, and possibilities continue to appear.

In much of the existing discourse, *AI literacy* is framed as a singular, unified competency that can be "achieved," rather than as a set of evolving, context-specific literacies. Widely circulated frameworks such as Digital Promise's *Understand • Evaluate • Use* model (Digital Promise, 2024), Barnard College's *Framework for AI Literacy* (Hibbert et al., 2024), and the Digital Education Council's *AI Literacy Framework* (Digital Education Council, 2024) offer valuable entry points and, in some cases, emphasize ongoing professional learning. However, they still position "AI literacy" as one named capacity to be built across a community. This unitary framing is easily interpreted as a simple threshold to be crossed, which can set up a dangerous binary of AI literate versus AI illiterate that often shapes institutional responses. The pitfalls of this binary are discussed later in the chapter.

This one-size-fits-all orientation has seeped into institutional strategy, where the prevailing impulse is to "get everyone AI literate" by learning a specific tool or completing a baseline course, checklist, or resource. The implicit assumption is that, once completed, the problem is solved and that faculty and staff will be ready to advance AI literacy across their institution. The challenge is that tools, practices, and processes will continue to shift. Without cultivating the broader skillsets and mindsets embedded in The Dimensions of AI Literacies taxonomy, faculty and staff risk being left behind as new tools emerge. Moreover, this approach creates a false binary—either one is "AI literate" or not—when, in reality, AI literacies are multifaceted, situational, and ever changing.

From Singular Literacy to Plural Literacies

The plural framing of AI literacies is rooted in socioculturally situated theoretical and conceptual framings of literacies development. Early definitions of literacy created a binary of literacy vs. illiteracy, a thesis challenged by Street (1984) who argued for a new understanding of literacies as multidimensional and inclusive of the cultural systems that determined how literacies were expressed and enacted. This plurality was echoed by Gee (1989), affirming that literacies are grounded in sociocultural norms, sparking the New Literacy Studies which surfaced a "social turn" where literacies were then seen as connected to their cultural origins. Collins and Blot (2003) work documenting the social turn extended this pluralistic view of literacies, stating that literacies are never neutral technical skills but historically situated social practices bound up with institutions, power, and identity. Their work illuminated that early understandings of literacy as a binary exacerbated discriminatory practices against traditionally marginalized groups, including but not limited to poverty-affected learners, BIPOC learners, and learners from the global south.

This act of marking the societal turn towards culture in learning spaces continued to expand over the years. Kathy Mills (2010) furthered these ideas, exploring the "digital turn" or how the practices and pedagogy of literacy study were shifting from traditional analog to digital media, mirroring a sociocultural grounding. Gunder's work on open remix (2021) collectively bound open educational practices to digital literacies, highlighting an "open turn" towards recognizing the products, practices, and perspectives of educators leveraging digital literacies in their engagement in open pedagogy. And Doug Belshaw (2012; 2023) further extended this thinking into both digital and AI contexts, arguing that literacies are plural, contextual, and value-laden rather than monolithic skills. Read alongside Collins and Blot's (2003) distinction between "official" and vernacular literacies, Belshaw's (2012) critique of top-down, standardized definitions points the same way: literacies should be locally negotiated rather than fixed as a single checklist or one-off experience.

The Dimensions of AI Literacies taxonomy builds on this trajectory, positioning AI literacies as plural, socioculturally situated, and relational: plural, because the literacies needed to engage with AI vary across roles, disciplines, and contexts; socioculturally situated, because AI systems are embedded in and shaped by cultural norms, histories, and power structures; and relational, because AI use in education is never purely individual but rather emerges through connections between people, technologies, institutions, and communities. Attending to these dynamics keeps AI literacies accountable to power and practice rather than drifting toward universality (Collins & Blot, 2003).

Interconnected Skillsets and Mindsets

This plural view of AI literacies recognizes that effective engagement with AI requires more than operational, technical, or one-off know-how. It involves an interdependence of clustered skillsets (tangible, demonstrable abilities that allow an educator to use AI effectively) and mindsets (orientations that shape how those skills are applied, sustained, and expanded over time) that work together. Without the mindset to question outputs, seek multiple perspectives, or adapt workflows, even the most advanced technical skillset can stagnate.

Furthermore, these dimensions are not static. Just as a skillset can be deepened through new learning, mindsets can evolve through experience, reflection, and dialogue. This evolution situates AI literacies as a moving target, not in the sense of a need to chase every new tool, but in continually refining the ways we interact with, shape, and make meaning from AI systems that align with and support our goals, both personally and professionally.

The Dynamic Exchange Between AI Literacies

The development of AI literacies is not a one-way transfer of knowledge from expert to learner. It is a dynamic exchange between the literacies individuals already bring to their engagement with AI and the literacies they gain through use. Faculty, for example, may arrive with strong pedagogical design knowledge, a commitment to accessible practices, and well-honed communication instincts—assets that shape how they judge model outputs, set boundaries, and integrate AI into authentic tasks. Through sustained use, they may gain additional capacities such as multimodal composition, data-informed decision-making, orchestration of human–AI workflows, and the confidence to experiment, iterate, and explain choices to learners and colleagues.

This interplay varies by role and context, producing distinct clusters of AI literacies growth: in some settings, ethical discernment and community impact become the early drivers; in others, making, remixing, and expressive communication take the lead. The point is not to progress through a fixed sequence, but to strengthen the connections among these facets so that practice and perspectives become more adaptive, reflective, and purpose-driven over time.

This dynamic also clarifies why one-off, tool-focused training is insufficient. A baseline course can train learners on today's interfaces, but it cannot anticipate future actions and attitudes that will emerge as individuals engage AI within their disciplines, communities, and institutional constraints. Nor can a techno-solutionist approach sustain growth without structures for ongoing practice, feedback, and reflection—role-aware pathways, authentic problems, and communities of practice that keep development active as tools and norms evolve. In other words, what people bring and what they gain continually form new constellations, strengthening practical judgment and expanding possibilities for teaching and learning.

Constellating Literacies: A Non-Linear Model of Growth

We describe this process of AI literacies combining into patterns of usage and development as *constellating AI literacies* (Gunder, 2024). Like stars forming patterns in the night sky, literacies emerge in clusters rather than in a fixed sequence. In one setting, an educator's critical, civic, and cultural literacies may develop early, driven by concerns about bias or equity. In another, cognitive, constructive, and creative literacies may take shape first, prompted by a need to create real-world assignments for the classroom. These clusters are not isolated; over time, they connect and illuminate new pathways for action.

Constellating AI literacies reframe a singular view of AI literacy as pluralistic—non-linear, personalized, and contextually driven. It acknowledges that a common shared goal can be reached through many possible configurations of literacies, depending on the needs and strengths of the individual and the environment in which they work. For institutional strategy, this means creating professional learning ecosystems that can flex to support varied pathways, rather than prescribing a single checkbox route to "readiness."

Table 1. From Technique to Table: Connecting Skills with Purpose

From Technique to Table: Connecting Skills with Purpose
We might think of our work moving beyond singularity and checkboxes to only learning the sauté when it has to work with the whole dish—not just in isolation. Teaching someone to sauté isn't enough. They also need to understand why they're doing it in the context of the entirety of the dish. The same is true for AI. Knowing how to use a single tool or execute a specific workflow can be useful in the moment, but without the broader mindset to place that skill in context—how it supports a larger goal, complements other abilities, and adapts to changing circumstances—the learning has limited staying power. In cooking, techniques are learned in relation to one another: sautéing, roasting, seasoning, plating. Over time, these individual skills form a repertoire that can be recombined in new ways to suit different menus, tastes, and occasions. Similarly, AI literacies develop in clusters. An educator might first master prompt refinement (the sauté) but only later see how it connects to critical evaluation (the seasoning) or ethical decision-making (the choice of ingredients). This is the essence of the act of constellating: skills and mindsets connecting over time to form a flexible, adaptive capacity. In both cooking and AI, the goal is not to perfect one recipe and declare mastery, but to cultivate a way of thinking and working that can adapt to whatever ingredients, tools, or opportunities the future brings.

The Dimensions of AI Literacies taxonomy provides one such ecosystemic approach. By defining and interlinking discrete literacies, we make visible the full spectrum of capacities that educators need to navigate AI's evolving landscape. More importantly, we design for continued learning and growth—not completion—recognizing that AI literacies will shift alongside the technologies, policies, and cultures that shape them.

THE DIMENSIONS OF AI LITERACIES

A Model for Reflexive and Remixable Practice

In a landscape where institutions often seek a definitive model for readiness or fluency, the field of education must take a deliberate stance to ground AI literacies development in the unique strengths, values, and priorities of individualized, local communities. It is through this alignment—rather than through standardization—that institutions and individuals are best positioned to navigate AI's rapid evolution in resilient and empowering ways.

Each dimension within the taxonomy can be activated in different ways depending on who is engaging with AI and for what purpose. An educational developer updating course content, a faculty member refining assessment design, a student composing multimodal assignments, or a leader developing campus-wide guidelines may all draw upon different literacies—or the same literacies expressed in contextually distinct forms. Furthermore, AI literacies are not only enacted by individuals with prior expertise; they are also developed through use. In this way, the taxonomy reflects a push and pull dynamic: individuals bring literacies to their encounters with AI, and they also cultivate new literacies through those engagements.

Exploring the Eight Dimensions of AI Literacies

What follows is a closer examination of each of the eight dimensions of AI literacies. Each entry offers an expanded interpretation of the definition, examines how the dimension surfaces in educational practice, and considers its expressions across multiple stakeholder roles. Together, these snapshots demonstrate how The Dimensions of AI Literacies taxonomy provides a flexible and pluralistic lens for shaping learning, strategy, and design in ways that are culturally responsive, pedagogically grounded, and human centered.

Cultural AI Literacies

Cultural AI literacies are recognizing the connections between people, AI-informed resources and tools, and points of engagement within AI tools and AI-enabled environments.

They involve understanding the contexts in which AI tools are used, and the sociocultural norms, histories, and institutional dynamics that shape those contexts. These literacies require attentiveness to how learners, educators, and leaders interact with AI in culturally situated ways—how prompts are written, what data sets are leveraged, and how outputs are interpreted and applied. Cultural AI literacies engage with both the inputs (e.g., how a user formulates a question or selects an AI tool), the processes (e.g., dialoguing iteratively with large language models), and the outputs (e.g., the generated text, image, or video)—and how each of these is influenced by local practices, languages, worldviews, and lived experience.

At their core, these literacies encompass both skillsets and mindsets. On the skillset side, cultural AI literacies include the capacity to use AI to develop culturally affirming content—for example, prompting AI to generate examples that reflect students' community knowledge, adapting activities for linguistic inclusivity, or translating guidance into locally resonant idioms. On the mindset side, cultural AI literacies require a reflective stance toward how AI systems encode dominant ideologies, how outputs may unintentionally marginalize or erase cultural perspectives, and how algorithmic "neutrality" often privileges one worldview over others. They prompt users to ask not only "What can this tool do?" but also "Whose norms are embedded in what it produces?"

Cultural AI literacies are not only employed by those who already possess them—they also emerge through use. A designer experimenting with AI-assisted feedback tools may initially focus on efficiency, but through iteration begin to notice that tone and terminology shift based on linguistic patterns the model has learned from dominant data sets. That insight can catalyze a new literacies dimension: the awareness of how automated feedback might subtly misalign with a learner's cultural context. In this way, cultural AI literacies are both brought to and developed through AI interaction.

Their expression varies across roles and contexts. For instance:

- A **learner** might use generative AI to compare cultural perspectives on a historical event, analyzing how a model's summary differs based on prompt phrasing or source origin. They may also evaluate AI-generated images for visual tropes that reinforce stereotypes, cultivating an awareness of representational bias.

- An **educator or faculty development professional** may apply cultural AI literacies by tailoring course materials to reflect the cultural and linguistic diversity of their students. In online and hybrid course design, this might include generating culturally responsive discussion prompts or case scenarios that reflect students' lived experiences—particularly when teaching across borders, to refugee or immigrant populations, or in Indigenous communities.
- An **educational developer** might guide faculty through evaluating whether an AI-generated quiz bank includes examples that are culturally exclusionary or overly reliant on Western paradigms. In co-designing a course, they might encourage the use of AI to localize case studies to reflect regional priorities—public health challenges in Sub-Saharan Africa, for example, or sustainability practices in the Global South.
- An **academic leader or strategist** may draw on cultural AI literacies to develop responsible-use guidelines that acknowledge regional laws (e.g., data privacy in the EU vs. U.S.), linguistic diversity, or institutional histories related to race, gender, or colonialism. These guidelines might be co-developed with community members to reflect shared values rather than imposed from above.

In each case, the dimension is not simply about using AI more "safely" or "correctly," but about leveraging AI in culturally intentional, reflective, and responsive ways. As global classrooms become increasingly hybrid and AI-integrated, cultural AI literacies equip educational developers and designers to shape learning environments that do not default to dominant perspectives but instead elevate the multiplicity of ways learners think, communicate, and engage.

Cognitive AI Literacies

Cognitive AI literacies are expanding intellectual capabilities by engaging with AI-enabled processes and environments.

They encompass developing the knowledge and capabilities necessary to navigate, understand, and make meaning within AI-mediated systems. These literacies require users to build familiarity with AI tools and processes through experimentation, reflection, and engagement. Just as intellectual agility in academic work develops through iterative learning and critique, cognitive AI literacies are cultivated through active interaction with AI systems—asking questions, interpreting responses, testing boundaries, and evaluating reliability. They require not only the ability to use AI tools effectively but also the capacity to understand how and why those tools behave as they do.

As a skillset, cognitive AI literacies include navigating different AI environments (e.g., text generation, image synthesis, or data modeling), evaluating the structure of outputs, and triangulating those outputs with other forms of evidence or human judgment. They also involve recognizing how AI models process prompts, what types of data they're trained on, and how confidence scores or hallucinations signal underlying limitations. As a mindset, these literacies reflect a critical and curious orientation toward emerging technologies—a willingness to explore, to recognize when human intervention is needed, and to question assumptions about objectivity, accuracy, or expertise embedded in algorithmic outputs.

Cognitive AI literacies are both applied and acquired. A faculty member with deep disciplinary knowledge may use AI to brainstorm assignment scaffolds and, in doing so, begin to notice how generative outputs tend toward generic or majority viewpoints. Through this process, the user gains a more nuanced understanding of how large language models compress complexity into surface-level summaries. Conversely, a student who initially struggles to frame effective prompts may, through repeated experimentation, develop stronger pattern recognition and discernment about what questions elicit richer outputs—expanding both their technical fluency and their academic judgment. This recursive dynamic—between using AI and learning through AI—is a defining feature of cognitive literacies development.

Across roles and contexts, cognitive AI literacies take on varied expressions:

- A **learner** might use AI to generate explanations of complex theories in accessible language and then compare those explanations to peer-reviewed sources, thereby developing metacognitive awareness of when AI can clarify versus when it oversimplifies. In STEM or multilingual contexts, students may use AI to translate disciplinary vocabulary into more familiar terms, iteratively refining their understanding of foundational concepts.
- An **educator or faculty development professional** may integrate AI into the learning process by designing assignments that require students to evaluate the strengths and weaknesses of AI-generated arguments, promoting analytical reasoning and disciplinary discernment. In global classrooms, this might include using AI to simulate contrasting perspectives on an issue, allowing learners to explore conceptual nuance beyond a single cultural frame.
- An **educational developer** might analyze how faculty are using AI to support feedback or assessment and then facilitate learning labs that guide educators through comparing AI outputs with rubric-based criteria. Designers may also support the development of "AI critique" activities that build cognitive engagement into the learning design itself—positioning students not only as consumers of AI content but as analysts of its structure and source logic.

- An **academic leader or strategist** may use AI to synthesize institutional data into planning scenarios, but with a cognitive lens that asks: What assumptions are embedded in this output? What patterns are being privileged or omitted? Leaders demonstrating cognitive AI literacies resist accepting AI-generated forecasts at face value and instead use them to **interrogate possibilities**, identify risk, and support strategic foresight.

In all of these examples, the emphasis is on using AI not just as a shortcut to answers, but as a catalyst for inquiry. Cognitive AI literacies help stakeholders interpret how knowledge is represented, distorted, or flattened through AI, and how we might expand or refine our engagement with these tools accordingly. In rapidly evolving AI environments, this literacies dimension becomes especially critical: it sustains the capacity to adapt, learn, and remain intellectually agile as technologies change.

Constructive AI Literacies

Constructive AI literacies are utilizing AI tools to build, remix, and generate new content, applying AI capabilities.

Constructive AI literacies involve engaging with AI tools as collaborators in the processes of creating knowledge, developing content, designing experiences, and shaping educational strategy. These literacies include not just the ability to generate artifacts with AI, but also the judgment to evaluate their quality, trace their origins, and determine their appropriate use. Crucially, constructive literacies rely on an understanding of how AI systems function—their training data, generative logic, and limitations—because only by understanding how something works can individuals reliably build with it. In this sense, constructive literacies are closely tied to cognitive literacies: knowing how a tool works is foundational to using it responsibly and effectively in making.

As a skillset, constructive AI literacies encompass designing prompts to produce specific kinds of content, iterating and remixing outputs, and using AI across stages of a design or writing process. But constructive literacies also require a skill that is often overlooked: the ability to detect when an AI output is derivative, flawed, or ethically inappropriate, especially in terms of misinformation, unacknowledged sourcing, or biased framings. As a mindset, constructive literacies invite a stance of creative experimentation tempered by process-awareness and ethical responsibility, which values attribution, contextual integrity, and alignment with the user's goals and community norms.

Importantly, constructive literacies do not minimize the importance of authorship. On the contrary, they deepen the user's responsibility to understand the implications of AI-generated content: Is this output remixing copyrighted material without credit? Has it stripped attribution from open-licensed sources? Does the generated result reinforce problematic assumptions or erase community-authored knowledge? These are questions that sit at the heart of constructive judgment in AI-mediated spaces—especially for educators and designers working within open education, where sharing, reuse, and citation are carefully cultivated practices. To construct with AI is not to bypass authorship but to navigate it with rigor, intention, and care.

The push-pull dynamic of constructive literacies is especially visible in educational design contexts. An educator might bring years of pedagogical experience to the creation of a new assignment and use AI to prototype alternative formats or generative extensions. In doing so, they develop a sharper lens for what aligns with learning outcomes and where AI's suggestions fall short, expanding their design fluency in the process. A student, prompted to use AI to develop an outline for a presentation, may learn to rework the output into their own voice, verifying claims and integrating cited sources—gaining not just content but a deeper sense of ownership and creative control.

These literacies emerge across roles in varied ways:

- A **learner** might use AI to transform their research findings into a visual explainer, iterating across formats (slide deck, infographic, short script) while also comparing AI suggestions with course readings to ensure alignment and originality. In doing so, they develop not only communication skills but also **remix literacies**, learning what to accept, what to adapt, and what to discard.
- An **educator or faculty development professional** may use AI to generate sample questions or prompts, refining the outputs to ensure they are culturally responsive, correctly cited, and tied to course goals. In open pedagogy contexts, they may also teach students how to ethically co-create with AI—emphasizing attribution, creative commons principles, and collaborative authorship.
- An **educational developer** might use AI to co-develop course materials—say, a case study scaffold or interactive scenario—and then guide faculty through a validation process: checking for tone, alignment with course objectives, and accuracy of embedded references. Constructive literacies in this role mean not just producing content but shaping workflows that support ethical design and sustained quality assurance.
- An **academic leader or strategist** may draw on constructive AI literacies when creating documentation for institutional strategy—such as toolkits, policy drafts, or communication templates. But the literacies lie not only in drafting efficiently with AI, but in **reviewing and refining** those materials to reflect institutional voice, legal and accessibility standards, and community representation.

In every case, constructive AI literacies support the act of making with discernment. They position users as authors, remixers, and evaluators—not only of content but of the process through which it is shaped. In fast-moving digital learning contexts, where AI tools invite speed but not always scrutiny, constructive literacies offer a crucial pause: an opportunity to create with purpose, cite with care, and build in ways that reflect both technological possibilities and ethical commitments.

Communicative AI Literacies

Communicative AI literacies are leveraging AI technologies to convey ideas effectively, recognizing the sociocultural practices and nuances that AI interprets and influences in different settings.

Communicative AI literacies focus on how individuals use AI to express meaning, adapt messages for specific audiences, and refine their voice through iterative engagement with generative tools. These literacies go beyond the mechanical act of producing a message. They encompass the relational, rhetorical, and cultural dimensions of communication—how messages are shaped, interpreted, and received in diverse contexts.

As a skillset, communicative AI literacies include designing prompts for clarity and tone, translating and rephrasing outputs for specific audiences, refining style and register, and using multimodal features (e.g., visuals or audio) to augment meaning. As a mindset, they reflect an understanding that communication is not static or one-directional—it is a social practice informed by norms, histories, power, and positionality. This mindset is especially critical when working with AI tools that, while powerful, carry embedded assumptions in how they interpret language and generate responses.

A key developmental arc within communicative AI literacies is the shift from transactional prompting to dialogic co-construction. Many early users of generative AI approach it as an "answer bot," issuing single prompts and passively receiving outputs. But deeper communicative fluency emerges through a process of iterative prompting, refining, questioning, and co-shaping. Especially as LLMs increasingly support memory and recall, users can engage in longer arcs of discourse with AI, returning to prior ideas, revisiting earlier drafts, and building knowledge over time. This shift requires learning the discourse conventions of AI interaction—not unlike learning the idioms, nuance, and cultural signals of a new language. It is a move from "translation" to fluency, and from mechanical interaction to relational co-authorship.

Importantly, communicative AI literacies also include the ability to bridge human-to-human communication in new ways. AI tools can now assist with multilingual translation, real-time voice tone modulation, and culturally adapted phrasing—making collaboration possible across teams, institutions, and geographies that may previously have struggled to connect. These tools are not neutral and must be used with care—but when guided by communicative literacies, they can enable greater mutual intelligibility, inclusion, and connection.

The push-pull dynamic of communicative literacies is particularly salient here. For instance, an educator might use AI to revise a feedback message for clarity and tone and, through the process, begin to develop a more intentional communication style—one that foregrounds encouragement, clarity, and inclusivity. Alternatively, a student who starts with AI-generated templates for emails or cover letters may, over time, learn to articulate their own voice more confidently, drawing on AI's suggestions but making increasingly sophisticated rhetorical choices.

These literacies manifest across educational roles:

- A **learner** may use AI to draft an application letter or presentation script, refining the tone to suit academic, professional, or personal audiences. In multilingual settings, students might use AI to **translate their ideas into another language** while maintaining original nuance and cultural reference—a process that supports deeper understanding not just of vocabulary, but of **meaning systems**.
- An **educator or faculty development professional** might leverage AI to rephrase complex instructional content, write inclusive guidance for diverse learners, or co-create materials that reflect different regional or disciplinary voices. In a dialogic process with AI, they may also find new ways to scaffold student understanding, test tone in syllabus language, or model rhetorical decision-making as part of a course activity.
- An **educational developer** may use communicative AI literacies to help faculty adjust the tone of announcements, guidance, or feedback across modalities—ensuring consistency between synchronous and asynchronous voice. Designers may also support the co-creation of **language variants** (e.g., simplifying guidance for learners with varied language backgrounds or translating it for accessibility) as part of equitable course design.
- An **academic leader or strategist** may prototype campus-wide communications using AI, but communicative literacies ensure that these drafts are **attuned to audience**, **anchored in institutional values**, and **refined with feedback**. Leaders who leverage AI to support multilingual inclusivity or culturally affirming messaging demonstrate communicative literacies not as output efficiency, but as relational leadership.

In every case, communicative AI literacies offer more than tools for editing. They are capacities for shaping relationships through language—whether between humans and AI, or between humans across distance, difference, and domain. In a world of accelerated messaging, these literacies provide a human-centered compass, guiding us toward clarity, authenticity, and connection.

Confident AI Literacies

Confident AI literacies are developing the ability to solve problems and manage learning within AI-driven environments by understanding and harnessing their unique features and potentials.

Confident AI literacies are foundational to all other forms of AI engagement in education. Without confidence, users often hesitate to explore, unsure of what's allowed, what's possible, or what might happen if they get it "wrong." With confidence, however, users begin to experiment, iterate, and reflect—engaging AI not as a static tool but as a partner in process-based learning and design. This dimension centers the belief that educators, learners, and leaders can work with AI in intentional, values-aligned ways—even when the rules are still being written.

As a skillset, confident AI literacies involve choosing and testing tools, navigating uncertainty, adapting when something doesn't work, and incorporating feedback into evolving workflows. As a mindset, confidence is both individual and relational: it includes the willingness to take risks, the resilience to recover from error, and the trust that others will support rather than shame the learning process. Confidence also involves trusting ourselves to act ethically with AI and trusting that AI systems can be shaped to reflect our values when we engage them with care.

Importantly, confident AI literacies create the conditions for imaginative, future-facing work. Faculty who might once have clung to rigid design templates begin to tinker with prompts. Educational developers share early prototypes to get feedback before polishing. Students feel empowered to try out new ways of composing knowledge, even when uncertain of the exact outcome. This freedom to fail forward, and to share messy, in-progress work, is often what turns hesitancy into growth.

At the same time, confidence must be tempered. Overconfidence—both human and machine—can lead to premature conclusions, flawed outputs, or ethical blind spots. Generative AI systems often respond with fluent, convincing prose even when the content is inaccurate, misleading, or based on flawed assumptions. A confident user is not simply enthusiastic—they are also discerning, cautious, and aware of when not to trust AI at face value. Confidence, in this sense, is about balance: between curiosity and critique, speed and reflection, risk and responsibility.

Confidence also intersects with power and permission. In many institutions, users hesitate to try AI not because they lack skill, but because they lack clarity about expectations. Students may be unsure whether AI use in their coursework is permitted or punishable. Faculty may fear being seen as lazy, unethical, or naïve. These anxieties can suppress creativity and innovation. When institutional signals are inconsistent or absent, confidence becomes fragile—and that fragility disproportionately affects those already marginalized or scrutinized in academic systems.

This is why confident AI literacies must be cultivated collectively, not just individually. It is not enough to tell someone to "just try it." We must build environments where risk-taking is modeled, where "getting it wrong" is part of learning, and where transparent discussion about values and expectations is the norm. Confidence flourishes where there is psychological safety, mutual respect, and shared responsibility for AI integration.

Across stakeholder roles, confident AI literacies are expressed in distinct ways:

- A **learner** might use AI to brainstorm ideas, revise drafts, or explore unfamiliar formats. Initially unsure, they gain confidence by testing outputs, comparing results, and developing internal criteria for what feels authentic, accurate, and appropriate. Over time, they begin to take initiative—shaping AI engagement around their own goals and voice.
- An **educator or faculty development professional** may begin by tentatively prompting AI for teaching examples, then gradually take on more complex educational design tasks. With growing confidence, they shift from reliance on generic suggestions to **purpose-driven co-creation**—and they share their process with peers and students, modeling curiosity, humility, and ethical discernment.
- An **educational developer** might test out a prompt library or automate part of a workflow, then document what worked, where they hesitated, and what they would do differently next time. Designers with confident literacies don't hide their drafts—they invite critique, refine templates across use cases, and build reusable patterns that others can adapt.
- An **academic leader or strategist** might demonstrate confident AI literacies by **naming uncertainty**—acknowledging the limits of current policy, inviting feedback, and creating cross-role advisory groups to explore emerging use cases. Confidence here looks like **leadership without perfectionism**—setting direction while staying open to correction and course adjustment.

In each case, confident AI literacies serve as the bridge between intention and innovation. They empower users to try, to revise, to ask hard questions, and to keep learning. They also sustain communities through ambiguity—because when confidence is shared, not hoarded, it becomes a cultural condition, not just a personal trait.

Creative AI Literacies

Creative AI literacies are engaging in ideation and generative actions using AI, focusing on how AI can add value and introduce new possibilities within specific contexts.

Creative AI literacies are about harnessing AI not just to make things, but to imagine what has not yet been made. These literacies involve using AI to brainstorm, remix, iterate, and prototype ideas—extending the reach of human imagination through co-generative processes. But creative literacies also encompass something more foundational: the belief that creativity is available to everyone, and that it can be cultivated, practiced, and expanded through intentional engagement with tools, communities, and problems worth solving.

As a skillset, creative AI literacies include generating novel outputs across modes and genres, experimenting with tone and structure, using AI to iterate on speculative designs, and translating abstract concepts into communicable artifacts. Users demonstrate this skillset not by mastering a single mode of production, but by approaching unfamiliar tasks with curiosity and play—tinkering, trying, and remixing across boundaries of form, convention, or discipline. As a mindset, creative literacies begin with rejecting the assumption that creativity is fixed or innate. Instead, it views creativity as a habit of mind and a stance toward possibility—one that embraces uncertainty, celebrates experimentation, and invites joy in the making.

Creativity and confidence are intimately connected. Without the freedom to fail, creative risk is impossible. And without seeing oneself as capable of creative contribution, users are unlikely to engage deeply in exploratory work. Many educators, designers, and students carry the weight of past experiences that taught them they were "not creative"—that their value was in analysis, execution, or adherence to structure. Creative AI literacies ask us to put down that baggage and step into a more expansive view: that creativity is not reserved for artists or innovators but is present in the everyday decisions we make about how to say something, how to shape something, and how to imagine something different.

AI tools can support this process in powerful ways. When used intentionally, they can generate surprising connections, help users break out of ruts, and enable low-stakes experimentation at scale. A student unsure of how to begin a writing assignment might use AI to propose three different outlines; a faculty member revising a lecture might use AI to test metaphors or examples; a designer may use image generation to visualize abstract concepts or explore aesthetic alternatives. These acts of generative divergence help move creative ideas from intuition to articulation—not because AI provides the "right" answer, but because it opens doors that users may not have seen themselves.

The push-pull dynamic is again central here. A user brings their interests, values, and context to the interaction, and through AI engagement, discovers new connections, strategies, or ways of seeing. A faculty member designing a new assignment might start with a vague idea, use AI to prototype a first draft, and then critique that draft to clarify what they actually want. Through this process, the creativity isn't just in the output; it's in the back-and-forth, in the shaping and reshaping. Similarly, a student generating visual representations for a research project might learn to articulate visual literacies in ways that deepen their engagement with the topic—and their ownership of the project's meaning.

These literacies show up across stakeholder roles:

- A **learner** might use AI to brainstorm multiple ways of presenting an argument, compare how tone shifts across versions, or remix a research topic into an infographic, short video, or digital story. Over time, learners see AI not as a shortcut, but as a **mirror and amplifier** for their own expressive development.
- An **educator or faculty development professional** might co-create instructional materials that are not only functional but imaginative—using AI to simulate historical debates, generate case scenarios, or develop interactive narratives. Creative literacies in this context mean seeing beyond content delivery, and instead designing experiences that evoke **curiosity, emotion, and connection**.
- An **educational developer** may work with faculty to prototype learning activities that integrate generative AI—inviting students to analyze, revise, or remix AI outputs as part of a creative workflow. Designers might also use AI to generate speculative futures, aesthetic themes, or experimental formats for course environments, helping instructors **see what else is possible**.
- An **academic leader or strategist** might draw on creative AI literacies to explore alternative program models, narrative messaging, or institutional storytelling—especially when trying to engage new audiences or communicate complex change. Creativity at this level isn't ornamental; it's **strategic and sensemaking**, helping others imagine futures they can believe in.

And yet, creativity with AI is not without tension. Generative tools are trained on vast data sets filled with existing patterns—and so they tend to reproduce, not disrupt. Without critical engagement, AI may offer the illusion of creativity while merely repeating the past. True creative AI literacies require users to ask: Whose imagination is being amplified here? What norms are being reinforced? What possibilities are missing? This literacies dimension lies in knowing not only how to generate, but how to intervene, reframe, and reimagine—using AI not to conform, but to create with purpose.

Ultimately, creative AI literacies empower users to make meaning in ways that are expressive, experimental, and situated. They invite people to move beyond replication and toward invention. And perhaps most importantly, they remind us that creativity is not a gift to be discovered, but a practice to be reclaimed.

Critical AI Literacies

Critical AI literacies are examining the assumptions, power structures, and implications of AI usage, and identifying the impact and limitations of AI technologies.

Critical AI literacies form the ethical backbone of AI engagement in education. They involve scrutinizing not just what AI tools can do, but why they do it, for whom, and at what cost. This dimension asks users to interrogate the power embedded in data, algorithms, and outputs: to recognize that AI systems are not neutral, objective, or universal, but are shaped by the values, omissions, and historical biases of the systems that produced them. In this sense, critical literacies are not a separate skill or disposition—they are a constant practice of vigilance and reflection that undergirds every act of use, from prompting a chatbot to designing a strategy for institutional adoption.

As a skillset, critical AI literacies include evaluating sources and outputs for accuracy and bias, identifying the limitations of training data, detecting persuasive language or illusionary coherence in generative outputs, and questioning the epistemologies and value systems embedded in AI tools. These skills are especially vital when AI outputs appear plausible but problematic—when they "sound right" but reproduce existing hierarchies, erase nuance, or conceal error beneath fluent prose. As a mindset, critical literacies reflect a posture of sustained skepticism paired with hopeful responsibility: it asks not only "What's wrong here?" but "What might a better version look like—and how can I help build it?"

This was the first AI literacies dimension to surface prominently in our research—and for good reason. As AI entered the educational landscape, early adopters were struck not only by what these tools could generate, but by what they often got wrong: flattening cultural specificity, citing nonexistent sources, echoing dominant narratives, and amplifying biases under the guise of helpfulness. And even when tools worked "well," they prompted uneasy questions: Whose labor trained this model? Who is credited, and who is forgotten? What happens when surveillance, automation, or misinformation are quietly embedded in teaching and learning systems?

In this way, critical AI literacies are not reactive but foundational. They are the engine that keeps other literacies honest. Without them, confidence may become overconfidence, creativity may become mimicry, and construction may reinforce systems of exclusion rather than transformation. Critical literacies ensure that innovation is grounded in accountability, equity, and long-term social impact.

These literacies are also iterative: they must be tuned and re-tuned, because AI systems evolve, contexts shift, and norms change. A tool that seems innocuous in one moment may become a source of harm in another. This constant re-evaluation requires not just technical awareness but ethical imagination—a commitment to noticing, naming, and addressing the subtle ways AI shapes power in the classroom, the institution, and the world.

Examples of this dimension span all stakeholder roles:

- A **learner** may use critical AI literacies to evaluate how search results shift based on prompt phrasing, or to analyze whether image generation tools reproduce racial or gender stereotypes. They may question the absence of certain voices in AI-generated summaries, or trace how language is manipulated to create a false sense of authority.
- An **educator or faculty development professional** might teach students to interrogate AI-generated content, not just for correctness but for representational fairness—guiding them to ask, "*Whose story is missing? Whose knowledge is foregrounded?*" Educators also demonstrate critical literacies when they themselves push back against institutional pressure to adopt AI tools without sufficient transparency or control.
- An **educational developer** might evaluate whether embedded AI features in an LMS disproportionately benefit certain students, or whether auto-generated quiz banks introduce unacknowledged assumptions. Designers practicing critical literacies actively **de-risk AI use** by testing for fairness, flagging accessibility gaps, and advocating for community-informed development.
- An **academic leader or strategist** may draw on critical AI literacies to set boundaries around surveillance technologies, to demand bias audits from vendors, or to develop institutional guidelines that reflect not only compliance but **care**. These leaders elevate questions like: *How are data being collected and used? What harms are being prevented—or ignored?*

In all of these examples, critical AI literacies extend beyond critique to action. They call on us to not only question but also to intervene—to build alternatives, advocate for transparency, and co-create ethical norms. In this sense, critical literacies are both defensive and generative: they protect against harm while also planting the seeds of something better.

And perhaps most importantly, critical literacies remind us that success in AI is not the same as goodness. Just because a model delivers a smooth result doesn't mean that result is just, inclusive, or meaningful. True innovation requires us to ask harder questions: Who is this working for? Who is it leaving behind? And what new futures might we co-create instead?

Civic AI Literacies

Civic AI literacies are acting to shape AI's development and usage in ways that promote the common good, both within education and society at large.

Civic AI literacies are where reflection becomes responsibility. They encompass the capacity—and the commitment—to use AI not only for individual gain or institutional efficiency, but for the advancement of justice, inclusion, and societal wellbeing. This dimension centers the understanding that AI is not just a tool—it is a social force, one whose impacts ripple far beyond the screen. Engaging civically with AI means recognizing those impacts and then acting with others to shape them in ways that align with shared values.

As a skillset, civic AI literacies include organizing around ethical AI use, contributing to community knowledge, advocating for policy change, and developing resources or infrastructures that increase equitable access. They might involve facilitating workshops, co-creating charters for responsible use, or participating in global conversations about regulation and rights. As a mindset, civic literacies reflect an orientation toward stewardship: the belief that each of us has a role in shaping the digital ecosystems we inhabit—and that silence or inaction is a form of complicity.

While critical AI literacies ask us to examine harm, civic AI literacies invite us to repair and reimagine. They are future-facing, action-oriented, and deeply hopeful. They remind us that institutions are made of people, and that by transforming individual practice into collective movement, we can change the systems that govern how AI is developed, deployed, and experienced.

Civic literacies also challenge the idea that AI responsibility lies only with technologists or administrators. They assert that educators, students, designers, and leaders all have a civic stake in how AI shapes education and society. Whether that means pushing back against exploitative tools, expanding access to underrepresented communities, or teaching students how to organize for digital rights, this literacies dimension connects micro-level practice with macro-level change.

Across roles, civic AI literacies manifest in transformative ways:

- A **learner** may recognize that an AI tutoring system is reinforcing linguistic or cultural bias and raise the issue with peers, instructors, or tech support—sparking a broader dialogue about design. Or they may participate in digital literacies campaigns, contribute to public comment on AI policy, or co-create AI usage norms in student communities.

- An **educator or faculty development professional** might build curriculum that includes not only critical AI analysis but civic engagement—assigning students to propose policy improvements, contribute to open knowledge databases, or collaborate with community partners on AI-supported initiatives. Teaching civic literacies becomes an act of empowerment, cultivating agency alongside awareness.
- An **educational developer** may act as a bridge between institutional decision-makers and learning communities—ensuring that new tools are adopted only after stakeholder consultation, accessibility audits, and value alignment. Designers might also co-develop open educational resources on AI ethics, amplifying access and shared governance.
- An **academic leader or strategist** practicing civic literacies may establish cross-campus working groups to shape inclusive AI strategy, advocate for open-source alternatives to closed tools, or partner with policymakers to influence regional or national approaches. They model **transparency, collaboration, and distributed leadership**, showing that civic responsibility is not an add-on, but that it is the core of meaningful innovation.

Civic AI literacies are especially vital at this moment of accelerating change. As generative AI becomes embedded in everything from assessment to advising, institutions face mounting pressure to adopt quickly, often without considering long-term implications. Civic literacies press pause—not to halt innovation, but to infuse it with care, integrity, and shared vision. It asks: Who is at the table? Who decides what "good" looks like? And how might we broaden the circle to include those historically excluded?

And perhaps most beautifully, civic AI literacies transform what might otherwise feel like fear or futility into collective purpose. They offer a route through the exhaustion of critical analysis and into the energy of co-creation. They remind us that AI does not have to be a fate handed down—it can be a future we help build. Together.

Designing with Integrity and Purpose Through AI Literacies

Ethics in AI is often treated as an add-on, a separate chapter, a late-stage audit, or a checkbox tucked into a policy appendix. But in the context of AI literacies, ethics is not a supplement. It is the substance. It is the connective thread that links cultural sensitivity with civic responsibility, technological understanding with pedagogical care, and innovation with accountability. Ethics is not the thing we pause to consider—it's the reason we proceed with caution and intention. And it is the reason why AI literacies must be cultivated as deeply human practices, not just competencies.

Across the eight literacies dimensions outlined in this chapter, ethical and equity-centered considerations emerge again and again. Critical AI literacies offer the lens through which users examine power: who is building these systems, what data are being used, and whose values are embedded in the outputs? Cultural literacies help us consider how those outputs will be received, interpreted, and acted upon across diverse communities and contexts. And Civic literacies challenge us to move from recognition to responsibility—asking not just What is this tool doing? but What could it do in service of a more just and equitable society?

Taken together, these dimensions offer a relational model of ethical practice, one rooted in ongoing, situated dialogue rather than top-down compliance. Ethical AI use, in this sense, is not a static checklist or singular moment of decision-making. It is contextual, collaborative, and continuous. It requires awareness of harm, yes, but also imagination toward repair. It means examining the politics of "efficiency" that so often undergird educational AI tools—efficiency that may come at the cost of privacy, autonomy, or inclusivity. And it means challenging the myth of value-neutral AI implementation, particularly in learning environments that serve historically marginalized communities.

Educational developers are uniquely positioned to model this stance. In their day-to-day work, they shape not only materials and experiences but also norms and expectations. Their decisions about which tools to adopt, how to scaffold exploration, and how to frame risk and responsibility are all acts of ethical design. When professional learning strategies frame ethical inquiry as central to pedagogical innovation—not peripheral—they signal that values are not barriers to progress. They are what give progress meaning.

This approach does not demand perfection. It calls for discernment. The AI literacies taxonomy itself is built on this idea—that educators and learners can develop the judgment to know when a tool is helpful and when it is harmful, when automation supports accessibility and when it threatens authenticity, when generativity enhances creation and when it risks erasure. In the hands of a critically reflective community, the taxonomy becomes a way to surface ethical tensions, not suppress them.

Just as a good dish reflects care in every decision—how it's sourced, seasoned, prepared, and shared—ethical AI practice is a layered, intentional craft. It invites us to consider not only what we create with AI, but also how we create, with whom, and to what end.

Table 2. AI Ethics at the Head of the Table

AI Ethics at the Head of the Table
Ethical AI use is not a garnish—it's a base ingredient. Like choosing seasonal, sustainable, or fair-trade ingredients, our choices shape not only the taste but the values embodied in the meal. You can't correct harm by adding seasoning at the end. It matters how the dish is sourced, who it nourishes, and whose traditions it honors. In the same way, designing with AI means asking: Whose data built this tool? Whose values does it reflect? Who benefits—and who might be excluded?
Educational developers, faculty development professionals, and educators don't just select technologies. They make choices that echo through policy, pedagogy, and practice. Treating ethics as integral to AI literacies ensures that justice is baked in—not sprinkled on. Because when we say everyone should have a seat at the table, we should also ask: Who set the menu—and how can we make space for more voices in the kitchen?

Constellating, Localizing, and Living the Literacies: Remix in Practice

AI literacies do not exist in isolation. They move in clusters, they evolve in context, and they live through practice. To reflect that reality, the taxonomy developed by Opened Culture is not designed to be a rigid framework or standardized model. It is deliberately open—not only in licensing, but in philosophy. Drawing from "the open turn" (Gunder, 2021), remix in this context is not merely about making derivative products, but rather a way of making meaning through process, connection, and collaboration. It is as much about cultivating shared mindsets as it is about developing technical skillsets. To remix is to build something together, drawing from what exists in order to imagine what could be.

This is why AI literacies must be remixable—because institutions, communities, and learners are different. Contexts are different. Values are different. The literacies dimensions outlined in this chapter offer a shared vocabulary, not a fixed blueprint. They provide a constellation of possibilities, meant to be navigated and reconfigured to meet the challenges and aspirations of local ecosystems. As new tools emerge, policies shift, and collective understanding deepens, remix allows us to remain nimble. It enables adaptation without abandonment, structure without stagnation. It keeps the taxonomy alive—resilient, relational, and responsive.

Through our research and global conversations, we've seen particular constellations of literacies surface as especially generative in practice. One common triad is Constructive–Critical–Civic: educators and designers begin by asking how an AI tool works (constructive), then explore whether it reproduces harm or upholds certain power structures (critical), and finally consider how they might implement the tool in ways that align with community values and contribute to the public good (civic). This cluster often emerges in institutional AI strategy development, course policy design, and ethical tool evaluation. Another widely observed constellation is Cognitive–Confident–Creative: users first seek to understand what an AI tool does and how to navigate it (cognitive), then build the self-assurance to experiment and take risks (confident), and ultimately move into imaginative and divergent uses of the tool that expand what's possible in learning and design (creative). This grouping shows up in workshops, sandbox courses, and design studios where professional learning is scaffolded over time.

These constellations are not prescriptive or exhaustive—they are remixed in response to local needs, pedagogical cultures, and institutional values. Educational developers may emphasize creative and constructive literacies when co-building assignments with faculty. Students may lean on cultural and confident literacies when navigating unclear policies on AI usage. Academic leaders may need to balance civic and critical literacies when advocating for ethical vendor partnerships or participatory governance. The remix is both the design and the enactment—how we flex the taxonomy to reflect who we are, what we care about, and where we want to go.

The examples to follow in the next chapter showcase this spirit of remix in action. Collected from educators, designers, and leaders around the world, they reveal how AI literacies are already being adapted, expanded, and integrated into lived teaching and learning environments. These cases are not meant to be best practices—they are living practices: situated, iterative, and full of insight. Taken together, they offer a window into how AI literacies are being activated not only to meet the moment, but to shape more inclusive, collaborative, and hopeful educational futures.

Table 3. Of Cookbooks and Constellations: Remixing Recipes and Literacies

Of Cookbooks and Constellations: Remixing Recipes and Literacies
In many ways, remixing AI literacies is like remixing a recipe. You start with a base of shared knowledge—ingredients, techniques, and timing—and then adapt it to fit your own needs, tastes, or the community you're serving. A skilled cook knows when it's okay to substitute an ingredient or change the cooking method because they've developed not just a set of techniques, but a feel for how things come together. Similarly, educators and designers remix literacies not by following a rigid formula, but by drawing on experience, intuition, and context. And just as the most nourishing meals often come from local ingredients, techniques passed down across generations, and foods in season, AI literacies are richest when rooted in the cultural context and lived realities of a community. They are not generic or one-size-fits-all—they are situated practices, best aligned with the values, needs, and dreams of the people using them. Literacies, like food, are not only about survival. Their expression is about joy, identity, care, and creation. The taxonomy itself can be thought of as a spice rack: not every dish needs every spice but knowing what's available shapes wise decisions. You might reach for saffron to elevate a special moment, but you wouldn't use it in everything—or worse, use it poorly where turmeric would get the job done more efficiently. The same is true of AI: without discernment, we can waste time, energy, or resources using the wrong tools for the job. Treating a chatbot like a search engine, or offloading judgment to an LLM when human interpretation is essential, results not in innovation, but in confusion or dilution. The art of literacies development, like the art of cooking, is in knowing what to use, when to use it, and how to bring out the best in the whole. When we teach someone to cook, we rarely expect them to replicate our dish exactly. Instead, we offer principles, stories, and scaffolds. Over time, that person builds their own palate, their own rhythm, their own recipes. The same is true of AI literacies. Once learned, they are not static rules but living practices—meant to be recombined, adjusted, and even reinvented in new contexts. What matters most is not just what gets made, but how and why—and who is invited to the table.

ACTIVATING AI LITERACIES ACROSS ROLES AND PROFESSIONAL LEARNING ECOSYSTEMS

A taxonomy is only as powerful as the practices it animates. Used as a shared language and a set of lenses, The Dimensions of AI Literacies can organize day-to-day decisions across a campus—how courses are redesigned, how guidance is written, and how evidence is gathered. Activation means building institution-wide learning as an ecosystem: role-aware, iterative, and unfinished, with faculty, educational developers, leaders, and students working on the same problems from different angles. It also means refusing the silo—replacing handoffs between units with coordinated routines that erase barriers in moving ideas into practice. When literacies are enacted this way, they travel—through studios and sprints, coaching and clinics, communities of practice and the artifacts they produce—so adoption doesn't stall inside a single department or division. The aim is institutional capacity building rather than isolated pilots: collaborative rhythms, reusable templates, and support mechanisms that keep pace with changing tools, practices, and processes.

Activation isn't a checkbox, and it isn't a workshop you attend once. It's an attitudinal shift, or mindset, that assists you in seeing the world and your work differently. When the Dimensions influence how we think, they guide concrete moves—identifying content to provide multiple perspectives, redesigning one assessment to be more authentic, rewriting a paragraph of syllabus guidance with a more inclusive tone, evaluating the way you designed the experience in the LMS to meet student needs. Each move pairs a targeted constellation of literacies with a small artifact and a feedback loop that includes trying new things out, evaluating them, adjusting them, and sharing them with others. The value is the celestial trail: before/after examples, template snippets, and reflective notes about what worked and what didn't that others can use. When those traces live in a common place and are reviewed on a cadence, practice improves in the open and spreads without relying on a one-time course or compliance checklist.

Table 4. Running the Line: Designing AI Literacies Development as a Collaborative Service

Running the Line: Designing AI Literacies Development as a Collaborative Service
At a fine dining restaurant, plates land on time because a brigade knows who brings what and how pieces fit. The executive chef sets intent and secures ingredients. The sous-chef coordinates flow and quality. Station cooks own their dishes. The servers and sommeliers pair choices with context. Everyone shares a quick *family meal* before service so taste and timing are aligned.
An activation ecosystem works in the same way: leaders set direction and support; educational developers coordinate cadence and curate techniques; faculty build the course "dishes"; students act as test tasters and co-designers who keep the work honest and usable. Literacies combine at pace, and nothing sits in a silo.
● **Leaders play the executive-chef role.** They choose direction, set guardrails, fund time and tools, and keep the "menu" aligned with the institution's strategic vision, mission, and goals.
● **Educational developers work like sous-chefs/expediters.** They keep the cadence, translate strategy into learning experiences, resources, and opportunities to connect.
● **Faculty operate as chefs de partie.** They redesign an assessment, run a feedback workflow, write clear guidance, and share the after-action notes others can reuse.
● **Students serve as the tasting panel and co-designers.** They taste test, surface clarity and belonging, and flag what works and what does not in real contexts.
Each contribution adds to the dining experience. Leaders, playing their executive-chef role, bring the different roles together in a family meal to connect, inspire, and empower collaboration. When the brigade functions as a whole, handoffs turn into collaboration, and practices move from one station to the next without losing heat.

Patterns that Scale

With an overwhelming sociotechnical development like AI, it's easy to default to "offer a workshop." Instead, we need to fight this urge and leverage the best of human-centered design thinking (Boller & Fletcher, 2020) and backward design (Wiggins & McTighe, 2005), starting with the people we serve to build human-centered, work-based experiences that are designed with the end goal in mind.

One-off workshops don't build durable capacity. AI keeps changing, so professional learning must move with it: short, work-based experiences that fit real roles, run in multiple modalities (i.e., face-to-face, hybrid, asynchronous), and leave behind artifacts others can adopt. The goal is living in a continuous flow of learning where we understand there is always more to learn, not completion.

- **Communities of practice** (Wenger, McDermott, & Snyder, 2002). Regular, cross-role meetups surface challenges, solutions, and inspirations. Each meeting produces a tiny publication—a one-page note, a newsletter spotlight with links, a micro whitepaper, or a slide gallery—so insights travel beyond the room. Over time, these become a campus commons that normalizes iterative improvement and the power of continuous learning.
- **Studios and sprints.** Small, time-boxed cycles focus on a thin slice of practice—one assessment, one feedback loop, one guidance paragraph. Teams try something, evaluate outputs, adjust guardrails, and share a before/after with a short reflection. Because these cycles are lightweight, they repeat and spread without burning out participants.
- **Resource commons.** Self-help materials sit alongside people-based supports: template language, workflow examples with risk notes, "when to use/when to avoid" cues, and model-critique routines. Materials live where instructors work (e.g., LMS shells, Center for Teaching and Learning website) and are updated on a predictable rhythm so the guidance stays credible and relevant.
- **Faculty champions and coaching cascades.** Champions partner with the Center for Teaching and Learning, as well as their departments and colleges, to mentor peers, run short coaching cycles, and document wins every term. The emphasis is on teaching others to fish--simple playbooks, short check-ins, and artifacts that peers can find inspiration in, adapting to their context. Recognition and awards programs spotlighting both finished and in-flight work serves not only as a conduit for sharing successes but also encourages scale and continuous improvement.
- **Leaders' advisory groups.** Executive leaders (e.g., provosts) convene standing advisory committees to surface broad challenges, learn together, align principles, and turn strategy into course-ready guidance. Parallel groups at the college, department, or program level adapt that guidance to local contexts and surface edge cases. Membership stays cross-role—faculty, educational developers, students, librarians, accessibility staff, and technologists with data privacy experience—so decisions reflect real use. Students in particular ground advisory work in the user experience as opposed to the operational benefits. Without their representation initiatives are speculative at best. The outputs are practical: a campus policy-to-practice brief that clarifies what is permitted, encouraged, or requires consultation; discipline-specific

examples; and a short calendar of near-term priorities with 30- to 60-day goals, measurement, and reporting on return on investment. The Center for Teaching and Learning curates the artifacts in a shared home and brokers the two-way flow between local (e.g., department, program, college) insights and campus strategy and guidance.

Across these patterns, the throughline is the same: work on real problems, capture what changed, publish the traces, and review on a cadence. That's how practices travel across units and how institutional capacity grows while tools, practices, and processes keep shifting.

REIMAGINING EDUCATIONAL DEVELOPMENT IN THE AGE OF GENERATIVE TOOLS

Educational development has always been about intentionality. Learning is intentionally structured to be relevant and responsive to a particular context and specific needs. While educational developers have used templates, benchmarking resources, and established design models to facilitate that work, generative AI introduces a leap in supporting capacity while also allowing for more strategic and experience design work, understood as the intentional crafting of moments and interactions that shape how learners perceive and engage with their learning journey.

This framing of experience design draws from the influence of design thinking on the field, where empathizing with learners and prototyping for impact have become central to how learning environments are imagined and refined (Boller & Fletcher, 2020). While there are legitimate concerns brought to the forefront with questions around authorship, authenticity, and ethics, working with generative AI is reshaping the design process, expanding what can be produced and how. In this sense, experience design offers a useful lens for extending AI literacies into instructional practice, showing how reflective and values-driven approaches can guide when and how AI is integrated into the flow of learning.

Generative AI shifts the designer's role from primarily creating and delivering content to orchestrating learning environments where human creativity and machine capability intersect. This evolution aligns with J. Robert Rossman and Mat Duerden (2019)'s work in *Designing Experiences*, which emphasizes identifying and intentionally shaping key moments that define the overall arc of an experience (2019). It also resonates with Pine and Gilmore's Experience Economy (Pine & Gilmore, 2019) and Chip and Dan Heath's The Power of Moments (Heath & Heath, 2017), which explore how designing for "moments that matter" can transform perception, engagement, and memory. Seen through the frame of AI literacies, this orchestration requires not only technical facility but also reflective judgment about which dimensions of learning the use of AI should amplify.

In an instructional context, this experience design work means thinking beyond individual activities toward the entire journey of learning. With much of the content development work supported by generative AI, moments can be sequenced for impact and interstitial moments—those smaller but meaningful interactions that happen between major learning events—can be elevated. Feedback, reflection, and engagement can be embedded in ways that create lasting impact. The speed and scope of what AI can produce invites rethinking of workflows, but they also demand sharper attention to the alignment between design decisions, learning goals, and the emotional and cognitive journeys of learners. This also highlights the enduring role of human designers in shaping learning that is caring, authentic, and culturally affirming. This is the work that humanizes the classroom and ensures technology serves, rather than flattens, the diversity of student experience.

Table 5. Holding the Vision: Educational Developers as Head Chefs

Holding the Vision: Educational Developers as Head Chefs In a professional kitchen, the sous-chef doesn't just chop vegetables. They help pace the line, anticipate the needs of each course, and prepare components so the head chef can focus on the composition and timing of the overall meal. They may suggest a garnish, swap an ingredient, or prep an element in multiple ways, but they aren't deciding the flow of the evening or the experience the diners will have. When designing learning experiences, AI can operate as sous-chef, accelerating prep, generating variations, and keeping production moving, but the designer still determines the menu, sequences the courses, and ensures every element fits the experience they are crafting. The sous-chef expands capacity; the chef holds the vision.

This reframing of the design process and the role of the designer calls for a shift in how the work is approached. Instead of beginning with "What will I create for this unit?" the designer might now ask "What is the cognitive and affective arc I want learners to experience, and where does AI help me build that?" (Bloom, 1956; Krathwohl, 2002).

The Dimensions of AI Literacies taxonomy serves as a guide for this decision-making. Beginning with backward design (Wiggins & McTighe, 2005), the Cognitive, Constructive, and Communicative dimensions work together to support evaluation of whether AI-generated materials are accurate, adaptable, and aligned with the needs of the intended audience, while the Critical dimension foregrounds the importance of examining underlying assumptions and implications. The Civic dimension highlights how representation, accessibility, and culturally affirming practices can be intentionally woven into design choices, ensuring that AI supports inclusion rather than undermining it (Hammond, 2015). The Creative and Confident dimensions encourage experimentation and rapid prototyping, while also positioning the designer to shape pacing, sequencing, and coherence with intentionality and care across the learning experience.

Generative AI also alters the temporal dynamics of design. Tasks that once required days or weeks, such as developing case examples or creating draft visuals, can now be completed in hours. This compression of production time allows more attention to sequencing, scaffolding, and learner engagement strategies. Yet this efficiency is not automatic. It depends on knowing how to use the tools effectively and on developing the Confident and Critical dimensions of AI literacies that help designers understand the timing involved in using AI well. Prompting, refining, and validating outputs still take time, and learning when that investment improves the design—and when it does not—is part of the ongoing professional judgment required. Experience design principles remind us that more content does not necessarily equal better learning; rather, the intentional arrangement of moments often produces the most meaningful outcomes.

The ability to prototype rapidly also supports more iterative design cycles. Multiple variations of a learning asset can be generated, tested, and refined based on feedback. This accelerates improvement while requiring literacies that focus on critical evaluation, ethical alignment, and adaptability. Confident literacies development is essential here, enabling designers to experiment without becoming overly reliant on initial AI outputs.

Looking ahead, the promise of generative AI lies not just in speeding up workflows but in enabling experiences that are intentionally designed to transform learners. When paired with deeper AI literacies, these tools can help designers move beyond efficiency into a future where learning journeys are more adaptive, more inclusive, and more memorable. Experience design reminds us that transformation requires shaping not only content, but also the emotional and cognitive arcs of learning. Generative AI has the potential to support that transformation by making it possible to test, refine, and orchestrate learning in ways that were once out of reach. If guided by intentionality and care, AI can expand educational development into a practice that produces not just courses, but lasting shifts in how people think, feel, and act—experiences that echo the most powerful transformations learners carry forward into their lives.

EDUCATIONAL DEVELOPERS AS CATALYSTS FOR CULTURAL TRANSFORMATION

Educational developers have often been the unsung heroes of teaching and learning amidst external factors such as shifting learner expectations, workforce development needs, and technological changes, all alongside internal factors like shrinking budgets and leaner operations. In the context of AI integration, this role becomes even more pivotal. The work is exciting but complex, involving pedagogy, technology, and strategy in ways that guide communities toward thoughtful adoption rather than reactive implementation.

The Dimensions of AI Literacies taxonomy gives its users language that crosses disciplinary and functional boundaries, enabling faculty, educational developers, faculty development professionals, technologists, and administrators to approach AI integration with common reference points. This shared vocabulary helps position AI literacies not as isolated skills, but as cultural capacities that can be embedded across professional learning ecosystems. These literacies rarely develop in linear order; they cluster and interact like constellations, forming patterns that reflect institutional priorities and local contexts. Seeing literacies this way reinforces that AI integration is not about checking off competencies, but about cultivating interconnected capacities that guide sustainable, values-aligned transformation.

Cultural transformation occurs when these capacities are enacted collectively, a process that can be framed through the "Three C's" of educational development: Collaboration, Creation, and Connection (Gunder, 2024). Collaboration emerges through shared learning experiences where participants engage in hands-on AI exploration, exchange perspectives, and identify relevant literacies in practice. Creation takes shape in the co-design of plural resources, frameworks, and exemplars that reflect institutional values and adapt to local contexts. Connection develops through sustained communities of practice where ideas circulate, experiments are shared, and collective capacity grows over time (Wenger, McDermott, & Snyder, 2002).

Transformation of this kind is rarely rapid. It requires building trust, shifting habits, and creating structures that endure beyond individual initiatives. Experience design principles apply here as well, yet the aim goes beyond crafting impactful moments. The next level is transformation. Experiences move from being memorable to fundamentally altering perspectives, behaviors, and capabilities. In this context, work to cultivate AI literacies that is led by educational developers is not simply about improving discrete activities or programs. It is about reshaping the culture of teaching and learning so that engagement with AI becomes part of an institution's identity, sustaining both innovation and integrity over time.

The positioning of educational developers often reflects what Kezar and Eckel (2002) describe as "coming in from the margins," influencing institutional change through lateral, relationship-driven work rather than top-down authority. This vantage point allows developers to navigate across boundaries, build coalitions, and introduce new practices such as AI literacies into existing structures in ways that feel contextually relevant and non-threatening. In the context of AI, this side-entry approach is particularly effective for embedding values-aligned practices into teaching, policy, and professional learning ecosystems.

Table 6. The Educational Developer as Host

The Educational Developer as Host
A skilled party host does far more than provide a space. They anticipate needs, set the atmosphere, and orchestrate the flow of the evening so that everyone feels included and engaged. They think carefully about who to invite and how different personalities might connect, curate the music and menu to reflect shared values, and adjust on the fly when the unexpected happens. While they may not serve every dish or lead every conversation, their unseen labor shapes the tone, coherence, and memory of the gathering.
Educational developers operate in a similar way. They don't deliver every piece of content or write all guidance, but they shape the conditions in which others thrive. They invite faculty, staff, and students into spaces of shared exploration, set the cadence for collaboration, and create an environment where AI literacies can take root and flourish. Like a host who curates a meaningful gathering, developers cultivate belonging, steward shared values, and help the event feel larger than the sum of its parts.

By treating AI integration as a sociocultural process rather than a purely technical upgrade, educational developers can help institutions build distributed capacity that is adaptable and aligned with their mission. The aim is not necessarily uniform fluency with a set of tools, but to build a community able to navigate emerging technologies with discernment, creativity, and ethical clarity. In this work, educational developers act as catalysts by aligning collaboration, community, and connection so that AI adoption strengthens rather than dilutes the human-centered values at the heart of education.

CONCLUSION

As educational developers, along with their colleagues and learners at their institutions, continue to grapple with the rapidly shifting realities of AI in education, the need to move beyond technical compliance and toward a more culturally affirming, human-centered approach is urgent. The Dimensions of AI Literacies taxonomy provides a way to meet this need—not through rigid frameworks or prescriptive mandates, but by illuminating a constellation of interdependent and interconnected AI literacies that evolve through practice, reflection, and situated experience. These literacies are not additive enhancements to existing pedagogical norms, but reorienting forces—ones that challenge us to reimagine the purposes, values, and relationships at the heart of education.

To treat AI literacies as sociocultural practice is to resist simplification. It means understanding that literacy is never neutral, never merely a matter of technical mastery, and never a binary. It is always shaped by power, access, and identity—by who defines competence, whose ways of knowing are privileged, and whose participation is made possible or precluded. In centering this perspective, we assert that AI integration is not simply an instructional or infrastructural concern, but a cultural project that implicates every corner of the academic ecosystem.

The eight dimensions articulated in this chapter—cultural, cognitive, constructive, communicative, confident, creative, critical, and civic AI literacies—offer not only a vocabulary for interpreting AI's impact on teaching and learning, but also a compass for designing with integrity. When activated collectively, these literacies shape inclusive ecosystems of practice: learning environments where creativity is scaffolded, critique is encouraged, care is practiced, and values are made visible. They help us surface the ethical, relational, and political questions that too often remain implicit in institutional strategy: What does this tool assume? Whom does it serve? Who is left out? What might we do differently?

This taxonomy has deliberate boundaries. It doesn't prescribe specific tools or platforms because those change too rapidly. It doesn't offer compliance checklists because those reduce complex literacies to mechanical tasks. And it doesn't resolve the fundamental tension between efficiency and criticality. Some contexts demand rapid AI adoption; others require slow, careful consideration. The taxonomy provides language for navigating these tensions, not resolving them, through human insight and intelligence.

We close not with answers, but with an invitation. AI literacies, like the culinary metaphors that run throughout this chapter, require attention to process, ingredients, and the communities we aim to serve. They demand shared preparation, intentional composition, and the willingness to adapt recipes to local needs and evolving conditions. They are cultivated in practice—through collaboration, experimentation, and the courage to question inherited norms. In the face of uncertainty, AI literacies offer not certainty, but possibility. Not a singular path forward, but a generative model for ongoing dialogue, care-filled design, and collective transformation. If we are to harness AI in ways that align with the highest aspirations of education, then we must lead not with fear or compliance, but with connection, curiosity, and a deep commitment to the people we serve. That is the promise of AI literacies—not as endpoints, but as entry points to more just, imaginative, and resilient futures.

REFERENCES

Belshaw, D. (2012). *The essential elements of digital literacies.* CreateSpace Independent Publishing.

Belshaw, D. (2023, March 18). *AI literacy.* Doug Belshaw's blog. https://dougbelshaw.com/blog/2023/03/18/ai-literacy/

Bloom, B. S. (Ed.). (1956). *Taxonomy of educational objectives: The classification of educational goals. Handbook I: Cognitive domain.* Longmans, Green.

Boller, S., & Fletcher, L. (2020). *Design thinking for training and development: Creating learning journeys that get results.* Association for Talent Development.

Collins, J., & Blot, R. K. (2003). *Literacy and literacies: Texts, power, and identity.* Cambridge University Press.

Digital Education Council. (2024). *Digital Education Council AI literacy framework.* https://www.digitaleducationcouncil.com/post/digital-education-council-ai-literacy-framework

Digital Promise. (2024). *AI literacy: A framework to understand, evaluate, and use emerging technology.* https://digitalpromise.org/2024/06/18/ai-literacy-a-framework-to-understand-evaluate-and-use-emerging-technology/

Gee, J. P. (1989). Literacy, discourse, and linguistics: Introduction. *Journal of Education, 171*(1), 5–17. DOI: 10.1177/002205748917100101

Gee, J. P. (1999). The new literacy studies and the "social turn." [ERIC document]. https://files.eric.ed.gov/fulltext/ED442118.pdf

Gunder, A. (2021). *The open turn: Portraits, practices, and perspectives on the remix of open educational resources* [Doctoral dissertation, The University of Arizona]. http://hdl.handle.net/10150/663131

Gunder, A. (2024). *Constellating AI literacies: Illuminating the sociocultural and pluralistic dimensions of AI in education.* Opened Culture.

Gunder, A., Herron, J., Weber, N., Chelf, C., & Birdwell, S. (2024). *Dimensions of AI literacies.* Opened Culture. https://openedculture.com/projects/dimensions-of-ai-literacies/

Hammond, Z. (2015). *Culturally responsive teaching and the brain: Promoting authentic engagement and rigor among culturally and linguistically diverse students.* Corwin.

Heath, C., & Heath, D. (2017). *The power of moments: Why certain experiences have extraordinary impact*. Simon & Schuster.

Hibbert, M., Altman, E., Shippen, T., & Wright, M. (2024, June 3). *A framework for AI literacy*. In EDUCAUSE Review. EDUCAUSE. https://er.educause.edu/articles/2024/6/a-framework-for-ai-literacy

Kezar, A., & Eckel, P. D. (2002). Coming in from the margins: Faculty development's emerging organizational development role in institutional change. *The Journal of Higher Education, 73*(1), 26–48. DOI: 10.1080/00221546.2002.11777132

Krathwohl, D. R. (2002). A revision of Bloom's taxonomy: An overview. *Theory into Practice, 41*(4), 212–218. DOI: 10.1207/s15430421tip4104_2

Lawrence-Lightfoot, S., & Davis, J. H. (1997). *The art and science of portraiture*. Jossey-Bass.

Mills, K. A. (2010). A review of the "digital turn" in the new literacy studies. *Review of Educational Research, 80*(2), 246–271. DOI: 10.3102/0034654310364401

Pine, B. J., & Gilmore, J. H. (2019). *The experience economy: Competing for customer time, attention, and money* (Updated ed.). Harvard Business Review Press.

Rossman, J. R., & Duerden, M. D. (2019). *Designing experiences*. Columbia Business School Publishing.

Street, B. V. (1984). *Literacy in theory and practice*. Cambridge University Press.

Wenger, E., McDermott, R., & Snyder, W. (2002). *Cultivating communities of practice: A guide to managing knowledge*. Harvard Business Review Press.

Wiggins, G. P., & McTighe, J. (2005). *Understanding by design* (2nd ed.). Pearson.

KEY TERMS AND DEFINITIONS

AI Literacies: The skills needed to comprehend, utilize, and critically evaluate AI within complex environments; AI literacies are to be distinguished from AI literacy (singular) due to the latter creating a harmful binary between "literacy" and "illiteracy" that has historically been used to discriminate and marginalize specific populations, communities, and cultures

AI Mindsets: Attitudinal and dispositional orientations that shape how individuals approach, sustain, and make meaning from their interactions with AI

AI Skillsets: Tangible, demonstrable actions and abilities that enable individuals to effectively engage with AI tools, systems, and environments within educational contexts

Civic AI Literacies: Employing AI knowledge and skills to contribute positively to society, using AI to foster community empowerment, engagement, and societal progress

Confident AI Literacies: Developing the ability to solve problems and manage learning within AI-driven environments by understanding and harnessing their unique features and potentials.

Cognitive AI Literacies: Expanding intellectual capabilities by engaging with AI-enabled processes and environments

Communicative AI Literacies: Leveraging AI technologies to convey ideas effectively, recognizing the sociocultural practices and nuances that AI interprets and influences in different settings

Constellating AI Literacies: A grouping of skill sets and mindsets that, when connected, help us navigate the complex realities of AI in education and society

Constructive AI Literacies: Utilizing AI tools to build, remix, and generate new content, applying AI capabilities

Creative AI Literacies: Engaging in ideation and generative actions using AI, focusing on how AI can add value and introduce new possibilities within specific contexts

Critical AI Literacies: Examining the power dynamics and ethical considerations inherent in AI practices, reflecting on the broader societal impacts of AI-driven decisions and actions

Cultural AI Literacies: Recognizing the connections between people, AI-informed resources and tools, and points of engagement within AI tools and AI-enabled environments

Literacies (plural): A theoretical and conceptual orientation that recognizes literacies as pluralistic, contextual, interconnected, and socially constructed dimensions rather than a single state or universal

Chapter 3
Balancing AI-Driven Innovation With Authentic Learning in Higher Education

O. Bhaskaru
https://orcid.org/0000-0001-6495-3327
Vignan's Foundation for Science, Technology, and Research, India

K. Lalitha
https://orcid.org/0009-0004-9735-7205
Santhiram Engineering College, India

ABSTRACT

Artificial Intelligence (AI) is increasingly shaping higher education by enhancing instructional design, assessments, and student engagement. While AI offers benefits like adaptive learning, predictive analytics, and smart feedback, it also challenges the preservation of authentic learning, which values real-world relevance, critical thinking, collaboration, and student agency. This chapter examines how educators and institutions can balance AI innovation with maintaining authentic pedagogy by proposing a framework that integrates AI tools while supporting core authentic learning principles. It draws on educational theory, case studies, and practical examples to show how AI can enhance teaching without undermining learning quality. Additionally, it addresses challenges such as faculty readiness, ethical issues, and policy gaps, offering recommendations for professional development, curriculum updates, and policy to ensure responsible AI use. The aim is to help educators and administrators foster environments where AI-driven innovation and authentic learning coexist effectively.

DOI: 10.4018/979-8-3373-4129-3.ch003

INTRODUCTION

Higher education is undergoing a profound transformation due to the rapid advancement and integration of Artificial Intelligence (AI) technologies. AI applications now influence teaching, learning, and institutional management. Adaptive learning platforms personalize educational content, while predictive analytics forecast student performance. Together, these innovations promise to revolutionize how knowledge is imparted and acquired.

Yet, this technological revolution poses significant questions for the nature and quality of learning itself. While AI systems offer efficiencies and enhanced engagement opportunities, there is an urgent need to preserve the authenticity of learning experiences—those that encourage real-world relevance, critical thinking, collaboration, and learner autonomy. Authentic learning environments are essential for producing graduates capable of solving complex problems and adapting to dynamic global challenges.

This chapter introduces the critical tension between the adoption of AI-driven innovations and the preservation of authentic learning in higher education. It sets out to explore the potential synergies and conflicts inherent in this intersection and proposes an analytical lens to understand and guide balanced integration. Key objectives include:

- Contextualizing the rise and scope of AI applications in education
- Defining the principles and characteristics of authentic learning.
- Articulating the chapter's focus on achieving a balanced, human-centered approach.

The following sections will delve deeper into these themes and set the foundation for the rest of the chapter series.

Rise of AI in Educational Contexts

Artificial Intelligence, broadly defined as machines' ability to simulate human cognitive processes, has been steadily integrated into education since the early 2000s. Recent advances in machine learning, natural language processing, and data analytics have accelerated the adoption of AI-powered tools in higher education settings.

Key AI Applications in Higher Education

- **Adaptive Learning Systems**: Platforms such as Smart Sparrow and Knewton use AI to analyze individual learners' knowledge gaps and preferences. These systems dynamically adjust instructional content and pacing to provide a personalized learning path. By tailoring lessons to the learner's needs, adaptive systems enhance engagement and help ensure mastery before moving forward (Woolf, 2010).

- **Intelligent Tutoring Systems (ITS)**: ITS provide customized, interactive feedback similar to a personal tutor. They assess student responses in real time, diagnose misconceptions, and offer targeted hints and scaffolding. This individualized support promotes critical thinking and deeper understanding without simply giving answers, fostering learner independence (VanLehn, 2011).
- **Predictive Analytics**: AI examines historical and current student data—such as grades, attendance, and participation—to identify students who might struggle or drop out. Institutions can then offer early support and interventions to improve retention and academic success (Arnold & Pistilli, 2012).
- **Automated Grading and Feedback** Using natural language processing, AI can assess essays and written assignments quickly and objectively, providing timely feedback on structure, grammar, and content quality. This helps students improve continuously while reducing grading workload for instructors (Shermis & Burstein, 2013).
- **Virtual Teaching Assistants**: Chatbots like Georgia Tech's "Jill Watson" answer student queries about course logistics and content at any time, offering instant support and reducing instructor burden. This continuous accessibility helps maintain student engagement outside regular class hours (Goel & Polepeddi, 2016).

Table 1. AI Applications in Higher Education

Application Type	Description	Benefits	Examples
Adaptive Learning	Personalized content delivery	Increases engagement and retention	Smart Sparrow, Knewton
Intelligent Tutoring Systems	AI-driven individualized tutoring	Supports mastery learning	Carnegie Learning, ALEKS
Predictive Analytics	Early detection of student success/failure	Enhances student support	Civitas Learning
Automated Assessment	AI-based grading of assignments	Saves instructor time	Turnitin Revision Assistant
Virtual Assistants	AI chatbots for student support	Improves accessibility	Jill Watson (Georgia Tech)

Table 1 illustrates key AI-driven applications currently transforming higher education, including adaptive learning systems, intelligent tutoring, predictive analytics, automated grading, and virtual teaching assistants. For each application type, the figure outlines its primary functions, the benefits offered—such as personalized learning, improved student support, and increased operational efficiency—and examples of prominent platforms. This overview highlights how AI technologies are enhancing educational experiences while emphasizing the need for thoughtful integration to preserve authentic and human-centered learning.

While these AI-driven innovations offer remarkable opportunities to enhance personalized learning and operational efficiency, they also introduce challenges that higher education institutions must carefully navigate. Over-automation can risk depersonalizing the learning experience, reducing opportunities for meaningful human interaction and critical reflection. There are concerns about algorithmic biases that may unintentionally reinforce inequities among diverse student populations (Zawacki-Richter et al., 2019). Moreover, reliance on AI tools without adequate faculty preparedness or institutional support could undermine pedagogical integrity and ethical standards.

Thus, while AI technologies present exciting prospects, their adoption must be accompanied by critical reflection to preserve the human-centered and authentic qualities essential to higher education.

Need for Authenticity in Learning

Authentic learning emphasizes meaningful, contextualized tasks that connect to real-world challenges and promote learner agency, collaboration, and reflection. The following section explores its characteristics in greater depth (Herrington et al., 2010).

Core Characteristics of Authentic Learning:

1. Ensure real-world relevance by designing tasks that mirror actual challenges and highlight the practical value of knowledge.
2. Build on a constructivist foundation where learners actively construct understanding through exploration, interaction, and collaboration.
3. Encourage collaboration by engaging students in teamwork, discussions, and joint problem-solving that reflect real-world knowledge creation.
4. Promote student agency by giving learners the freedom to set goals, make choices, and take ownership of their learning process.
5. Foster reflection by prompting learners to assess their progress, identify gaps, and refine their understanding for continuous growth.

While these characteristics provide a strong foundation for authentic learning, integrating them with AI presents challenges. For instance, AI tools may facilitate collaboration through group-matching algorithms, but they cannot fully replicate the nuance of human interaction, negotiation, and trust-building that authentic teamwork requires (Zhang, Kizilcec, & Chen, 2021).

Table 2 demonstrates how authentic learning fundamentally differs from traditional education models. Whereas traditional methods often involve passive learning in decontextualized environments, authentic learning promotes active, situated experiences that mirror real-world practices. Teachers act more as facilitators than transmitters of content, while students are co-creators of knowledge rather than mere recipients. Furthermore, authentic learning emphasizes performance-based assessments aligned with real-world competencies rather than rote memorization or standardized tests.

As AI tools become more prevalent in higher education, it is crucial to use them to enhance—rather than replace—authentic learning. Institutions must balance technology with meaningful education to ensure students build critical, reflective, and collaborative skills for lifelong success

Table 2. Comparison of Traditional vs. Authentic Learning

Dimension	Traditional Learning	Authentic Learning
Learning Approach	Passive reception of information	Active construction of knowledge
Assessment	Standardized tests	Performance-based, real-world tasks
Role of Teacher	Knowledge transmitter	Facilitator and guide
Student Role	Recipient of information	Active participant and collaborator
Learning Context	Classroom, abstract	Realistic, contextualized

Objectives and Scope of the Chapter

This chapter aims to explore the complex relationship between AI and authentic learning in higher education, focusing on how institutions can adopt innovative AI technologies without compromising essential pedagogical values. It addresses the challenge of integrating AI in a way that supports meaningful, student-centered learning experiences.

The primary objectives of this chapter include:

1. **Examining the transformative potential of AI in instructional design, assessment, and student engagement:**

The chapter investigates how AI technologies are reshaping education by enabling personalized learning, enhancing assessment processes through automation and intelligent feedback, and increasing student interaction and motivation via tools like intelligent tutoring systems and virtual assistants. This examination highlights how AI can improve educational outcomes and efficiency.

2. **Identifying essential elements of authentic learning that need to be maintained:**

Despite AI's expanding role, the chapter emphasizes preserving key aspects of authentic learning, including real-world relevance of tasks, fostering critical thinking and problem-solving skills, promoting collaboration and social engagement, and encouraging student ownership of their learning. These elements are crucial for preparing students to address real-life challenges effectively.

3. **Proposing a balanced framework that aligns AI tools with core authentic learning principles:**

The chapter introduces a framework to guide the responsible integration of AI, ensuring technological advancements complement rather than diminish authentic learning. This framework helps educators and institutions use AI to enhance, rather than replace, meaningful teaching and learning.

4. **Highlighting practical challenges related to faculty readiness, ethics, and institutional policies:**

The chapter identifies obstacles in AI adoption such as gaps in faculty skills and training, ethical concerns including privacy and algorithmic bias, and the lack of clear institutional policies. Addressing these challenges is necessary to ensure the responsible and equitable use of AI in education.

5. **Offering strategic recommendations for educators and administrators:**

To support effective AI integration, the chapter provides recommendations on professional development, curriculum redesign, and policy creation. These strategies help build faculty competence, update curricula to integrate AI thoughtfully, and establish guidelines for ethical AI use in education.

Scope of the chapter:

This chapter covers relevant educational theories related to authentic learning, reviews AI applications in higher education, and draws on case studies and practical examples. It addresses both the opportunities and risks associated with AI to equip academic leaders with the insights needed to navigate AI's evolving role in education thoughtfully and effectively.

While AI offers significant opportunities for efficiency and personalization, scholars caution that over-reliance on automation risks reducing education to mechanical transactions rather than meaningful human learning (Bayne, 2015; Selwyn, 2019). This tension between technological innovation and authentic pedagogy underscores the importance of striking a balance. The next section therefore examines why authenticity remains a vital concern in AI-driven higher education

UNDERSTANDING AUTHENTIC LEARNING

Authentic learning has become a central focus in higher education as institutions strive to prepare students for complex real-world challenges. This chapter examines the key characteristics of authentic learning, its grounding in constructivist learning theories, and the vital role educators play in fostering authentic learning environments.

Characteristics of Authentic Learning

Authentic learning focuses on meaningful experiences that connect closely with real-world contexts. Unlike traditional learning that often relies on memorization, authentic learning encourages active engagement, critical thinking, and practical application of knowledge.

The key features include:

1. Real-World Relevance:

Learning tasks reflect actual challenges students might face outside the classroom. This connection helps increase motivation by showing the practical importance of what they are learning (Herrington, Reeves, & Oliver, 2014).

2. Complex, Ill-Structured Problems:

Students work on open-ended problems that require them to analyze, evaluate, and synthesize information rather than just recall facts. These problems mirror the ambiguity and complexity of real-life situations (Newmann, Marks, & Gamoran, 1996).

3. Collaboration:

Learning happens through social interaction, where students negotiate ideas and create shared understanding. This helps develop teamwork and communication skills essential for real-world success (Lave & Wenger, 1991).

4. Student Agency and Reflection:

Learners take control of their own learning by setting goals and reflecting on their progress. This encourages self-awareness and helps students become independent thinkers (Paris & Paris, 2001).

5. Interdisciplinary Integration:

Tasks often require applying knowledge from multiple subject areas, reflecting how real-world problems involve many different fields. This helps students think broadly and connect ideas across disciplines (Brown, Collins, & Duguid, 1989).

While these characteristics define the ideal of authentic learning, integrating them with AI remains challenging. For example, AI systems may support collaboration through group formation tools, but they cannot fully replicate the complexity of human relationships and social negotiation that authentic teamwork requires (Zhang, Kizilcec, & Chen, 2021).

Relevance of Constructivist Theories

Authentic learning is rooted in constructivism, where learners actively build knowledge.

- **Cognitive Constructivism** (Piaget, 1954) focuses on how individuals internally construct understanding by engaging with experiences and reflecting on them. Learners create mental models based on their interactions with the world, gradually refining their knowledge through exploration and critical thinking.
- **Social Constructivism** (Vygotsky, 1978) views learning as a social process where knowledge is built through interaction with others. The Zone of Proximal Development (ZPD) describes how learners progress with the help of guidance and collaboration.

Together, these views align with authentic learning's emphasis on real-world contexts, social interaction, and learner autonomy, allowing students to build understanding collaboratively and meaningfully.

The Educator's Role in Promoting Authenticity

Educators play a crucial and multifaceted role in fostering authentic learning experiences. Their responsibilities extend far beyond simply delivering content; they are instrumental in designing, facilitating, and nurturing learning environments that truly reflect the complexities of the real world. By carefully crafting these learning experiences, educators help students develop the skills, knowledge, and mindset needed to navigate authentic challenges.

Key roles of educators in promoting authentic learning include:

- **Reflecting Real-World Challenges:** Educators design tasks and problems that mirror actual situations learners will face beyond the classroom. These challenges require higher-order thinking skills such as analysis, synthesis, and evaluation rather than rote memorization. This alignment with real-life scenarios helps students see the relevance of their learning and prepares them for future professional and personal contexts (Herrington & Oliver, 2000).
- **Fostering Collaboration and Peer Learning:** Social interaction and collaboration are fundamental components of authentic learning. Educators encourage students to work together, share diverse perspectives, engage in discussions, and solve problems collectively. Such peer learning promotes deeper understanding and mimics the collaborative nature of knowledge creation in the real world (Brown, Collins, & Duguid, 1989).
- **Providing Scaffolding and Feedback:** Learning complex skills and concepts requires appropriate support. Educators offer scaffolding—temporary guidance and support structures—that help learners move from their current level of understanding to more advanced mastery. Through timely and constructive feedback, educators guide students' growth, helping them identify strengths and areas needing improvement (Wood, Bruner, & Ross, 1976).
- **Encouraging Reflection and Metacognition:** Reflection is a critical part of authentic learning. Educators prompt students to think about their own learning processes, evaluate their progress, and develop self-awareness about their thinking strategies. This metacognitive practice enables learners to become self-directed, better understand their knowledge gaps, and continually improve (Schön, 1983).
- **Balancing Structure with Learner Autonomy:** While guidance and structure are essential, authentic learning also requires giving students the freedom to make choices about their learning. Educators balance providing enough direction to keep students on track with allowing autonomy to foster independence, creativity, and ownership over the learning process (Hmelo-Silver, Duncan, & Chinn, 2007).

By fulfilling these roles, educators create rich, authentic learning environments that prepare students not just to memorize facts but to think critically, collaborate effectively, and solve complex problems—skills essential for success in the real world.

In summary, authentic learning represents a fundamental shift from traditional, passive models of education toward experiences that are meaningful, contextualized, and driven by students themselves. Grounded in constructivist educational theories, this approach requires educators to carefully design and facilitate learning opportunities that nurture critical thinking, collaboration, and student agency. These foundational principles are crucial when considering how emerging technologies, such as AI tools, can be integrated into education without compromising the authenticity of learning. The following chapters will explore this integration in greater detail.

AI IN HIGHER EDUCATION — OPPORTUNITIES AND CONCERNS

The integration of AI into higher education is rapidly transforming how teaching, learning, and assessment are conducted. This chapter explores the multifaceted opportunities AI presents in educational contexts while critically examining the concerns associated with over-automation, ethical considerations, and equity implications. Understanding this balance is crucial for institutions aiming to leverage AI's benefits while preserving educational quality and authenticity.

AI Applications in Learning and Teaching

AI technologies are transforming higher education by enabling personalized, adaptive, and efficient learning experiences. The key applications below illustrate their growing influence.

- Adaptive Learning Systems: AI-driven platforms dynamically tailor content, difficulty, and pacing based on individual learner profiles, improving engagement and outcomes (Woolf, 2010). For example, platforms like Knewton or Smart Sparrow adjust lessons to meet student needs in real time.
- Intelligent Tutoring Systems (ITS): ITS provide automated guidance, feedback, and hints, simulating one-on-one tutoring (VanLehn, 2011). These systems can diagnose misconceptions and scaffold learning effectively.
- Predictive Analytics: AI models analyze data such as attendance, grades, and participation to predict student performance and identify at-risk learners, enabling timely interventions (Baker & Inventado, 2014).

- Automated Assessment and Feedback: AI facilitates rapid grading of assignments, especially multiple-choice and short answer formats, and can provide personalized feedback on writing or problem-solving (Shermis & Burstein, 2013).
- Natural Language Processing (NLP): Chatbots and virtual assistants can answer student queries, provide academic advising, and support learning outside class hours (Kerly, Ellis, & Bull, 2007).
- Content Creation and Curation: AI tools help educators develop customized learning materials or summarize vast resources, streamlining curriculum development (Chen, Xie, & Yang, 2020).

To consolidate these diverse applications, Table 3 provides an overview of the AI-enhanced learning ecosystem, highlighting core components, their functions, and representative tools used in contemporary higher education settings.

Table 3. AI-Enhanced Learning Ecosystem

Components	Description	Example Tools
Adaptive Learning	Personalized content delivery	Knewton, Smart Sparrow
Intelligent Tutoring	Automated guidance and scaffolding	Carnegie Learning, ALEKS
Predictive Analytics	Early detection of at-risk students	Civitas Learning, Blackboard Predict
Automated Assessment	Fast grading and feedback	Gradescope, Turnitin
Chatbots/NLP	Student support and Q&A	IBM Watson Assistant, Google Dialogflow
Content Creation	Material generation and curation	Squirrel AI, Content Technologies

Risks of Over-Automation and Depersonalization

Despite the many advantages AI offers in education, increasing dependence on it carries risks that may diminish the essential human aspects of learning. Excessive automation can result in several challenges:

- **Loss of Human Interaction:** Heavy reliance on AI can reduce meaningful conversations and mentorship between students and educators, weakening social learning experiences (Selwyn, 2019).
- **Algorithmic Bias:** AI systems trained on biased or incomplete data risk perpetuating inequalities or unfairly stereotyping certain student groups (Baker et al., 2020).

- **Reduction in Critical Thinking:** Overuse of AI-generated hints or answers may discourage students from engaging deeply with problems, limiting their creativity and independent reasoning (Williamson & Piattoeva, 2021).
- **Dehumanizing Assessment:** Automated grading tools might miss subtle nuances in student work or fail to consider cultural contexts, which can affect the fairness of evaluations (Williamson, 2017).
- **Erosion of Student Agency:** When AI rigidly dictates learning pathways, it can reduce learners' autonomy and motivation, undermining their active participation in their own education (Bayne, 2015).

These concerns highlight the importance of designing AI systems that support and enhance authentic learning, ensuring technology complements rather than replaces the human elements of education.

Ethical and Equity Considerations

The integration of AI in higher education brings important ethical concerns that institutions must carefully address:

- **Data Privacy and Security:** It is crucial to protect student data collected by AI systems from misuse, unauthorized access, or data breaches, ensuring confidentiality and trust (Cummings & Ferris, 2021).
- **Transparency and Explainability:** AI-driven decisions, particularly those related to assessments or predictive analytics, need to be transparent and understandable to both educators and students to foster confidence and accountability (Burrell, 2016).
- **Inclusivity and Access:** AI tools must be designed to serve all learners, including those with disabilities, and avoid widening existing digital divides or creating new barriers to education (Selwyn, 2019).
- **Accountability:** Institutions should establish clear policies defining who is responsible when AI-based decisions negatively affect students, ensuring fair and ethical use of technology (Floridi et al., 2018).

Addressing these ethical and equity considerations is essential for fostering trust and fairness in AI-enhanced learning environments.

To summarize these concerns, Table 4 outlines the core ethical principles relevant to AI in higher education, their educational implications, and common challenges that arise when these principles are not upheld.

Table 4. Ethical Principles in AI for Higher Education

Ethical Principle	Educational Implication	Example Concern
Privacy & Data Security	Secure data collection and storage	Unauthorized data sharing
Transparency	Clear AI decision-making processes	Black-box algorithms
Equity & Inclusion	Equal access and bias mitigation	Accessibility barriers, bias
Accountability	Defined responsibility for AI outcomes	Who is liable for incorrect predictions

In conclusion, AI offers transformative potential for higher education through adaptive, efficient, and scalable solutions. However, without intentional design and policies, it risks diminishing the human-centered, authentic learning experience. Balancing innovation with these concerns is essential for responsible AI integration—a theme explored in the upcoming framework chapter.

FRAMEWORK FOR BALANCED AI INTEGRATION

The rapid integration of AI in higher education demands a carefully constructed framework that ensures technological innovation complements rather than compromises authentic learning. This chapter presents foundational principles, decision-making models, and institutional policies to guide educators and administrators in adopting AI tools responsibly and effectively, maintaining the integrity of pedagogy centered on real-world relevance, critical thinking, collaboration, and student agency.

Principles of Harmonization

Balancing AI-driven innovation with authentic learning requires following several important principles:

1. **Human-Centered Design:** AI tools must be implemented to empower both learners and educators by supporting, not replacing, the teaching and learning process. They should enhance engagement, provide meaningful insights, and reduce routine workload while preserving the essential human elements of education. As Selwyn (2019) emphasizes, technology must serve pedagogy, ensuring that educators retain control and agency in guiding authentic learning experiences.
2. **Transparency and Explainability:** AI systems must deliver clear and understandable results that can be easily interpreted by both educators and learners. Transparency builds trust and ensures that teachers can use AI-generated insights responsibly in their decision-making. As Holstein, McLaren, and Aleven (2019)

highlight, explainability is essential for educators to correctly interpret outcomes and apply them in ways that genuinely support learning.

3. **Ethical Responsibility:** AI use in education should always be guided by principles of fairness, data privacy, and equity. Institutions must ensure that sensitive student data is protected and that algorithms do not reinforce bias or exclude vulnerable groups of learners. As Williamson and Piattoeva (2021) emphasize, ethical responsibility is critical to creating inclusive and trustworthy AI-enhanced learning environments.
4. **Alignment with Learning Goals:** AI tools must be designed to directly support the core aims of authentic learning, including problem-solving, collaboration, and reflective practice. Technology should enhance meaningful educational outcomes rather than reduce learning to automated tasks. As Herrington, Reeves, and Oliver (2014) argue, aligning AI with authentic pedagogy ensures that innovation strengthens critical thinking, teamwork, and student agency instead of undermining them.
5. **Flexibility and Adaptability:** AI solutions should be customizable so that educators can adjust them to suit diverse learners, subjects, and teaching contexts. Flexible systems allow instructors to adapt content, pathways, and assessments to different needs, avoiding rigid algorithms that may limit pedagogical effectiveness. As Luckin et al. (2016) note, adaptability is essential for ensuring that AI supports inclusive, responsive, and context-sensitive learning environments.

However, many existing AI systems lack the transparency or adaptability needed to realize these principles in practice. Proprietary algorithms often function as 'black boxes,' making it difficult for educators to interpret results or adjust tools to diverse contexts, which raises doubts about whether harmonization can be fully achieved without stronger accountability measures (Burrell, 2016; Floridi et al., 2018).

Model for Decision-Making in AI Adoption

Institutions can apply a structured, iterative decision pathway to evaluate AI tool adoption, as depicted in Figure 1:

Figure 1. Decision pathway for AI tool adoption in higher education

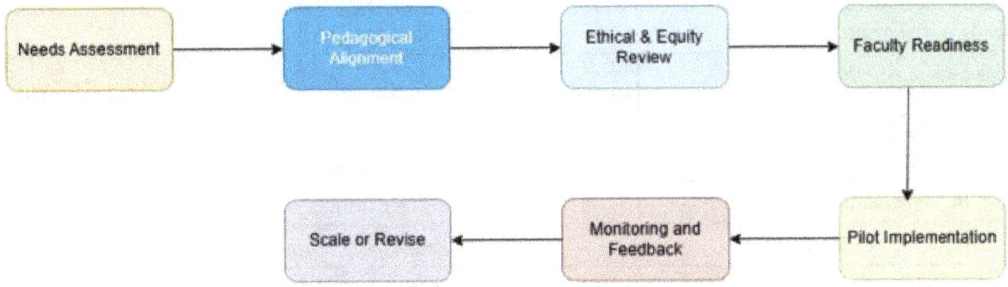

1. **Needs Assessment:** First, institutions identify specific educational challenges or gaps where AI could provide meaningful benefits. Examples include creating personalized learning experiences or offering real-time feedback to students.
2. **Pedagogical Alignment:** Next, it is essential to ensure that the selected AI tools support the principles of authentic learning and genuinely enhance desired learning outcomes.
3. **Ethical & Equity Review:** This stage involves evaluating important ethical considerations, such as safeguarding data privacy, minimizing algorithmic biases, and ensuring the AI tools are accessible to all students.
4. **Faculty Readiness:** Institutions must provide adequate training to educators and assess their preparedness to effectively use AI in their teaching practices.
5. **Pilot Implementation:** Small-scale trials or pilot programs allow for observing the actual impact of AI tools in controlled settings before wider adoption.
6. **Monitoring & Feedback:** Continuous evaluation is crucial to measure effectiveness, identify any unintended consequences, and gather input from all stakeholders.
7. **Scale or Revise:** Based on the evidence collected, institutions decide whether to expand the use of the AI tool or make necessary revisions to improve its implementation.

This model promotes responsible and evidence-based AI adoption, balancing innovation with the preservation of educational quality.

To complement the visual model, Table 5 provides a summary of each step in the decision pathway along with its core considerations, serving as a practical reference guide for academic leaders and IT administrators.

Table 5. Decision Pathway Steps with Key Considerations

Step	Key Considerations
Needs Assessment	Define goals, identify problems
Pedagogical Alignment	Match with authentic learning objectives
Ethical & Equity	Privacy, bias, fairness
Faculty Readiness	Training, attitudes, technical skills
Pilot Implementation	Small-scale testing, collect feedback
Monitoring & Feedback	Data analysis, learner outcomes
Scale or Revise	Decision to expand or refine

Institutional Policies and Faculty Readiness

For AI integration to be sustainable and effective, institutions need a strong and comprehensive framework:

- **Policy Formation:** Establishing clear policies on data privacy, consent, intellectual property rights, and ethical AI use is crucial. These regulations protect students, faculty, and the institution, creating a trustworthy environment for AI adoption (European Commission, 2020).
- **Faculty Development:** Ongoing professional development is essential to equip educators with the knowledge and skills to use AI tools effectively. Workshops, peer coaching, and communities of practice foster educators' confidence, encourage innovation, and help them understand both the possibilities and limitations of AI in teaching (Bai & Wang, 2022).
- **Interdisciplinary Collaboration:** Engaging educators, technologists, ethicists, and students in collaborative efforts brings diverse perspectives that improve the design, implementation, and ethical considerations of AI applications in education (Ferguson, Clow, & Macfadyen, 2021).
- **Resource Allocation:** Providing sufficient resources—including infrastructure, time, and technical support staff—is vital for enabling experimentation with AI tools and for scaling successful AI-enhanced teaching practices.

Together, these elements build a supportive institutional environment that prepares faculty and supports responsible, innovative use of AI in education

Integrative Use Case: Decision Pathway for AI Tool Adoption

Imagine a university seeking to implement an AI-driven adaptive learning platform to improve personalized instruction:

- After a needs assessment, the university identifies gaps in accommodating diverse learning paces.
- The platform is evaluated for alignment with pedagogical goals, supporting scaffolded, authentic problem-solving activities.
- An ethical review highlights concerns about algorithmic bias; thus, human oversight is incorporated.
- Faculty readiness is addressed through targeted professional development.
- A pilot phase tests the platform in select courses with feedback loops.
- Monitoring and feedback reveal positive engagement but some accessibility challenges, prompting adjustments.
- Based on results, the platform is scaled up institution-wide with accompanying policy support.

This case exemplifies how the decision pathway balances innovation with authenticity.

By embedding these principles and processes into institutional culture, higher education can navigate the complexities of AI adoption responsibly. The goal is a dynamic synergy where AI tools empower educators and learners without undermining the authentic learning experience.

Building upon this framework, the next section focuses on practical strategies for educators to design and implement authentic learning experiences enriched by AI, including reflective assessments and ongoing professional growth to maintain student-centered pedagogy.

STRATEGIES FOR EDUCATORS

With the institutional framework and decision-making models in place for responsible AI integration, this chapter focuses on actionable strategies educators can employ to design authentic learning experiences enhanced by AI technologies. These strategies support educators in harnessing AI to facilitate critical thinking, collaboration, and student agency, while preserving pedagogical authenticity and ensuring student-centered learning.

Designing AI-Supported Authentic Tasks

Authentic learning tasks engage students in meaningful, real-world problem solving that connects theory to practice (Herrington & Oliver, 2000). When integrating AI tools, educators can:

- **Leverage Adaptive Learning Systems:** AI platforms that adjust content difficulty and learning pathways based on student performance encourage individualized mastery while preserving authentic inquiry (Baker et al., 2020).
- **Create Project-Based Scenarios:** AI-driven simulations and virtual labs provide dynamic environments where students can experiment, reflect, and receive intelligent feedback, mimicking professional contexts (Dede, 2014).
- **Promote Collaborative Learning:** AI tools that facilitate group formation, peer feedback, and communication analytics can deepen social learning without supplanting human interaction (Zhang et al., 2021).
- **Support Metacognitive Skills:** Intelligent tutoring systems that prompt reflection, self-assessment, and goal setting help learners develop higher-order thinking essential for authentic engagement (Aleven et al., 2016).

For example, a biology course might use an AI simulation allowing students to model ecosystems and predict outcomes, fostering authentic scientific inquiry while receiving tailored guidance.

Reflective Use of AI in Assessments and Feedback

Assessment plays a vital role in authentic learning by supporting both evaluation and ongoing development. AI can enhance this process by delivering timely, personalized feedback, but it must be thoughtfully integrated to avoid excessive dependence on automated grading systems.

1. **Formative Feedback:** AI-driven tools can assess student work—such as writing, coding, or problem-solving—and offer immediate, specific feedback that helps learners revise their work and deepen their understanding (Gikandi, Morrow, & Davis, 2011).
2. **Reflective Assessment:** Educators can leverage AI analytics to encourage students to reflect on their learning journey, identify challenges, and develop self-regulation skills, fostering metacognitive growth (Winne & Hadwin, 2013).
3. **Avoiding Depersonalization:** It is important to blend AI-generated feedback with instructor insights to maintain the personal, motivational, and relational

aspects of assessment, ensuring students feel supported (Nicol & Macfarlane-Dick, 2006).

4. **Ensuring Fairness:** Awareness of potential AI biases is crucial for equitable assessment. Employing diverse assessment methods alongside AI helps to create a more balanced and just evaluation of student performance (Williamson, 2021).

Together, these approaches promote a reflective and balanced use of AI in assessment that supports authentic learning without compromising fairness or personal connection.

To illustrate these principles in practice, Table 6 summarizes key AI-enhanced assessment strategies, detailing how each supports authentic learning and fosters reflective engagement.

Table 6. AI-Enhanced Assessment Strategies

Strategy	Description	Authentic Learning Connection
Adaptive Quizzing	AI adjusts difficulty based on responses	Personalized challenge
Peer Review Facilitation	AI organizes and manages peer feedback	Collaborative learning and reflection
Automated Feedback on Drafts	Immediate suggestions for improvement	Supports revision and metacognition
Learning Analytics	Insights into student progress and struggles	Informs targeted support and self-awareness

Professional Development and Continuous Learning

Educator readiness is essential for the successful integration of AI in education. Continuous professional development (PD) ensures that faculty remain updated on the latest AI tools and pedagogical methods. Important aspects of PD include:

- **Workshops and Training Programs:** These targeted sessions focus on developing AI literacy, ethical use, and instructional design skills, helping educators build necessary competencies (Bai & Wang, 2022).
- **Communities of Practice:** Facilitating peer learning and the sharing of experiences promotes confidence and encourages innovative approaches among educators (Wenger, 1998).
- **Reflective Practice:** Encouraging educators to critically assess AI's impact on teaching and learning nurtures adaptive expertise and ongoing improvement (Schön, 1983).

- **Institutional Support:** Allocating time, providing incentives, and offering technical assistance are vital for sustaining effective professional development efforts (Darling-Hammond et al., 2017).

Educators who are well-equipped through these efforts can create learning environments that effectively incorporate AI tools, enhancing student engagement without compromising authenticity.

As educators gain expertise in thoughtful AI integration, the next chapter will showcase real-world case studies illustrating how institutions balance AI innovation with authentic learning, emphasizing successes, challenges, and lessons learned.

CASE STUDIES AND PRACTICAL INSIGHTS

As educational institutions increasingly adopt AI technologies, examining real-world examples of balanced AI integration offers valuable insights. This chapter presents case studies from universities that have successfully merged AI-driven innovation with authentic learning, explores key success factors and challenges, and discusses lessons for scalability and sustainability. These practical insights inform how institutions can navigate the evolving educational landscape while maintaining pedagogical integrity.

University Examples of Balanced AI Use

The adoption of AI in higher education varies widely depending on institutional goals, faculty readiness, and available resources. While some universities have aggressively integrated AI-driven tools across curricula, others have taken a cautious, pedagogically grounded approach to ensure authentic learning remains central. The following case studies illustrate how diverse institutions have effectively balanced technological innovation with the preservation of authentic learning experiences. These examples highlight different disciplines, AI applications, and strategies for maintaining human-centered education in an increasingly digital landscape.

By examining these real-world implementations, we can identify common approaches that support engagement, critical thinking, collaboration, and ethical use of AI. This analysis also sheds light on how institutional culture and policy frameworks play pivotal roles in facilitating balanced AI integration.

Case Study 1: Stanford University — AI-Supported Project-Based Learning

Stanford implemented AI tools within its engineering courses to enhance project-based learning. Using an AI-powered collaboration platform, students received real-time feedback on design iterations and peer communication analytics that supported team dynamics. Faculty reported that AI tools increased student engagement and allowed personalized mentorship without compromising the collaborative nature of projects (Smith et al., 2022). However, some students expressed concerns that algorithm-driven team suggestions limited their autonomy in forming groups, showing the need to balance AI guidance with learner choice.

Case Study 2: University of Edinburgh — Adaptive Learning for Humanities

The University of Edinburgh incorporated adaptive learning platforms in its humanities curriculum, blending AI-driven content customization with instructor-led discussions and reflective assignments. The approach preserved critical thinking and authentic interpretation skills while leveraging AI's ability to scaffold learning pathways. Student feedback highlighted the value of tailored pacing and meaningful human interaction (Jones & Patel, 2021). However, faculty cautioned that over-reliance on adaptive algorithms could risk narrowing exposure to diverse perspectives, which is central to developing critical interpretation skills in the humanities.

Case Study 3: National University of Singapore — Ethical AI in Assessment

At the National University of Singapore, AI was integrated into assessment design for a business ethics course. AI tools provided automated formative feedback on case study analyses, but final evaluations were completed by instructors to ensure contextual fairness and ethical considerations. This hybrid approach balanced efficiency with authenticity, fostering deeper ethical reflection (Tan & Lee, 2023). However, faculty noted that maintaining human oversight in every assessment cycle required additional time and effort, raising questions about scalability in larger courses and resource-constrained environments.

Success Factors and Pitfalls

An analysis of various real-world examples reveals several common success factors that contribute to effective AI integration in higher education:

1. **Faculty Engagement and Training:** Successful AI adoption heavily depends on the active involvement of educators throughout the process. When faculty members participate in selecting AI tools and receive comprehensive training, they can better align these technologies with specific pedagogical objectives. This engagement empowers instructors to adapt AI applications to support authentic learning rather than simply using technology for its own sake (Bai & Wang, 2022).
2. **Student-Centered Design:** AI implementations that prioritize learner autonomy tend to be more successful. By providing students with choices and opportunities for reflection, rather than encouraging passive consumption of content, AI tools can foster deeper engagement and critical thinking. This learner-focused approach respects student agency, a key element of authentic learning environments (Herrington & Oliver, 2000).
3. **Ethical Oversight:** Institutions that establish clear policies and mechanisms for monitoring AI use ensure fairness, data privacy, and bias mitigation. This ethical oversight builds trust among all stakeholders—students, faculty, and administrators—and addresses concerns that might otherwise limit adoption. Maintaining transparency around data use and algorithmic decisions is crucial for responsible AI integration (Williamson, 2021).
4. **Blended Approaches:** Combining AI technologies with human facilitation preserves the essential relational and social dimensions of authentic learning. Human instructors remain vital in providing guidance, emotional support, and personalized feedback that AI alone cannot replicate. This hybrid model leverages the strengths of both AI and educators to create enriched learning experiences (Nicol & Macfarlane-Dick, 2006).

However, alongside these success factors, several pitfalls have been identified that can undermine AI integration efforts:

1. **Overdependence on AI:** Relying too heavily on automation and AI-driven processes risks depersonalizing education. When students engage with AI in isolation or when AI replaces critical human interactions, it can reduce motivation, diminish critical engagement, and limit the development of higher-order thinking skills (Dede, 2014).
2. **Inadequate Infrastructure:** Many institutions face technical challenges such as insufficient hardware, unreliable internet connectivity, or lack of ongoing technical support. Without a robust infrastructure, AI tools cannot function effectively, leading to frustration for both educators and learners and ultimately limiting the impact of AI initiatives (Baker et al., 2020).

3. **Resistance to Change:** Adoption of AI often encounters reluctance from both faculty and students due to unfamiliarity with the technology or distrust in its benefits. This resistance can slow down or block the integration process. Overcoming this barrier requires thoughtful change management strategies, including clear communication, demonstrations of AI's value, and continuous support to build confidence among users (Darling-Hammond et al., 2017).

By understanding and addressing these success factors and pitfalls, institutions can better navigate the challenges of integrating AI while preserving the authenticity and quality of education.

Lessons for Scalability and Sustainability

For AI to effectively and sustainably support authentic learning on a larger scale, institutions need to adopt strategic approaches:

- **Iterative Implementation:** Introducing AI tools through pilot programs in selected courses allows institutions to collect feedback, address issues, and refine the technology before expanding its use broadly (Zhang et al., 2021).
- **Cross-Functional Collaboration:** Successful AI adoption requires cooperation among IT specialists, educational designers, and ethics committees to ensure that technical capabilities, pedagogical goals, and ethical standards are all carefully balanced (Baker et al., 2020).
- **Continuous Evaluation:** Ongoing monitoring and assessment of AI's effects on student learning outcomes, engagement levels, and equity issues are essential. This continuous feedback loop helps in making informed adjustments to improve effectiveness (Gikandi, Morrow, & Davis, 2011).
- **Student Involvement:** Involving students as active participants and co-designers in the AI integration process promotes greater ownership of their learning experiences and helps ensure diverse learner needs are addressed (Dede, 2014).

Together, these lessons support the development of AI initiatives that are scalable, sustainable, and aligned with authentic learning principles.

Table 7 presents a summary of key lessons and recommended implementation strategies for sustainable AI integration. It identifies important aspects such as pilot testing, multidisciplinary teamwork, transparency in AI use, and promoting student agency. For each, practical strategies are suggested to support effective adoption.

Table 7. Key Lessons for Sustainable AI Integration

Aspect	Lesson	Implementation Strategy
Pilot Testing	Start small and iterate	Course-level pilots with feedback loops
Multidisciplinary Teams	Include diverse expertise	Establish steering committees with varied roles
Transparency	Communicate AI use and data policies	Clear communication channels and training
Student Agency	Empower students in AI-supported tasks	Involve students in design and decision-making

By learning from practical implementations, institutions can foster environments where AI tools enrich authentic learning experiences without supplanting essential human elements.

As the practical insights clarify how AI can be balanced with authentic pedagogy, the next chapter will synthesize key recommendations and explore future directions to guide ongoing transformation in higher education.

CONCLUSION AND FUTURE DIRECTIONS

This chapter demonstrated that while AI offers efficiency, personalization, and innovation, it also risks reducing authenticity if not carefully aligned with pedagogy and ethics. The key challenge is achieving balance between innovation and authenticity.

Summary of Key Recommendations

To successfully balance the integration of AI technologies with authentic learning principles, institutions and educators must take several key steps:

1. **Prioritize Pedagogical Alignment:** It is crucial that AI tools are selected and implemented to support the fundamental elements of authentic learning. This means ensuring that AI enhances aspects like real-world relevance, encourages critical thinking, fosters collaboration among students, and promotes learner autonomy and agency. AI should act as a facilitator of these learning experiences rather than replacing or overshadowing them (Herrington et al., 2014; Luckin et al., 2016).
2. **Invest in Faculty Development:** Continuous and ongoing professional development is essential to prepare educators for the evolving landscape of AI in education. Training programs should help faculty build AI literacy, understand both the capabilities and limitations of AI tools, and develop skills to critically

assess how these technologies impact teaching and learning. Such programs empower educators to confidently integrate AI in ways that are pedagogically sound and ethically responsible (Zawacki-Richter et al., 2019).

3. **Develop Clear Institutional Policies:** Institutions must establish clear AI policies addressing ethics, privacy, transparency, and equal access to ensure trust and protection for all stakeholders (Holmes et al., 2021).
4. **Foster Human-Centered AI Design:** Collaboration between educators, AI developers, and technologists is vital to designing AI solutions that truly enhance learning. The goal is to create AI systems that support and enrich human interaction, creativity, and personalized learning experiences, rather than diminishing the essential human elements of education. Such human-centered design approaches prioritize the needs of both learners and educators, preserving the core values of authentic learning (Dede, 2016; Williamson & Piattoeva, 2022).
5. **Encourage Reflective Practice:** Both students and educators should be encouraged to engage in reflective use of AI tools. Reflective practice involves critically examining how AI influences learning processes and outcomes, maintaining a focus on authentic engagement. This ongoing reflection helps prevent over-reliance on AI and promotes thoughtful, purposeful integration of technology to enhance critical thinking and learner autonomy (Boud & Molloy, 2013).

The Future of AI and Authentic Pedagogy

Looking forward, the future of AI in education depends on its thoughtful integration into pedagogical frameworks that value learner autonomy and meaningful engagement. Emerging technologies like generative AI, immersive simulations, and intelligent tutoring systems offer exciting possibilities but also require ongoing scrutiny to prevent over-automation or depersonalization (Seldon & Abidoye, 2018; Chen et al., 2020).

Faculty roles will evolve from knowledge transmitters to facilitators and ethical guides who harness AI's insights to personalize learning pathways while preserving critical inquiry and collaboration (Selwyn, 2019). Institutions will need agile policies and infrastructures capable of adapting to rapid technological advancements, always with a commitment to equity and inclusion (Williamson & Piattoeva, 2022).

Ultimately, AI should serve as a catalyst for deepening authentic learning rather than an end in itself.

CONCLUSION

Balancing innovation and authenticity is not a static achievement but a continuous process requiring dialogue, experimentation, and reflection. Educators, administrators, and policymakers must work collaboratively to create environments where AI enriches the educational experience without undermining the human elements essential for meaningful learning (Brown, 2020).

By embracing this dual commitment, higher education can prepare students not only to thrive in a technologically advanced world but also to remain critical thinkers, creative problem-solvers, and ethical contributors to society.

The evolving landscape of AI in education invites us to rethink and redefine teaching and learning in ways that honor both innovation and authenticity—ensuring that technology serves as a powerful partner in fostering lifelong, human-centered learning. This chapter ultimately argues that the future of AI in education must be guided not by technological determinism but by deliberate pedagogical choice, ensuring that innovation remains accountable to authenticity and the deeper purposes of higher learning.

REFERENCES

Aleven, V., McLaughlin, E. A., Glenn, R., & Koedinger, K. R. (2016). Instruction based on adaptive learning technologies. In Sawyer, R. K. (Ed.), *The Cambridge handbook of the learning sciences* (2nd ed., pp. 522–549). Cambridge University Press.

Arnold, K. E., & Pistilli, M. D. (2012). Course signals at Purdue: Using learning analytics to increase student success. *Proceedings of the 2nd International Conference on Learning Analytics and Knowledge*, 267–270.

Bai, X., & Wang, S. (2022). Faculty development for AI integration in higher education: Strategies and challenges. *Journal of Educational Technology*, *43*(2), 123–138. DOI: 10.1016/j.jedt.2022.01.004

Baker, R. S., Hawn, A., Ritter, S., Corbett, A. T., Aleven, V., & Fancsali, S. (2020). Algorithmic bias in education. *Harvard Educational Review*, *90*(2), 1–28.

Baker, R. S., & Inventado, P. S. (2014). Educational data mining and learning analytics. In Larusson, J. A., & White, B. (Eds.), *Learning analytics* (pp. 61–75). Springer.

Bayne, S. (2015). What's the matter with "technology-enhanced learning"? *Learning, Media and Technology*, *40*(1), 5–20.

Boud, D., & Molloy, E. (2013). *Feedback in higher and professional education: Understanding it and doing it well.* Routledge.

Brown, J. S., Collins, A., & Duguid, P. (1989). Situated cognition and the culture of learning. *Educational Researcher*, *18*(1), 32–42.

Brown, M. (2020). *Education and technology: Critical perspectives, possible futures*. Routledge.

Burrell, J. (2016). How the machine "thinks": Understanding opacity in machine learning algorithms. *Big Data & Society*, *3*(1), 1–12. DOI: 10.1177/2053951715622512

Chen, X., Xie, H., & Yang, L. (2020). AI in education: Content creation and curation. *Journal of Educational Technology*, *14*(3), 45–60.

Cummings, C., & Ferris, M. (2021). Data privacy in AI-powered education systems. *Journal of Learning Analytics*, *8*(2), 33–49.

Darling-Hammond, L., Hyler, M. E., & Gardner, M. (2017). Effective teacher professional development. Learning Policy Institute. https://learningpolicyinstitute.org/product/effective-teacher-professional-development-report

Dede, C. (2014). *The role of digital technologies in deeper learning. Students at the Center: Deeper Learning Research Series*. Jobs for the Future.

Dede, C. (2016). Learning in the 21st-century: Digital technologies and pedagogy. In Clayton, S. D. (Ed.), *The Cambridge handbook of the learning sciences* (pp. 701–726). Cambridge University Press.

European Commission. (2020). Ethics guidelines for trustworthy AI. https://digital-strategy.ec.europa.eu/en/library/ethics-guidelines-trustworthy-ai

Ferguson, R., Clow, D., & Macfadyen, L. (2021). Interdisciplinary approaches to AI in education: Challenges and opportunities. *International Journal of Artificial Intelligence in Education, 31*(4), 567–586. DOI: 10.1007/s40593-020-00226-2

Floridi, L., Cowls, J., Beltrametti, M., Chatila, R., Chazerand, P., Dignum, V., & Vayena, E. (2018). AI4People—An ethical framework for a good AI society. *Science and Engineering Ethics, 24*(1), 103–130. DOI: 10.1007/s11948-017-9901-2 PMID: 30930541

Gikandi, J. W., Morrow, D., & Davis, N. E. (2011). Online formative assessment in higher education: A review of the literature. *Computers & Education, 57*(4), 2333–2351.

Goel, A., & Polepeddi, L. (2016). Jill Watson: A virtual teaching assistant for online education. Georgia Tech Technical Report.

Herrington, J., & Oliver, R. (2000). An instructional design framework for authentic learning environments. *Educational Technology Research and Development, 48*(3), 23–48.

Herrington, J., Reeves, T. C., & Oliver, R. (2010). *A guide to authentic e-learning*. Routledge.

Herrington, J., Reeves, T. C., & Oliver, R. (2014). Authentic learning environments. In Spector, J. M., Merrill, M. D., Elen, J., & Bishop, M. J. (Eds.), *Handbook of research on educational communications and technology* (pp. 401–412). Springer.

Hmelo-Silver, C. E., Duncan, R. G., & Chinn, C. A. (2007). Scaffolding and achievement in problem-based and inquiry learning: A response to Kirschner, Sweller, and Clark (2006). *Educational Psychologist, 42*(2), 99–107.

Holmes, W., Bialik, M., & Fadel, C. (2021). *Artificial intelligence in education: Promises and implications for teaching and learning*. Center for Curriculum Redesign.

Holstein, K., McLaren, B. M., & Aleven, V. (2019). Intelligent tutors as teachers' aides: AI systems to support classroom instruction. *ACM Transactions on Computer-Human Interaction, 26*(6), 1–28. DOI: 10.1145/3359183

Jones, A., & Patel, R. (2021). Blending adaptive learning with traditional humanities education: A case study. *Journal of Higher Education Innovation, 15*(3), 45–59.

Kerly, A., Ellis, R., & Bull, S. (2007). CALMsystem: A conversational agent for learner modelling. *Knowledge-Based Systems, 20*(2), 139–148.

Lave, J., & Wenger, E. (1991). *Situated learning: Legitimate peripheral participation*. Cambridge University Press.

Luckin, R., Holmes, W., Griffiths, M., & Forcier, L. B. (2016). Intelligence unleashed: An argument for AI in education. Pearson Education. https://www.pearson.com/content/dam/corporate/global/pearson-dot-com/files/innovation/Intelligence-Unleashed-Publication.pdf

Newmann, F. M., Marks, H. M., & Gamoran, A. (1996). Authentic pedagogy and student performance. *American Journal of Education, 104*(4), 280–312.

Nicol, D. J., & Macfarlane-Dick, D. (2006). Formative assessment and self-regulated learning: A model and seven principles of good feedback practice. *Studies in Higher Education, 31*(2), 199–218.

Paris, S. G., & Paris, A. H. (2001). Classroom applications of research on self-regulated learning. *Educational Psychologist, 36*(2), 89–101.

Piaget, J. (1954). *The construction of reality in the child*. Basic Books.

Schön, D. A. (1983). *The reflective practitioner: How professionals think in action*. Basic Books.

Seldon, A., & Abidoye, O. (2018). *The fourth education revolution: Will artificial intelligence liberate or infantilise humanity?* University of Buckingham Press.

Selwyn, N. (2019). Should robots replace teachers? AI and the future of education. *Polity*.

Shermis, M. D., & Burstein, J. (2013). *Handbook of automated essay evaluation: Current applications and new directions*. Routledge.

Smith, T., Liu, M., & Ramirez, J. (2022). AI-enhanced collaborative learning in engineering education at Stanford University. *International Journal of Engineering Pedagogy, 12*(1), 76–89.

Tan, H., & Lee, K. (2023). Integrating ethical AI assessment tools in business education. *Journal of Business Ethics Education*, *20*(1), 101–118.

VanLehn, K. (2011). The relative effectiveness of human tutoring, intelligent tutoring systems, and other tutoring systems. *Educational Psychologist*, *46*(4), 197–221.

Vygotsky, L. S. (1978). *Mind in society: The development of higher psychological processes*. Harvard University Press.

Wenger, E. (1998). *Communities of practice: Learning, meaning, and identity*. Cambridge University Press.

Williamson, B. (2017). Big data in education. *Sage (Atlanta, Ga.)*.

Williamson, B., & Piattoeva, N. (2021). Education governance and datafication. *Learning, Media and Technology*, *46*(1), 1–8.

Williamson, B., & Piattoeva, N. (2022). Objectivity as standardization in data-scientific educational governance: Grasping the global through the local. *Learning, Media and Technology*, *47*(1), 1–15. DOI: 10.1080/17439884.2022.2032512

Winne, P. H., & Hadwin, A. F. (2013). *Metacognition in education: A focus on self-regulated learning*. Routledge.

Wood, D., Bruner, J. S., & Ross, G. (1976). The role of tutoring in problem solving. *Journal of Child Psychology and Psychiatry, and Allied Disciplines*, *17*(2), 89–100. PMID: 932126

Woolf, B. P. (2010). *Building intelligent interactive tutors: Student-centered strategies for revolutionizing e-learning*. Morgan Kaufmann.

Zawacki-Richter, O., Marín, V. I., Bond, M., & Gouverneur, F. (2019). Systematic review of research on artificial intelligence applications in higher education—Where are the educators? *International Journal of Educational Technology in Higher Education*, *16*(1), 39. DOI: 10.1186/s41239-019-0171-0

Zhang, J., Kizilcec, R. F., & Chen, B. (2021). Enhancing collaboration with AI-supported group formation in online learning. *Computers & Education*, *165*, 104134. DOI: 10.1016/j.compedu.2021.104134

KEY TERMS AND DEFINITIONS

Adaptive Learning Systems: AI-driven platforms that adjust content delivery and learning paths in real-time based on student responses and performance.

Adaptive Learning Systems: Platforms that adjust the presentation of educational material based on the learner's performance in real-time.

AI Literacy: The ability to understand, critically evaluate, and effectively use AI technologies within an educational context.

AI-Driven Innovation: The use of artificial intelligence technologies to drive new approaches, systems, or processes in education that enhance learning, administration, and student engagement.

Artificial Intelligence (AI): The simulation of human intelligence processes by machines, especially computer systems. In education, AI is used for tasks like personalized learning, grading automation, predictive analytics, and tutoring systems.

Authentic Learning: A learning approach centered on real-world problems and meaningful tasks that replicate professional practice. It encourages critical thinking, collaboration, and student engagement.

Decision-Making Model: A structured process or tool to help institutions evaluate the benefits, risks, and ethical implications of AI implementation.

Personalized Learning: Educational methods and AI tools that tailor learning experiences, content, and pacing to individual student needs.

Chapter 4
AI-Enhanced Instructional Design and Curriculum Development for Next-Generation Learning Ecosystems in Higher Education

Aliye Saraç
https://orcid.org/0000-0002-0697-790X
Istanbul Topkapi University, Turkey

ABSTRACT

This chapter examines Artificial Intelligence (AI) as a transformative force in higher education, focusing on instructional design and curriculum development. AI is framed as a human-centered, ethical, and pedagogically aligned partner for creating flexible, inclusive, and future-ready ecosystems. Using models such as ADDIE, TPACK, and UDL, it highlights AI's role in learner analysis, adaptive content, real-time monitoring, and personalized evaluation. Applications include adaptive platforms, AI-driven feedback, and inclusive design, supported by LMS, LXP, analytics, and advising. Ethical issues like privacy, fairness, and accessibility are emphasized, presenting AI as a catalyst for adaptive and coherent education.

DOI: 10.4018/979-8-3373-4129-3.ch004

INTRODUCTION

Higher education has undergone significant transformations due to rapid technological advancements and evolving societal expectations. This chapter examines the development of next-generation learning ecosystems and the increasing need for innovation in higher education, highlighting the transformative role of artificial intelligence (AI) in instructional design, curriculum development, and academic practices. The discussion begins with an overview of higher education in the age of AI and then explores the paradigm shift in instructional design. This includes an examination of the theoretical foundations and practical applications that integrate AI into established models, such as ADDIE, and frameworks like TPACK. Additionally, it incorporates principles of Universal Design for Learning (UDL) to enhance both personalization and accessibility. Subsequent sections provide scenario-based examples that demonstrate AI-assisted lesson and course design, while also analyzing the technological components of AI-enhanced learning ecosystems. These components include learning management systems, analytics dashboards, and academic advising tools. The chapter further addresses AI-driven curriculum development, emphasizing flexible, competency-focused, and data-informed approaches. It also delves into the assessment aspect of AI-supported instructional design. Finally, the discussion considers the limitations of AI, including ethical responsibilities, accessibility concerns, and the role of educators. Strategic recommendations for the effective implementation of AI in higher education are then presented. Collectively, these sections offer a framework for understanding the intersections of AI, pedagogy, and institutional change, guiding readers through both conceptual foundations and practical applications.

1. NEXT GENERATION LEARNING ECOSYSTEMS AND THE NEED FOR TRANSFORMATION IN HIGHER EDUCATION

Higher education is presently placed in an epoch characterized by the swift transformation of knowledge production, transmission, and sharing, coinciding with the digitization of societal institutions. It is moving away from a classroom-based system where teachers simply give knowledge to students; learning is becoming a multi-channel, adaptive, and data-driven process. In this setting, traditional higher education is being replaced by next-generation learning ecosystems that focus on the learner, are more adaptable, recognize the importance of lifelong learning, and utilize technology smartly and effectively. These ecosystems are places where the digital and social aspects of education intersect to form a complex structure with numerous interactions among learning tools, content, stakeholders, and technology infrastructures.

Learning ecosystems are defined as structures where elements such as people, content, technology, strategy, and learning culture come together holistically and interactively to create personalized, continuous, and productive learning environments to enhance students' learning experiences (Ismail, 2024). Today, next-generation learning ecosystems are viewed as flexible platforms that support diverse learning experiences by integrating people, content, technologies, data, culture, strategy, and governance. This paradigm encompasses official educational programs, informal information exchange, digital learning settings, and in-person encounters within a comprehensive context. As students' profiles evolve, digitalization accelerates, and the job market demands new skills, these ecosystems have become a necessity in higher education, rather than a choice. Universities may provide long-lasting value for both individuals and the institution as a whole by creating learning environments that align with strategic goals, are continually evolving, and can easily adapt to future needs.

Today's student profiles consist of more flexible individuals who are self-directed in their learning and highly proficient in digital literacy skills. This shift reinforces the view—advocated by contemporary educational approaches—that education cannot be reduced to the mere delivery of digitized content; somewhat, it must be grounded in meaningful, contextual, and personalized learning experiences. Within this framework, artificial intelligence (AI) technologies play a central role in both data analytics and personalizing learning experiences. AI enhances the efficiency, accessibility, and inclusivity of learning processes by offering opportunities for interaction, adaptability, and personalization, thereby transcending its role as a mere technical tool. Instead, AI serves as a strategic partner in learning processes, strengthening pedagogical decision-making and making strategic contributions to instructional design.

In the context of next-generation learning ecosystems, the role of lecturers also needs to be reconsidered. Human-AI collaboration in education requires faculty members to assume the roles of learning guides, learning designers, and data literates, not just knowledge transmitters. Instead of replacing teachers, AI applications should support their decision-making processes, increase educational impact, and enrich the learning experience. Within this framework, technological transformation should be structured around pedagogical values, focusing on learning rather than technology.

At this point, instructional technologies stand out as a strategic field that strengthens the theoretical foundations and enriches the practical dimension of the transformation in higher education. At the center of this field is the understanding that technology can produce better quality learning outcomes in education by radically reshaping the processes of knowledge transfer, interpretation, and translation into practice (Kohen-

Vacs et al., 2024; Malik, 2023). Current trends focus on designing highly interactive and engaging learning experiences that align with students' real-life contexts and needs, and this approach constitutes a key component of the Technology-Enhanced Learning and Training (TEL) framework (Kohen-Vacs et al., 2024).

In conclusion, the integration of AI into instructional design and curriculum development within next-generation learning ecosystems is not merely a digitalization process; it is also a reconfiguration of higher education based on human, ethical, and pedagogical values. This transformation aims to deliver inclusive, data-driven, and flexible learning experiences that unlock learners' potential. In the education of the future, AI should be regarded not just as a tool but as a strategic partner in building equitable and accessible learning systems. These issues will be further discussed in the following sections.

2. HIGHER EDUCATION IN THE AGE OF ARTIFICIAL INTELLIGENCE

Artificial intelligence (AI) is an interdisciplinary field that has evolved at the intersection of disciplines such as neuroscience, psychology, linguistics, philosophy, mathematics and computer science, focusing on machines or computer systems that mimic cognitive functions, and has become one of the strategic technologies of the contemporary information society with its capacity to process information, perceive its environment and react in a human-like manner (Kökver et al., 2025). The historical development of artificial intelligence (AI) began with systems based on symbolic representation and logical inference, a period referred to in the literature as the “symbolic AI era” (Adami, 2021). From the 1990s onward, the rise of machine learning and data-driven approaches laid the groundwork for redefining AI not merely as a technical problem-solving tool but as a socio-technical system (Radanliev, 2024). In the contemporary era, deep learning-based generative AI models have had a transformative impact on both technological and societal levels, thanks to their capacity to generate text, images, and decisions (He et al., 2025). Accordingly, the history of AI reflects not a linear progression but a cyclical evolution in which each phase overcomes the limitations of previous approaches and redefines cognitive representation, learning processes, and productive capacity. This multidimensional definition and historical evolution demonstrate that AI is not only a technical innovation but also a strategic element that transforms the functions, methods, and purposes of higher education.

The role of AI in the context of higher education is critical in terms of its mission to provide the knowledge, skills, and competencies required by the age. Higher education in the age of AI necessitates a transformation that extends beyond adapting to technological developments, encompassing pedagogical, theoretical, and ethical dimensions in a holistic manner (Qayyum et al., 2025; Adesiji, 2024). In the field of education, AI is not merely an automation tool. AI is also considered a paradigm that redefines the nature of learning processes, forms of information access, and models of academic interaction. AI provides real-time data processing and decision support mechanisms by leveraging multi-layered architectures enabled by technologies such as cloud computing, big data analytics, machine learning (ML), and deep machine learning (DML) (Kohen-Vacs et al., 2024). AI tools save time for students in learning activities, such as idea development, content generation, problem-solving, and simulation, as well as for instructors in preparing course materials, evaluation, and feedback processes (Tillmanns et al., 2025). In this context, strengthening the technology infrastructure in higher education institutions, developing data management systems, and adapting the curriculum to the requirements of the digital age form the basis of sustainable transformation strategies (Adesiji, 2024; Anvari et al., 2024).

AI systems undertake multidimensional functions, such as decision-making in the context of learning, providing personalized recommendations, offering instant feedback, and monitoring learning processes. However, the integration of these systems into higher education is not only a matter of technical infrastructure; it is also a pedagogical design problem that needs to be understood in relation to learning theories. At this point, Piaget's cognitive constructivist approach, Vygotsky's social constructivism, and Siemens' connectionism theory are the prominent theoretical grounds in explaining the educational role of AI (Qayyum et al., 2025). According to the constructivist approach, learning occurs through an individual's active participation and the integration of new information with prior knowledge. By analyzing data from the learner's previous learning experiences, AI provides personalized content recommendations and creates adaptive learning paths tailored to each individual. In this way, learning becomes a process of actively constructing meaning, rather than merely consuming content. The social constructivist approach suggests that learning develops through social interactions, shared problem-solving, and the use of cultural tools and resources. In this context, natural language processing-based chatbots, collaborative digital platforms, and virtual learning communities support student-to-student interaction and convergent development (Chen et al., 2020). Moreover, AI-generated scenarios and problem sets encourage students to engage actively with real-world situations, thereby developing critical thinking and problem-solving skills. AI can pose thought-provoking questions, guide students through critical thinking exercises, and support their personal development by enabling them to consider different perspectives (Guan et al., 2023). AI strengthens the dynamics of the learning ecosystem by positioning the student as a producer and distributor of knowledge in the network structure. In the AI era, learners build their own learning networks through interaction with digital resources, algorithms, and other learners. This is especially advantageous in the management of interdisciplinary, multisourced, and rapidly updated information environments, supporting the theory of connectionism that explains learning on networks.

A significant aspect of the pedagogical impact of AI in higher education is its relationship to learning analytics. By analyzing students' interaction data in the online environment, academic success can be predicted, interests can be identified, and the learning experience can be restructured according to individual needs. Thus, instructors can make timely and effective interventions with data-driven decisions (Qayyum et al., 2025). This approach replaces intuitive decisions in education with measurable, evidence-based pedagogical planning.

AI is not only a technology that supports individual learning processes; it is a systemic force contributing to the redefinition of institutional structures, curricula, and teaching roles in higher education. AI in higher education has the potential to transform business practices, from automating administrative tasks to enhancing curriculum development and assessing educational outcomes (Ramos et al., 2024). However, the quality and sustainability of this transformation is possible through technological integration, theoretical depth, ethical awareness, and pedagogical coherence. Therefore, strengthening the AI literacy of teaching staff is a critical necessity. UNESCO's "Artificial Intelligence Competency Framework for Teachers" defines five core competency areas: (1) human-centered mindset, (2) AI ethics, (3) AI foundations and applications, (4) AI pedagogy, and (5) AI for professional development (UNESCO, 2024). These competencies aim to equip lecturers with the knowledge and skills to ensure both the pedagogical integration of technology and its ethical, transparent, and fair use. In this respect, higher education in the age of AI, supported by conceptual clarity and theoretical underpinnings, as well as practices aligned with ethical and pedagogical principles, gives higher education a new direction and meaning in the complexity of the digital age.

3. THE PARADIGM SHIFT IN INSTRUCTIONAL DESIGN IN THE AGE OF ARTIFICIAL INTELLIGENCE

Digitalization in higher education is redefining teaching styles and the processes of planning, structuring, and implementing instruction. Instructional design, one of the concepts at the center of this transformation, is not only about organizing content or sequencing instructional activities. Traditional instructional design models have guided structured and systematic educational practices for many years. These models have been effective in planning the instructional process, utilizing approaches based on a specific sequence and linear logic, which enables the clear identification of learning outcomes, the structuring of content, and the definition of assessment criteria. However, these models have become inadequate in the face of changing learner profiles, the digitalization of learning environments, and the development of data-driven applications (Visscher, 2021). In this context, understanding the three stages of digital evolution-digitization, digitalization, and digital transformation—is essential for understanding the scope of digitalization in higher education (Reinitz, 2020). Digitization refers to the conversion of analog information into digital formats, such as scanning paper records and storing them online for archiving and retrieval. Digitalization involves using digital technologies to enhance or transform individual teaching or administrative processes, such as course delivery, student assessment, or research administration. However, these steps alone do not constitute a complete digital transformation. Digital transformation (Dx) requires a strategic and coordinated effort to reshape institutional practices, learning environments, and curriculum design, integrating technology, data analytics, and pedagogical innovation. It entails deep, aligned changes in culture, workforce, and technological infrastructure. Higher education institutions must often undertake substantial digitization and digitalization efforts before successfully implementing comprehensive digital transformation, ensuring that teaching, learning, and assessment practices are systematically aligned with their strategic educational objectives.

Today, learning processes are no longer predictable, fixed, or uniform scenarios; they have become complex, variable, and individualized. In this context, instructional design has gained a new meaning as a pedagogical engineering process that holistically designs the learning experience, putting the learner at the center, and is supported by technological opportunities. It is also a technical process that organizes instructional materials. Especially with the integration of AI technologies into education, there has been a significant paradigm shift in the understanding of instructional design (Mousa, 2025). This paradigm shift necessitates a reevaluation of both the structure of processes and the creation and evaluation of learning outcomes.

The new generation instructional design approach is data-driven and adaptive. The digital traces created by students throughout the learning process can be analyzed using various variables, such as participation level, interaction intensity, content preferences, and achievement graphs. Individualized instructional scenarios can then be developed based on these findings. At this point, AI can intervene in almost every stage of instructional design. An AI-supported instructional design approach breaks the linear structure offered by traditional models, providing agile, iterative, and feedback-oriented processes (Novita, 2025). This approach transforms the learning experience from a "design, implement, measure, improve" cycle into a structure that is constantly evolving and reshaped according to the learner's immediate needs.

In this context, not only does technology need to be integrated into education, but the relationship between pedagogy and technology also needs to be redefined and continuously improved. While in traditional understandings, technology was positioned as a tool in the service of pedagogy, today this relationship has transformed into a mutually interactive structure. The TPACK model is one of the leading frameworks conceptualizing this transition. This model, which combines the components of technological knowledge (TK), pedagogical knowledge (PK), and content knowledge (CK), also enhances the instructional designer's ability to integrate AI in alignment with the pedagogical purpose (Çelik, 2023). Similarly, the Universal Design for Learning (UDL) framework advocates that instructional design should be structured in a way that is accessible and engaging for all individuals (Novita, 2025). At this point, AI becomes an effective solution partner in increasing content accessibility, developing alternative presentation formats, and making adaptations based on individual differences (Kalaigian et al., 2024). The collaboration between the human mind and AI in the design process will make education both more inclusive and more effective.

Instructional design in the age of AI represents a restructuring process in which not only the tools but also the ways of thinking are changing. This paradigm shift moves instructional design away from standardized solutions. It transforms it into a data-driven structure that is learner-sensitive, integrates technology with pedagogical goals, and continually evolves.

4. THEORETICAL APPROACHES IN AI-ENHANCED INSTRUCTIONAL DESIGN AND SAMPLE APPLICATIONS FOR CURRICULUM DEVELOPMENT

This section focuses on three widely discussed approaches in instructional design—ADDIE, TPACK, and UDL—selected to capture the essence of the topic. Each subsection concludes with a scenario-based implementation that illustrates the concepts with practical examples.

4.1. The ADDIE Model and AI Integration

The ADDIE model, widely adopted among traditional instructional design models, appears to be a suitable model for integrating AI technologies into the restructuring process brought about by digitalization in higher education. Comprising five stages—Analysis, Design, Development, Implementation, and Evaluation—this model retains its theoretical robustness while gaining flexibility and effectiveness when reinterpreted through AI-enhanced solutions. The following outlines each stage along with how AI can be integrated, supported by examples.

Analysis Phase: In-Depth Learner Needs Analysis through AI

The first and fundamental phase of the ADDIE model, the analysis phase, traditionally focuses on identifying audience characteristics, the learning environment, and needs. Integrating AI into this phase enables a more in-depth quantitative and qualitative analysis process. This is where data mining, machine learning, and learner profiling applications take center stage. Data obtained from students' digital traces such as their data on online forums in learning management systems (LMS) or learning experience platforms (LXP), video streaming records, and exam performances (Tillmanns et al., 2025) can be analyzed by AI algorithms to identify students' learning styles, strengths/weaknesses, interests and learning gaps (Mahamuni & Tonpe, 2024). For example, a learner analytics study conducted in a university's engineering department using previous course records, exam results, and forum interactions could reveal common difficulties in understanding certain concepts. This data can help shape the design process in a more precise and targeted way.

Design Phase: Planning Content Flow and Learning Paths with AI

The design phase is the process in which fundamental instructional decisions are made, such as defining learning objectives, sequencing content, and determining interaction strategies. In this process, AI-enhanced systems can provide content flow recommendations based on learner profiles (Krouska et al., 2024; Ramos et al., 2024). Furthermore, automated content mapping algorithms can analyze the relationships between topics at a conceptual level (Mahamuni & Tonpe, 2024) and suggest learning paths that will make the learning journey more meaningful. For example, when an instructional designer wants to create a concept map of a biology course, a natural language processing (NLP) system can generate a suggested content sequence based on pre-loaded content and learning objectives. Furthermore, AI tools can create alternative learning pathways for different learner types—for example, video-rich paths for visual learners and reading-heavy paths for verbal learners.

Development Phase: Automating Content Production

This is one of the most visible stages for AI integration, involving the creation of learning materials. This is where the production of learning materials takes place, and AI both accelerates this process and enables the production of individualized content. Applications such as text-to-video conversion (Winder et al., 2024), automatic slide creation, exam question generation (Tillmanns et al., 2025), and personalized test scenario development (Trilaksana & Soelistiono, 2024) are among the significant contributions AI offers to the content creation process. For instance, an instructor might use an AI-based video creation tool to convert lecture notes into visual and auditory content, broadening sensory engagement. Question bank tools can detect key concepts in the content and generate open-ended, multiple-choice, or comparative questions aligned with Bloom's taxonomy.

Implementation Phase: Interactive, Guidance-Focused Learning Environments

The application phase represents the learning process in which the student is engaged with the designed content and experiences. AI technologies can offer guidance mechanisms that increase the level of interaction at this stage and direct the learning process. Virtual assistants (Rezaie et al., 2025), chatbots (Qayyum, 2025), interactive learning guides (Chanyi et al., 2025), and automated feedback systems (Mousa, 2025; Lee, 2023; Kerres & Buntins, 2020) can offer real-time solutions to the problems the student encounters during the application phase (Alenezi, 2023). For example, an AI assistant in a language learning platform can offer immediate grammar corrections, reducing instructor workload while fostering learner autonomy. Similarly, in AI-based virtual classrooms, the system can automatically suggest content repetitions or create personalized development plans based on the student's learning history. These environments have the potential to go beyond the transfer of information and function as structures that guide, stimulate, and support the learning experience.

Evaluation Phase: AI's Role in Assessment Processes

The final phase of the ADDIE model, the evaluation phase, involves measuring the effectiveness of the instructional design and analyzing learner performance. One of the most significant advantages offered by artificial intelligence at this stage is the development of automatic assessment systems (Ozogul et al., 2025). Beyond multiple-choice exams, it is possible to evaluate open-ended responses with natural language processing (Wei, 2025), to understand the emotional variables of the learner in the learning process with sentiment analysis (Akintayo et al., 2024), and to trace the development of learning over time with learning journey visualization systems (Kerres & Buntins, 2020). For example, an AI-supported platform can provide both the student and the instructor with a holistic view of the learning process by visualizing all the interactions, activity participation, and assessment results of the student throughout a semester on a timeline. The aspects that need improvement in instructional design can be revealed through AI by analyzing the data.

These stages demonstrate that traditional instructional design frameworks, such as the ADDIE model, when integrated with AI, both maintain their theoretical validity and dynamically respond to contemporary learning needs. This integration enhances the instructional design by making it more efficient, personalized, and effective.

Scenario-Based Implementation: "Digital Literacy" Lesson Developed with AI-Assisted Instructional Design within the Framework of the ADDIE Model

A Faculty of Education at a public university plans to launch a mandatory "Digital Literacy" course for all second-year students. The course targets a heterogeneous group with varying ages, digital skills, and learning histories, and is delivered in a hybrid format (combining face-to-face and online components). To address this diversity and improve student outcomes, instructors decide to design the course using the ADDIE model with AI integration.

Analysis Phase

AI Components: Learning Analytics, Recommendation Systems

Prior to the start of the course, historical records from the university's Learning Management System (LMS), pre-test results, and student self-reported survey data are integrated and analyzed using AI algorithms. Digital learner profiling systems generate profiles for each student based on factors such as frequency of technology use, predisposition to online learning, past academic performance, and personal interests.

In the scenario, AI analysis categorizes students into three groups: *basic-level participants*, *intermediate-level participants*, and *advanced-level participants*. Distinct learning objectives and content depths are established for each group. Additionally, peer-mentoring clusters are designed to foster social learning.

Design Phase

AI Components: Knowledge Mapping, Conceptual Relationship Analysis

AI-based content mapping tools identify conceptual relationships among subtopics related to digital literacy, which are then used to construct recommended learning pathways. For instance, for basic-level participants, the proposed sequence is *Computer Hardware Fundamentals File Management Security*, whereas for advanced-level participants, the sequence is *Data Privacy Source Evaluation Digital Ethics*.

Differentiated learning scenarios are also developed for each group. For example, advanced learners might collaboratively engage in an authentic *deepfake detection project*, while basic-level learners work on simplified case analyses concerning email security.

Development Phase

AI Components: Automated Content Generation, Natural Language Processing (NLP)

While instructors prepare the core textual content for the course, AI-enabled tools automatically convert these materials into instructional videos, infographics, and presentation slides. The system also generates assessments, including quizzes, fill-in-the-blank exercises, and short written-response questions, based on key concepts within the content.

Moreover, AI can dynamically produce "on-demand" supplementary resources according to students' engagement patterns. For example, if a student spends an extended period on the concept of *cyberbullying*, the system could recommend a short animated explainer video alongside two alternative academic articles on the topic.

Implementation Phase

AI Components: Chatbots, Real-Time Personalized Feedback Systems

In the online component of the course, an AI-powered virtual assistant maintains continuous interaction with students. This assistant instantly answers frequently asked questions, directs students to relevant learning materials, reminds them of assignment deadlines, and provides alternative explanations for complex concepts.

Students can also take short quizzes through the chatbot and receive explanatory feedback on incorrect responses. The bot monitors individual progress and offers motivational prompts such as "You are doing very well" or "You should review this topic again" to encourage persistence.

Evaluation Phase

AI Components: NLP-Based Assessment, Learning Analytics Visualization

At the end of the semester, the system generates a visual representation of each student's learning journey. The report includes indicators such as interaction intensity, content completion rate, topics presenting difficulty, and frequency of feedback requests.

NLP technologies assess students' written assignments through semantic analysis, scoring them on dimensions such as content coherence, topic relevance, and argument development. This reduces the instructors' grading workload while ensuring timely, high-quality feedback for learners.

Additionally, aggregated data reveal areas that require improvement within the course design. These insights are used to inform curriculum revisions, enabling instructors to prepare data-driven improvement plans.

This scenario demonstrates that AI applications can be meaningfully integrated into each stage of the ADDIE model, benefiting both instructors and students.

Personalization of the learning experience, automation of feedback processes, and increased flexibility in instructional design are among the key advantages of AI integration.

Recommendations

- AI-supported content should be balanced with human guidance to sustain learner motivation.
- Peer mentoring structures should be systematically designed to strengthen social learning.
- Data security protocols should be explicitly communicated to students at the outset of the course.

4.2. Pedagogy-Technology Integration with AI in the TPACK Framework

In the age of AI, instructional design requires more than simply appending technology to education; it entails integrating these technologies with pedagogical reasoning and content expertise. These developments, supported by various digital tools and methodologies, have enriched educational processes and outcomes by creating innovations in the way knowledge is transmitted and used (Usher et al., 2021; Kohen-Vacs et al., 2025). One of the prominent approaches to make sense of this integration at the theoretical level is the TPACK model. Explained as Technological Pedagogical Content Knowledge (TPACK), this model examines the effectiveness of teaching at the intersection of three fundamental knowledge domains: content knowledge (CK), pedagogical knowledge (PK), and technological knowledge (TK) (Swallow & Olofson, 2017). This model argues that the use of technology should not only be incorporated into the teaching process but should also be internalized in accordance with pedagogical goals and the nature of the content.

The TPACK framework offers a powerful conceptual tool for understanding how instructors can establish meaningful relationships with technology. Within TPACK, a balanced synthesis of TK, PK, and CK is crucial for designing innovative content that meets the diverse needs of learners. However, as AI becomes increasingly integrated into teaching processes, the model requires further refinement. Extending TPACK to include AI requires educators to integrate digital tools with AI systems that can process data, generate predictions, and guide learning processes for pedagogical purposes.

In this regard, "Smart TPACK" (Mishra et al., 2023)—which adapts educational content to student needs—has matured to incorporate both the ethical and pedagogical dimensions of AI tools. The TPACK+AI framework enables instructors to base pedagogical decisions on both content expertise and the outputs of data-driven technological systems. The adoption of AI technologies has transformed teaching and learning practices; the integration of tools such as generative AI has also deepened our understanding of how technology, pedagogy, and content intersect. For example, an instructor teaching an online history course might use AI analytics to examine students' prior engagement with course materials and performance levels, then design differentiated learning paths for distinct groups of learners. Here, the alignment of content knowledge, pedagogical strategy, and technological tools directly reflects TPACK+AI competence.

The integration of AI and pedagogical technology should focus on both tools and learner interaction. AI systems can continuously monitor learner behavior, adapt to individual performance, and engage directly with learners. For example, a chatbot system can not only answer questions; it can also decide which resources the learner should be directed to based on their previous interactions or provide messages that support learning motivation. However, challenges in this process, such as a lack of technical competence, ethical concerns, and risks of overdependence on AI tools, suggest the need for a balanced approach (Lakhe Shrestha et al., 2025). By emphasizing the irreplaceable role of human interaction and critical thinking in education, teachers advocate the use of AI as a complementary tool, not a substitute (Lakhe Shrestha et al., 2025).

Within the TPACK framework, AI-supported lesson-planning tools require teachers to combine content and pedagogical expertise with the ability to critically evaluate AI outputs, modify them as needed, and ensure their alignment with learning goals (Chatterjee & Bhattacharjee, 2020; Novita, 2025). The TPACK+AI approach aims to position educators not merely as consumers of AI in the classroom but as intentional designers who preserve the human-centered essence of teaching while innovating for 21st-century learners (Lakhe Shrestha et al., 2025).

Scenario-Based Implementation: "Climate Change and Society" Course Designed with the TPACK+AI Model

Offered within the Faculty of Social Sciences, "Climate Change and Society" is an interdisciplinary elective enrolling students from diverse departments. The course aims to analyze the social, political, and economic dimensions of climate change, develop data-informed thinking skills, and encourage students to devise solutions to societal challenges.

Design Using the TPACK+AI Approach

- **Content Knowledge (CK):** Topics include climate policy, sustainability, carbon footprint, and climate-induced migration. The instructor possesses deep academic expertise in these areas.
- **Pedagogical Knowledge (PK):** The course employs project-based learning, collaborative discussions, and case analyses, leveraging interaction-focused pedagogical strategies to enhance student learning.
- **Technological Knowledge (TK):** Delivered via an online platform, students access resources through an LMS, participate in discussion forums, and prepare digital presentations.
- **AI Integration (AI):**
    - **Scenario 1 – Learner Profiling:** The AI system analyzes students' interests and prior performance, recommending differentiated starting points and personalized reading lists tailored to their needs.
    - **Scenario 2 – Climate Crisis Simulation:** Students engage in an interactive simulation where scenarios evolve based on their decisions. The AI provides feedback such as: *"An increase in deforestation has rapidly reduced biodiversity in the region. Would you like to implement ecosystem restoration measures?"*
    - **Scenario 3 – Automated Composition Analysis:** Students write essays on course-related topics. An NLP algorithm assesses textual coherence, argument quality, and expressive clarity, offering instant feedback.
    - **Scenario 4 – Learning Journey Visualization:** At the end of the term, the AI system visualizes each student's learning journey, including resources read, videos watched, forum contributions, and project milestones, in a graphical format.

This scenario illustrates how the TPACK+AI approach, when coupled with pedagogical sensitivity, can transform instruction. The creation of a student-centered, data-driven, technologically rich, and ethically aware learning environment is among the most significant benefits of integrating AI into instructional design.

Recommendations

- Simulation scenarios should be adapted for different cultural contexts.
- Peer discussions should be enriched by critically evaluating AI outputs.
- Pedagogical strategies should be continuously updated to align with evolving technologies.

4.3. Personalization and Accessibility with UDL (Universal Learning Design)

As higher education learning environments grow increasingly heterogeneous, inclusivity and flexibility have become central requirements in instructional design. Educators working with students who vary in abilities, learning styles, linguistic proficiency, cognitive tendencies, and cultural backgrounds are increasingly encountering the limitations of "one-size-fits-all" approaches.

In this context, Universal Design for Learning (UDL) advocates for flexible, customizable, and multimodal instructional structures to enable all students to succeed (Novita, 2025). The UDL framework rests on three principles: 1) Providing multiple means of accessing information. 2) Offering multiple ways to process and express knowledge. 3) Supporting multiple forms of engagement in learning. AI applications can directly support these principles by creating multimodal content, offering differentiated instructional suggestions based on learner data, and generating alternative assessment methods (Novita, 2025). This enables educators to design inclusive lesson plans that accommodate diverse needs without producing entirely separate materials for each student.

For example, in a history course, the same content could be delivered in multiple formats: text-to-speech narration for students with reading difficulties, interactive, map-based tools for visual learners, and micro-content modules with a low cognitive load for those with attention challenges. Producing such differentiated content manually is both time- and expertise-intensive; however, AI-enabled systems can analyze interaction data to determine which presentation formats are most effective for each learner and adapt accordingly.

AI also enhances accessibility through features such as captions, automated translation, and simplified text formatting (Chemnad & Othman, 2024; Chakraborty et al., 2023). For individuals with physical disabilities, reformatting materials into screen–reader–compatible HTML or auto-generating subtitles for video content plays a crucial role in ensuring equitable access (Acosta-Vargas, 2024). From an affective and motivational perspective, AI can analyze indicators such as login frequency, content completion rates, and interaction durations to assess engagement levels (Hooda et al., 2022). If low motivation is detected, the system can offer alternative pathways, such as shorter modules, varied media formats, or gamified learning elements (Alenezi, 2023)—directly supporting UDL's "multiple means of engagement" principle. Additionally, NLP algorithms can simplify complex academic texts, creating low–cognitive–load versions that make difficult material more accessible and engaging. Such solutions contribute to making learning both more inclusive and more democratic.

Ultimately, the UDL+AI combination transforms instructional design in higher education from a fixed, information-transmission model into a learning architecture that prioritizes each individual's potential. This architecture—responsive to varied learner needs, offering multiple learning pathways, and shifting students from passive recipients to active participants—is a foundational element of next-generation learning ecosystems. However, to realize this potential effectively, educators need pedagogical competence in UDL principles along with the technological awareness required to select and adapt AI tools appropriately. Therefore, an "UDL+AI Pedagogical Alignment" framework for instructors should define competencies that address both tool-use proficiency and the pedagogical purposes these tools serve.

Scenario-Based Implementation: "Scientific Literacy" Course Designed with UDL+AI

Developed for first-year students from various departments within the Faculty of Science, "Scientific Literacy" aims to foster critical engagement with scientific knowledge, interpret information, and effectively evaluate digital resources. The student cohort is highly heterogeneous: some have strong cognitive abilities, while others face specific learning difficulties; some prefer visual content, while others prefer textual materials.

Design Using the UDL+AI Approach

1. **Content Delivery via Multiple Representations:** The course content is hosted on an AI-supported learning platform. Based on prior interaction data and learning preferences, the system delivers personalized versions of the materials:
   - Detailed articles for students with strong reading skills.
   - Animated short videos for those with attention difficulties.
   - Simplified interfaces with low color contrast for students with sensory sensitivities.
2. **Engagement-Enhancing Feedback Loops:** The AI analyzes engagement patterns to detect drops in motivation. For students who have been inactive for extended periods, the system sends notifications, such as: *"A new topic that might interest you is ready for you to explore!"* Immediate, explanatory feedback is provided after each completed module, tailored to prior errors and paired with alternative learning materials.
3. **Accessibility Solutions:**
   - All materials have been reformatted into screen–reader–compatible HTML for visually impaired students.
   - Automatic subtitles and summary transcripts for videos to support deaf and hard-of-hearing learners.

- o Simplified versions of complex content via NLP for those with cognitive challenges.

4. **Continuous Learning Tracking:** The AI monitors time spent on tasks, areas of difficulty, and successful learning strategies, compiling personalized progress reports for each student. These reports enable students to self-monitor their growth while allowing instructors to adapt course content accordingly.

This scenario demonstrates how UDL principles can be operationalized through AI-driven instructional design. Dimensions such as content differentiation, feedback loops, accessibility solutions, and personalized learning analytics illustrate how AI can strengthen the inclusive character of education. AI-integrated UDL applications have the capacity to promote individual achievement while also advancing broader educational equity goals.

Recommendations

- Pedagogical objectives should bound AI content-adaptation features.
- Mixed-ability group work should be encouraged.
- Accessibility standards should be periodically reviewed to remain aligned with technological advancements.

5. EXAMPLE TECHNOLOGICAL COMPONENTS OF AI-ENHANCED LEARNING ECOSYSTEMS IN HIGHER EDUCATION

5.1. Learning Management Systems (LMS) and Learning Experience Platforms (LXP)

Traditional learning management systems (LMSs) have been used in higher education for many years to distribute course content, collect assignments, and conduct assessment processes. Systems such as Moodle, Blackboard, and Canvas are examples of this structure. However, the limitations of these systems arise in areas such as holistic monitoring of the student experience, dynamic interventions in the learning process, and personalization.

In this context, a new generation of platforms called Learning Experience Platforms (LXPs), supported by AI, has emerged. LXPs are learner-centered platforms that enable students to tailor their learning paths to their interests, performance history, and learning preferences. Academic studies have shown that the LXP model can increase personalized learning experiences and educational impact (Shamsudin & Hoon, 2024). In addition, LXPs protect students from cognitive overload and provide them with individualized learning paths through content-based, collaborative, and session-based recommendation systems (Dahal et al., 2025).

These systems provide real-time content recommendations to students throughout their learning experience, suggest new resources based on their learning behaviors, and offer support materials for areas of difficulty. The integration of LMSs and LXPs is valuable for higher education institutions to realize both their institutional and pedagogical goals. Such an integration goes beyond static content delivery, enabling an interactive, personalized, and continuously evolving learning experience.

5.2. Learning Analytics and Dashboards

One of the most powerful components of an AI-enhanced learning ecosystem is the data generated through learning analytics. Learning analytics refers to the analysis of diverse data—such as students' interactions with the platform, content completion rates, examination performance, and forum participation—to provide predictive and explanatory insights for both students and instructors. Long and Siemens (2011) define this approach as *"the process of collecting, measuring, analyzing, and reporting data about learners and their contexts, with the aim of understanding and optimizing learning and the environments in which it occurs."*

For example, learning analytics-based dashboards can show instructors, in real time, which modules students find challenging or which activities generate the most engagement. Simultaneously, dashboards can present students with their own learning graphs, raising awareness of their progress, unfinished content, and areas of strength. This dual feedback loop allows instructional design improvements while encouraging students to take an active and responsible role in their learning process.

Advanced learning analytics systems can identify at-risk students before course failure occurs through predictive modeling. Such proactive support, facilitated by early warning systems (Liz-Domínguez et al., 2019; Herodotou et al., 2019), aims to prevent academic failure. Learning analytics also supports data-driven instructional design by employing natural language processing (NLP) techniques to analyze students' textual outputs—such as forum contributions and assignment reflections. Furthermore, automated content generation algorithms can suggest instructional materials, reducing the workload on content developers and accelerating instructional design processes. Collectively, these functions represent powerful AI solutions that support the instructional designer's decision-making process.

5.3. AI-Enhanced Advising and Guidance Systems in Academic Counseling

Academic advising is a vital process in higher education that offers students personalized support. However, high student–advisor ratios often make it difficult for advisors to manage individualized planning, guidance, and follow-up effectively (Soomro et al., 2025). At this point, AI-based guidance systems can significantly improve the process by offering data-driven, scalable, and proactive solutions for academic and career planning (Bilquise & Shaalan, 2022).

These systems can analyze multidimensional data—such as students' academic performance, interests, past academic choices, and engagement with online learning platforms—to generate personalized course recommendations, career path planning, and matching of internship or certification programs (Iatrellis et al., 2024). For instance, an engineering student with a pronounced interest in algorithmic content could be guided toward additional or elective courses in data science or artificial intelligence. In this manner, the recommendations are aligned with both academic objectives and career trajectories that foster the student's professional growth and domain-specific competencies (Bilquise & Shaalan, 2022).

One of the most important contributions of AI-based advising systems is their ability to support student autonomy by enabling learners to consciously shape their own learning trajectories (Soomro et al., 2025). Moreover, early warning mechanisms can detect risk indicators such as low performance or declining motivation before they manifest, enabling advisors to intervene proactively (Iatrellis et al., 2024). These systems can also automatically report students' challenges or motivational issues to their advisors, strengthening communication and allowing advisors to reach students in need more quickly (Bilquise & Shaalan, 2022). This integrated approach enhances both student success and the efficiency of academic advising services (Soomro et al., 2025).

The components discussed in this section demonstrate that AI-enhanced learning ecosystems have evolved beyond mere content delivery to become holistic systems capable of monitoring, transforming, and personalizing all dimensions of the learning process. The integration of LMS and LXP systems, learning analytics dashboards, and AI-based advising tools is reshaping the student learning experience in a data-driven, interactive, and guiding manner. In this context, AI is not merely a learning support tool but a strategic partner that accompanies both faculty and students in decision-making processes.

6. AI-ENHANCED CURRICULUM DEVELOPMENT: FLEXIBILITY, COMPETENCE, AND DATA FOCUS

Traditional higher education curricula have typically followed a linear structure, providing students with a standardized learning pathway. However, evolving societal, digital, and professional contexts have led to a diversification of learners' goals and needs. As students now progress at varying paces and pursue increasingly multidimensional skill sets, higher education institutions are compelled to adopt more flexible, competency-based, and data-informed curriculum models. In this context, AI emerges as a transformative force that reshapes learning processes as well as the overall conception and design of curricula.

The new generation of curriculum design no longer assumes that all students will follow the same sequence of courses but is instead grounded in modular and scalable structures that allow learners to choose their own pathways. In this context, micro-credentials and competency-based learning approaches emerge as key components of flexible curriculum design. Micro-credentials are short, intensive, and outcome-oriented learning packages that target specific skills or areas of knowledge. Students can select such modules according to their interests and career goals, combining them to form personalized academic pathways (Orman et al., 2023; Hunt et al., 2020). Within these structures, AI plays a dual role: analyzing learners' interests and competency levels to provide tailored recommendations, and facilitating the integration of content between modules. For instance, systems that recommend technical courses alongside complementary skill areas such as communication and teamwork can significantly enhance the effectiveness and adaptability of modular curricula. Such structures also enable better alignment between labor market demands and individual learning pathways.

One of the significant shortcomings of traditional curricula lies in their inability to measure how effectively students acquire specific competencies systematically. Artificial intelligence provides a powerful solution to this issue by creating competency maps based on learners' data (Hochstetter-Diez et al., 2025). Each interaction within the learning environment—be it a completed task, feedback exchange, or assessment—contributes to a digital footprint that reflects the learner's progress. Through the analysis of these data, AI can identify which competencies a student has already mastered, highlight areas that need further development, and propose tailored learning pathways. For instance, an AI-based system might recognize that a student exhibits strong analytical thinking skills yet performs less effectively in written communication. In response, the system could recommend specific modules, assignments, or projects designed to enhance writing abilities in the next phase of learning. In this way, the curriculum evolves from a static framework for content delivery into a dynamic, adaptive system that continuously guides and supports learners in developing their competencies.

While traditional curricula are often designed around instructors' plans, learner-centered curricula place students' goals, interests, and needs at the forefront. AI supports this shift through tools such as scenario generation, learning pathway simulation, and module matching. Based on students' previous academic data, AI-driven curriculum scenarios can be developed. For example, for a student in a teacher education program, the system could identify an interest in early childhood education and firm performance in project-based learning, recommending modules such as child development, play-based teaching strategies, and technology-supported early childhood education. This personalized scenario provides a systematic approach not only to achieving the student's goals but also to developing their strengths, while preventing one-dimensional growth by addressing weaker areas through targeted modules.

Academic units can simulate alternative curriculum sequences for different learner profiles, making programs more flexible and goal-oriented. AI-supported scenarios can also be applied in corporate and lifelong learning contexts, extending their relevance beyond formal education.

Scenario-Based Implementation: Personalized Learning Experience through AI-Enhanced Flexible Curriculum Design

A public university's Department of Information and Records Management has initiated a restructuring of its undergraduate curriculum to align with 21st-century competencies. The new framework will be built around micro-credentials, competency orientation, and learner-centered design. The faculty decides to pilot an AI-enhanced learning analytics system to create differentiated curriculum pathways tailored to each student's past achievements, interests, and learning styles, delivering content flows aligned with individual learning goals.

AI Components and Implementation Process:

1. **Competency Mapping and Student Profiling:** Data on students' past course performance, project outcomes, and engagement with the LMS are collected. An AI-enhanced analysis system usses these data to create a "competency profile" for each student. For example:
    - *Student A*: High in research methods, moderate in digital archiving, low in written communication.
    - *Student B*: Strong in technical tools, struggles with theoretical content, and has developed in analytical thinking.

2. **Creating Personalized Learning Pathways:** The system combines 6–8 ECTS micro-modules based on each profile to recommend alternative learning routes. Example pathway for Student A:
    - o "Basic Statistics for Data Visualization" (competency gap)
    - o "Effective Academic Writing" (development need)
    - o "Information Classification with Artificial Intelligence" (growth potential)
    - o "Information Ethics" (deepening existing competence)
3. **AI-Based Scenario Generation and Alternative Module Structures:** Each module is offered with alternative content, assessment, and interaction formats tailored to different learner profiles. For example, in the *Information Retrieval Strategies* module:
    - o Infographics and video simulations for visual learners
    - o Case-based academic readings for textual learners
    - o Mini-projects with problem-solving scenarios for experiential learners
4. **Embedded Assessment and Continuous Feedback:** Each module integrates AI-supported embedded assessment tools. For instance, during online scenario analyses, the system evaluates not only correct/incorrect answers but also the reasoning processes behind decisions. At the end of the process, students receive detailed reports on their strengths, progress, and modules requiring review.

Institutional Implementation and Strategic Outcomes:

Following the pilot, the faculty reports that 85% of students achieved higher module completion rates in personalized pathways and that real-time data from embedded assessments made it easier for instructors to revise module content. Systematic tracking of competency development also provided a significant advantage in accreditation processes by enabling the monitoring of student learning outcomes. Plans for improvement in subsequent years are based on these data.

This scenario illustrates how AI can support individualized learning in curriculum development while driving strategic transformation at the institutional level. It demonstrates how flexible modular structures, when combined with AI, can become personalized learning pathways, and how data-driven assessment and continuous improvement cycles can enhance pedagogical quality. Such examples signal the growing adoption of a *learning engineering* approach at the program level in the future.

Recommendations:

- Module transitions should be planned to support holistic learning goals.

- AI recommendation algorithms should be designed with flexibility to introduce non-random variation in learning pathways.
- Students with similar competency gaps could form learning communities.
- Instructors should use AI-generated data for one-on-one mentoring.
- Transparent policies and consent processes should be applied for data security.

7. THE ASSESSMENT DIMENSION OF AI-ENHANCED INSTRUCTIONAL DESIGN

Assessment and evaluation processes are not just a step that documents the results of instructional design, but play a guiding and transformative role in all phases of learning. In this transformation, the possibilities offered by AI, combined with the automation of assessment tools, enable the monitoring of the learning process individually and instantaneously, the recognition of faulty learning patterns, active participation in student self-assessment processes, and the structuring of pedagogical interventions based on data. AI-enhanced assessment systems have reached a level where they can not only answer the question "has it been learned?" but also "how has it been learned?", "What difficulties have been encountered?" and "How can the learning process be improved?".

Traditional assessment and evaluation approaches are primarily summative in nature, aiming to document the level of knowledge a student has achieved at a particular point in time. However, this approach has often overlooked the conceptual difficulties that students encounter throughout the process, as well as the deficiencies in learning strategies or individual learning paths. However, the "process-oriented" learning approach emphasized by contemporary learning theories has brought formative assessment tools to the forefront, and technological developments have made it possible to use these tools more effectively. At this point, AI redefines formative assessment through its ability to process instant data during the learning process, generate continuous feedback, and offer adaptive intervention suggestions (Mousa, 2025; Hooda et al., 2022).

Feedback has traditionally been regarded as the presentation of information comparing expected and actual outcomes. Over time, its importance in academic settings has grown, with particular emphasis on the role of formative feedback in enhancing teaching quality and learning outcomes (Steinberg & Sartain, 2015). However, in higher education environments—especially in large-enrolment courses—the inadequacy of timely and meaningful feedback has been a persistent criticism (Boud & Molloy, 2013). Here, AI emerges as a powerful component capable of alleviating the feedback burden on educators while increasing students' access to actionable, high-quality feedback that can improve their work (Lee, 2023).

Recent studies have shown that integrating AI into formative assessment enhances personalized learning experiences and improves instructional effectiveness by providing educators with meaningful, data-informed insights into student progress (Mousa, 2025). Formative assessment, as a key component of learner-centred education, promotes students' active engagement in their own learning. When learners receive timely feedback, they can better track their development, recognize areas where further effort is needed, and sustain motivation throughout the process (Villegas-Ch et al., 2025). Moreover, formative assessment within learner-focused settings enables instructors to adjust their teaching strategies to the needs of each student, thereby nurturing a learning environment grounded in trust, responsibility, and self-regulation (Lai, 2024). The use of adaptive learning environments and AI-based analysis tools further strengthens this process by providing focused feedback and informed guidance aimed at addressing specific learning challenges (Trajkovski & Hayes, 2025). For instance, an online assessment system supported by AI might do more than simply determine whether a student's response is correct or incorrect. It can identify recurring patterns of error, detect conceptual difficulties, and compare a learner's progress with that of peers following similar trajectories. Based on such information, the system could suggest a brief explanatory video, a relevant simulation, or a short practice activity to reinforce understanding. In this way, assessment moves beyond its traditional role of evaluating past performance to become a proactive and continuous instrument for learning improvement.

AI-enhanced assessment systems play a crucial role in identifying recurring learning errors. When students consistently make similar mistakes on specific topics, this may signal gaps in understanding, weaknesses in cognitive strategies, or even learning-related anxiety. These complex patterns often remain unnoticed through traditional observation methods, making AI-based analysis a valuable complement to conventional assessment practices. However, AI systems, using pattern-recognition algorithms on large datasets, can identify these behaviours and generate informative reports for both students and instructors. This increases the possibility of early intervention and enhances the quality of the learning process.

AI has become an essential tool in the development of assessment instruments. In automated test generation, the system suggests questions that correspond to the learning objectives and topics established by the instructor. By applying pedagogical frameworks such as Bloom's Taxonomy, these systems can design items that measure various cognitive levels, ranging from basic knowledge to more complex skills, including analysis, synthesis, and evaluation (Elkins et al., 2024). In addition, AI technologies can create personalized test sets based on students' previous responses and performance trends. When assessing open-ended answers, AI-based text analysis tools evaluate aspects such as semantic accuracy, coherence, clarity, and the use of relevant examples, providing educators with meaningful information to refine their teaching practices. Techniques such as the Naïve Bayes theorem, Random Forest algorithms, sentiment analysis, and semantic analysis have been successfully applied to scoring free-form texts and essays (Wahyuningsih et al., 2024; Liang et al., 2022; Azahar & Ghauth, 2022).

Selecting the appropriate type of assessment depends on the nature of the learning outcomes and the course objectives. Effective feedback practices directly contribute to student success by enhancing self-regulation, motivation, academic performance, and engagement (Hooda et al., 2022). In higher education, assessment is not limited to formative and summative approaches—it also includes self-assessment, peer assessment, and e-assessment. These methods prevent unidirectional evaluation and highlight that, alongside AI, human relationships, intuitions, and perspectives remain valuable components of learning environments.

Collectively, these examples illustrate that AI-enhanced assessment systems are not merely technological conveniences; they are catalysts for pedagogical transformation. By making learning more visible, assessment more meaningful, and instructional processes more effective, these tools strengthen the quality of decision-making by complementing instructors' intuitive observations with data. Nonetheless, ethical boundaries—particularly those related to automated scoring, data privacy, and fairness in assessment—must be carefully addressed. Every AI-generated output should be interpreted through a pedagogical lens, with final decisions grounded in human-centred approaches. AI-enhanced assessment is evolving from a process that measures students' achievement levels into a multi-layered system that monitors and guides the nature, process, and effectiveness of learning. Accordingly, higher education institutions must not only redesign their assessment tools but also rethink their assessment philosophy, integrating these systems into data-driven learning ecosystems. AI is poised to be one of the architects of this new philosophy.

8. THE LIMITS OF AI: ETHICS, ACCESSIBILITY, AND RESPONSIBILITY

The possibilities that artificial intelligence (AI) offers for instructional design, curriculum development, and the restructuring of learning environments in higher education are unquestionably transformative. However, this transformation is incomplete if it is evaluated only in terms of technical competencies and functional benefits. AI is not just a tool in education; it is an actor that needs to be repositioned in terms of pedagogical, sociocultural, and ethical aspects. Therefore, ethical sensitivity, the principle of accessibility, and professional responsibility should be considered as key determining factors in the development of AI-enhanced learning systems (Kasztelnik, 2024; Holmes et al., 2019).

The integration of AI into decision-making processes inevitably has an impact on individuals through the use of algorithmic structures. One of the most critical issues here is algorithmic bias. Since machine learning systems are trained with historical data, they tend to reproduce the social biases and inequalities inherent in that data. For example, if historical data on socioeconomic status has an indirect influence on a student's learning performance, this may be reflected in the recommendations of AI systems. This can lead to certain groups being systematically held to lower expectations or having their access to alternative learning pathways limited (Boateng & Boateng, 2025). Therefore, ensuring equality in learning opportunities is not only a technical but also an ethical responsibility.

The digital divide is another major limiting factor. Inequalities in access to digital tools and internet connectivity can restrict the effectiveness of AI in education. Policymakers and investors must work to ensure equal access to technology for all learners, supporting low-cost, low-hardware, or offline-capable AI-based solutions (Katona & Gyonyoru, 2025).

Data security and student privacy are also central to the development of AI-enabled systems. Personal information, such as interaction data, performance reports, textual feedback, and even emotional responses, are essential to the functioning of AI systems. However, the way in which this data is collected, for what purpose it is processed, with whom it is shared, and how long it is stored should be clearly, transparently, and accountably defined within the framework of data ethics principles. Educational institutions should consider these principles when designing AI systems. However, the literature also contains findings that student autonomy and self-regulation skills may be weakened by AI-enhanced recommender systems (Le-Nguyen & Tran, 2024; Shah & Asad, 2024). Although recommender systems aim to improve the learning process by providing guidance, they may overshadow students' independent decision-making skills. Therefore, the balance between external guidance and individual autonomy needs to be carefully considered in the design process.

The fact that AI becomes an active actor in instructional design also redefines the nature of human-machine collaboration. In this framework, the ethical balance is not only about technological efficacy, but also about the question of who should bear pedagogical responsibility. The recommendations offered by AI should not replace instructional designers and academics, but rather be a support mechanism that enriches their decision-making processes. However, non-transparent algorithmic processes may make it difficult for teachers to understand how and why the system provides specific recommendations, potentially undermining trust (Wang et al., 2024). Moreover, AI's transformation of teaching roles requires a redefinition of professional competencies. It is not enough to use digital tools alone; specialization in data literacy, algorithmic thinking, ethical decision-making, systemic analysis, and digital accessibility is mandatory (Qayyum et al, 2025). In addition to these, high costs associated with the implementation process and the need for professional development for teachers to adapt to technology are also significant barriers (Wei et al., 2025). In this context, continuous professional development programs and institutional policy development processes need to be carried out in an integrated manner.

Despite its pedagogical benefits, AI in education presents challenges for both teachers and students. Teachers' primary concerns include data privacy, the protection of intellectual property rights, and the potential weakening of critical thinking skills (Mousa, 2025). Over-reliance on AI can limit students' capacity for independent thought, problem-solving, and creativity (Zhang, 2025; Trilaksana & Soelistiono, 2024). Moreover, AI-generated content may contain inaccuracies or misleading information due to data gaps or algorithmic biases. This situation makes it increasingly challenging for students to distinguish between factual information and AI-generated content, while simultaneously amplifying teachers' concerns about diminished classroom interaction and the potential devaluation of their professional authority (Trilaksana & Soelistiono, 2024). Trust in AI is closely tied to the transparency and contextual appropriateness of its outputs. Responsible, ethical, and pedagogically balanced integration of AI into education is therefore critical.

Consequently, the integration of AI in higher education is more than a technical innovation; it is a value-based restructuring process. This process should be based on a system that recognizes students' individual differences, promotes equal opportunities, prioritizes data security, and aligns technological decisions with pedagogical objectives (Nguyen & Tuamsuk, 2022). No matter how sophisticated AI systems are, the subject and ultimate custodian of education is the human being. Therefore, shaping technological possibilities with ethical awareness will ensure sustainability in terms of trust, inclusiveness, and quality in future education systems.

CONCLUSION AND STRATEGIC RECOMMENDATIONS

AI-enhanced instructional design and curriculum development in higher education represent a multifaceted transformation that extends beyond technological innovation, encompassing shifts in pedagogical philosophy, learning environments, and the evolving responsibilities of academic professionals. The chapters in this book examine the impact of artificial intelligence on instructional design processes at all stages, from analysis to implementation, from evaluation to structuring ethical principles. The main finding is that AI has gone beyond being a tool and has become a strategic component of learning ecosystems.

In the future of higher education, instructional design will be shaped by a paradigm in which humans and machines learn, make decisions, and evolve together. In this context, AI should be viewed not simply as an automator of processes, but as a partner that personalizes learning experiences, diversifies learning pathways, and enriches decision-support systems. However, this partnership can only be sustained through an approach that aligns with pedagogical values, is balanced by ethical responsibility, and prioritises accessibility.

For higher education institutions to participate effectively in this transformation, they need an institutional-level strategic plan for integrating AI. Such a plan must extend beyond upgrading technological infrastructure to include enhancing faculty members' digital pedagogical competencies, promoting a culture of data-driven learning, and institutionalising decision-making based on learning analytics. Furthermore, AI solutions should be adopted in open-source, transparent, and pedagogically driven forms rather than purely commercial products. Institutions must integrate this transformation into their high-level strategic documents and embed AI-supported teaching into their governance structures.

Within this transformation, concrete calls to action are inevitable for faculty members, instructional designers, and policymakers. Faculty should develop competencies in data literacy, algorithmic thinking, and digital ethics. Instructional designers should take responsibility for aligning AI technologies with pedagogical models. Policymakers should establish comprehensive policy frameworks that address both the technical dimensions and the social and pedagogical consequences of AI integration.

In conclusion, AI-enhanced instructional design and curriculum development have the potential to enhance accessibility, inclusivity, and flexibility in higher education. Realizing this potential requires attention to the human, ethical, and strategic responsibilities involved. The higher education of the future will be shaped by human-centred technological transformation, data-driven pedagogical commitment, and collaborative wisdom. AI should not merely be a tool in this new order—it should be a co-learner, a companion on the shared journey of education.

REFERENCES

Acosta-Vargas, P., Acosta-Vargas, G., Salvador-Acosta, B., & Jadán-Guerrero, J. (2024). Addressing web accessibility challenges with generative artificial intelligence tools for inclusive education. In *2024 Tenth International Conference on eDemocracy & eGovernment (ICEDEG)* (1-7). IEEE. https://doi.org/DOI: 10.1109/ICEDEG61611.2024.10702085

Adami, C. (2021). A brief history of artificial intelligence research. *Artificial Life*, *27*(2), 131–147. DOI: 10.1162/artl_a_00349

Adesiji, T. T. (2024). Integrating Artificial Intelligence in Nigerian University Curricula: Challenges, Opportunities, and Future Prospects. *In 2024 IEEE 5th International Conference on Electro-Computing Technologies for Humanity (NIGERCON)* (1-7). IEEE. https://doi.org/DOI: 10.1109/NIGERCON62786.2024.10927366

Akintayo, O. T., Eden, C. A., Ayeni, O. O., & Onyebuchi, N. C. (2024). Integrating AI with emotional and social learning in primary education: Developing a holistic adaptive learning ecosystem. *Computer Science & IT Research Journal*, *5*(5), 1076–1089. DOI: 10.53022/oarjms.2024.7.2.0025

Alenezi, A. (2023). Teacher perspectives on AI-driven gamification: Impact on student motivation, engagement, and learning outcomes. *Information Technologies and Learning Tools*, *97*(5), 138–148. DOI: 10.33407/itlt.v97i5.5437

Anvari, R., Moradi, F., & Shirvani, A. (2024). Digital learning ecosystem at educational institutions: a 4-university perspective. *Professional studies: theory and practice*, 28(1), 100-110.

Azahar, M. Z. A. B., & Ghauth, K. I. B. (2022). A hybrid automated essay scoring using NLP and random forest regression. In *International Conference on Computer, Information Technology and Intelligent Computing (CITIC 2022)* (448-457). Atlantis Press.

Bilquise, G., & Shaalan, K. (2022). AI-based academic advising framework: A knowledge management perspective. *International Journal of Advanced Computer Science and Applications*, *13*(8).

Boateng, O., & Boateng, B. (2025). Algorithmic bias in educational systems: Examining the impact of AI-driven decision making in modern education. *World Journal of Advanced Research and Reviews*, *25*(1), 2012–2017. DOI: 10.30574/wjarr.2025.25.1.0253

Chakraborty, N., Mishra, Y., Bhattacharya, R., & Bhattacharya, B. (2023). Artificial Intelligence: The road ahead for the accessibility of persons with Disability. *Materials Today: Proceedings*, *80*, 3757–3761. DOI: 10.1016/j.matpr.2021.07.374

Chanyi, L., Mokhtar, M. M., & Ayub, A. F. M. (2025). The 5P Funnel Framework: An AI-Integrated Instructional Design for Enhancing Teacher Professional Development. *Journal of Public Administration and Governance*, *14*(2), 78–96. DOI: 10.5296/jpag.v14i2S.22590

Chatterjee, S., & Bhattacharjee, K. K. (2020). Adoption of artificial intelligence in higher education: A quantitative analysis using structural equation modelling. *Education and Information Technologies*, *25*(5), 3443–3463. DOI: 10.69557/ujrra.v3i4.124

Chemnad, K., & Othman, A. (2024). Digital accessibility in the era of artificial intelligence—Bibliometric analysis and systematic review. *Frontiers in Artificial Intelligence*, *7*. Advance online publication. DOI: 10.3389/frai.2024.1349668

Chen, X., Xie, H., Zou, D., & Hwang, G. J. (2020). Application and theory gaps during the rise of artificial intelligence in education. *Computers and Education: Artificial Intelligence*, *1*, 100002. DOI: 10.1016/j.caeai.2020.100002

Çelik, I. (2023). Towards Intelligent-TPACK: An empirical study on teachers' professional knowledge to ethically integrate artificial intelligence (AI)-based tools into education. *Computers in Human Behavior*, *138*, 107468. DOI: 10.1016/j.chb.2022.107468

Dahal, P., Nugroho, S., Schmidt, C., & Sänger, V. (2025). AI-Based Learning Recommendations: Use in Higher Education. *Future Internet*, *17*(7), 285. DOI: 10.3390/fi17070285

Elkins, S., Kochmar, E., Cheung, J. C., & Serban, I. (2024). How teachers can use large language models and bloom's taxonomy to create educational quizzes. *Proceedings of the AAAI Conference on Artificial Intelligence*, *38*(21), 23084–23091. DOI: 10.1609/aaai.v38i21.30353

Guan, J., Zhang, J., & Zhang, X. (2023). The Influence of Generative Artificial Intelligence on High School Students' Academic Planning–ChatGPT. *Lecture Notes in Education Psychology and Public Media*, *24*(1), 205–210. DOI: 10.54254/2753-7048/24/20230705

He, R., Cao, J., & Tan, T. (2025). Generative artificial intelligence: A historical perspective. *National Science Review*, *12*(5). Advance online publication. DOI: 10.1093/nsr/nwaf050

Herodotou, C., Rienties, B., Verdin, B., & Boroowa, A. (2019). Predictive learning analytics 'at scale': Guidelines to successful implementation in Higher Education based on the case of the Open University UK. *Journal of Learning Analytics, 6*(1), 85–95. DOI: 10.18608/jla.2019.61.5

Hochstetter-Diez, J., Negrier-Seguel, M., Diéguez-Rebolledo, M., Candia-Garrido, E., & Vidal, E. (2025). From Mapping to Action: SmartRubrics, an AI Tool for Competency-Based Assessment in Engineering Education. *Sustainability, 17*(13), 6098. DOI: 10.3390/su17136098

Holmes, W., Bialik, M., & Fadel, C. (2019). *Artificial intelligence in education promises and implications for teaching and learning*. Center for Curriculum Redesign.

Hooda, M., Rana, C., Dahiya, O., Rizwan, A., & Hossain, M. S. (2022). Artificial intelligence for assessment and feedback to enhance student success in higher education. *Mathematical Problems in Engineering, 2022*(1). https://doi.org/DOI: 10.1155/2022/5215722

Hunt, T., Carter, R., Zhang, L., & Yang, S. (2020). Micro-credentials: The potential of personalized professional development. *Development and Learning in Organizations, 34*(2), 33–35. DOI: 10.1108/DLO-09-2019-0215

Iatrellis, O., Samaras, N., Kokkinos, K., & Panagiotakopoulos, T. (2024). Leveraging generative AI for sustainable academic advising: Enhancing educational practices through AI-driven recommendations. *Sustainability, 16*(17), 7829. DOI: 10.3390/su16177829

Ismail, O. S. (2024). Empowering the modern learning ecosystem: Integrative approaches for a holistic educational experience. In *Revitalizing the Learning Ecosystem for Modern Students* (pp. 145–167). IGI Global Scientific Publishing.

Kalaigian, M., Thompson, M. S., VanLone, J., & Nickel, R. (2024). *Using Generative AI to Implement UDL Principles in Traditional STEM Classrooms. In 2024 IEEE Frontiers in Education Conference (FIE) (1-9)*. IEEE., DOI: 10.1109/FIE61694.2024.10893115

Kasztelnik, K. (2024). Artificial Intelligence-Assisted Curriculum Development: Innovations in Designing Educational Content for the 21st Century Learner. *Journal of Higher Education Theory and Practice, 24*(11), 51–59.

Katona, J., & Gyonyoru, K. I. K. (2025). AI-based Adaptive Programming Education for Socially Disadvantaged Students: Bridging the Digital Divide. *TechTrends, 69*, 925–942. DOI: 10.1007/s11528-025-01088-8

Kerres, M., & Buntins, K. (2020). Recommender in AI-enhanced learning: An assessment from the perspective of instructional design. *Open Education Studies, 2*(1), 101–111. DOI: 10.1515/edu-2020-0119

Kohen-Vacs, D., Amzalag, M., Weigelt-Marom, H., Gal, L., Kahana, O., Raz-Fogel, N., & Usher, M. (2024). Towards a call for transformative practices in academia enhanced by generative AI. *European Journal of Open. Distance & E-Learning, 26*(1), 35–50. DOI: 10.2478/eurodl-2024-0006

Kökver, Y., Pektaş, H. M., & Çelik, H. (2025). Artificial intelligence applications in education: Natural language processing in detecting misconceptions. *Education and Information Technologies, 30*(3), 3035–3066. DOI: 10.1007/s10639-024-12919-1

Krouska, A., Troussas, C., Voyiatzis, I., Mylonas, P., & Sgouropoulou, C. (2024, November). ChatGPT-based recommendations for personalized content creation and instructional design with a tailored prompt generator. In *2024 2nd International Conference on Foundation and Large Language Models (FLLM)* (295-299). IEEE. https://doi.org/DOI: 10.1109/FLLM63129.2024.10852487

Lai, J. W. (2024). Adapting self-regulated learning in an age of generative artificial intelligence chatbots. *Future Internet, 16*(6), 218. DOI: 10.3390/fi16060218

Lakhe Shrestha, B. L., Dahal, N., Hasan, M. K., Paudel, S., & Kapar, H. (2025, June). Generative AI on professional development: a narrative inquiry using TPACK framework. In *Frontiers in Education* (Vol. 10). https://doi.org/DOI: 10.3389/feduc.2025.1550773

Lee, A. V. Y. (2023). Supporting students' generation of feedback in large-scale online course with artificial intelligence-enabled evaluation. *Studies in Educational Evaluation, 77*, 101250. DOI: 10.1016/j.stueduc.2023.101250

Le-Nguyen, H. T., & Tran, T. T. (2024). Generative AI in terms of its ethical problems for both teachers and learners: Striking a balance. In *Generative AI in teaching and learning* (pp. 144–173). IGI Global Scientific Publishing.

Liang, C., Zhang, B., Gong, X., Li, M., Guo, H., & Li, R. (2022). A Survey of Automated Essay Scoring System Based on Naive Bayes Classifier. In *Artificial Intelligence in Education and Teaching Assessment* (pp. 247–250). Springer Singapore., DOI: 10.1007/978-981-16-6502-8_21

Liz-Domínguez, M., Caeiro-Rodríguez, M., Llamas-Nistal, M., & Mikic-Fonte, F. A. (2019). Systematic literature review of predictive analysis tools in higher education. *Applied Sciences (Basel, Switzerland), 9*(24), 5569. DOI: 10.3390/app9245569

Long, P., & Siemens, G. (2011). Penetrating the fog: Analytics in learning and education. *EDUCAUSE Review*, *46*(5), 31–40. https://er.educause.edu/articles/2011/9/penetrating-the-fog-analytics-in-learning-and-education

Mahamuni, A. J., & Tonpe, S. S. (2024). Enhancing educational assessment with artificial intelligence: Challenges and opportunities. In *2024 International Conference on Knowledge Engineering and Communication Systems (ICKECS)* Vol. 1. (1-5). IEEE. https://doi.org/DOI: 10.1109/ICKECS61492.2024.10616620

Malik, R. (2023). Impact of technology-based education on student learning outcomes and engagement. In 2023 *10th International Conference on Computing for Sustainable Global Development (INDIACom)* 784-788. IEEE. Electronic ISBN:978-93-80544-47-2

Mishra, P., Warr, M., & Islam, R. (2023). TPACK in the age of ChatGPT and Generative AI. *Journal of Digital Learning in Teacher Education*, *39*(4), 235–251. DOI: 10.1080/21532974.2023.2247480

Mousa, M. (2025). AI-Supported Formative Assessments: Enhancing Student-Centered Learning and Teacher Perceptions. *Journal of Pedagogy and Education Science*, *4*(02), 127–141.

Nguyen, L. T., & Tuamsuk, K. (2022). Digital learning ecosystem at educational institutions: A content analysis of scholarly discourse. *Cogent Education*, *9*(1), 2111033. DOI: 10.1080/2331186X.2022.2111033

Novita, R. (2025). AI in Lesson Planning: Improving Teacher Efficiency and Instructional Design. *Jurnal Riset Rumpun Ilmu Pendidikan*, *4*(2), 192–202. DOI: 10.55606/jurripen.v4i2.5560

Orman, R., Şimşek, E., & Kozak Çakır, M. A. (2023). Micro-credentials and reflections on higher education. *Higher Education Evaluation and Development*, *17*(2), 96–112. DOI: 10.1108/HEED-08-2022-0028

Ozogul, G., Zheng, X., Min, W., Lee, S., Carpenter, D., & Lester, J. (2025). Towards AI-Enhanced Classroom Response System Eliciting Self-Explanations in Computer Science Courses. *The Journal of Applied Instructional Design*, *14*(2).

Qayyum, A., Rafique, Z., Shah, S. S. W. A., Ahmad, S., & Haider, Z. (2025). Artificial intelligence (AI)-driven curriculum development in early childhood education: Educators' insights, barriers, and policy pathways. *Research Journal of Psychology*, *3*(1), 713–733. DOI: 10.59075/rjs.v3i1.102

Radanliev, P. (2024). Artificial intelligence: Reflecting on the past and looking towards the next paradigm shift. *Journal of Experimental & Theoretical Artificial Intelligence*, •••, 1045–1062. DOI: 10.1080/0952813X.2024.2323042

Ramos, R. F., De Angel, R. M., Ruetas, A. P., Lagman, A. C., Morano, J., Payongayong, R. T., & Enrile, J. C. (2024, August). Effective Lesson Planning and Assessment Design Using Leveraging Microsoft Copilot Implementation. In *2024 IEEE 15th Control and System Graduate Research Colloquium (ICSGRC)* (331-336). IEEE. https://doi.org/DOI: 10.1109/ICSGRC62081.2024.10691289

Reinitz, B. (2020). *Consider the Three Ds When Talking about Digital Transformation*. Retrieved from: https://er.educause.edu/blogs/2020/6/consider-the-three-ds-when-talking-about-digital-transformation

Rezaie, F., Asino, T. I., & Panwar, K. (2025). Leveraging Instructional Design Models for Corporate Training and Professional Development using Artificial Intelligence (AI). *The Journal of Applied Instructional Design*, *14*(2).

Shah, S. S., & Asad, M. M. (2024). Impact of Critical Thinking Approach on Learners' Dependence on Innovative Transformation Through Artificial Intelligence. In *The Evolution of Artificial Intelligence in Higher Education: Challenges, Risks, and Ethical Considerations* (pp. 161–182). Emerald Publishing Limited.

Shamsudin, N. M., & Hoon, T. S. (2024). Exploring the Synergy of Learning Experience Platforms (LXP) with Artificial Intelligence for Enhanced Educational Outcomes. In *International Conference on Innovation & Entrepreneurship in Computing, Engineering & Science Education (InvENT 2024)* (pp. 30-40). Atlantis Press.

Soomro, A. A., Khan, M. H., Umar, M., Khan, S., & Ali, O. (2025). AI-Driven Academic Advising in Higher Education: Leveraging Intelligent Systems to Personalize Student Support, Improve Retention, and Optimize Career Pathways. *The Critical Review of Social Sciences Studies*, *3*(2), 229–248. DOI: 10.59075/vy3v7k17

Steinberg, M. P., & Sartain, L. (2015). Does teacher evaluation improve school performance? Experimental evidence from Chicago's Excellence in Teaching project. *Education Finance and Policy*, *10*(4), 535–572. DOI: 10.1162/EDFP_a_00173

Swallow, M. J., & Olofson, M. W. (2017). Contextual understandings in the TPACK framework. *Journal of Research on Technology in Education*, *49*(3-4), 228–244. DOI: 10.1080/15391523.2017.1347537

Tillmanns, T., Salomão Filho, A., Rudra, S., Weber, P., Dawitz, J., Wiersma, E., Dudenaite, D., & Reynolds, S. (2025). Mapping Tomorrow's Teaching and Learning Spaces: A Systematic Review on GenAI in Higher Education. *Trends in Higher Education*, *4*(1), 2. DOI: 10.3390/higheredu4010002

Trajkovski, G., & Hayes, H. (2025). AI-Assisted Formative Assessment and Feedback. In: AI-Assisted Assessment in Education. Digital Education and Learning. (283-312) Springer Nature Switzerland. Palgrave Macmillan, Cham. https://doi.org/ DOI: 10.1007/978-3-031-88252-4_7

Trilaksana, H., & Soelistiono, S. (2024). Campus Learning Based on AI: Implementation of ChatGPT in AILS and Its Implications for Curriculum Development in Indonesia. *Influence: international journal of science review, 6*(1), 63-72.

UNESCO. (2024). *AI competency framework for teachers*. UNESCO Publishing., DOI: 10.54675/ZJTE2084

Usher, M., Hershkovitz, A., & Forkosh-Baruch, A. (2021). From data to actions: Instructors' reflections about learners' data in online emergency remote teaching. *British Journal of Educational Technology*, *52*(4), 1338–1356. DOI: 10.1111/bjet.13108

Villegas-Ch, W., Buenano-Fernandez, D., Navarro, A. M., & Mera-Navarrete, A. (2025). Adaptive intelligent tutoring systems for STEM education: Analysis of the learning impact and effectiveness of personalized feedback. *Smart Learning Environments*, *12*(1). Advance online publication. DOI: 10.1186/s40561-025-00389-y

Visscher, A. J. (2021). On the value of data-based decision making in education: The evidence from six intervention studies. *Studies in Educational Evaluation*, *69*. Advance online publication. DOI: 10.1016/j.stueduc.2020.100899

Wahyuningsih, T., Manongga, D., Sembiring, I., & Wijono, S. (2024). Comparison of effectiveness of logistic regression, naive bayes, and random forest algorithms in predicting student arguments. *Procedia Computer Science*, *234*, 349–356. DOI: 10.1016/j.procs.2024.03.014

Wang, D., Bian, C., & Chen, G. (2024). Using explainable AI to unravel classroom dialogue analysis: Effects of explanations on teachers' trust, technology acceptance and cognitive load. *British Journal of Educational Technology*, *55*(6), 2530–2556. DOI: 10.1111/bjet.13466

Wei, Z., Zhang, G., Zhang, M., & Cui, W. (2025). The Symbiotic Integration of Cognitive-Enhanced Artificial Intelligence and University Education: Building the Future Intelligent Learning Ecosystem. In *Proceedings of the 2025 4th International Conference on Big Data, Information and Computer Network* (434-439). https://doi.org/DOI: 10.1145/3727353.3727424

Winder, G., Bass, S., Schiele, D., & Buchner, J. (2024). Using large language models for content creation impacts online learning evaluation outcomes. In *International Journal on E-Learning* (305-318). Association for the Advancement of Computing in Education (AACE). https://doi.org/DOI: 10.70725/423664moqcrd

Zhang, J. (2025). Generative AI in Higher Education: Challenges and Opportunities for Course Learning. [REMOVED HYPERLINK FIELD]. *Advances in Social Sciences Research Journal, 12*(01), 11–18. DOI: 10.14738/assrj.1201.18121

Chapter 5
The Role of AI in Reshaping Curriculum Structures for Future Learners

Punam Kumari
https://orcid.org/0000-0001-8144-7573
Amity University, India

ABSTRACT

This chapter will explore how Artificial Intelligence (AI) is fundamentally transforming curriculum design, development, and delivery in educational systems worldwide. Traditional curriculum structures often lack the flexibility to accommodate diverse learner needs, evolving job markets, and interdisciplinary knowledge demands. Through AI-driven insights, institutions can create dynamic, adaptive, and personalized curricula that continuously evolve based on learner performance data, emerging industry trends, and societal needs. The chapter highlights models of AI integration, ethical concerns, and future directions for curriculum innovation.

1. INTRODUCTION

1.1 Why Curriculum Innovation is Needed

Education is at a pivotal moment in history, driven by rapid technological advances, evolving societal needs, and an increasingly interconnected global economy. Traditional curriculum structures, which were largely designed for the industrial age, often struggle to prepare learners for the dynamic and uncertain realities of the 21st

DOI: 10.4018/979-8-3373-4129-3.ch005

century. The pace of change in the workplace particularly the demand for digital literacy, critical thinking, creativity, and adaptability has outstripped the capacity of static curricula to remain relevant (Uhran et al., 2005). Several pressing factors make curriculum innovation a necessity rather than a choice:

Technological Disruption – Emerging technologies such as artificial intelligence (AI), robotics, blockchain, and the Internet of Things (IoT) are transforming industries at unprecedented speed. Skills that were highly sought after a decade ago may now be obsolete, while new roles and competencies emerge continuously.

Changing Workforce Demands – Employers increasingly seek interdisciplinary problem-solvers who can collaborate across domains, think analytically, and learn continuously. The ability to adapt, unlearn, and reskill has become more important than memorizing static bodies of knowledge.

Globalization and Cultural Fluency – The modern professional environment requires collaboration across cultural, geographic, and disciplinary boundaries. Curricula must prepare students to navigate diversity, work in global teams, and appreciate the ethical dimensions of decision-making.

Sustainability and Societal Challenges – Issues like climate change, economic inequality, and public health crises demand holistic, systems-level thinking. Learners must be equipped not only with technical expertise but also with the ethical frameworks and civic responsibility to address such challenges.

Learner-Centric Paradigms – Today's learners expect personalized, flexible, and engaging educational experiences. The one-size-fits-all model of teaching is increasingly incompatible with diverse learning styles, paces, and aspirations.

Curriculum innovation, therefore, is not merely about adding new subjects or replacing textbooks. It requires a rethinking of what we teach, how we teach, and why we teach, with an emphasis on relevance, adaptability, and lifelong learning. This is where AI presents itself as a transformative force—not just as a subject of study but as an enabler of change in how curriculum is designed, delivered, and continuously refined.

1.2 Overview of AI's Potential Role in Education

Artificial intelligence has already begun to redefine the possibilities within education, extending far beyond automating administrative tasks or providing basic e-learning tools. AI's potential lies in its ability to analyze vast amounts of data, recognize patterns in learner behavior, and adapt instruction to individual needs at scale (Hubballi et al., 2025).

1. Personalizing Learning Paths

AI can power adaptive learning platforms that tailor content, pace, and assessment to each student's strengths, weaknesses, and learning preferences. This is particularly significant in diverse classrooms where students may have widely varying abilities, prior knowledge, and learning speeds. For example, AI-driven systems can identify when a learner is struggling with a concept and offer alternative explanations, visualizations, or practice exercises to reinforce understanding.

2. Data-Driven Curriculum Design

By analyzing student performance data over time, AI can help educators and curriculum designers pinpoint gaps in understanding, emerging trends in skill requirements, and content areas that need revision. Instead of relying solely on periodic curriculum reviews, educators can continuously refine and optimize courses to keep them relevant and effective.

3. Enhancing Assessment and Feedback

AI-based tools can provide timely, formative feedback that supports learning in real time. This not only reduces the workload on educators but also enables learners to self-correct and deepen their understanding more quickly. Natural language processing (NLP) algorithms, for instance, can assess open-ended responses, essays, or coding assignments with high accuracy, offering feedback on both technical correctness and conceptual depth.

4. Simulating Real-World Scenarios

AI can bring experiential learning into the curriculum by enabling immersive simulations and virtual environments. In fields ranging from medicine to engineering to environmental science, learners can engage with realistic problem-solving tasks that mirror the complexities of the real world. These AI-driven simulations also allow for safe experimentation and failure without real-world consequences, promoting deeper learning.

5. Supporting Lifelong Learning and Reskilling

As career paths become less linear, AI can support microlearning and modular curriculum structures that allow individuals to acquire skills just in time for emerging opportunities. AI-powered recommendation systems can suggest new courses, certifications, or learning materials based on a learner's goals, performance history, and industry trends.

6. Promoting Equity and Inclusion

AI tools, when designed with ethical considerations, can help identify and address educational inequities. For instance, predictive analytics can flag learners who may be at risk of dropping out or falling behind, enabling targeted interventions. AI-powered translation and accessibility tools can also break down language and disability barriers, broadening participation and inclusivity.

7. Curriculum as a Living System

Perhaps the most transformative aspect of AI's role in curriculum is its ability to make learning systems adaptive and self-improving. Instead of a static, fixed syllabus, AI enables a dynamic curriculum that evolves in response to learner data, societal changes, and emerging knowledge domains. This shifts education from a "set-and-forget" model to one that is continuously responsive and future-ready.

The urgency for curriculum innovation is rooted in the mismatch between traditional educational structures and the demands of a rapidly changing world. AI offers unprecedented opportunities to bridge this gap by enabling personalization, adaptability, and continuous improvement in both what and how we teach. For future learners, this means not only gaining relevant skills but also developing the capacity to thrive in a world where learning never stops. The subsequent sections of this chapter will explore specific strategies, case studies, and frameworks for integrating AI into curriculum design, ensuring that education remains a driver of innovation, equity, and societal progress.

2. TRADITIONAL VS AI-DRIVEN CURRICULUM STRUCTURES

2.1 Fixed vs Adaptive Curriculum Models

For decades, education systems across the world have relied on fixed curriculum models carefully structured, standardized sequences of content and assessments, often designed to cover a predefined set of topics within a fixed timeframe. This model has been instrumental in promoting uniformity, ensuring that all learners meet minimum competency standards, and aligning education with accreditation requirements (Chu & Ashraf, 2025). However, it comes with inherent limitations.

In a fixed curriculum model, learning objectives, course materials, and assessment methods are typically determined well in advance and remain unchanged for years. While this stability can be beneficial for quality control, it does not easily accommodate changes in industry demands, emerging technologies, or the unique learning trajectories of individual students. In such systems:

- Content updates often occur only after lengthy review cycles.
- Instruction is delivered at a uniform pace, regardless of learners' readiness or prior knowledge.
- Assessment is usually summative, evaluating learning after instruction rather than adapting during the process.
- Learners with different abilities and backgrounds often receive the same materials and teaching methods, which can lead to disengagement or knowledge gaps.

In contrast, **AI-driven curriculum models** represent a shift toward adaptivity, personalization, and continuous improvement. An adaptive curriculum does not treat all learners the same; rather, it uses real-time data to adjust content, difficulty level, pacing, and instructional approach to suit each learner's needs. Instead of adhering strictly to a one-size-fits-all syllabus, adaptive systems respond dynamically to a learner's progress, gaps, and goals.

In AI-enhanced adaptive models:

- Content delivery is fluid, adjusting as the learner interacts with the material.
- Feedback is immediate, allowing students to understand mistakes and correct them in real time.
- Learning paths are non-linear, enabling students to explore topics in a sequence that suits their personal learning style.
- The curriculum itself is iterative, updating regularly based on both learner data and industry developments.

For example, a traditional mathematics course might follow a rigid chapter-by-chapter schedule for an entire class, whereas an AI-driven platform could identify that some students are ready to skip certain foundational concepts while others need additional practice before moving forward. In doing so, AI-driven curricula aim to optimize time-on-task, maintain engagement, and improve mastery.

2.2 Role of Data and Predictive Analytics in Curriculum Evolution

Data is the lifeblood of AI-driven curriculum innovation. In traditional models, curriculum revisions are often informed by periodic reviews, standardized test results, and occasional stakeholder feedback. While these methods provide valuable information, they tend to be lagging indicators—revealing what has already happened rather than predicting what needs to happen next (Awasthi, R., & Tiwari, A. 2024). Predictive analytics, powered by AI, shifts this paradigm by using historical and real-time data to forecast learner needs, identify emerging skill gaps, and anticipate industry trends before they become urgent.

Some key ways data and predictive analytics contribute to curriculum evolution include:

1. **Early Identification of Learning Gaps**

AI systems can track learner interactions with course materials in granular detail—time spent on each topic, frequency of errors, patterns in assessment results—and flag students who are struggling long before final exams. This allows for targeted interventions such as personalized assignments, supplementary resources, or peer tutoring.

2. **Curriculum Responsiveness to Industry Changes**

By analyzing labor market data, job postings, and skill demand trends, predictive analytics can signal when certain competencies are becoming more important in the workplace. Educational institutions can then update their curricula proactively rather than reactively, ensuring graduates are equipped with relevant skills.

3. **Optimizing Instructional Sequences**

Data from thousands of learners can reveal which content sequences lead to better comprehension and retention. AI can recommend restructuring lessons or introducing concepts in alternative orders to improve learning outcomes.

4. **Supporting Continuous Feedback Loops**

Instead of revising curricula in multi-year cycles, AI enables a continuous improvement process. Feedback from learner performance, engagement metrics, and instructor input can feed into curriculum updates at regular intervals—even in the middle of an academic term.

5. **Personalization at Scale**

While a single instructor may struggle to customize materials for hundreds of students, AI systems can analyze data patterns across cohorts to deliver personalized learning experiences without overburdening educators.

6. **Forecasting Future Learning Needs**

Predictive models can go beyond immediate performance data to forecast the types of skills learners will likely need in the future, based on technological advancements, policy changes, or economic shifts. For example, an AI system might suggest integrating AI ethics modules into engineering programs ahead of regulatory changes in the industry.

Example: Imagine a traditional curriculum where a new programming language is only introduced after an official syllabus review, which happens every three years. By the time it's implemented, industry demand for that skill may have peaked or evolved. In an AI-driven environment, real-time analysis of tech job postings could flag a surge in demand for that language, prompting its integration into coursework within the next semester.

Table 1. Comparison of Traditional vs AI-Driven Curriculum Models

Aspect	Traditional (Fixed) Curriculum	AI-Driven (Adaptive) Curriculum
Structure	Predetermined, static sequence of topics and assessments	Flexible, adjusts content and sequence based on learner needs
Pace of Learning	Uniform for all learners	Personalized pace tailored to individual progress
Content Updates	Occur in multi-year cycles after formal reviews	Continuous updates based on data, industry trends, and learner performance
Assessment	Primarily summative (end-of-term exams, fixed assignments)	Formative and ongoing, with real-time feedback and adaptive quizzes
Personalization	Limited; same resources for all learners	High; tailored resources, alternative explanations, and varied formats
Role of Data	Minimal use of learner data beyond grades	Extensive use of real-time data and analytics to inform instruction
Industry Alignment	Often reactive; updates lag behind market changes	Proactive; predictive analytics integrate emerging skills early

continued on following page

Table 1. Continued

Aspect	Traditional (Fixed) Curriculum	AI-Driven (Adaptive) Curriculum
Instructor Role	Content delivery focused	Facilitator and mentor, supported by AI insights
Learner Engagement	Passive reception of content	Active, interactive, and learner-driven exploration
Curriculum Evolution	Fixed until formal revision	Living system, constantly evolving through AI feedback loops

3. FRAMEWORKS FOR AI-BASED CURRICULUM DESIGN

3.1 Adaptive Learning Paths and Intelligent Content Recommendation

One of the most transformative aspects of AI-based curriculum design lies in its ability to generate adaptive learning paths that respond to the unique needs, pace, and aspirations of each learner. Traditional curricula generally assume a linear, one-size-fits-all learning progression, but adaptive frameworks allow for non-linear, personalized trajectories.

An adaptive learning path begins with a diagnostic phase, where AI-driven assessments determine a learner's prior knowledge, skill levels, and preferred learning modalities. Based on this data, the system designs a customized sequence of topics, resources, and assessments. This path is not static—it evolves as the learner progresses, using continuous performance monitoring to adjust content difficulty, presentation style, and pacing.

AI-powered intelligent content recommendation systems function similarly to the algorithms behind streaming services or online shopping platforms, but in an educational context, they recommend learning materials—videos, articles, simulations, case studies—that align with the learner's needs and goals. These systems rely on:

- **Learner Profile Data** (academic history, strengths, weaknesses, interests)
- **Real-Time Interaction Data** (time spent on activities, assessment scores, engagement patterns)
- **Content Metadata** (difficulty level, prerequisites, skill alignment)

For example, a student struggling with statistical concepts in a data science course may automatically receive recommendations for interactive simulations, additional problem sets, or targeted video explanations. Conversely, a learner excelling in a topic may be offered advanced materials or interdisciplinary applications to deepen their understanding.

Such intelligent systems not only improve learning outcomes but also foster learner autonomy, allowing students to take an active role in navigating their educational journey.

3.2 Skill-Mapping with Industry Requirements Using AI Algorithms

A critical challenge in curriculum design is ensuring that what learners study aligns with the skills demanded by the labor market. Traditionally, this alignment has been achieved through consultations with industry experts, employer surveys, or alumni feedback—methods that, while useful, are often slow to capture emerging trends.

AI-powered skill-mapping frameworks offer a faster, data-driven approach. These systems use natural language processing (NLP) and machine learning algorithms to analyze vast amounts of labor market data—job postings, professional profiles, industry reports—and extract insights on in-demand skills, tools, and competencies.

The process typically involves:

1. **Data Collection** – Aggregating job advertisements, internship postings, and corporate training requirements from multiple online platforms.
2. **Skill Extraction** – Using NLP to identify explicit skill keywords (e.g., "Python programming," "data visualization") and implicit skills inferred from job descriptions (e.g., problem-solving, team leadership).
3. **Trend Analysis** – Applying time-series and clustering algorithms to track the growth, decline, or transformation of specific skills over time.
4. **Curriculum Alignment** – Comparing extracted skill requirements with existing course content to identify gaps and opportunities for integration.

For instance, if AI analytics reveal a growing demand for AI ethics expertise in the technology sector, universities can integrate ethics modules into computer science, law, and business courses well before regulatory or social pressures make it mandatory.

Moreover, predictive skill-mapping enables institutions to prepare learners for skills that are not yet mainstream but are projected to become significant within a few years—future-proofing graduates against rapid industry changes.

3.3 AI for Interdisciplinary Learning Programs

The problems of the 21st century—climate change, global health crises, sustainable urban development—are interdisciplinary by nature. They require collaboration across domains, blending knowledge from science, engineering, humanities, social sciences, and the arts. AI can play a pivotal role in designing, delivering, and sustaining interdisciplinary learning programs.

AI-driven systems can:

- **Identify Knowledge Overlaps** – By analyzing curricular databases across departments, AI can highlight thematic or skill-based intersections (e.g., the shared relevance of data visualization in both public health and economics).
- **Facilitate Cross-Departmental Collaboration** – Intelligent scheduling and content-sharing platforms can help faculty from different disciplines co-create and co-deliver courses.
- **Recommend Interdisciplinary Modules** – Based on a student's primary field of study, AI can suggest complementary subjects from other disciplines that enhance employability and problem-solving capacity.
- **Integrate Real-World Problems into Learning** – AI can curate datasets, case studies, and problem scenarios from global repositories to create project-based learning opportunities that require multiple disciplinary perspectives.

For example, an AI-driven interdisciplinary course on "AI for Sustainable Agriculture" might combine elements of computer science (machine learning algorithms for crop prediction), environmental science (climate modeling), and economics (market trend analysis for agricultural products).

Furthermore, AI can facilitate interdisciplinary capstone projects, matching students from diverse academic backgrounds to work on real-world challenges. Using project-matching algorithms, AI can ensure that teams have a balanced mix of technical, analytical, and creative skills.

4. AI TOOLS AND TECHNIQUES IN CURRICULUM STRUCTURING

- Machine learning models for learner profiling
- Natural Language Processing (NLP) for syllabus updates
- Learning analytics dashboards for curriculum feedback loops

Artificial Intelligence (AI) is no longer a futuristic concept confined to tech labs; it is actively shaping how educators design, deliver, and refine curriculum structures worldwide. By combining data-driven decision-making with adaptive algorithms, AI tools provide unprecedented insights into student needs, syllabus relevancy, and curriculum adaptability. This section explores three crucial AI applications in curriculum structuring: machine learning models for learner profiling, Natural Language Processing (NLP) for syllabus updates, and learning analytics dashboards for curriculum feedback loops. Together, these tools offer a foundation for creating agile, inclusive, and globally competitive education systems.

4.1 Machine Learning Models for Learner Profiling

Concept and Importance of Learner Profiling

Learner profiling refers to the process of creating detailed, data-backed representations of students' skills, learning preferences, pace, and needs. Traditionally, educators relied on manual observations and periodic tests to understand learners. Today, machine learning (ML) enables the automation and enhancement of this process. ML algorithms analyze diverse datasets—academic performance, engagement metrics, attendance patterns, and even socio-economic background—to cluster students into distinct profiles (Montebello M., 2024). These profiles guide curriculum adjustments, ensuring that learning is personalized and relevant.

How It Works in Curriculum Structuring

- Data Collection: Student data from Learning Management Systems (LMS), online quizzes, projects, and behavioral logs.
- Feature Engineering: Variables such as average grades, submission delays, question difficulty success rates, and interaction frequency.
- Model Application: Clustering algorithms (e.g., K-Means, DBSCAN) to group learners into categories like "fast learners," "concept-oriented learners," or "practice-intensive learners."
- Curriculum Alignment: Customizing assignments, pacing, and supplemental materials based on each cluster.

Machine learning (ML) is a cornerstone of AI-driven curriculum restructuring because it enables systems to adapt to diverse student needs. Learner profiling refers to building a detailed, data-driven representation of a student's abilities, preferences, learning pace, and potential challenges. With such profiles, educators and AI systems can create personalized learning paths, ensure targeted interventions, and make curriculum updates more dynamic.

4.1.1 Purpose of Learner Profiling

Before diving into the models, it's important to clarify why learner profiling matters:

- Personalization: Tailoring course material based on student needs.
- Early Intervention: Detecting struggling learners before they fail.
- Optimized Resource Allocation: Ensuring students get the right content at the right time.
- Career Path Guidance: Matching learning progress with career-oriented skills.

4.1.2 Commonly Used Machine Learning Models

A. Supervised Learning Models

These models work with labeled data—where student features (e.g., attendance, quiz scores) are linked to known outcomes (e.g., pass/fail, grade categories) (Nafea et al., 2024).

(i) Decision Trees

- How it works: Splits data into branches based on feature values until it reaches a decision.
- Use in learner profiling: Predicts whether a student is at risk of failing based on multiple features like class participation, assignment completion, and quiz performance.
- Example: A university uses decision trees to classify students into "High Performer," "Average," and "Needs Intervention" categories.

(ii) Random Forests

- How it works: An ensemble of decision trees that reduces overfitting by averaging predictions from multiple trees.
- Use in learner profiling: Improves accuracy of risk prediction and identifies the most important learning indicators.

- Example: An EdTech platform like Byju's uses a random forest to predict the probability that a student will complete a course successfully.

(iii) Logistic Regression

- How it works: Estimates probabilities for binary outcomes using a logistic function.
- Use in learner profiling: Classifies students into "Likely to Succeed" vs. "Likely to Struggle."
- Example: Used in MOOCs to predict dropout likelihood from early engagement data.

B. Unsupervised Learning Models

These models work without labeled outcomes, discovering patterns in student data (Ersozlu et al., 2024).

(i) K-Means Clustering

- How it works: Groups students into clusters based on similarity in their learning behaviors.
- Use in learner profiling: Segments students into groups like "Fast Learners," "Moderate Learners," and "Needs Support."
- Example: In an Indian engineering college, K-means clustering was used to group students based on lab performance, which helped the faculty assign targeted remedial classes.

(ii) Hierarchical Clustering

- How it works: Creates a tree-like structure (dendrogram) to show data grouping at different levels.
- Use in learner profiling: Useful for grouping students at multiple granularity levels—e.g., based on both academic performance and extracurricular engagement.
- Example: An online coding bootcamp used hierarchical clustering to create peer-learning groups.

C. Deep Learning Models

These models are useful for large and complex datasets where patterns are not easily detectable (Zhang et al., 2025).

(i) Artificial Neural Networks (ANN)

- How it works: Mimics human brain structure to capture complex patterns in data.
- Use in learner profiling: Detects nuanced learning difficulties by analyzing multi-source data such as clickstream behavior, quiz patterns, and discussion forum activity.
- Example: Coursera uses neural networks to recommend personalized course sequences.

(ii) Recurrent Neural Networks (RNN) & LSTMs

- How it works: Specially designed to handle sequential data, remembering past information for future predictions.
- Use in learner profiling: Predicts a student's performance trajectory based on time-series learning data.
- Example: Used in adaptive learning platforms to forecast when a student is likely to disengage from the course.

D. Reinforcement Learning

- How it works: Learns by interacting with an environment and receiving feedback (rewards/penalties).
- Use in learner profiling: Creates adaptive learning paths that change in real time based on how the student responds.
- Example: An AI tutor adjusts the difficulty of problems depending on how quickly and accurately the student answers.

Real-Life Case Studies

Case Study 1: Global – Pearson's AI-Driven Learner Profiling

Pearson, a leading education company, uses a combination of random forest models and deep learning to analyze learning data from millions of students. The AI system predicts performance, identifies skill gaps, and recommends targeted learning resources. This has significantly improved retention rates in online courses (Alfarra et al., 2024).

Case Study 2: India – NPTEL & SWAYAM

In India, the SWAYAM online learning platform uses ML models such as logistic regression and K-means clustering to (Khajuria et al., 2023):

- Identify students at risk of dropping out.
- Group students for peer-learning activities.
- Recommend additional learning material based on individual progress.

Case Study 3: Duolingo

Duolingo uses reinforcement learning to adjust the difficulty level of language exercises in real-time, maintaining the learner's engagement and progression pace (Vega et al., 2024).

Case Study 4:

India At Amity University, Noida, an ML-based learner profiling system was integrated into its Amity Learning Management System (ALMS). The model, trained on student engagement and grade data, could identify at-risk students within the first three weeks of the semester. This allowed instructors to adapt the curriculum mid-course—offering remedial video lectures to some and advanced research projects to others.

Case Study 5:

The Open University (UK) uses ML algorithms in its "OU Analyse" system to predict student performance. Data from thousands of learners informs tailored weekly study recommendations, enabling a flexible curriculum that evolves for different learner segments.

Challenges in ML-Based Learner Profiling

While machine learning offers great promise, several challenges exist:

- Data Privacy: Sensitive student data must be protected.
- Bias and Fairness: Models may unintentionally favor certain groups.
- Explainability: Deep learning models can be hard to interpret for educators.
- Data Quality: Incomplete or noisy data can mislead profiling.

Future Outlook

The next generation of learner profiling models will likely be:

- More interpretable through explainable AI (XAI).
- More inclusive, addressing bias and ensuring fairness.
- More integrative, combining academic, social, and emotional learning data for holistic profiling.

4.2 Natural Language Processing (NLP) for Syllabus Updates

Concept and Importance

Curriculums often struggle to stay relevant in the face of rapid industry evolution. Updating syllabi traditionally involves lengthy manual reviews by faculty committees, risking outdated content by the time revisions are approved. Natural Language Processing (NLP) changes this by automatically scanning and comparing syllabus content with emerging trends in academic literature, industry job descriptions, and skill requirements (Alhawiti, 2014).

How It Works in Curriculum Structuring

- Text Mining: NLP algorithms analyze current syllabi, extracting key topics and learning outcomes.
- Trend Analysis: Cross-referencing extracted content against sources like research papers, online courses (Coursera, edX), and job postings from LinkedIn or Naukri.com.
- Gap Identification: Highlighting missing or outdated concepts, such as "deep learning" in a machine learning course or "quantum cryptography" in cybersecurity programs.
- Recommendation Engine: Suggesting new modules, keywords, and references to integrate into the updated syllabus.

Case Study 1

In India IIT Madras partnered with the National Programme on Technology Enhanced Learning (NPTEL) to use NLP-based syllabus comparison. The system identified that their Computer Science curriculum needed to add transformer-based architecture in NLP courses to align with global AI developments. This update reduced the skill gap for graduating students entering AI-driven industries.

Case Study 2

Arizona State University (USA) uses an NLP-powered curriculum review tool that continuously scans online academic publications and industry job postings to update its syllabus recommendations. This enables a dynamic curriculum, reducing the update cycle from years to months.

4.3 Learning Analytics Dashboards for Curriculum Feedback Loops

Concept and Importance

Curriculum structuring is not a one-time activity it requires ongoing refinement based on student performance and engagement feedback. Learning analytics dashboards serve as the bridge between curriculum design and student outcomes, visualizing actionable data for educators and administrators (Bodily & Verbert, 2017).

How It Works in Curriculum Structuring

- Data Integration: Pulling information from LMS, attendance systems, grading software, and surveys.
- Visualization: Creating dashboards that track metrics like module completion rates, assessment scores, and participation.
- Feedback Loops: Curriculum committees use these insights to adapt lesson plans, modify assessment methods, or re-sequence topics.

Case Study 1

In India At Manipal Academy of Higher Education, a learning analytics dashboard was implemented to monitor the effectiveness of new modules in their Data Science program. Early analytics revealed that students struggled with advanced statistics introduced in Week 2. In response, faculty shifted the topic to Week 5, following a foundation-building sequence in programming and algebra.

Case Study 2

University of Melbourne (Australia) uses its Learning Analytics Dashboard (LAD) to identify courses with high dropout rates. The dashboard automatically correlates these rates with curriculum elements, such as overly compressed content or insufficient prerequisite knowledge, enabling rapid restructuring.

Integration of Tools for Holistic Curriculum Structuring

The real transformative power of AI in curriculum structuring lies in the synergy between these tools:

- Machine Learning profiling identifies learner needs.

- NLP syllabus analysis ensures up-to-date content.
- Learning analytics dashboards provide continuous feedback to validate and refine curriculum changes.

For example, an engineering department could profile students at the start of the semester (ML), align course modules with emerging technologies like Industry 5.0 (NLP), and monitor real-time performance to adjust pacing (dashboard analytics).

Challenges and Ethical Considerations

While these AI tools are powerful, their implementation in curriculum structuring must address:

- Data Privacy: Protecting sensitive learner data used for profiling.
- Bias Mitigation: Ensuring ML models do not reinforce socio-economic or cultural biases.
- Faculty Training: Educators must be skilled in interpreting AI-generated insights.

AI-driven tools and techniques represent a paradigm shift in curriculum structuring. By automating learner profiling, accelerating syllabus updates, and providing real-time feedback through analytics, AI enables dynamic, relevant, and personalized education ecosystems. Indian institutions like IITs and Manipal Academy are already demonstrating this potential, aligning national curricula with global standards. In the long run, these tools will not just restructure syllabi they will redefine the relationship between educators, students, and knowledge itself.

5. ETHICAL AND PRACTICAL CHALLENGES

While AI offers unprecedented possibilities in education, it also brings ethical dilemmas and practical barriers that must be addressed to ensure sustainable, fair, and safe adoption. These challenges can be grouped into three primary areas: data privacy and student profiling risks, bias in AI systems, and balancing automation with human educator roles.

5.1 Data Privacy and Student Profiling Risks

AI-based curriculum systems often require large amounts of student data from performance metrics to behavioral analytics to deliver personalized learning experiences. While this data can enhance learning, it also exposes students to potential privacy violations and misuse of information. AI systems can generate detailed "student profiles" that may follow learners throughout their academic journey and, in some cases, beyond. Such profiling can lead to unintended consequences, such as pigeonholing students into certain tracks or limiting their opportunities based on early performance metrics.

Ethical Concern

If not properly regulated, profiling may perpetuate inequality, labeling students as "low potential" and affecting their confidence or access to resources. Moreover, educational institutions must comply with data protection laws like GDPR (General Data Protection Regulation) in Europe or FERPA (Family Educational Rights and Privacy Act) in the U.S. to avoid legal repercussions.

Practical Challenge

Many schools and universities lack the technical expertise and secure infrastructure needed to store and manage sensitive data. Additionally, cloud-based AI systems may store information in multiple jurisdictions, creating complex legal compliance issues.

Real-Life Case Study Cambridge Analytica's Data Misuse & Lessons for Education

In 2018, the Cambridge Analytica scandal revealed how personal data from millions of Facebook users was harvested and misused for political purposes without consent. While not directly related to education, this incident served as a wake-up call for all sectors dealing with personal data — including schools. If similar unauthorized access occurred in an educational AI system, sensitive student information (e.g., academic records, behavioral patterns) could be exploited by third parties, leading to discrimination in university admissions or job opportunities.

Mitigation Strategies

- Use privacy-by-design principles in AI system development.
- Implement anonymization and encryption for all stored data.
- Ensure informed consent before collecting or analyzing student information.
- Conduct regular security audits to detect and fix vulnerabilities.

5.2 Mitigating Bias in AI Systems

AI systems learn from data — and if that data reflects historical inequalities or cultural biases, the resulting recommendations may inadvertently reinforce those biases. For example, if an AI-powered career recommendation system is trained primarily on historical employment data where men dominate engineering roles and women dominate nursing roles, it might unintentionally discourage female students from STEM careers or male students from nursing programs.

Ethical Concern

Bias in AI can perpetuate social stereotypes, widen gender and racial gaps in education, and limit diversity in academic and professional fields.

Practical Challenge

Bias detection and correction require both technical sophistication and domain expertise. Many educational institutions lack diverse datasets that truly represent all student populations, particularly in countries with regional disparities.

Real-Life Case Study – The Amazon AI Recruiting Tool

Amazon developed an AI-based recruiting tool that inadvertently downgraded resumes containing the word "women's" (as in "women's chess club captain") because it was trained on historical data reflecting male-dominated tech hiring. The tool was eventually scrapped. This example highlights the dangers of biased training data — if similar issues occur in AI-based curriculum design, certain student groups could be systematically disadvantaged, receiving fewer opportunities or less challenging coursework.

Mitigation Strategies

- Use diverse and representative datasets for training AI models.
- Implement bias detection algorithms and fairness audits.
- Encourage human oversight for AI-driven decisions, ensuring teachers can challenge or override recommendations.
- Collaborate with ethics committees to regularly review AI outputs.

5.3 Balancing Automation with Human Educator Roles

AI can automate many aspects of teaching from grading assignments to tailoring course content but this raises concerns about reducing the role of human educators in the learning process.

While automation can save time and allow teachers to focus on more complex student needs, over-reliance on AI risks creating impersonal learning environments where students feel disconnected from their instructors. Emotional intelligence, empathy, and mentorship essential parts of education cannot be fully replicated by machines.

Ethical Concern

A purely automated approach might undermine teacher-student relationships, which play a critical role in student motivation and mental well-being. Additionally, job displacement fears among educators may create resistance to adopting AI tools.

Practical Challenge

Finding the right balance between AI automation and human interaction requires clear role definition. Teachers must be trained to work alongside AI, interpreting outputs and adding human judgment where necessary.

Real-Life Case Study – Duolingo's AI Language Learning Platform

Duolingo uses AI to personalize language learning for millions of users worldwide. While its adaptive algorithms have helped many learners progress faster, some users report feeling that the platform lacks human connection, leading them to also seek traditional tutoring. This example shows that while AI can optimize learning efficiency, human educators still play a critical role in motivation, cultural context, and personalized feedback.

Mitigation Strategies

- Use AI to augment, not replace, human educators.
- Offer blended learning models combining AI-driven modules with live teacher sessions.
- Train teachers in AI literacy so they can effectively integrate technology without losing human touch.

- Foster continuous student feedback loops to ensure emotional and social needs are met.

6. CASE STUDIES AND EMERGING TRENDS

Artificial intelligence is rapidly transforming learning environments, not just by augmenting traditional classroom instruction but by enabling entirely new curriculum paradigms. This section explores notable AI-driven curriculum initiatives from universities and EdTech startups, followed by emerging trends in lifelong and competency-based learning powered by AI integrating real-world examples from India and around the world.

6.1 AI-Driven Curriculum Initiatives in Universities and EdTech Startups and beyond

Indian Case Study: Symbiosis Artificial Intelligence Institute (SAII)

Symbiosis International University (Pune) recently launched its Symbiosis Artificial Intelligence Institute (SAII), aiming to democratize AI education across disciplines. Rather than confining AI learning to computer science, SAII offers interdisciplinary undergraduate programs that integrate AI with domain-specific insights—such as healthcare, agriculture, and media. The institute emphasizes ethical, responsible AI use and collaborates with tech companies and research institutions to provide experiential learning. This initiative reflects a practical, inclusive approach in preparing socially conscious, AI-empowered graduates.

Indian Case Study: Universal AI University

India's first dedicated **Universal AI University** (Karjat, Maharashtra) embodies a full-scale AI-informed curriculum model Universal AI. This institution embeds AI across undergraduate to doctoral programs, with features such as AI-personalized learning pathways, virtual AI tutors, real-time feedback loops, AI-driven curriculum updates, and placement assistance tailored by AI-based skill-market alignment Universal AI. This represents an ambitious experiment in AI-centric higher education, creating dynamic and responsive learning ecosystems.

Indian EdTech Example: LEAD School

LEAD School, an EdTech unicorn serving over 3.5 million K–10 students in India, employs AI-driven personalized learning tools, regular progress evaluations, and teacher training to improve learning outcomes in under-resourced settings. Its integrated model combines digital content, AI analytics, and capacity-building—demonstrating scalable, equity-focused curriculum enhancement.

Global Case Study: Squirrel AI Learning (China)

In China, Squirrel AI Learning (Yixue Group) has developed an Intelligent Adaptive Learning System that breaks subjects into thousands of granular knowledge points. Through diagnostic assessments and knowledge graphs, it tailors individualized learning paths at scale across over 2,000 centers in 200+ citie. Recognized with UNESCO and MIT awards, this AI-driven system exemplifies precision-driven, large-scale curriculum personalization.

Global Academic Initiative: NTUA Adaptive Engineering Education (Greece)

At the National Technical University of Athens (NTUA), a framework combining spaced-repetition loops, virtual reality labs, and a virtual subject expert enabled personalized reinforcement of engineering concepts through AI-facilitated virtual environments. This model illustrates how AI can merge immersive technologies, learning science principles, and adaptive algorithms to reinforce complex subject matter.

Case Study: AI-Powered Personalized Learning in Rural Schools (India)

In rural Indian schools, where teacher shortages and large class sizes are common, AI-driven adaptive learning platforms such as **Mindspark** have been deployed to bridge learning gaps. Mindspark uses AI algorithms to personalize practice questions based on each student's performance, providing instant feedback even in low-resource environments. A large-scale study demonstrated that students using Mindspark showed significant improvement in mathematics and language scores compared to traditional teaching methods.

- **Key Impact:** Enhanced learning outcomes despite limited teacher availability.
- **Relevance to Curriculum Reshaping:** Demonstrates how AI can adapt curriculum delivery to individual learners in contexts where human resources are limited.

Case Study: AI-Enabled Early Warning Systems in K–12 Classrooms (Sub-Saharan Africa)

In many Sub-Saharan African countries, student dropout is a pressing issue due to economic challenges and resource limitations. AI-enabled early warning systems have been piloted in certain K–12 settings to analyze attendance, assessment data, and engagement patterns. For instance, UNESCO's **"AI for Education in Africa"** initiative has documented projects where machine learning models helped teachers identify at-risk students early. This allowed timely interventions such as mentoring or financial aid, reducing dropout rates in low-resource schools.

- **Key Impact:** Improved retention and targeted support for vulnerable learners.
- **Relevance to Curriculum Reshaping:** Highlights how AI can complement existing curricula by embedding predictive analytics for inclusive education.

6.2 Future Vision: AI in Lifelong and Competency-Based Learning

AI is not just reshaping formal education—it is fundamentally redefining lifelong and competency-based learning. Institutions and platforms are increasingly adapting AI to create modular, skills-driven, and career-aligned learning journeys.

Global Corporate Learning Example: Accenture LearnVantage

Accenture's LearnVantage platform uses AI for personalized employee training, including micro-certifications and simulations customized to role and experience level. The result: a 32% faster skill acquisition and a 47% reduction in time to proficiency compared to conventional methods. This corporate case shows the potential of AI in continuous learning and upskilling.

Global Higher-Ed Study: AI Tutoring for Distance Learners

The Syntea AI-powered assistant, deployed at IU International University of Applied Sciences, reduced study time by 27% in distance learning courses while significantly enhancing learning efficiency and personalization. This demonstrates AI's capacity to scale and customize learning in higher education.

Global EdTech Platforms: Coursera & DreamBox

Platforms like DreamBox Learning (adaptive K–8 math) and Coursera (adult learners' course suggestions) use AI to deliver personalized learning paths and contextual course recommendations. These platforms show how AI facilitates competency-based progression and lifelong learning alignment with career goals.

Emerging Trend: Competency-Based Education in Singapore (SIT)

Singapore Institute of Technology (SIT) has adopted competency-based education with stackable micro-credentials powered by AI and big data. The system aligns courses directly with industry needs, enables recognition of prior learning, and supports adult learners with flexible, skills-first pathways. This model represents a forward-looking, modular approach that integrates AI insights for responsive curriculum design.

Global Equity Initiative: Digi-Wise and Ferby Chatbot

Nonprofits, including Qatar's **Education Above All**, have launched **Digi-Wise**, an AI literacy program and chatbot (**Ferby**) adapted for linguistic and cultural diversity, particularly in India. The focus is on open-source, inclusive engagement with AI and developing critical AI literacy without sidelining human educators. This approach positions AI within the broader agenda of equity and global skill-building.

6.4 Implications for Future Learners and Institutions

These case studies and trends provide a roadmap for future curriculum structures:

- **Universities** can evolve into living learning systems, dynamically updated with real-time insights and tailored to student needs.
- **EdTech startups** play a pivotal role in accelerating innovation, often bridging education with agile development of AI tools.
- **Workforce learning** benefits from shorter, targeted competency vehicles, enabling lifelong adaptability in a swiftly evolving job market.
- **Ethical design** and inclusion must remain central—ensuring AI empowers, rather than excludes, diverse learners.

AI-driven curriculum initiatives—from interdisciplinary AI institutes and adaptive EdTech platforms to competency-aligned lifelong learning systems—are reshaping education at multiple levels. From India's Universal AI University and SAII to

China's Squirrel AI, from Accenture's corporate learning platforms to Singapore's micro-credentialing framework, each case illuminates a facet of the emerging AI-enabled curriculum landscape.

As we build curricula for future learners, AI offers the means to craft smarter, more responsive, and inclusive education but only if institutions engage with these technologies thoughtfully, ethically, and in alignment with real-world human needs.

7. CHALLENGES AND IMPLEMENTATION CONSIDERATION

While the transformative potential of Artificial Intelligence (AI) in reshaping curriculum structures is undeniable, practical challenges remain that must be addressed before large-scale integration can succeed. These challenges include infrastructural barriers, teacher preparedness, student experiences, and the broader policy frameworks that guide adoption.

Cost and Infrastructure: One of the foremost barriers is the cost of implementing AI-based educational systems. Schools, particularly in low- and middle-income countries, often lack reliable internet access, adequate hardware, and the technical infrastructure required to support AI-driven platforms. Even in developed regions, sustaining these technologies requires ongoing investment in maintenance, software updates, and cybersecurity (UNESCO, 2021). Without equitable funding models, AI integration risks exacerbating existing educational inequalities rather than reducing them.

Teacher Training and Professional Development: Teachers play a critical role in mediating AI tools within the classroom. However, many educators report limited confidence in using advanced digital technologies for instruction. Professional development programs that focus not only on technical skills but also on pedagogical strategies for integrating AI are essential (Holmes et al., 2021). Without targeted training, there is a danger that AI will be underutilized or misapplied, reducing its potential benefits.

Student Perspectives and Experiences: Learners often perceive AI as engaging when it provides personalized pathways, immediate feedback, and gamified experiences. Yet, students have also expressed concerns about reduced human interaction and the risk of being "tracked" or labeled by algorithms (Luckin, 2018). Including student voices in curriculum design ensures that AI adoption enhances, rather than diminishes, the learner experience. This highlights the need for a balanced approach where AI augments teacher-led instruction rather than replacing it.

Policy and Regulatory Frameworks: At a systemic level, the absence of clear policy guidelines for AI in education poses risks related to ethics, data privacy, and accountability. International organizations like UNESCO and OECD are beginning to provide policy recommendations that emphasize transparency, inclusivity, and safeguarding of student data (OECD, 2021). National education systems must adapt these frameworks to their specific contexts to ensure responsible implementation.

Recommendations: To move forward, governments and institutions should prioritize investments in infrastructure, develop structured teacher training programs, and incorporate student feedback into curriculum planning. Policymakers should establish robust frameworks to regulate the ethical use of AI. Only by addressing these challenges comprehensively can AI become a sustainable and equitable force in reshaping curricula for future learners.

8. CONCLUSION

Artificial Intelligence (AI) has emerged as more than just a technological tool—it is now a critical driver of transformation in how knowledge is delivered, accessed, and applied in educational settings. Across the world, AI technologies are reshaping curriculum structures by enabling personalized learning paths, adaptive content delivery, and real-time feedback mechanisms that were unimaginable just a decade ago.

In traditional educational models, curriculum design has largely been linear, standardized, and slow to adapt to societal changes. This rigidity often left learners struggling to align their acquired skills with the rapidly evolving demands of industries. AI disrupts this model by introducing dynamic curriculum structures that can be tailored to each learner's abilities, pace, and career aspirations. Through advanced analytics and machine learning algorithms, AI can identify skill gaps, recommend targeted learning materials, and even adjust difficulty levels to keep learners both challenged and motivated.

Furthermore, AI's impact is not limited to improving individual learning outcomes—it is also transforming curriculum development processes themselves. Educators and institutions can now draw insights from massive datasets, including learner performance metrics, industry job trends, and global academic benchmarks. These insights allow for evidence-based curriculum updates that ensure learners are acquiring not just theoretical knowledge, but also industry-relevant skills in real time.

For example, in India, AI-powered platforms like Byju's and upGrad are already integrating data-driven learning analytics to continuously adapt course materials. Globally, universities like Arizona State University have adopted AI to create adaptive mathematics and engineering courses that respond to individual student performance. Such developments illustrate that AI is no longer a supplementary aid—it is central to the redefinition of curriculum design for the 21st century.

Reimagining Education for a Dynamic, Global Future

The future of education will not be defined by rigid course outlines or static syllabi but by fluid, competency-based learning ecosystems that evolve alongside global technological, economic, and social changes. AI plays a central role in enabling this vision.

One of the most profound shifts AI brings to curriculum design is the move from time-based to mastery-based learning. Instead of progressing through a syllabus based on academic calendars, learners can advance only when they have mastered each competency. This approach ensures deeper understanding and practical application of skills, rather than superficial completion of topics. AI facilitates this model by offering instant assessments, personalized feedback, and targeted remedial resources.

Moreover, in a globalized economy, skills are becoming universal currencies. AI can bridge educational divides by providing access to world-class curriculum resources to learners anywhere in the world, regardless of location or socio-economic background. This democratization of education enables students in rural India to access the same AI-curated courses as those in Silicon Valley or Singapore.

Another critical aspect is interdisciplinary learning. AI-driven curriculum models can blend subjects in ways traditional education often resists—combining, for instance, computer science with environmental studies, or humanities with data analytics—reflecting how problems in the real world are multifaceted and require cross-domain expertise. By analyzing global research trends, labor market needs, and learner interests, AI systems can propose customized interdisciplinary tracks that prepare students for the complex challenges of the future.

The integration of AI ethics and digital literacy into every curriculum will also be essential. As AI becomes more prevalent, future learners must be equipped not only with technical know-how but also with the ability to navigate its societal, ethical, and cultural implications. This ensures that AI adoption in education remains aligned with human-centric values rather than purely technological capabilities.

Looking Ahead

As we step into an era where change is the only constant, the role of AI in education must be envisioned not as a disruptor to be feared, but as a partner in progress. The successful reshaping of curriculum structures will depend on how well educators, technologists, policymakers, and learners themselves collaborate to harness AI's capabilities responsibly.

AI's power lies in its adaptability—it can cater to diverse learning needs, adjust to evolving industries, and incorporate emerging disciplines into existing curricula. When combined with the creativity and empathy of human educators, AI has the potential to make education more inclusive, future-ready, and globally connected than ever before.

In reimagining curriculum structures, we must embrace the idea that education is no longer a one-time preparation for life but a lifelong journey. AI will play a vital role in enabling this shift, supporting learners at every stage of life, whether they are in primary school, pursuing higher education, or reskilling in mid-career. Lifelong and competency-based learning, powered by AI, will become the standard—not the exception.

The journey ahead will require us to rethink not just the "what" of education (curriculum content) but also the "how" (delivery mechanisms) and "why" (purpose and outcomes). With AI as a catalyst, the future of education holds the promise of being more personalized, relevant, and equitable, preparing learners for roles and challenges we cannot yet fully imagine.

Ultimately, the integration of AI into curriculum structures is not just a technological upgrade—it is a philosophical transformation. It calls upon us to reimagine education as a dynamic, interconnected, and responsive ecosystem that empowers learners to thrive in a rapidly changing, globalized world. The decisions we make today about AI in education will define the learning landscapes of tomorrow—and with thoughtful implementation, we can ensure that future learners are not just equipped for the future but are ready to shape it.

REFERENCES

Alfarra, A. H., Amhan, L. F., Mosa, M. J., Alajrami, M. A., El Kahlout, F., Abu-Nasser, B. S., & Abu-Naser, S. S. (2024). AI-driven learning: Advances and challenges in intelligent tutoring systems.

Alhawiti, K. M. (2014). Natural language processing and its use in education. *International Journal of Advanced Computer Science and Applications*, *5*(12), 72–76.

Awasthi, R., & Tiwari, A. (2024). Role of Data Mining in Redesigning the Existing Curriculum: A Survey Based Literature Review. *Journal of Computational Analysis and Applications*, *33*(7).

Bodily, R., & Verbert, K. (2017). Review of research on student-facing learning analytics dashboards and educational recommender systems. *IEEE Transactions on Learning Technologies*, *10*(4), 405–418.

Chu, T. S., & Ashraf, M. (2025). Artificial Intelligence in Curriculum Design: A Data-Driven Approach to Higher Education Innovation. *Knowledge (Beverly Hills, Calif.)*, *5*(3), 14.

Ersozlu, Z., Taheri, S., & Koch, I. (2024). A review of machine learning methods used for educational data. *Education and Information Technologies*, *29*(16), 22125–22145.

Holmes, W., Bialik, M., & Fadel, C. (2021). *Artificial Intelligence in Education: Promises and Implications for Teaching and Learning*. Center for Curriculum Redesign.

Hubballi, R. B., Selvakumar, P., Seenivasan, R., Dinesh, N., & Seelam, P. K. (2025). Overview of Current AI Technologies in Education. In *Transformative AI Practices for Personalized Learning Strategies* (pp. 1–26). IGI Global Scientific Publishing.

Khajuria, R., Sharma, A., & Sharma, A. (2023). A detailed survey regarding the usage of different ICT technology modes adopted by higher education institutions. *Indonesian Journal of Electrical Engineering and Computer Science*, *29*(3), 1634–1641.

Luckin, R. (2018). *Machine Learning and Human Intelligence: The Future of Education for the 21st Century*. UCL Institute of Education Press.

Montebello, M. (2024). Learner Profiling and Pedagogical Customization. In *Encyclopedia of Educational Innovation* (pp. 1–5). Springer.

Nafea, A. A., Alameri, S. A., Majeed, R. R., Khalaf, M. A., & Al-Ani, M. M. (2024). A short review on supervised machine learning and deep learning techniques in computer vision. *Babylonian Journal of Machine Learning*, *2024*, 48–55.

OECD. (2021). *AI in Education: Challenges and Opportunities*. OECD Publishing.

Uhran, J. J., Batill, S. M., & Silliman, S. E. (2005, October). A curriculum renovation revisited. In *Proceedings Frontiers in Education 35th Annual Conference* (pp. F1D-10). IEEE.

UNESCO. (2021). AI and Education: Guidance for Policy-makers. Paris: UNESCO. https://unesdoc.unesco.org/ark:/48223/pf0000376709

Vega, J., Rodriguez, M., Check, E., Moran, H., & Loo, L. (2024, July). Duolingo evolution: From automation to artificial intelligence. In *IEEE Colombian Conference on Applications of Computational Intelligence* (pp. 54-71). Cham: Springer Nature Switzerland.

Zhang, F., Wang, X., & Zhang, X. (2025). Applications of deep learning method of artificial intelligence in education. *Education and Information Technologies, 30*(2), 1563–1587.

Chapter 6
Artificial Intelligence as Faculty Development and Learning Innovation

Parveen Sharma
https://orcid.org/0000-0002-7351-0525
Lovely Professional University, India

ABSTRACT

Artificial intelligence (AI) has been taking over the higher education sector and is likewise playing a role that defines the professional growth of faculty members. This chapter discusses how campus-wide AI based solutions can be used to enable faculty to grow through improved training, advanced learning analytics and to offer personalized professional learning at scale. A conceptual model is proposed to identify the 3 key pillars of AI in faculty development, including (i) AI in training and skill enhancement delivered via intelligent platforms, virtual simulations, etc; (ii) AI-based learning analytics to obtain actionable insights out of classroom interactions, with assessments, and predictive performance tools; and (iii) personalized professional learning driven by adaptive modules, AI tutors, and career pathway guidance. In addition, an AI benefits map is presented to show how these applications can be used to serve faculty responsibilities in the context of teaching, research, administration and mentoring.

1. INTRODUCTION

Artificial Intelligence (AI) is one of the most disruptive trends of the 21 st century that is altering industries, economies, and societies faster than ever before. Education, which is usually one of the slowest sectors to employ technological change compared

DOI: 10.4018/979-8-3373-4129-3.ch006

to the financial and healthcare sectors, is currently getting transformed faster than ever before because of the integrated AI (Harry,2023).. Colleges, universities, and schools around the world are trying to use AI as a means of not only greater results in student learning but also a means of stimulating faculty development and innovation in teaching related practices. The impact of artificial intelligence on contemporary academic life has grown over the years as it has allowed teachers to use adaptive learning systems and automation of menial academic tasks (Harry, 2023).

Earlier, the understanding of educational transformation was based on curriculum development, testing and assessment, and development of facilities. Recent literature emphasized the evolution of AI applications in education that moved from experimental AI tools towards more integrated practice supporting teaching and assessment, as well as, individualisation of learning (Holmes and Tuomi, 2022). A ten-year retrospective study identified that AI use in education was primarily in the creation of intelligent tutoring systems, learning analytics, and adaptive assistance of learners (Zhai et al., 2021).Faculty were expected to adjust gradually, usually through workshops or professional training programs. Though such solutions resulted in gradual improvements, they were not necessarily dynamic enough to meet rapid changes in learning environments. The increasing role of AI has increased opportunities to close this gap. Faculty members, the backbone of educational systems, have now the twin responsibility of adjusting to the use of AI-facilitated tools, and using them to expand not only their own professional expertise, but also enrich students of the learning experiences.

1.1 Brief Overview of AI in Education

Artificial Intelligence in education can generally be described as taking machine learning, natural language processing, and data analytics finding solutions and intelligent systems to aid teaching, learning, and administrative functions. The initial use of educational technologies involved major emphasis on online platforms, E-learning and online courses. But the current adoption on AI has penetrated further into how education is administered but also in how educators themselves gain the ability, form the strategies of their teaching, and coordinate their learning obligations. It has also been applied in the quest to make education more personal, enhance administrative effectiveness, and to come up with more engaging learning opportunities (Nguyen, 2023).

Among the most widespread ways of effective AI application in education, the following may be listed (Pedro et al., 2019):

- Adaptive Learning Platforms-Smart systems which alter learning content as per a student progress.

- Intelligent Tutoring Systems (ITS) -AI supported tutors to offer individual support beyond the classroom.
- Automated Assessment Tools - Any system that can evaluate assignments, include tests and even essays with a minimum human input.
- Predictive Analytics - Applications that determine which students are at risk and offer early solutions.
- AI- Enhanced Research Support- Systems that would help faculty in literature reviews, data analysis and publication strategies.

These technologies are beyond the technology that they employ to teach their students, but an ecosystem that directly affects them in the realms of professional development. Faculty may use AI-based analytics to receive feedback on their performance as teachers, AI-based platforms to design interactive teaching content, and automation can help faculty save time on other common administration activities, among others. Scientists have also emphasized the need to be cautious as despite the potential beneficial, AI has certain ethical, social and pedagogical concerns in the field of education (Selwyn, 2022). In this aspect, AI not only transforms the experience the students have in the contemporary learning setting, but also transforms the work and career directions of the educational sector professionals.

1.2 Need for Faculty Growth and Innovation in Teaching

Faculty shape the core of a mission of education. The quality of education provided is directly influenced by their level of innovativeness and understanding of changing trends that require delivery of education through new teaching methods and the level at which they upgrade their subject knowledge. The innovative use of AI in the higher education field has enhanced teaching efficiencies, decision-making, and improved governance of the institution (Ge and Hu, 2020). Some have argued that AI must not only be embraced in the field of education but must also equip learners with the ethical and critical reflexion they need to interact with AI-driven societies (Schiff, 2022) Past studies indicated that AI tools in the classroom focused mostly on intelligent tutoring systems and problem-solving workshops (Beck et al., 1996). The emergence of AI has become a challenge as well as an opportunity to the career growth of the college teacher because they need new skills and adaptive tactics (Wang, 2020).

In most education systems, however, growth of faculty has been hampered by a number of issues:

1. Speed of Increase in Knowledge: knowledge in different fields of study is increasing more rapidly than ever before. Professors find it difficult to follow such

changes and maintain the tempo in their commitments to teaching, research and administration.

2. The Dynamic Student Population: The current generation of students is digital and demands an interactive, customized, and technology-enabled learning. Their expectations have changed that they no longer correlate with the traditional lecture-based methods.
3. Increasing Administrative Burdens: They place more responsibilities on faculty administratively, including grading, documentation, and compliance related tasks, and have minimal time to spend in professional growth or innovative instructing arts.
4. Globalization in Higher Education: As the cross-border collaborations and competition grow, faculty will be expected to stay globally competent not only in their area of expertise but also in technological application.
5. Lifelong Learning Imperative: Immediately, Lifelong Learning is required of faculty, not only to ensure their abilities keep pace with developments in their subject domain, but also in digital pedagogy, data literacy, and AI-based tools.

It is in the light of this that AI presents new territories of faculty development. It offers scalable, data-driven and personalized professional development solutions. With Learning platforms that have AI, instructors get personalized training, they see their progress, and they can change their approach to teaching according to feedback. In addition, AI applications make it possible to put innovative practice into practice by faculty members so that they could improve the results of their students, which, on the other hand, also positively affect the professional profile of faculty members (Khalid et al., 2024)..

Teacher innovation is not an option anymore and it is a must. Universities and schools not empowering their faculty with AI-powered tools will jump the gun of their rivals in a competitive educational marketplace. Faculty members that adopt AI-guided professional development are in a better position to promote creativity, critical inquiry, and problem solving by students- qualities that are crucial in the modern service economy.

1.3 Purpose of the Chapter

This chapter is aimed at exploring Artificial Intelligence as an agent of faculty development and improvements in education. Although the evidence on the positive effect of AI on the educational process is quite extensive, little has been done to study how AI affects the growth of the faculty and their empowerment. This chapter attempts to bridge that gap by exploring the potential positivity of the opportunities that AI technologies present:

- Make professional development of the faculty more individual with the support of personalized learning and the focus on skills.
- Promote the adoption of new pedagogical methods by the faculty.
- Less claims processing paperwork with the result that time is available to have more creative teaching and research.
- Acknowledge educational issues that teachers encounter when trying to incorporate AI in their development as educators.
- Provide trends on what the future of AI- enabled faculty development will look like.

In the chapter, there will be a holistic approach that will weigh out the possibilities and positive aspects of AI against the problems and ethical issues surrounding it. Tables will be included to contrast traditional and AI-driven faculty development schemes, enlist AI tools adjuvant pedagogical innovation and identify issues and countermeasures to them. Numbers will be used to demonstrate the conceptual models and benefit maps, and assist in realizing how AI can be used to develop faculty.

Finally, the chapter contends that rather than acting as a substitute to faculty, AI will become kind of an enabler and catalyst to professional development and pedagogical evolution. When used wisely and ethically, AI can level the playing field to help faculty achieve excellence in teaching, bring innovation to research, and teach students how to deal with an AI-enabled future.

2. THE CHANGING LANDSCAPE OF HIGHER EDUCATION

Tradition and innovation are two things that have always been combined in higher education. College institutions used to be strong on centuries-old methods of transmitting information - which involved lectures in the physical classroom and knowledge transfers via printed books and face-to-face communications. Artificial intelligence in higher education helped the process of digital transformation that has changed the landscape of learning, research, and institutional management (Lytras et al., 2024). Although such a model was effective in the past, the nature of the environment in higher education has changed greatly as a result of more dynamic society, as well as technological disruptions. In the contemporary context, the advent of online education tools, artificial intelligence (AI), and data-based educational working are transforming the textbook recipe of how learning and education take place.

At the centre of such change is faculty members. They are not only expected to make sure that academic excellence is achieved but also that the students are prepared to live in a society which is dominated by technology. However, the transformations that have been witnessed in the field of higher education are enormous to educationists. Devoted to switching the old educational routine to digital and, last but not least, the redesign of the classroom to an AI-sensitive, the process requires constant professional training, adaptability, and willingness to take an innovative step and introduce the new technology. This part explains these changes, the pressures on faculty and why there is need to intertwine technology change with faculty development.

2.1 Shifts from Traditional to Digital and AI-Enabled Classrooms

The historical basis of higher learning has been subjected to the traditional model that faculty member is the only bearer of truth and sits to lecture his students who receive information in a passive manner. Primarily assessments were conducted in forms of examinations or write-ups and in professional development of faculty there were only a few opportunities other than attending courses and workshops, research publications, and serving in curriculum committees

This model started changing since the emergence of digital technologies late in the XX century and early in the XXI century. Digital libraries, online course management systems and e-Learning platforms offered new platforms of teaching and learning. The classroom became bigger than the literal space of a university. Faculty members were now supposed to incorporate multimedia presentations, online discussion board, and assessments in their courses. Although this transformation was enormous, it remained to a large extent, the traditional teacher-centered set-up. Adaptive learning, such as I-driven adaptive learning has been cited as an integral contributor to sustainable education change where inclusivity and long-term learning outcomes are achieved (Strielkowski et al., 2025).

It was the disruption of artificial intelligence. In contrast to the previously existing digital tools, AI-based technology introduced learning to provision intelligent, flexible, and customized learning. Classrooms in the contemporary world no longer exist to disseminate learning information to just one party. They can be classified as active ecosystem because the AI systems have an interaction with the faculty in the following ways:

- Individualize learning experiences according to the need of the individual student; modify content and pace.
- Offer real-time reporting which monitors the progress of students, pointing out where learners are weak.
- Automated routine processes e.g. grading, clerical paperwork making faculty time available.

- Help in creation of content like developing quizzes, creating summaries or producing case studies.
- Improve student participation using intelligent tutoring systems, virtual assistants and interactive simulations.

On the part of faculty, this change is entailing that the role of a faculty is more than delivery of content but facilitation, mentorship and guidance. Their role is no longer limited to sources of knowledge but they are also interpreters of AI-generated insights, learning experience designers, mentors to guide their students who live in a world becoming more intricate due to the increase in machine decision-making and data processing.

2.2 Pressure on Faculty to Adapt to Emerging Technologies

The meteoric rise of digital and AI tools has added to the opportunities and pressures that the faculty members have to work under. As noted by the perspectives of the teachers, awareness, trust, and perceived usefulness are among factors that can play an important role in adopting AI tools in higher education (Al-Mughairi and Bhaskar, 2024). Contrary to the examples of the previous technological changes which took place over a long period of time, the implementation of AI has been rapid, and, in certain instances, destructive. Faculty now find themselves pressured in many different ways:

1. Institutional Pressure: Universities and colleges are feel obligated to appreciably and keep up with the contemporary training market. This tends to convert into the requirements to faculty to accept AI-enabled tools, build new courses, and demonstrate technology-enhanced delivery.
2. Stakeholder Expectations Expectation of the current students are the digital natives who demand the technology enabled learning facilities today. They like active, individualized and unorthodox learning. Faculty members relying exclusively on pedagogical strategies that are more traditional may end up losing such students.
3. Professional Competition: There is a growing trend in evaluation not only by research and publications but also by teaching innovation and utilization of modern tools of competition. Failure to adapt exposes one to stagnation or even being out-thought by colleagues who have adopted the ways of AI-empowered practices.
4. Workload Management: Though AI can ease the administrative work, it still takes time and effort to learn how to work with it. Faculty members also find it

difficult to find time to engage in teaching, research, service, and also undertake the need to learn new technologies.

5. Cultural Resistance: Depending on how long individuals have been working in traditional education, they may find learning to use AI to be a radical change of culture. Fear of being out of job due to the use of machines and inability to trust digital tools are also among the major obstacles to the adoption of the change.

The members of the faculty who can adjust to these new pressures are the ones that are most likely to be successful and thrive in this newly developed environment. They are open to new technologies, experiment with new ways of teaching, and constantly improve their competencies, which makes them the leaders of the academic community. Flexibility has thus turned not only to be an attractive characteristic, but it is also a pre-requisite to a long-term professional development.

Meanwhile, the institutions are becoming more aware that combining digital and AI-focused practices is not a practice that can be successfully implemented by a single person. Instructors should be enabled in terms of the well-organized assistance with delivering specific training courses, accessing up-to-date technological supplies, and receiving continuously a chance to enhance their professionalism. This institutional support minimizes resistance, instills confidence in the usage of high-tech tools, and makes sure that the teachers will be motivated to be innovative. Adaptation, in this regard, is a collective responsibility a proactive faculty and supportive institutions establish a sustainable pathway of AI implementation in higher education collectively.

2.3 Link to Continuous Professional Development

The change in higher education highlights the need to have continuous professional development (CPD) of the faculty. In traditional models, professional development was intermittent and in most cases, this involved visiting annual conferences, sporadic workshops or training programs. A systematic review postulated that AI-based frameworks will be helpful in promoting the continuous professional growth of teachers through personalized learning routes and feedback (Fakhar et al., 2024). Such methods cannot be enough nowadays in the era of AI, where technologies are quick-changing and educators should regularly upgrade their competencies in order to be efficient.

The continuous professional development in an AI-enabled environment comprises:

- Continuous Learning: Faculty should have access to AI- enabled platforms which will offer continual staff training, to teach within their limits.

- Data-Driven Feedback: AI software can provide data-based feedback on teaching performance to make the faculty aware of the student engagement, learning rates, and weakness areas to improve.
- Collaborative Learning: through AI-enabled systems, faculty groups enhance the cross-institutional and cross-disciplinary sharing of knowledge.
- Data Skills Proliferation: In addition to subject proficiency, faculty will need to acquire the skills of data literacy, online teaching, and ethical application of artificial intelligence.
- Adaptability and Resilience: CPD needs to make the faculty adaptable to the current tools as well as resilient in case of any change in technology in future.

In this regard, AI does not only present an opportunity of instructing students but also serving as a co-faculty developer. With the help of AI, faculty will be able to create individualized development roadmaps, gauge real-time progress in their career practice, and stay nimble when it comes to fulfilling emerging teaching demands. The table 1 shows the comparison of the traditional faculty development and the AI driven one.

Table 1. Comparison of Traditional Faculty Development vs. AI-Driven Faculty Development

Aspect	Traditional Faculty Development	AI-Driven Faculty Development
Mode of Training	Periodic workshops, conferences, and seminars	Continuous, personalized training through AI platforms
Feedback Mechanism	End-of-course evaluations and peer reviews	Real-time analytics and adaptive feedback on teaching effectiveness
Content Delivery	Standardized, one-size-fits-all modules	Customized learning paths tailored to faculty needs
Focus Areas	Subject expertise and pedagogy	Subject expertise, digital pedagogy, data literacy, and AI competencies
Accessibility	Limited to scheduled events and physical presence	Available anytime, anywhere through digital platforms
Scalability	Difficult to scale across large faculty groups	Highly scalable with automated AI-driven solutions
Outcome Measurement	Subjective and periodic	Objective, data-driven, and continuous
Innovation Potential	Limited, incremental	High, enabling innovative teaching and research practices

The terrain of higher education is changing in a deep-based way. The transformation that took place in the industry from the traditional classroom, to digital learning, and currently to the AI supported ecosystem is transforming the roles and responsibilities of faculty members. As much as these changes are accompanied by such setbacks like pressure to learn new technologies and cope with changing expectations of the students, they also open a new realm of professional development and innovation.

The notion of continuous professional development has also become inseparable, and AI can do much to support the faculty members and enable them to prepare their plans in a more personified, data-driven, and scalable way. AI warrants that faculty is not left behind but rather equipped to lead the next era of institutional change and fills the gap between conservation and innovation by making the most of both worlds in terms of synergy created by a combination of two distinctly different elements, i.e., combining technology and the art of perfecting the old school of thought, which in turn bridges the above-mentioned gap and becomes the most relevant aspect of change between both the worlds, aka conservative and innovative world of thought.

3. APPLICATIONS OF AI IN FACULTY GROWTH

The role of Artificial Intelligence in higher education has frequently been discussed in its student-centered form context-how using adaptive learning, intelligent tutoring systems, and AI-based higher education increases student learning outcomes. In the future, the author believes that the use of AI will also transform the faculty performance evaluation process through data-driven, transparent processes and more detailed forms of assessment (Alakoum et al., 2024). But just as important of a dimension is how the introduction of AI contributes to the intellectual nourishment and empowerment of faculty members. Educators use AI in learning as more than a proponent of educational training but also as the agent of career development, skills build-up, innovative teaching, and learning.

In this segment, the authors will discuss a host of ways in which AI can aid faculty development in three broad categories: AI to train and develop skills, AI-enabled learning analytics to improve performance, and individualized professional learning using artificial intelligence tutors. The conceptual model of AI applications to faculty development is presented in Figure 1. All of these applications create an active ecosystem that has the potential to change the way faculty development was traditionally understood into a data-driven, individualized and future proofed process.

3.1 AI in Training and Skill Enhancement

On-going training is something that has been a mainstay of faculty development. Traditionally, this training used to be organized by professional workshops, annual conferences and certification courses. These methods were helpful, but were characterized by limitations including limited customization, sporadic schedules and inability to be applied immediately. Education in the AI age can be viewed as a global shift, where the focus is placed on skill upgrading, coping with the emerging concerns, and finding the balance between international trends and national possibilities (Chen et al., 2024). Faculty-oriented training tools are being transformed into new forms of A.I-based training that fit into the needs of individual faculty members and are flexible and scalable.

a) AI-Enabled Training Platforms

AI-aided platforms have the capability of customising training modules as per faculty requirements. As an example, a faculty member interested in enhancing his or her digital pedagogy will be provided with suggestions such as modules on design instruction, interactive resources, and administration of online classrooms. The AI systems evaluate the faculty profiles, previous training record, and experience when teaching to develop customised learning paths.

b) Virtual Simulations for Teaching Practice

VR and AR virtual reality simulations supported by AI would enable faculty to train on teaching in the low-stakes environment. As an example, a simulator equipped by AI can simulate a classroom setting where students will have various types of learning styles and behavioral issues. The faculty may experiment with various instructional features and get the system feedback on their performance.

c) Automated Content Development

AI is also facilitative in development of skills in content creation. Machine aids in the form of natural language generation (NLG) and AI-driven design helpers allow faculty to prepare quizzes, case studies, and multimedia presentations in a more time-efficient way. Learners no longer have to waste hours creating materials; they instead devote their time to practice how to deliver them and ignite interest.

d) Research and Publication Support

Besides instruction, AI is used to facilitate research by the faculty. The use of intelligent applications like intelligent literature review software, plagiarism detection software, and analytical applications powered by AI improves the quality of the output being provided by faculty members. This does not only help in augmenting professional development but also helps in building prestige to the institution.

The contribution that AI can make to the training process as well as the development of skills is to enable the faculty to keep up with the dynamical academic world where the new tools, methodologies, and expectations set by students are introduced at a rapid rate. Through the provision of individualized learning modules, adaptive training platforms, and intelligent feedback systems, AI helps to make sure that educators will be able to keep integrating new skills into the teaching process with ease and never feel overwhelmed by the pace of the changes. Meanwhile, AI is an important way to eliminate the load of non-value-added or monotonous tasks, including regular grading, content formatting, or administrative reporting. This will enable faculty to spend more of their time and efforts on other productive academic pursuits such as novel teaching, research and mentoring. This makes AI not only a supporting tool but a facilitator of professional development, in this manner, educators can succeed both in a dynamic educational ecosystem..

3.2 AI-Based Learning Analytics for Faculty Performance Improvement

Among the most impactful AI has had on faculty development is the data-informed information it gives on the teaching performance. With the help of IAI-augmented learning platforms, employee training has changed to adaptive skill building and ongoing professional development (Rahayu and Bablu, 2023). Traditionally, faculty performance evaluation has been based either on student feedback surveys and/or peer reviews of faculty performance or administrative assessment. These are sometimes subjective, inconstistent and narrow scoped methods. Learning analytics using AI have the capacity to get around these drawbacks by providing objective feedback, real-time feedback, and actionable feedback.

a) Classroom Interaction Analytics

AI will be able to monitor trends in faculty-student dynamics in online or hybrid courses. Levels of engagement with a student, question frequencies, and engagement in discussions can be measured to offer a line of feedback on the effectiveness of teaching. As another example, analytics can show faculty that students start losing interest after 20 minutes of lecture, prompting the redesign of sessions with active sessions to be provided every 20 minutes.

b) Assessment Data and Feedback Loops

Grading systems powered by AI or AI-augmented grading do not only automate the process of assessing work done by students but also help to isolate trends in student error. These graphical patterns can bring to focus the areas that require improvement as regards teaching methods. An example is in case a significant proportion of students continue to fail in particular concept, then faculty can revise the manner in which that information is presented.

c) Predictive Performance Insights

Prior to their implementation, there is the possibility of IA predicting the effectiveness of the teaching strategies that are offered. Predictive models, for example, may be used to model how various teaching interventions may impact on students. This gives faculty the option of making evidence-based decisions regarding course design, instead of making decisions based on intuition.

d) Faculty Development Dashboards

The problem that has seen many institutions move to the adoption of AI-based dashboards is to consolidate the information about faculty performance in one place. These dashboards could have student feedback, classroom engagement, and research contributions. Faculty is able to monitor their progression over time and get improvement recommendations.

The shift to quantitative standards and increase in performance becomes a significant break in the way of faculty development. Using quantifiable measures and information-driven knowledge, the institutions are able to enhance the degree of objectivity in the assessment of teaching performance and career development. This minimizes the impact of subjective interpretation or the personal bias, and, thus, the evaluation of the faculty development is evidence-based, objective, and impartial. A system of such a kind is able not only to ensure the reliability of development pathways but also to make much more specific recommendations based on the needs and circumstances of individuals.

In addition to assessment, this change also fosters a larger culture of life-long, ongoing learning in the faculty. Educators can also be motivated to be more reflective in their teaching practice and embrace continuous self-development when they get feedback on performance in real-time. Data-driven systems help the faculty to detect any gaps at the initial stages, explore the new approaches, and incorporate the innovative practices into their classes. With this purpose, the focus on quantitative and performance based measures is not merely an observation of the progress but a proactive factor that encourages the educators to stay flexible, prospective and dedicated to the revision of the technological and pedagogical changes..

3.3 Personalized Professional Learning with AI Tutors

Personalization has been a buzzword in student learning but AI offers the same value to faculty in the form of personalized professional development (PPD). Training of faculty is usually on a formulaic basis and does not take into account individual needs, strong or weak areas and career objectivities. The results of incorporating AI into teacher professional development have demonstrated the possibility of interactive and individual education on a large scale (Copur-Gencturk et al., 2024). The tuts however can offer bespoke tutoring in the manner that they are offered to students.

a) Adaptive Learning for Faculty

The professional development content can be adapted according to the faculty progress by I tutors. Healthy example is when an educator learns the basics of digital pedagogy quite fast; the AI tutor can then proceed to more in-depth modules, such as the use of AI to design assessments or ethics of using AI. Faculty that need more time on some specific areas can be given sufficient time to practice and get assistance.

b) On-Demand Learning

Faculty are subjected to time management issues, since they have teaching, research and administrative assignments. Instructors provide just-in-time microlearning with brief training sessions that faculty members can view when they have time. As an example, each learner can receive a 10-minute refresher on designing interactive assessments immediately before a class through AI tutor.

c) Intelligent Feedback and Mentoring

The advantage of AI tutors is not only in the provision of the content but also serves as a mentor giving motivating immediate feedback. As an example, once a faculty member has completed a practice lecture in a simulation tool, the AI teacher can examine voice deployment, lecture pace, student engagement and use of digital tools, and make recommendations.

d) Career Pathway Guidance

Tutors have the opportunity to draw professional development road maps to the faculties. As an example, in case a faculty member wants to become a full professor in addition to his/her current assistant professor position, the AI tutor will have recommendations to the training modules, research projects, and publishing activities corresponding with this career advancement.

The use of AI tutors in personalized learning guarantees that the faculty development will be personalized, efficient, and oriented to the future. It shifts beyond generic mass training, to contextual and adapting learning.

Figure 1. Conceptual model of AI applications for faculty development

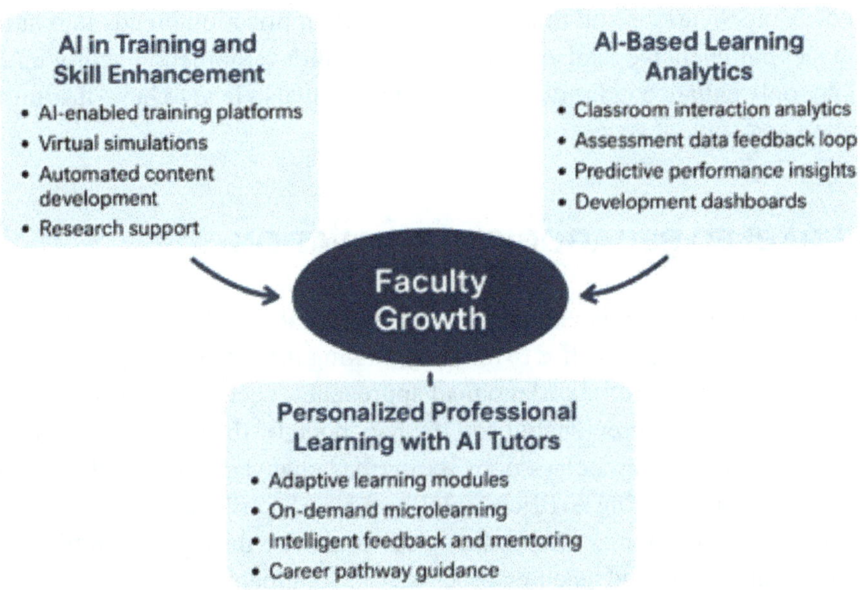

(Author's own creation).

The instances of AI application to faculty development show that technology is no longer a technical support to the educational process of teachers; it has also become a partner in many instances. Instead of being a support system in the background, AI is actively actively involved in professional development now, offering adaptive training opportunities, boosting instructional design, and assisting in real-time decision-making. It allows constantly enhancing faculty competencies with its own modules, as well as provides performance feedback that is not based on a subjective assessment but on actual data.

AI also enhances the career path of a teacher by automating redundant office tasks, allowing the teacher to innovate and interact with students. It assists faculty in identifying their strengths, working on their weaknesses, and aligning themselves to institutional goals in a more effective way through the use of intelligent dashboards, predictive analytics, and automated feedback. The establishment of personalized learning channels and the ability to test new educational methods account to the fact that, with the help of Artificial Intelligence, faculty members not only keep current with the latest trends but also become capable of academic innovation. By doing so, AI will be used as a reliable companion in the formation of adaptable, future-proofed educators that will always be on the front lines of their profession. The idea in the conceptual implementation provided in this section is to display the interconnected nature of AI applications and thus reveal that each application blends into another to form a comprehensive landscape of professional development. Faculty enabled via AI not only enhance individual competencies but also lead to huge institutional innovation and student success.

4. AI-ENABLED PEDAGOGICAL INNOVATION

Teaching and learning is central to higher education and it is a challenge that faculty members have always had to meet; by making the process of learning engaging and effective. Traditional pedagogical approaches, such as lectures, textbooks, and examinations have previously been the backbone of the classroom, but as the situation of the learner and classroom setting has changed, so have the demands placed on the faculty. Rising Artificial Intelligence (AI) promises the yet unrealized possibilities to revolutionize the pedagogical practices through permitting more intelligent content, enabled teaching processes and augmented student interactions. The use of AI in pedagogy, such as AI-TEACH pattern, is emerging and transforming education with novel educational tools that amplify the quality of education and interaction between the learners (Siddiqui et al., 2025).

Pedagogical innovation acting under the influence of AI is not intended to succeed faculty. Rather, it gives them strength to move beyond the mechanical work and concentrate on higher levels of teaching: cultivating creativity, thinking, and life-long learning in children. This section considers the factors supporting the pedagogical innovation through the AI the most significant to give some practical insights into the example.

4.1 Smart Content Creation (AI-Assisted Lesson Planning and Assessments)

Designing and creating course material is one of the tedious tasks that the faculty face. Designing lecture slides, building quizzes, assignments and case studies consume a lot of time that should be devoted to other activities. The 20-year data points to the constant rise in AI solutions in education, with most of them focusing on intelligent tutoring, learning analytics, and adaptive systems (Guan et al., 2020). AI tools have disrupted this field by helping to smartly create content, thereby enabling faculty to design more interesting and inclusive content and save more time dedicated to the higher-level educational work.

a) AI in Lesson Planning

The AI-powered systems have the ability to create a well-developed curriculum based on a particular learning goal. The faculty enters information – including the area of knowledge, learning objectives, and student competency level, and the system offers lesson structures, important concepts, and supplemental materials. Even some platforms incorporate multimedia such as videos and infographics as well as interactivity to bolster engagement.

Another example is that AI can propose a weekly schedule of an introductory course on economics in which lectures, discussions, case studies, and assessment activities are balanced. It is also able to provide reading lists and additional reading materials aligned to the course objectives.

b) Automated Assessment Design

It is possible to produce questions that are based on Bloom taxonomy or according to specific learning outcomes. The questions can be multiple choices, case-based and developed with the help of adaptive quizzes within a few minutes. Instead of trying to develop such assessments on their own, faculty can then narrow and authenticate them.

Even Infused AI tools permit dynamic evaluation, at which point the complexity of the assessment becomes something automated upon the student feedback. This way the students are adequately stretched and faculty provided with diagnostic information about student performance in a better position than ever before.

c) Content Personalization

The AI content generators tailor learning content according to the needs of learners of different characters. As an example, AI can generate simplified representations when dealing with students who have trouble with a complex idea or advanced readings when dealing with students who are performing well. Faculty have the freedom of providing differentiated instruction without having to develop versions of each.

d) Research-Driven Teaching Material

With the use of AI, literature review tools enable faculty to incorporate the latest research in the teaching materials. Rather than carefully scrutinizing hundreds of scholarly articles, faculty can turn to Artificial Intelligence and have it summarize the findings of each, spot any current trends, and suggest new studies that they should consider in the lectures.

Smart content creation ultimately serves to increase quality teaching and ensures that faculty gets more time to meaningfully interact with students.

4.2 Adaptive Teaching Methods Using AI Tools

Not only does AI facilitate the processes of content creation but it also changes the way this gets delivered. Adaptive teaching techniques incorporate AI to make sure the teaching technique becomes dynamically changing according to the demands of the students. Adaptive learning with the use of AI has been highlighted as the basis of transformational and sustainable change to emphasize equity, efficiency, and lifelong learning (Strielkowski et al., 2025). As compared to a traditional classroom where teaching may take a linear approach, AI-facilitated adaptive course delivery enables faculty members to adapt their teaching patterns to the various types of learners and each individual student at his or her own pace.

a) Real-Time Learning Analytics

AI systems can measure student engagement in classes—his/her attention span, participation rates, and question response time. Based on such information faculty can make adjustments to teaching strategically immediately. For example, if analytics reveal that students' engagement tends to fall off during the theoretically focused parts, faculty can add interactive polls or case studies to get students more engaged.

b) Personalized Learning Pathways

Adaptive platforms will allow each student his / her individual learning path. Faculty can push core materials but AI will suggest supplementary materials to fulfill specific needs. As an example, with a programing course, AI can provide introductory coding to one group of learners and advanced algorithm tasks to another group of learners.

c) Dynamic Classroom Management

One useful application is in terms of lecture query handling; AI assistants might be able to take care of straightforward requests, whether it is clearing up a definition or explaining an idea, leaving faculty to engage in higher level interactions. Other schools have experimented with AI-powered chatbots included in learning management systems to better respond in real time to students without overloading the instructor.

d) Inclusive Pedagogy

AI-based accessibility tools help instructors to teach inclusively, i.e., by creating real-time subtitles, translating the material into various languages, or reading the text aloud. Faculty can thus be certain that their instructions reach all of the students with a variety of needs, including international and students with disabilities.

Adaptive instruction does not just individualize the learning process to meet the pace, needs and abilities of individual students but it further expands accessibility to education in a more inclusive and equitable manner. Adaptive teaching allows students with varying levels of skills and background to gain the same benefits by adapting the content delivery and engagement tracking with the help of AI-based tools and offering personalized materials. This methodology will allow breaking down of barriers to students who may have difficulties in a standard classroom and will at the same time challenge the high-performing students with a challenging task, which will result in a balanced and fair setting that helps everyone to achieve success.

4.3 Enhanced Student Engagement Through Intelligent Systems

Learning success is a major factor that is influenced by student engagement. Conventional methods tended to focus on classroom activity, group work, or project work. Even though they are still useful, AI-based intelligent systems introduce innovative and innovative means of maintaining students engaged in the learning process.

a) Gamification and Interactive Learning

Gamified learning can be a way of motivating employees using AI-powered gamification platforms. Faculty can create AI-enabled quizzes, challenges and simulations, which offer students badges or progress points. The pedagogy encourages learning especially in the subjects that might otherwise be abstract or should be considered difficult.

b) Intelligent Tutoring Systems (ITS)

ITS assist students with one-on-one direction out of the classroom. These intelligent systems mimic a human tutor role, responding to queries, providing a feedback, and offering extra practice. Faculty also benefit since they are able to monitor how students are engaging with such systems and change certain methods of instruction towards them based on that engagement.

c) Virtual and Augmented Reality

A combination of VR/AR can help to develop immersive learning with faculty. As an example, medical faculty would provide students with virtual dissections, and history faculty would give tours of exotic civilizations of ancient times. This kind of innovations makes learning more fun and memorable.

d) Sentiment and Engagement Tracking

Even some AI applications will be able to examine student moods by facial recognition or emotion reading text. Table 2 presents the examples of the AI Tools that should help in teaching innovation. Teaching styles and the effectiveness of course materials in your courses can be monitored by the faculty to provide timely feedback to keep the students motivated.

Through incorporating intelligent engagement technology, instructors guarantee that learning is not one-way, it's two-way, dynamic and student focused.

Table 2. Examples of AI Tools Supporting Teaching Innovation

Area of Innovation	AI Tool/Platform	Application in Teaching
Smart Content Creation	ChatGPT, Jasper, Quizizz	Generates lesson plans, quizzes, and assessments; assists in creating interactive learning content
Adaptive Teaching Methods	Squirrel AI, Knewton, Smart Sparrow	Provides personalized learning pathways; adapts teaching content based on student performance
Classroom Support	Google AI Assistant, Microsoft Copilot	Assists in classroom management; answers routine queries; supports faculty in multitasking
Student Engagement	Kahoot!, Classcraft, Carnegie Learning ITS	Gamifies learning; provides intelligent tutoring; enhances real-time engagement
Accessibility & Inclusivity	Otter.ai, Google Translate, AI Captioning Tools	Real-time transcription, translation, and speech-to-text for diverse learners
Immersive Learning	Labster, AI-powered VR/AR tools	Creates virtual labs, simulations, and immersive subject experiences

Pedagogical innovation has been influenced by AI which has changed the meaning of teaching in the 21 st century. Whether by developing intelligent content or adaptive pedagogy and engagement systems, AI can help faculty develop classrooms that become more personalized, inclusive and engaging. Such innovations do not only enhance the level of students results but also benefit the faculty through heightening creativity and proficiency in teaching.

Table 2 provides a variety of examples of practical tools that can be applied by the faculty members due to AI. The obstacles are not in the facilitation of these tools but the fact that faculty is not ready, the institution is not ready and the capability to practice AI in an ethical and meaningful sense has not happened yet.

5. OPPORTUNITIES AND BENEFITS OF AI FOR FACULTY

By incorporating artificial intelligence in higher education, professors have been given a wide range of opportunities. As the research literature has demonstrated, ICT can contribute to faculty development, providing the tools that can increase the level of teaching and, consequently, student success overall (Morton, 2026). In addition to its use as an instrument of automation, AI has emerged as a facilitator of creativity, efficiency and collaboration in academia. These advantages cut across teaching, research, administration and professional growth by providing faculty members with the opportunity to work more creatively and constructively. The benefits map is provided in Figure 2, and it denotes how the field of AI can help out the faculty members in the education system.

5.1 Personalized Development Pathways

One problem with the traditional faculty development programs is that the programs tend to be generalized programs of training that are held as workshops and seminars and thus, they may fail to respond to particular strengths, weaknesses or career goals. Its capabilities allow AI to change this universal mode of development into a more individual developmental process.

- AI-based systems are able to monitor faculty interactions, the way they are teaching, as well as student feedback and then suggest specific learning resources or courses.
- Faculty have access to AI-driven professional growth dashboards, which give them tailored recommendations at the time (e.g., complete an online workshop on blended learning, utilize a new simulation tool, sharpen skills in data analytics).

- This kind of personalization keeps things moving so that the faculty matures steadily, stably, and right on track with institutional priorities, as well as personal career plans.

Not only does this make things more efficient but it also inspires the faculty members who get to experience direct value in their professional development work

5.2 Time-Saving in Routine Academic Tasks

The first practically beneficial advantage of AI to faculty is that it can alleviate the chores of repetitive activities that can be time-consuming.

- The use of AI-assisted grading systems enables the assessment of multiple-choice tests, essays, and presentations, as well, which allows the faculty to have more time to engage in the critical thinking activities and mentoring.
- Scheduling programs on AI can be used to schedule office hours, research meetings, and class schedule automatically, eliminating administrative burnout.
- Natural language processing (NLP) tools are also able to summarize long reports, extract references and even create the draft of academic writing materials, speeding up the process of writing and documentation.

By automating these repetitive tasks, AI will release faculty members so that they can focus more of their energy in higher-level academic duties like mentorship, curriculum design, and pedagogical ingenuity

5.3 Improved Research and Publication Support

Research is at the center of the higher education but it can be a stressing process to faculty members due to the escalating demands of quality publications. This is an area that I am well supported by IAI:

- AI-driven literature review tools have the potential to read through thousands of research articles, point out areas of interest and make summaries, saving time on background research.
- Predictive analytics would be useful to the researcher, as it is likely to reveal emerging areas of research, through analysis of emerging patterns in the existing bodies of literature, and also through identification of gaps in existing literature.

- The quality and accuracy of a manuscript may be enhanced and checked using AI writing assistant and reference managers as they provide grammar polishing, plagiarism detection, and citation updates.
- Machine-learning-based data analysis tools make it possible to process massive and complicated amounts of data with higher exactness as compared to manual processes.

The applications assist faculty in remaining prolific in their research and contributes to the advancement of knowledge in their fields without being overburdened with technical or clerical issues.

5.4 Collaboration and Global Networking

AI does not only contribute to the personal efficiency and career development of individual members of the faculty, but also is essential to team building and encouraging international networking. Intelligent collaboration platforms mean that AI will be able to match educators with other colleagues both within institutions and even beyond, propose their possible research partners, indicate areas of interest, and simplify communication. This provides the chance of cross-cultural education, collaborative work, and expansive academic interactions, which carry the influence of the faculty growth not just at an individual but at collective and global levels.

- Intelligent platforms suggest potential research partners globally based on their commonality of research interests, their citations or their common co-authorship networks.
- Artificial intelligence is employed in virtual collaboration environments to help manage projects with absolute ease, communicate on a multilingual basis and share knowledge in real time.
- Faculty members will be able to participate in global learning community where AI will bring relevant discussions, forums or conferences to assure that members are updated on major developments.

These networking opportunities facilitate cross-cultural learning and provide the possibility of joint projects, co-authorship of publications, and international collaboration and relationship, thereby placing the faculty members in the international academic system of relationships and interrelationships.

Figure 2. Benefits map – how AI supports faculty roles

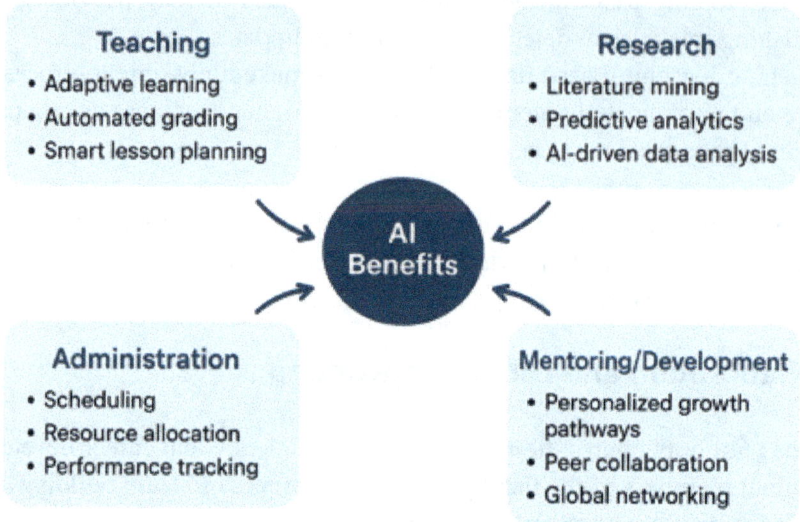

(Author's own creation).

This benefits map visually communicates that AI acts as a unifying force, reducing barriers and enhancing effectiveness in nearly every aspect of academic work.

6. CHALLENGES AND ETHICAL CONSIDERATIONS

The fact that Artificial Intelligence (AI) religiously entered the sphere of higher education has generated indubitable benefits, but sets down numerous challenges and ethical questions. The potential of AI in the educational sector is huge, but there are also certain issues associated with ethical, doctrinal, and ethical considerations of the responsible use of AI (Eden et al., 2024). Faculty development makes use of personalized learning systems, intelligent tutoring, automated academic supports, although they require consideration of the risk and complexity that surrounds these systems. Without being addressed, these challenges can not only inhibit the professional development of faculty members but also pose obstacles in the way of institutions, which aim at responsible adoption of AI.

6.1 Data Privacy and Security Issues

Computer-aided systems require massive amounts of student and faculty data input and Analysis to be effective. Every training module, performance analytics, and intelligent system are being based on sensitive data. This creates major issues in regard to privacy, confidentiality and ownership of information. Faculty could also be concerned of how their records of the teaching performance are stored, whether they are being used to be able to do an evaluation of them without any consent, and even the situation that said records could be revealed to third parties. The impact of breach in data security is damaging to both professional reputations and trust within an institution. In this way, it behooves to have strong policies on the governance of data, anonymization, and ethical data use as well.

6.2 Over-Reliance on AI vs. Human Judgment

As much as AI can be effective in viewing trends and coming up with suggestions, excessive trusting technology can degrade human instinct in instructing and coaching. The knowledge offered by AI has to be combined with professional judgment and knowledge of values operating within specific contexts by a faculty member. As an example, an AI system can propose a generalized form of teaching that is not suitable to accommodate the diverse learners in a specific environment. Without the element of human intuition and empathy, the academic process can be very robotic as opposed to dynamically life-altering. Hence, AI must be an enabler rather than a substitute to faculty decision-making.

6.3 Resistance to Change among Faculty

Not every member of the faculty eagerly warms to technological change. Others might be a victim of the growing importance of AI where they might feel that their work is being undermined by the automation or that they risk becoming obsolete. Other individuals might have doubts regarding AI-generated knowledge or fear moving towards a radically redefined mechanism of teaching and learning. Faculty who have been exposed to digital tools in their academic lives is particularly resistant to the implementation of digital tools. This stresses the importance of change management efforts, institutional incentive, and peer-supporting system to drive gradual adoption.

6.4 Skill Gaps in AI Adoption

The effectiveness of the deployment of AI in faculty development requires the digital knowledgeability and preparedness of teachers. A number of faculty members would not be able to communicate with AI platforms due to the lack of technical skills. This lack of skills might deny them the opportunity to enjoy the adaptive teaching materials, Research information systems and even the smart grading systems. Unless specifically trained and consistently professionally developed, institutions can contribute to an intensifying gap between instructors who are successfully utilising technology and those that are not coping. The table below describes (Table 3) the challenges of adopting AI in faculty development and the possible mitigation strategies.

Table 3. Challenges of AI Adoption in Faculty Development with Possible Mitigation Strategies

Challenge	Description	Possible Mitigation Strategies
Data Privacy and Security	Sensitive faculty and student data collected by AI may be misused, leaked, or stored without consent.	Establish strong data governance policies, ensure encryption, promote transparency, and adopt ethical data-sharing practices.
Over-Reliance on AI	Risk of diminishing human judgment and intuition in academic decisions.	Position AI as a supportive tool, maintain faculty authority, and encourage hybrid decision-making approaches.
Resistance to Change	Faculty skepticism or fear of AI replacing traditional roles and responsibilities.	Provide incentives, conduct awareness programs, and introduce peer-led adoption initiatives to build confidence.
Skill Gaps	Faculty lack of technical expertise to effectively engage with AI platforms.	Offer continuous professional development, AI-literacy workshops, and institution-supported training modules.

This section illustrates that faculty development in the era of AI can not be considered as a technical problem only. Ethical, cultural, and professional aspects need to be considered as well to make sure the integration of AI will not be unfair, opaque, and empowering.

7. FUTURE DIRECTIONS

Even though the use of artificial intelligence in post-secondary education is still a new area, its opportunities are far-reaching. The future lies in AI-driven educational systems where smart systems facilitate faculty development, pedagogic, and research. It is believed that colleges and universities will progressively adopt AI in their mainstays like learning management systems, assessment platforms, and professional training systems.

It needs faculty preparation both in terms of mindset and skill to prepare them to such an ecosystem. Ethical practices, teamwork, and learning across disciplines should be trained along with AI literacy. Institutions will be required to assist faculty with training on a continuous basis, digital infrastructure, and the ability to experiment with the new technologies. The future development of faculty in AI-based setting can be sustainable provided that the humanistic values are kept at the focus. Although AI will make work faster and more personal, teachers will not be substitutable by mentoring, guiding, and critical thinking. The expected AI opportunities in faculty development can be summed up and presented in Table 4 below.

Table 4. Future AI Trends in Faculty Development

Future Trend	Implication for Faculty
AI-driven personalized learning	Tailored training plans based on individual needs
Intelligent research assistants	Faster literature reviews, data analysis, and writing
Virtual AI mentors & tutors	On-demand guidance for teaching and skill growth
Predictive analytics for careers	Early identification of skills required for future roles
Immersive AI tools (AR/VR + AI)	Enhanced experiential teaching and training methods
Ethical AI frameworks	Responsible use of AI in teaching and research

8. CONCLUSION

Intelligent robots are transforming graduate school and faculty training. This chapter has discussed the role of AI in assisting faculty development by using adaptive training platforms, data-based feedback, individualized professional learning, and AI-based pedagogical innovation. Enhanced efficiency, creative instruction, research support, and international cooperation are among the benefits mentioned, whereas such issues as the privacy of data, ethical issues, and change resistance are essential. The most important value of this discussion is that it demonstrates AI is not a replacement of faculty but enables them instead. Implemented responsibly, AI improves the professional growth, promotes innovation in higher education and strengthens the teaching practice. Finally, the future of faculty development is balancing to create efficiencies when enabled by AI with human values of empathy and mentorship, and creativity. Schools that facilitate such equilibrium will be in a better position to succeed in AI-facilitated academic world.

REFERENCES

Al-Mughairi, H., & Bhaskar, P. (2024). Exploring the factors affecting the adoption AI techniques in higher education: insights from teachers' perspectives on ChatGPT. *Journal of Research in Innovative Teaching & Learning*.

Alakoum, A., Nica, E., & Abiad, M. (2024). Revolutionizing faculty performance evaluation: The future role of AI in higher education. *Journal of Self-Governance and Management Economics*, *12*(1), 25–49.

Beck, J., Stern, M., & Haugsjaa, E. (1996). Applications of AI in Education. *XRDS: Crossroads. The ACM Magazine for Students*, *3*(1), 11–15.

Chen, N. S., Smyrnova-Trybulska, E., Morze, N., Ślósarz, A., Glushkova, T., Przybyła-Kasperek, M., & Gubo, Š. (2024). Education in the Era of AI, Enhancing Skills, Challenges and Perspectives–International Context and National Experience. *International Journal of Research in E-learning*, *10*(2), 1–30.

Copur-Gencturk, Y., Li, J., & Atabas, S. (2024). Improving teaching at scale: Can AI be incorporated into professional development to create interactive, personalized learning for teachers? *American Educational Research Journal*, *61*(4), 767–802.

Eden, C. A., Chisom, O. N., & Adeniyi, I. S. (2024). Integrating AI in education: Opportunities, challenges, and ethical considerations. *Magna Scientia Advanced Research and Reviews*, *10*(2), 006-013.

Fakhar, H., Lamrabet, M., Echantoufi, N., & Ajana, L. (2024). Towards a New Artificial Intelligence-based Framework for Teachers' Online Continuous Professional Development Programs: Systematic Review. *International Journal of Advanced Computer Science and Applications*, *15*(4).

Ge, Z., & Hu, Y. (2020, April). Innovative application of artificial intelligence (AI) in the management of higher education and teaching. [). IOP Publishing.]. *Journal of Physics: Conference Series*, *1533*(3), 032089.

Guan, C., Mou, J., & Jiang, Z. (2020). Artificial intelligence innovation in education: A twenty-year data-driven historical analysis. *International Journal of Innovation Studies*, *4*(4), 134–147.

Harry, A. (2023). Role of AI in education. *Interdiciplinary Journal & Hummanity (INJURITY)*, *2*(3).

Holmes, W., & Tuomi, I. (2022). State of the art and practice in AI in education. *European Journal of Education*, *57*(4), 542–570.

Khalid, U., Kashif, H., Alamdar, R., & Naseer, F. (2024). Redefining faculty roles in an AI-driven educational ecosystem with implications for teaching and curriculum development. *Journal of Media Horizons*, *5*(4), 127–139.

Lytras, M. D., Serban, A. C., Alkhaldi, A., Aldosemani, T., & Malik, S. (2024). Digital transformation in higher education in times of artificial intelligence: Setting the emerging landscape. In *Digital Transformation in Higher Education, Part A* (pp. 1-22). Emerald Publishing Limited.

Morton, T. B. (2026). Enlightening Educators: Unlocking the Benefits of AI in Faculty Development. In *Harnessing AI's Potential to Support Student Success and Teaching Excellence* (pp. 109-128). IGI Global Scientific Publishing.

Nguyen, N. D. (2023). Exploring the role of AI in education. *London Journal of Social Sciences*, (6), 84–95.

Pedro, F., Subosa, M., Rivas, A., & Valverde, P. (2019). Artificial intelligence in education: Challenges and opportunities for sustainable development.

Rahayu, S., & Bablu, T. A. (2023). AI-Augmented Learning and Development Platforms: Transforming Employee Training and Skill Enhancement. *Journal of Computing Innovations and Applications*, *1*(01), 19–38.

Schiff, D. (2022). Education for AI, not AI for education: The role of education and ethics in national AI policy strategies. *International Journal of Artificial Intelligence in Education*, *32*(3), 527–563.

Selwyn, N. (2022). The future of AI and education: Some cautionary notes. *European Journal of Education*, *57*(4), 620–631.

Siddiqui, M. T., Mansoori, M. V., Siddiqui, M. A., & Yadav, A. (2025). AI-enabled pedagogy: Advancing education through innovative teaching tools and the AI-TEACH model. *Journal of Informatics Education and Research*, *5*(1), 2526–2539.

Strielkowski, W., Grebennikova, V., Lisovskiy, A., Rakhimova, G., & Vasileva, T. (2025). AI-driven adaptive learning for sustainable educational transformation. *Sustainable Development*, *33*(2), 1921–1947.

Wang, L. (2020, May). Artificial intelligence and career development of college teachers: Challenge and countermeasures. [). IOP Publishing.]. *Journal of Physics: Conference Series*, *1550*(2), 022030.

Zhai, X., Chu, X., Chai, C. S., Jong, M. S. Y., Istenic, A., Spector, M., & Li, Y. (2021). A Review of Artificial Intelligence (AI) in Education from 2010 to 2020. *Complexity*, *2021*(1), 8812542.

Chapter 7
From Automation to Innovation: AI as a Catalyst for Faculty Growth

Amrik Singh
https://orcid.org/0000-0003-3598-8787
Lovely Professional University, India

ABSTRACT

Artificial intelligence (AI) in higher education, moving beyond the automation of routine tasks to fostering genuine innovation in faculty roles and professional development. AI-driven tools ranging from automated grading systems to intelligent tutoring platforms are reshaping the responsibilities of educators, enabling them to focus on mentorship, critical thinking facilitation, and the ethical integration of technology in pedagogy. The discussion highlights the shift from traditional knowledge transmission to knowledge facilitation, emphasizing the importance of AI literacy and continuous professional development for faculty. By automating administrative and repetitive instructional tasks, AI empowers educators to dedicate more time to creative curriculum design, personalized student engagement, and collaborative learning environments. The chapter also addresses the challenges and opportunities presented by generative AI, including the need for ethical guidelines, the development of new assessment strategies, and the cultivation of a growth mindset among faculty.

INTRODUCTION

The future of technological advancement in higher education is not impressive, as the introduction of Artificial Intelligence (AI) to the processes of service delivery is currently a reality. However, instead of being a simple technology that helps to

DOI: 10.4018/979-8-3373-4129-3.ch007

automatize routine tasks, AI is becoming a potent driver of faculty development that helps redefine educators as the creators of innovative learning experiences (Sharma & Singh, 2024; Nuong et al., 2024; Singh, 2024a; Singh, 2024b). The chapter discusses the complex possibilities of how AI can empower faculty, support their career growth, research, and teaching models, eventually resulting in a more vibrant and successful educational ecosystem.

Background of the study

The rapid infusion of artificial intelligence (AI) into higher education marks a transformative shift from simple automation of routine tasks toward enabling deeper pedagogical innovation and professional growth among faculty. Historically, educational technology focused on efficiency automating administrative duties such as grading, attendance tracking, and content distribution to reduce faculty workload. While these developments delivered measurable time savings, they often treated technology as a tool for substitution rather than transformation. The current AI wave is different: machine learning, generative models, intelligent tutoring systems, and analytics platforms not only automate but also augment human judgment, provide personalized teaching insights, and open new avenues for scholarly inquiry (Singh, 2024c; Garg et al., 2024; Singh et al., 2024). This reframing positions AI as a catalyst that can accelerate faculty development in teaching, research, and service. Faculty growth is a multi-dimensional construct comprising pedagogical competence, research productivity, digital literacy, and professional identity. Traditional faculty development programs—workshops, mentoring, and peer observation remain essential, but they struggle to scale and to keep pace with rapid technological change. AI systems promise scalable, data-informed interventions: adaptive learning platforms that reveal student misconceptions; analytics dashboards that surface patterns in engagement and outcomes; writing assistants that help refine grant proposals and manuscripts; and simulation tools that allow risk-free experimentation with novel teaching strategies. These capabilities can help faculty iteratively refine practice, identify research opportunities, and extend their scholarly reach. However, the promise of AI for faculty growth is neither automatic nor universal. Institutional readiness, digital infrastructure, faculty attitudes, and ethical considerations shape adoption and impact. Concerns about deskilling, loss of academic autonomy, algorithmic bias, data privacy, and the commodification of teaching are real and must be addressed (Singh & Sihmar, 2025; Singh & Kumar, 2024). Moreover, faculty development mediated by AI requires new competencies interpreting analytics, integrating AI tools into curriculum design, and critically assessing algorithmic outputs. Without intentional professional learning frameworks, AI may deepen existing inequities rather than mitigate them. The literature on educational technology suggests that meaningful improvement occurs when tools are integrated into a broader ecology of practice where policy, training, incentives, and community support align. Applying that lens to AI, research must examine not only what the tools can do, but how they are implemented, who benefits, and what unintended consequences emerge. Comparative studies across disciplines and institution types are needed because faculty roles, class sizes, and research expectations vary widely. Equally important is longitudinal inquiry that tracks how faculty competence and identity evolve as AI becomes embedded in everyday academic work. This study situates itself at the intersection of innovation studies, educational technology, and faculty development. It explores how AI moves institutions from automation freeing time and reducing transaction costs to innovation generating new pedagogies, research agendas, and modes of professional growth (Singh, 2024c; Garg et al., 2024; Singh et al., 2024). By focusing on the enabling conditions, barriers, and ethical dimensions of AI adoption, the research aims to produce actionable insights for administrators, professional developers, and faculty themselves. Ultimately, understanding how AI can catalyze faculty growth is not just a technical question but a strategic one: it determines whether higher education will harness AI to expand human creativity, equity, and intellectual advancement, or merely to optimize old processes in newer wrappers.

The Shifting Paradigm: Beyond Efficiency

To most teachers, introducing Artificial Intelligence (AI) into education settings is usually linked to such activities as auto-grading, learning software, or management efficiencies. It is true that these applications enhance operational effectiveness which liberate the desirable time and minimizing redundant activities. Nonetheless, these applications, despite their potential positive benefits, are just the tip of the iceberg in AI applications in education. The difference between what AI can accomplish concerning faculty is not just the extent of what it can accomplish, but what AI can empower them to be creators, strategists, mentors, and researchers on a whole new level of impact (Mitrache et al., 2024). AI provides teachers with a chance to redefine their functions beyond the transactional processes. Faculty can also achieve a lot in real-time through machine learning algorithms and data analytics tools to understand the learning patterns of students, pinpoint areas of weaknesses in understanding, and make adjustments to instruction. This degree of individualization was not possible in large-scale previously (Singh, 2024c; Garg et al., 2024; Singh et al., 2024; Singh & Sihmar, 2025; Singh & Kumar, 2024). More to the point, it causes a change in the focus of the educator as he or she is no longer concerned with the execution of tasks but with strategic intervention and curriculum innovation. AI-tools can be used to curate and offer variousiation strategies, simulate classroom conditions to use during training, and thus enable teachers to become more dynamic in their methods (Mutambik, 2024). In addition to teaching, AI makes research innovative. Faculty are now able to analyze huge amounts of data to do research, simplify literature reviews through natural language processing tools, and even co-write research proposals with AI-generated suggestions. These tools supplement the information processing process, raising the production of scholarly works and making cross-disciplinary cooperation processes, which used to be information-intensive, more possible. Moreover, AI can contribute to inclusive education by supporting the needs and different learning styles (Mitrache et al., 2024; Nuong et al., 2024; Singh, 2024a; Singh, 2024b; Singh & Kumar, 2024). Faculty can use AI to create more accessible learning opportunities that will make education genuinely equitable. With the reduction of routine pressure, teachers are liberated to invest further in the areas of mentorship, facilitating critical thinking, and thought leadership. After all, it is not only a shift of efficiency but of evolution. AI will allow faculty to become change facilitators, rather than information dispensers. It is no longer about what AI paves the way, but rather about what it augments creativity, empathy, strategic vision, and human connection (Garg et al., 2024; Singh et al., 2024; Singh & Sihmar, 2025). With the evolving power of AI, those teachers who will adopt it to its fullest power will be on the leading edge of a pedagogical revolution, and pedagogy will be redefined as a highly human activity, not eroded by intelligent technology.

Streamlining Technology and Technology

Automation is emerging as a disruptive enabler in the dynamic world of education and not the final answer. Automation of the everyday academic routine, including grading multiple-choice quizzes, assembling attendance data, or creating a simple performance report is considered a major change in the role of educators (Aithal &Maiya, 2023). These are time-consuming and low-order processes that can be automatically done now by intelligent devices, and faculty can regain their precious time and intellectual resources. Nevertheless, the increase in efficiency should not be interpreted as a final stage (Deri et al., 2024; Singh, 2024c; Garg et al., 2024). Instead, it needs to be viewed as the platform on which innovation, creativity, and pedagogical progress can thrive. The release of faculty members of repetitive tasks provides the opportunity to redirection of the effort to more complex and meaningful tasks such as mentoring students, creating interdisciplinary curricula or conducting applied research. These activities require not only the knowledge of the subject but also emotional intelligence, critical thinking, and the ability to adapt to the situation, which are not duplicated by machines. Automation, in turn, allows redefining the role of an educator and turns them into a provider of learning and innovation rather than delivery. Furthermore, the underlying change leads to opportunities of exploring newer teaching strategies, including flipped classes, immersive learning, and AI-implemented personalized learning (Nuong et al., 2024; Singh, 2024a; Singh, 2024b; Deri et al., 2024). Faculty will be able to spend additional time on determining subtle student needs, developing creativity, and giving individualized feedback to help students grow personally (Aithal &Maiya, 2023). Automation therefore provides a supportive structure towards constant advancement in pedagogy, developing an atmosphere that allows the teachers as well as the learners to experience greater interactions and engagement.The cultural change in academic institutions is also important. Automation can also become an incentive to reconsider the work process and disorganize the old standards. The facilities investing in automation not merely to reduce expenditures but to inform their human resources have a greater chance of scoring points in the long run (Sharma & Singh, 2024; Singh, 2022; Singh, 2024; Nuong et al., 2024; Singh et al., 2024; Singh & Sihmar, 2025; Singh & Kumar, 2024). This is not to oust teachers, but to empower them by liberating them to concentrate on high value additions, which demand judgment, empathy, and innovation.

LITERATURE REVIEW

To conclude, automation in education cannot be regarded as the ultimate goal but rather the foundation to a more vibrant and considerate academic ecosystem. It marks the beginning of a greater change that one which enables teachers to overcome administrative overloads and provides them with meaningful and human-focused advances to learning and teaching.

More Intense Interaction with Students

The automation of habitual academic activities, e.g. grading objective tests or producing reports, has created the possibility of faculty members devoting more significant time to students. No longer under the pressure of being slaves of repetitive jobs, teachers are now able to devote their time and effort to developing more academic relationships and making learning experiences memorable. Among the greatest benefits, one can distinguish the possibility to hold one on one consultations (Long et al., 2024). Such individualized interactions will help the teacher know the individual learning style, difficulties, and goals of a student, which will make it possible to offer more customized direction and assistance in the end (Singh et al., 2024; Singh & Sihmar, 2025; Singh &Kumar, 2024). t. Faculty members will also be in a better position to offer detailed and constructive feedback on more complex assignments including the essay, research and case studies with more time at their disposal. This form of feedback is unlike the standardized grading that involves critical analysis, situational knowledge and individualized recommendations, which are all factors that aid students in their academic development and critical thought processes. This enhanced feedback loop, besides increasing the confidence of the students, enhances their capacity to reflect, revise and improve.

Figure 1. Conceptual framework on automation to innovation

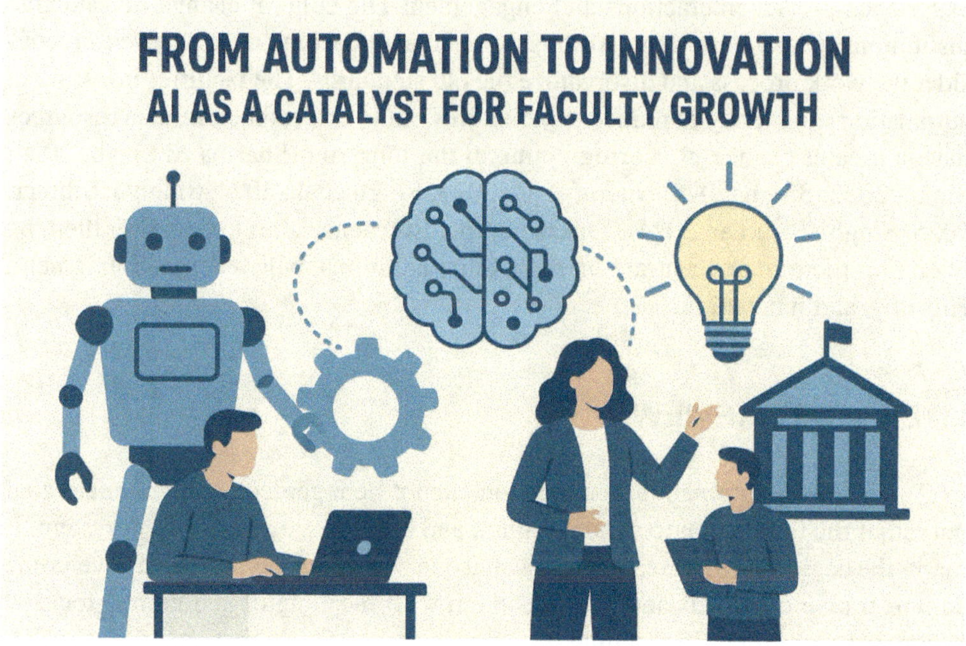

Author's Own Elaboration

Moreover, automation helps to create classroom settings in which more substantial discussions are possible. The educators have an opportunity to spend more time on creating interactive lessons, conducting debates, and promoting collaborative problem-solving activities (Voronov et al., 2023). Such activities will help to develop features of higher-order thinking, emotional intelligence, and communication skills that are necessary to succeed in the modern world (Sharma & Singh, 2024; Singh, 2022; Singh, 2024). The time saved on the automation process can eventually be used on positive interaction that can take the teaching-learning relationship to the next level. The students have more access to mentors and the faculty get a new sense of purpose and attachment to the academic mission. This way, automation does not take away the role of the educator; on the contrary, it empowers him or her to concentrate on the human aspect of education that really matters.

Curriculum Improvement and Creation

Automation and its incorporation in the education sector, especially in the management of repetitive and time-consuming activities, presents the faculty with a promising chance to redirect their attention towards curriculum improvement and improvement. As routine grading and administrative processes are transferred to the AI systems, educators receive the liberty to perform intellectually engaging tasks that help to bring academic innovation and relevance. Designing innovative and future-prepared courses is one of the most notable regions, in which this time may be redirected (Ogunbodede & Atchrim, 2025). Faculty are able to re-conceptualize course design to be more interactive, practical and in line with the real world. They can also integrate the components of experiential learning, project-based learning, and technology-based modules (augmented reality (AR), virtual simulation, or game-based evaluation) instead of using the traditional lecture-based format exclusively (Deri et al., 2024; Singh, 2024c; Garg et al., 2024; Singh et al., 2024). These aspects promote involvement and increase the learning results. Besides, time can provide the possibility of more interdisciplinary approach of curriculum design. Academics can also work across disciplines to combine the knowledge of various disciplines, thus producing hybrid courses that reflect the interdependence of modern issues like greenness or information ethics or international hospitality. This is because such courses are not just expanding the student outlook, but also stimulating critical and integrative thinking. Also, teachers will be able to keep abreast of the new research and industry developments and bring them to their learning resources. This makes it possible to have up to date learning content that is also evidence based and responsive to the needs of the employers and society. Another type of customized resources that can be designed by faculty is digital modules, interactive case studies, and video lectures that address the needs and preferences of diverse learners (Garg et al., 2024; Singh et al., 2024; Singh & Sihmar, 2025; Singh & Kumar, 2024). In short, automation preconditions the creation of a dynamic academic climate within which the curriculum becomes more and more enriched following the course of innovation. It will enable the faculty to go beyond content delivery and be architects of transformative education that will prepare students to the challenges of the modern world.

Specialize in High-Impact Research

As the robots replace the administrative and monotonous academic activities, the faculty will have the priceless time-time that can be used to conduct high-impact research. No longer bound by the daily responsibilities of grading, report creation, and data input, teachers can dedicate more time to academic research and can now indulge in intellectual activity more fully and ambitious research agendas can be pursued (Willard & Hutson, 2024). This transition will allow faculty to conceptualize and come up with more complex and interdisciplinary research projects that can answer pressing global issues. Faculty now has access to research questions that involve a lot of reading, teamwork, and critical thinking no matter the topic they are researching, sustainability in hospitality, the implications of artificial intelligence in education, or the sociocultural dynamics of tourism (Sharma & Singh, 2024; Singh, 2022; Singh, 2024a; Nuong et al., 2024; Singh, 2024a). Time is also associated with increased ability to apply to competitive grants, develop academic networks, and participate in conferences to exchange ideas and develop professionally. Also, automation enables researchers to put more energy into the analysis of large and complex sets of data which is a significant element of evidence-based scholarship. Using the assistance of AI-powered tools, they will be able to discover patterns, come up with insights, and prove hypotheses even more effectively and without losing the intellectual rigor required in academic research. The increased interest of the faculty in research has the added benefit of providing a new body of information in their fields as well as improving the overall academic status of the institution and its influence on the policy and industry. Moreover, this research-based method might lead to the enhancement of classroom experience (Deri et al., 2024; Singh, 2024c; Garg et al., 2024; Singh et al., 2024; Singh & Sihmar, 2025; Singh & Kumar, 2024). Active researching faculties provide new insights, practical examples, and recent discoveries in the classroom, which provide the students with a dynamic and up-to-date education. In brief, automation is an accelerating factor in conducting high-impact research since it reduces distractions in administration (Garg et al., 2024). It enables faculty to enhance their academic input, become innovative, and influence the future of their fields eventually creating a culture of research wherein depth, creativeness, and societal applicability are greatly valued.

Individualized Learning Design

The adoption of automation in learning has transformed faculty-mediated development of customized learning opportunities. Automating data collection and analysis of student engagement, student assessment outcomes, student attendance, and student engagement in activities gives educators access to countless insights into the learning process of students that they can use. Such observations are the basis of individualizing pedagogical approaches and learning materials to students based on their needs (Willard & Hutson, 2024). Instead of basing their work on one-size-fits-all methods, faculty members are now able to learn more about the strength, weaknesses, and learning preferences of students, as well as the direction of their learning process. As an example, when information shows that a learner is actually always weak in conceptual applications in addition to being strong in memorization-based tasks, the instructor can change his or her lesson to incorporate more visuals, real life examples or even give that learner one-on-one lessons. Such a degree of customization will improve the outcomes of learning, motivation, and student satisfaction. Adaptive learning pathways are also possible with automated systems, in which the course content dynamically adjusts according to the student performance (Singh, 2024b; Deri et al., 2024; Singh & Sihmar, 2025; Singh & Kumar, 2024). Faculty are able to adopt the technique of differentiated instruction, issue remedial or accelerated courses on demand, and even restructure the assessment styles to match various learning profiles. Such plans are inclusive, and they will benefit all students in spite of their background and access to their educational potentials. Furthermore, the design of personalized learning with the help of automation promotes a more active and reactive model of teaching. Faculty are able to act before students become at risk of being behind schedule with data showing that the student is in danger, providing necessary support through extra resources, feedback or mentorship. This will improve retention and add to a conducive learning atmosphere. Essentially, automation will enable the faculty members to get out of the traditional metrics and be able to relate to students in a more meaningful way. It allows developing a learner-oriented ecosystem, where the teaching procedure is informed by data, flexible, and responsive to open the path to a more fair and efficient learning process.

Artificial Intelligence and Pedagogical Development

Artificial Intelligence (AI) is not just a technological resource it is becoming quickly a collaborative member of the pedagogical revolution of the higher education. To the faculty members, AI is an unprecedented chance to revolutionize the traditional teaching method and reorganize the role of the educator in the process of meaningful learning. The greatest influence of AI is the potential to facilitate the innovation of instructional designs, delivery, and assessment and thereby make a faculty develop more engaging, personalized and more effective learning experiences (Singh, 2024; Nuong et al., 2024). The AI-powered platforms include both dynamic content curation and adaptive learning paths and intelligent tutoring systems that react to the needs of a particular student on a case-by-case basis. These technologies help faculty to leave behind their rigid lesson plans and explore various formats through flipped classes, blended learning, gamification and simulations. Considering large volumes of learning data, AI can emphasize the gaps in the knowledge of pupils, propose individual resources, and even help develop micro-learning modules based on particular results. This will enable teachers to plan a curriculum that will develop in tandem with student development that encourages a learner-centered approach

(Flores et al., 2023). Also, AI facilitates the ongoing enhancement of pedagogy by offering practical advice. Predictive analytics can be used by the faculty to pick at-risk students early on and take proactive action. The insights provided by AI can guide the instructional methods, allowing a teacher to improve his or her approach in a classroom through feedbacks using the current classroom dynamics but not post-semester assessments (Deri et al., 2024; Singh, 2024c; Singh & Kumar, 2024). This responsive teaching model does not only improve the performance of students but also the development and satisfaction of the faculty. The interdisciplinary innovation and cooperation on a global level are also promoted by AI. Teachers are able to leverage other facilities to discuss AI-based learning methods or to co-create content or research on the effectiveness of teaching. Such tools as AI-led discussion boards, automatic translation, and virtual teaching assistant allow making inclusive and accessible education more accessible than ever (Garg et al., 2024). Overall, AI is not a substitute of the teacher but it is a booster of pedagogical development.

Research Problem

The integration of Artificial Intelligence (AI) in higher education has shifted from automating administrative and repetitive tasks to fostering innovation in teaching, research, and faculty development. However, despite this potential, there remains a limited understanding of how AI actually contributes to faculty growth in real academic contexts. Most existing studies focus on student-centered applications such as personalized learning or assessment automation while the faculty perspective is often underexplored. Faculty members encounter challenges related to digital competence, ethical use, trust in AI systems, and institutional support. The central research problem, therefore, lies in identifying how AI functions as a catalyst for faculty growth enhancing pedagogical innovation, research productivity, and professional identity while also examining the barriers and enabling factors influencing its effective adoption. Addressing this gap is crucial for designing faculty development frameworks that align technological advancement with academic values and institutional missions.

RESEARCH METHODOLOGY

This study adopts a secondary data methodology to critically analyze the role of AI in promoting faculty growth. The approach involves collecting and synthesizing existing academic literature, policy reports, institutional case studies, and global higher education surveys published in reputable databases such as Scopus, Web of Science, ERIC, and Google Scholar. Sources include peer-reviewed journal articles, government and organizational white papers (e.g., UNESCO, OECD, World Economic Forum), and institutional reports from universities implementing AI-driven teaching and research tools. Data will be analyzed through thematic content analysis, identifying patterns related to AI-enabled innovation, challenges, ethical implications, and faculty development strategies. By integrating insights from diverse global contexts, the study seeks to construct a conceptual framework that explains how AI transitions from an automation tool to an innovation enabler for faculty. This secondary data-driven approach ensures depth, reliability, and a comprehensive understanding of global trends shaping the future of academic growth in the AI era.

DISCUSSION AND INTERPRETATION

With AI as a collaborator, faculty members can break the traditional borders and become the pioneers of education changing the learning landscape by making it intelligent, adaptive, and, as a matter of fact, student-centered. This collaboration is an indication that automation is being used to ensure efficiency, and AI is being used to empower students and teachers, which represents a new dawn of innovation in teaching and learning.

Data-Based Pedagogy and Individualized Learning

AI is particularly strong in data processing and analysis of large volumes, and this feature may transform the decision-making process in pedagogy.

Learning Analytics: AI Learning analytics apps may give faculty real-time feedback on student engagement, trends in performance, and problem areas. The data can be used to make haste changes to instructional plans, learners who need more attention, and determine the effectiveness of various teaching practices (Lhakard, 2024).

Adaptive Learning Platforms: AI-led platforms have the potential to individualize the learning process of every student and customize the content, speed, and evaluation according to student progress and learning preferences (Sharma & Singh, 2024). These platforms can give faculty the opportunity to not only deliver content, but also to create and manage highly customized learning journeys, which liberates faculty to focus on mentoring and higher-level skill development.

Intelligent Tutoring Systems: Artificial intelligence tutors can offer real-time and personalized feedback to students regarding challenging problems explaining and steering them through difficult issues (Singh, 2022; Singh, 2024). Through these systems, faculty can incorporate these systems to enhance their instruction and therefore be able to concentrate on helping the students gain insight and be able to think critically instead of just correcting them.

Improved Content Production and Competing

The use of AI is revolutionizing the process of faculty development and presentation of instructional material, and it is becoming more vibrant, reachable and interactive.

AI-Generated Content and Material: AI may help produce first drafts of lecture notes, various collections of practice problems, summaries of research articles, or even produce virtual simulation (Singh, 2024). Although human supervision is essential, this saves a lot of time in coming up with the initial content and the faculty can refine and contribute their own input.

Interactive Learning Modules: AIs can be used to assist faculty to create and deliver interactive learning modules, such as chatbots (FAQs), customized quizzes, and responsive feedback loops, and make the learning process more interactive and reactive.

Accessibility and Inclusivity: AI tools are capable of creating captions to instructed videos automatically, translating materials into other languages, and adjusting the content to the learning requirements of disabled students, facilitating a more inclusive learning process (Nuong et al., 2024).

Project-Based Learning and Experiences

Within the modern learning environment, the promotion of experiential and project-based learning (PBL) has become one of the most effective methods of training students in the skills of the real world, critical thinking, and problem-solving. With the growing automation and the digital tools that replace the more mundane academic functions, faculty is more and more enabled to rethink learning spaces that do not rely on the one-way delivery of knowledge to the learner but instead provide the learner with active and three-dimensional instruments of learning. PBL and experiential approaches introduce the aspect of prioritizing practice over theory, which allows students to be able to learn through doing, reflecting and collaborating (Ogunbodede & Atchrim, 2025; Willard & Hutson, 2024). Experience-based learning provides students with the real life situations like internship, simulation, case studies, and field work which replicate real-life experiences of the professional challenge. The method facilitates the process of narrowing the gap between classroom education and the requirements of the industry, promoting greater comprehension and memorization of the concepts (Singh & Kumar, 2024). Having greater time to spend out of the administrative load, faculty can create and oversee meaningful experiences, partner with the industry, and take students through reflective practices that support learning outcomes. Project-based learning, in its turn, focuses on complex and open-ended questions making students work as teams, research and use interdisciplinary knowledge to come up with answers. Professional work in any other industry is frequently reflected in tangible deliverables such as reports, prototypes, or presentations, which are also the outcome of these projects (Singh & Sihmar, 2025). PBL is not only building the academic skills but also cultivating the key soft skills including communication, collaboration, project management, and leadership. Additionally, the new technologies that have appeared such as virtual and augmented reality, collaborative digital platforms, and AI-centered analytics can now be introduced by faculty into the format of experience and projects. Such platforms make it more authentic, interactive, and scaled so that students could experiment with situations, which they otherwise could not access because of logistical or financial limitations. Through these student-centered pedagogies, teachers can build more meaningful and rich learning experiences by investing time in them. They turn classrooms into a place of innovation that involves students in the process of their active learning (Singh, 2024a; Singh, 2024b). Finally, experiential and project-based learning can equip students to not only excel in school, but also flourish in a highly diversified, rapidly evolving workforce in the global economy (Flores et al., 2023; Lhakard, 2024). Through AI, it is possible to make learning more authentic and immersive, and it is no longer limited to the traditional lecture-based learning.

Virtual and Augmented Reality Simulations: AI forms the foundation of advanced VR/AR simulations, where students can learn more about complicated concepts and can perform virtual experiments, or learn a real-world skill in a safe and controlled setting. These technologies can be used by the faculty to develop very engaging and experiential learning opportunities (Deri et al., 2024).

AI-Based Project Management and Collaboration tools: AI will be helpful in running student projects, assisting with roadblock detection, and enabling more efficient group work, which will enable the faculty to run complex projects more efficiently and knowingly.

Real-World Data Analysis: With the capabilities of AI to work with big data, faculty can use real-world data in their courses, giving the students a chance to work with real data and conduct research.

Research and Scholarship Booster

Artificial Intelligence (AI) has also become a disruptive technology in the field of academic research and academic activity, changing the process of generating, distributing, and assessing knowledge (Singh, 2024c). The AI is a catalyst that makes all the research phases faster starting with literature reviews and data collection and analysis, writing and publication to enable scholars to work faster and more creatively (Mitrache et al., 2024; Mutambik, 2024). The ability to process a large volume of data in previously unheard of speeds is one of the most important contributions of AI. Using tools based on the natural language processing (NLP), researchers can perform literature reviews in a fraction of the time it previously required to accomplish this, finding the relevant works, summarizing the findings, and even revealing the gaps in the body of knowledge that currently exist. It enables scholars to build on previous studies in a more strategic way and place their study in a more articulate position (Garg et al., 2024). During the data analysis process, AI can be used with strong capabilities based on machine learning algorithms and predictive analytics as well as pattern recognition. The tools are especially effective when data sets are large, be it qualitative or quantitative, and allow the researcher to reveal trends, test the hypothesis, and come up with insights that would not be revealed with ease with other methods. Besides, AI is able to assist in meta-analysis, sentiment analysis and content analysis with a high level of accuracy and consistency. The collaboration between disciplines is also encouraged through AI, which avails platforms that render complex data to an understandable form to scholars in other fields (Singh et al., 2024). Such innovations as visualization and AI-based simulations are used to present the results of the research in more compelling and user-friendly forms, which contribute to collaborative innovation and knowledge sharing. In addition to the analysis, AI models like language models can be used to help a writer in writing academic papers, by providing coherent structures, sharpening grammar, and even writing drafts (Willard & Hutson, 2024; Flores et al., 2023). This is especially useful in the case of non-native English speakers researchers, and it enables a more fair contribution to the international scholarly discourse. Also, AI facilitates detection of plagiarism, citation and formatting of a manuscript, simplifying the process of submitting a document. Moreover, AI-based research analytics, assist institutions and researchers to quantify effects, trace citations and spot potential research hot spots.These tools can help to make strategic decisions and increase the prominence and importance of scholarly work, as academic publishing turns more data-driven (Singh et al., 2024). Altogether, AI is not a tool, but a strategic ally in the promotion of academic studies. Improving the productivity, accuracy and also facilitating innovation, AI is transforming the world of research and scholarship into a better place by making it more inclusive, dynamic and impactful. Outside of the classroom, AI has limitless possibilities to bring faculty research to a faster pace and deepen the scope of knowledge in any field.

Research Assistance and Discovery

AI tools are transforming how research is done including literature review, data analysis and so on.

Smart Literature Review: AI is capable of searching and synthesizing large amounts of academic literature within seconds creating pertinent papers, trends, and research gaps and greatly shortening the preliminary phases of any research project.

Data Collection and Analysis: AI algorithms will be able to process large and complex data, discover patterns, give predictions and even come up with hypotheses, allowing faculty to do more advanced and informative research (Singh & Kumar, 2024). There is a change in this especially in areas such as social sciences, medicine and environmental studies.

Grant Proposal Support: AI will be able to help with finding appropriate funding sources, reviewing earlier successful grants, and even produce initial text to write a grant, which will help reduce the grueling grant writing process.

Academic Communication and Publication.

This is also in the area of communication within faculty on the dissemination of their research findings, which are also being affected by AI.

Automated Summarization and Abstract Generation: AI has the ability to create short-length summaries or abstracts of research articles, which helps in the fast dissemination and findability of the research.

Improvement of Language and Style: AI-based writing assistant may assist faculty to improve their academic writing, screen their grammatical mistakes and conform to a particular style manual, enhancing their publications.

Finding Publication Venues: AI can use the work of a faculty member to recommend which journals or conferences to be published, which will have a higher chance of success.

CHALLENGES AND IMPLICATIONS

With the rise of Artificial Intelligence (AI) into the academic world, it is simultaneously accompanied by a vast amount of potential and various challenges and ethical implications that will have to be carefully maneuvered. Although AI can be utilized to improve research, simplify administration, and individualize learning, the unregulated use of this emerging technology can potentially cause numerous issues regarding the aspects of bias, data security, academic dishonesty, and the decline of human cognition. The problem of bias within the AI systems is among the major problems (Singh & Sihmar, 2025; Singh & Kumar, 2024). As AI algorithms are taught using past data, they can be biased and, in fact, increase existing prejudices. It is especially an issue when it comes to fields such as admissions, grading, and research evaluation where biased algorithms may serve to support inequality instead of ensuring fairness. In order to reduce such risks, it is important to ensure transparency in the design of the algorithms and use of various datasets. Another important issue is the issue of data privacy. Neither academic institutions nor other organizations cease to use AI to analyze the behavior, performance, and preferences of students. The gathering and utilization of such information should however be subject to stringent privacy protocols. Researchers and students should be made aware of the use of their data and consent should be a core value of any AI usage. Breachs or abuse of data may undermine trust and harm the ethical culture of an academic institution (Deri et al., 2024; Singh, 2024c; Garg et al., 2024). AI is also a threat to the conventional standards of academic integrity. As the level of sophistication of AI-generated content grows, it is becoming hard to differentiate between human and machine-generated content. This creates some doubts regarding authorship, plagiarism, and the worth of original thought (Ogunbodede & Atchrim, 2025; Willard & Hutson, 2024). Academic policies of the institutions should be modified to accommodate these changes to ensure that AI tools are ethical and should not be used to compromise the sanctity of scholarly work. Furthermore, the excessive use of AI can reduce critical thinking and human judgment in the teaching and research processes. Although AI is capable of offering insights, it is too contextually insensitive, does not possess moral reasoning, and creativity that characterize human intelligence. The educators and researchers need to find a compromise and AI should be treated as an assistant but not as a substitute to human input. To address these barriers, the institutions should promote the culture of ethical AI literacy (Sharma & Singh, 2024; Singh et al., 2024). This involves educating faculty, students, and administrators on how to use AI responsibly, create clear guidelines and encourage interdisciplinary collaboration in solving new ethical issues. Finally, ethical approach to AI implementation can help in making sure that technology can be used to promote the underlying principles of academia as equity, integrity, and intellectual freedom (Willard & Hutson, 2024). Although the opportunities of AI in faculty development are enormous, it is essential to consider and cope with the issues of challenges and ethical concerns.

Training and Upskilling: Faculty will also need proper training and professional development in order to successfully introduce AI tools into their teaching and research. The institutions need to spend on intensive training programs.

Digital Divide: It is essential to provide fair access to AI technologies and the infrastructures required so that the existing gap would not be widened.

Ethical AI Application: Faculty should be taught about the ethical aspects of AI, such as bias in AI, data privacy, intellectual property, and academic integrity. It is necessary to create explicit guidelines and rules on AI application in education.

Human Connection: AI might be able to handle all the work, but there should be no human aspect of the teaching and mentorship process that it will do. Faculty should make sure that the technology supplements, and does not subtract, the real human interaction and compassionate counseling.

Over-reliance and Critical Thinking: Over-reliance on AI can also lead to the decrease in critical thinking and the ability to solve problems on your own unless regulated. The role of the faculty should be to instruct the students on how AI can be utilized as a learning tool and not its replacement.

Job Displacement Concerns: Although this chapter talks of growth, it is necessary to note that there are some faculty who will be concerned with job displacement. It will need to change the narrative of replacement to augmentation, making AI enable the faculty to work more on higher-value activities.

CONCLUSION

The journey from automation to innovation, catalyzed by AI, represents a transformative era for faculty in higher education. By strategically embracing AI, institutions can empower their educators to move beyond routine tasks and embrace roles as facilitators of deeper learning, innovators in pedagogy, and pioneers in research. The future of faculty growth is not about AI replacing educators, but rather about a powerful human-AI partnership. This collaboration will free faculty to dedicate their intellectual prowess, creativity, and empathy to the most impactful aspects of their profession: inspiring students, generating new knowledge, and shaping the next generation of leaders. By fostering a culture of continuous learning, ethical AI integration, and a clear vision for the human-AI synergy, universities can unlock unprecedented opportunities for faculty to thrive, leading to an enriched, more dynamic, and ultimately more effective educational experience for all. The catalyst is here; the journey of innovation has just begun.

SIGNIFICANCE OF THE STUDY

As universities worldwide adopt AI technologies to improve efficiency and competitiveness, the academic workforce stands at the center of this transformation. Faculty members are not only the implementers of technological change but also the innovators who can harness AI to reimagine teaching, research, and service. Thus, examining the significance of AI for faculty growth has both theoretical and practical implications for educational institutions, policymakers, and the broader academic community. At the institutional level, this study provides valuable insights for higher education leaders seeking to align digital transformation with faculty development strategies. While many universities invest in AI tools for automation such as grading systems, plagiarism detection, or administrative scheduling few evaluate how these technologies can foster creativity, innovation, and scholarly productivity among faculty. This research emphasizes that the true value of AI lies not merely in saving time but in enabling faculty to experiment with new pedagogies, engage in interdisciplinary research, and enhance academic mentoring. Findings from the study can inform institutional policies on faculty training, AI literacy programs, and ethical governance of digital technologies. From a faculty development perspective, the study underscores the need to reconceptualize professional learning in the AI era. By identifying how AI supports continuous learning, performance analytics, and personalized professional feedback, the research contributes to redefining what it means to grow as an academic in a technologically mediated environment. Faculty members can benefit from understanding how AI tools can augment their capabilities whether in course design, student engagement, or research collaboration while remaining critically aware of issues like bias, academic integrity, and digital dependency. The study also carries theoretical significance, as it bridges concepts from educational technology, innovation diffusion, and human capital development. It provides a conceptual framework explaining how AI transitions from a tool of automation to a driver of innovation in higher education. This framework can guide future empirical research on technology-enabled faculty development and help scholars explore the long-term transformation of academic work under AI influence. Furthermore, at the societal and policy levels, the study contributes to the global discourse on sustainable and equitable digital transformation in education. Governments and accreditation bodies are increasingly prioritizing AI integration, yet their policies often focus on infrastructure rather than human capability. By highlighting the human-centered aspect of AI adoption, this study emphasizes that empowering faculty with the right skills, attitudes, and ethical awareness is essential to achieving inclusive innovation in education. Finally, the study holds practical significance for the global academic community. As AI continues to reshape the boundaries of knowledge creation, collaboration, and dissemination, understanding its impact on faculty growth will help ensure that educators remain active agents of change rather than passive users of technology. In essence, this research advocates for a balanced approach where AI amplifies, rather than replaces, human intellect and creativity positioning faculty at the heart of educational innovation and institutional excellence in the 21st century.

FUTURE FORWARD

From the chalkboards of the past to the smartboards of the present, the role of a faculty member has always been one of evolution. But the advent of artificial intelligence (AI) signals a shift far more profound than any before, propelling faculty from the realm of automation to the frontier of innovation. In this future-forward paradigm, AI is not a replacement but a powerful catalyst for growth, a co-pilot that liberates educators and researchers from the mundane, allowing them to focus on what truly matters: human-centered pedagogy, deep mentorship, and groundbreaking discovery. AI's most immediate impact lies in its ability to automate administrative and routine tasks. Imagine a world where grading multiple-choice exams, providing basic feedback on essays, or scheduling office hours are handled by an intelligent agent. This frees up countless hours, enabling professors to reinvest their energy into designing more dynamic, personalized learning experiences. Instead of a one-size-fits-all curriculum, AI-powered tools can create adaptive learning paths that cater to each student's unique pace and style, providing instant feedback and supplemental resources precisely when and where they're needed. This data-driven insight allows faculty to identify students who are struggling and provide targeted interventions, transforming the classroom into a place of personalized support rather than generic instruction.Beyond the classroom, AI is revolutionizing the very fabric of academic research. Tools like AI research assistants can sift through vast databases of academic papers, identify key trends, and synthesize complex information in a fraction of the time it would take a human. This eliminates the tedious work of literature reviews and data analysis, allowing researchers to dedicate more time to formulating novel hypotheses, designing experiments, and engaging in interdisciplinary collaboration. AI is also democratizing access to complex research, enabling professors to explore new fields and tackle problems that were once prohibitively time-consuming. This shift fundamentally redefines the faculty member's role from a consumer of information to a creative orchestrator of knowledge, leveraging AI to explore uncharted intellectual territory.The true promise of AI in academia is the elevation of the human element. When routine tasks are automated, faculty can reclaim their most valuable function: fostering critical thinking, creativity, and ethical reasoning. The Socratic dialogue, the spirited debate, the one-on-one mentorship—these are the irreplaceable human interactions that AI cannot replicate. The future faculty member will be an expert not just in their subject, but in AI literacy, guiding students on how to ethically and effectively use these tools, and challenging them to go beyond what an algorithm can produce. This evolution is not about AI replacing teachers, but about AI empowering them to become more effective, innovative, and impactful educators and scholars, shaping a new generation of learners ready to navigate a world where human ingenuity and machine intelligence work in powerful, symbiotic harmony.

REFERENCES

Aithal, P. S., & Maiya, A. K. (2023). Innovations in higher education industry–Shaping the future. [IJCSBE]. *International Journal of Case Studies in Business, IT, and Education*, *7*(4), 283–311.

Deri, M. N., Zaazie, P., & Singh, A. (2024). Digital Future of the Hospitality Industry and Hospitality Education Globally. In Sharma, A. (Ed.), *International Handbook of Skill, Education, Learning, and Research Development in Tourism and Hospitality. Springer International Handbooks of Education*. Springer., DOI: 10.1007/978-981-97-4318-6_14

Flores-Chacón, E., Pacheco, A., Gonzales-Ortiz, Y., Moreno-Vega, L., del-Castillo-Palacios, F., & Perez-Rojas, E. (2023). Educational innovation: The architecture of digital technologies as a catalyst for change in university teacher training. *Scientific Reports*, *13*(1), 20991. PMID: 38017148

Garg, A., Singh, A., & Yanan, J. (2024). Exploring the Impact of Digital Detoxification on Higher Education Students' Learning. In Grima, S., Chaudhary, S., Sood, K., & Kumar, S. (Eds.), *Business Drivers in Promoting Digital Detoxification* (pp. 111–126). IGI Global Scientific Publishing., DOI: 10.4018/979-8-3693-1107-3.ch008

Lhakard, P. (2024). AI Catalyst: Revolutionizing Workforce Development-A Comprehensive Study of Intelligent Learning Systems. Asian Journal of Management. *Entrepreneurship and Social Science*, *4*(04), 331–346.

Long, K. C., Gunder, A., Robinson, B., Davis, V. L., Barth, D., Adams, T., & Ross, O. (2024). *Leading the AI Revolution: The Crucial Role of HBCUs in Steering AI Leadership*. Online Learning Consortium.

Mitrache, M. D., Spulbar, L. F., & Mitrache, L. A. (2024). The Influence of AI Technology in Stimulating Growth and Innovation in Business. *Revista de Stiinte Politice*, (81), 51–61.

Mutambik, I. (2024). The use of AI-driven automation to enhance student learning experiences in the KSA: An alternative pathway to sustainable education. *Sustainability*, *16*(14), 5970.

Nuong Deri, M., Singh, A., Zaazie, P., & Anandene, D. (2024). Leveraging Artificial Intelligence in Higher Educational Institutions: A Comprehensive Overview. *Education and Law Review*, (30). Advance online publication. DOI: 10.1344/REYD2024.30.45777

Ogunbodede, K. F., & Atchrim, I. A. (2025). Artificial Intelligence in Nigeria: A Catalyst for Economic Growth, Innovation, and Technological Advancement. *Faculty of Natural and Applied Sciences Journal of Computing and Applications*, *2*(2), 111–116.

Sharma, R., & Singh, A. (2024). Use of Digital Technology in Improving Quality Education: A Global Perspectives and Trends. In Nadda, V., Tyagi, P., Moniz Vieira, R., & Tyagi, P. (Eds.), *Implementing Sustainable Development Goals in the Service Sector* (pp. 14–26). IGI Global., DOI: 10.4018/979-8-3693-2065-5.ch002

Singh, A. (2022). Conceptual framework on Smart Learning Environment- An Indian perspective. *Journal of Education and Law*, (25). Advance online publication. DOI: 10.1344/REYD2022.25.36706

Singh, A. (2024a). The Role of Digital Transformation and Its Effects on the Education Sector. In Chakraborty, S. (Ed.), *Challenges of Globalization and Inclusivity in Academic Research* (pp. 92–99). IGI Global Scientific Publishing., DOI: 10.4018/979-8-3693-1371-8.ch007

Singh, A. (2024b). Endorsing Gamification Pedagogy for Nurturing Employability Skills in Higher Education Institutions (HEI). In Membrive, V. (Ed.), *Practices and Implementation of Gamification in Higher Education* (pp. 172–183). IGI Global Scientific Publishing., DOI: 10.4018/979-8-3693-0716-8.ch008

Singh, A. (2024c). Impact of E-learning on Student Motivation in Higher Education Institutions: An Indian Perspective. *Journal of Education and Law*, (29). Advance online publication. DOI: 10.1344/REYD2024.29.43214

Singh, A. (2024c). Students Wellbeing and Performance in Higher Education Institutions. In Aloka, P. (Ed.), *Factors Impacting Student Well-Being and Coping Tactics* (pp. 1–12). IGI Global Scientific Publishing., DOI: 10.4018/979-8-3693-8860-0.ch001

Singh, A., & Kumar, P. (2024). E-Learning Ecosystem in Higher Education Institutions: Trends and Practices. In Al Husseiny, F., & Munna, A. (Eds.), *Preparing Students for the Future Educational Paradigm* (pp. 1–18). IGI Global Scientific Publishing., DOI: 10.4018/979-8-3693-1536-1.ch001

Singh, A., & Sihmar, P. (2025). Higher Education Institution Sustainability: Role of Green Human Resource Management. In Adu-Gyamfi, M., Boateng, F., & Atiku, S. (Eds.), *Green HRM Awareness and Training in Higher Education Institutions* (pp. 1–14). IGI Global Scientific Publishing., DOI: 10.4018/979-8-3693-2956-6.ch001

Singh, A., Singh, D., & Chhikara, S. (2024). Online Learning: Challenges and Suggestions to Enhance Student Engagement in Higher Education Institutions. In Naidoo, V., & Verma, R. (Eds.), *Reshaping Entrepreneurial Education Within an Industry 4.0 Context* (pp. 59–80). IGI Global Scientific Publishing., DOI: 10.4018/979-8-3693-0409-9.ch004

Voronov, V. V., Menshikov, V. V., & Ruza, O. P. (2023). Artificial intelligence: A catalyst for entrepreneurship education in the Baltics. *Baltic Region*, *15*(3), 45–65.

Willard, J., & Hutson, J. (2024). Beyond Automation: AI as a Catalyst for New Job Creation in Software Development. International Journal Of Engineering Research And Development, 20(8).

KEY TERMS AND DEFINITIONS

Academic Innovation: The creative integration of new technologies, like AI, into academic work to improve learning outcomes, faculty efficiency, and institutional effectiveness.

Adaptive Learning Systems: AI-based platforms that dynamically adjust content and assessments based on real-time student performance and engagement.

AI-Powered Tools: Software and applications that use artificial intelligence to assist with tasks such as grading, content creation, personalized learning, or data analysis in educational settings.

Artificial Intelligence (AI): A branch of computer science that creates systems capable of performing tasks that typically require human intelligence, such as learning, problem-solving, and decision-making.

Automation: The use of technology to perform tasks with minimal human intervention, often improving efficiency and consistency in administrative and instructional processes.

Data-Driven Decision Making: The process of using data analysis and AI-generated insights to guide planning, teaching strategies, and faculty development initiatives.

Digital Pedagogy: The use of digital technologies, including AI, to enhance teaching practices, curriculum design, and student engagement.

Faculty Development: A range of activities and programs designed to enhance the teaching, research, and professional skills of academic staff.

Innovation in Education: The implementation of new methods, ideas, or tools to improve teaching, learning, and academic operations, often facilitated by emerging technologies like AI.

Personalized Learning: An instructional approach that uses data and AI to tailor educational experiences to the unique needs, pace, and learning styles of individual students.

Chapter 8
Personalized Professional Growth:
AI as a Mentor for Educators

Arun Agrawal
https://orcid.org/0000-0001-7233-6660
Institute of Technology and Management, Gwalior, India

Dhanashri Rohidas Londhe
Zeal College of Engineering and Research, Pune, India

Komal Vikrant Rajgude
https://orcid.org/0009-0004-8251-6744
Nutan Maharashtra Institute of Engineering and Technology, India

Vaibhavi Avachat
Nutan Maharashtra Institute of Engineering and Technology, India

Mukesh Kumar Tripathi
KIET Group of Institutions, Delhi, India

Brijendra Gupta
Siddhant College of Engineering, Pune, India

Deepak Gupta
https://orcid.org/0000-0003-3929-1362
Institute of Technology and Management, Gwalior, India

ABSTRACT

Professional growth is essential for educators to keep pace with evolving teaching practices and learner needs. Traditional faculty development programs often lack personalization and flexibility. This chapter explores how Artificial Intelligence (AI) can act as a mentor, offering tailored support for continuous learning and improvement. It examines AI applications such as adaptive learning platforms, real-time teaching feedback, and predictive analytics that guide educators toward targeted skill enhancement. Real-world examples highlight how institutions are using AI tools for training, performance improvement, and research support. The chapter

DOI: 10.4018/979-8-3373-4129-3.ch008

also discusses ethical considerations and the importance of balancing technology with human expertise. By embracing AI as a mentor, educators can build adaptive, future-ready skills that enhance both teaching quality and student outcomes.

1. INTRODUCTION

Educators need to continuously evolve to meet evolving teaching needs. Traditional teacher programs often lack personalization and fail to meet individual goals. Artificial intelligence can act as a mentor and provide solutions. It supports customized learning, provides timely feedback, and helps educators develop the right skills, thereby improving teaching quality and student outcomes.

1.1. Importance of Continuous Professional Growth for Educators

In today's rapidly evolving educational landscape, continuous professional growth is essential for educators to remain effective and relevant (Nisperos, 2025). Teaching is no longer limited to lectures or following a cookie-cutter lesson plan. Modern classrooms demand innovative teaching methods, digital fluency, and the ability to adapt to the diverse needs of students (Blyznyuk et al., 2025). To meet these demands, educators must view learning as a lifelong process.

Regular professional development helps teachers stay up-to-date on the latest knowledge, tools, and teaching strategies in their fields. This enables them to integrate new teaching methods, such as blended learning, project-based instruction, and digital resources, to create more engaging and effective learning experiences. This not only improves student performance but also strengthens teachers' confidence and ability to navigate changing classroom dynamics (Okumu & Opio, 2023).

Professional growth also contributes to career advancement and personal fulfillment. Educators who engage in continuous learning are more prepared to take on leadership roles, participate in research, or pursue specialized teaching areas (Fairman et al., 2022). This sense of progress fuels motivation and job satisfaction, which directly impacts the quality of education for students.

Another key aspect is inclusion. Continuous learning enables educators to develop strategies that meet the needs of students from diverse cultural, social, and academic backgrounds. By embracing new technologies and staying informed about emerging trends, teachers can ensure that every learner feels supported and valued.

Furthermore, ongoing professional development fosters collaboration. Through workshops, training programs, and peer learning communities, educators can share ideas, problem-solve together, and develop innovative solutions to classroom challenges. These networks strengthen professional connections and foster a culture of growth within institutions (Brennan & Gorman, 2023).

In a world of rapidly evolving technology, policies, and student expectations, stagnation is not an option. Continuous professional growth ensures educators not only stay relevant but also lead the future with confidence and creativity. This commitment to growth benefits teachers, their institutions, and, most importantly, the students they serve.

1.2. Limitations of Traditional Faculty Development Programs

Traditional teacher development programs have played a critical role in improving teaching practices, but they often fail to meet the evolving needs of modern educators. Their primary limitation lies in their one-size-fits-all approach. These programs often offer generic seminars or workshops that fail to address individual educators' unique skill gaps or goals.

Another issue is limited flexibility. Courses are often scheduled at fixed times and locations, making it difficult for busy educators to attend or fully engage. This rigid structure often reduces engagement and diminishes the effectiveness of training.

Traditional courses also tend to focus on theory rather than practice. Educators may acquire new knowledge, but they often struggle to effectively apply it in the classroom. The lack of follow-up or personalized feedback means that new skills are rarely reinforced or improved (Ang et al., 2021).

Furthermore, many programs lack integration with modern technology and teaching trends. As digital tools and data-driven instructional methods become increasingly crucial, traditional approaches fail to prepare educators to meet these demands.

Finally, these programs often fail to provide ongoing support. Growth is viewed as a one-time event rather than an ongoing process. Without ongoing guidance or adaptive coaching, educators miss opportunities for continuous development and effective refinement of their teaching practices.

1.3. How AI Can Act as a Mentor to Support Personalized Growth

Artificial intelligence (AI) has the potential to transform teacher development by becoming personalized mentors for educators. Unlike traditional programs, AI-powered systems can analyze educators' strengths, gaps, and preferences to create customized learning paths. This ensures teachers focus on the skills and knowledge areas most relevant to their roles and goals (Selvaraj, 2025).

AI tools can also provide real-time feedback on teaching practices (Jegede, 2024). For example, classroom analytics can highlight trends in engagement, student performance, or areas of instructional approach that require improvement. This timely insight helps educators make informed adjustments to improve teaching effectiveness.

Another advantage of AI tutoring is flexibility and convenience. Educators can learn at their own pace, using an adaptive platform that fits their schedule. This makes professional growth more tangible and doesn't interfere with their daily work (Das et al., 2025).

AI can also recommend resources and opportunities, such as courses, workshops, or research materials, tailored to educators' specific needs. By combining continuous learning with actionable insights, AI ensures that professional growth is a continuous and meaningful process.

As such, AI is more than just a tool; it's a partner, helping educators develop future-oriented skills and elevate the quality of their education.

2. THE NEED FOR PERSONALIZED PROFESSIONAL DEVELOPMENT

In today's rapidly changing educational landscape, the importance of personalized professional development (PPD) for educators cannot be overstated. Schools, colleges, and universities are undergoing a paradigm shift driven by technological innovations, evolving student needs, and the pursuit of more effective and inclusive teaching practices. While traditional teacher development programs provide a foundation for teacher growth, they often lack flexibility and personalization. This gap highlights the urgent need for a professional development model that recognizes each educator's unique challenges, goals, and background (Bitalo, 2024).

Personalized professional development goes beyond cookie-cutter workshops or rigid training programs. It focuses on creating learning opportunities tailored to educators' individual skills, teaching context, and career aspirations. This approach not only supports professional growth but also empowers teachers to adapt and innovate, resulting in a direct positive impact on student learning outcomes (Orgaer, 2024). The following chapters explore three key drivers that underscore the need for this shift: the diverse skills gap among educators, the limitations of "one-size-fits-all" training, and the growing demand for digital fluency and adaptive teaching methods.

2.1. Diverse Skill Gaps Among Educators

Educators vary widely in their academic backgrounds, teaching experience, and technological abilities. These differences create skills gaps that cannot be addressed with a single training approach (Dumont & Ready, 2023). For example, a senior professor with decades of teaching experience may struggle to integrate digital tools into classroom activities; while a younger teacher may be comfortable with technology but need guidance on classroom management, assessment design, or inclusive pedagogy.

These differences aren't limited to technical or pedagogical skills. Some educators may need support with research and publishing, while others may need leadership training to prepare for administrative or academic positions. Subject-specific skill gaps are also common. Rapid advances in disciplines like computer science, biotechnology, or data analytics often outpace curriculum delivery, forcing educators to regularly upgrade their skills to stay relevant (Opitz & Walles, 2021).

Furthermore, the diversity of the student population presents new challenges and requires specialized skills. Today, educators are tasked with teaching students with diverse cultural backgrounds, learning preferences, and technology proficiency. Personalized professional development allows teachers to focus on the specific skills needed to create inclusive classrooms, design accessible learning materials, and implement differentiated instructional strategies.

By identifying and addressing these individual skill gaps, PPD ensures every educator receives support aligned with their professional development journey. It transforms development from a standardized checklist to a meaningful, targeted process that builds confidence, competence, and innovation in students.

2.2. Challenges With One-Size-Fits-All Training

Traditional teacher development programs often adopt a one-size-fits-all approach, assuming that a single set of training activities will meet the needs of all educators. While convenient to organize, such programs often fail to achieve meaningful or sustainable results.

A key limitation is the lack of personalization. Generic seminars or workshops may cover broad topics that aren't relevant to every participant. For example, a course on basic classroom management techniques might not be very helpful to experienced educators, while an advanced course on digital tools might be overwhelming for participants still mastering the fundamentals. This mismatch often leads to lower participant engagement, reducing the effectiveness of the program.

Another challenge is limited engagement and follow-up. Most traditional training programs are delivered as short, intensive courses, leaving little room for ongoing support. Educators may emerge inspired but lack the guidance needed to implement new strategies in their classrooms. Without regular feedback or reinforcement, these ideas often die before they can be translated into improved teaching practices (Bartlett & Camba, 2024).

Logistical barriers further limit participation in one-size-fits-all programs. Fixed schedules and centralized locations make it difficult for educators to balance training with teaching, administrative, and personal responsibilities. This results in lower participation rates and missed opportunities for growth (Ellerbee, 2025).

Finally, these programs often lag behind advances in technology and teaching methods. As the education industry rapidly evolves, rigid, standardized training models can no longer keep pace with emerging trends like blended classrooms, competency-based learning, or data-driven instruction. Ultimately, educators are unable to adequately address modern challenges, widening the gap between institutional goals and classroom realities.

Personalized professional development addresses these challenges by providing flexible, adaptable, and contextually tailored learning experiences. It empowers educators to choose learning paths that meet their needs, ensuring that professional growth is actionable, relevant, and sustainable (Idowu, 2024).

2.3. Growing Demand for Digital Fluency and Adaptive Teaching Methods

The rise of educational technology has created a pressing need for digital fluency and adaptive teaching methods. Digital tools are no longer just optional extras but an integral part of modern pedagogy. From online learning platforms and interactive simulations to data-driven assessment tools, technology has revolutionized how knowledge is delivered and consumed (Ajani, 2024).

However, not all educators are equipped to navigate digital transformation. Many lack the confidence or skills necessary to effectively integrate technology into their teaching practices (Singun, 2025). For example, using learning management systems, creating multimedia content, or analyzing student performance data can be challenging for teachers with limited exposure to these tools. Without targeted training, this skills gap can lead to disparities in the quality of students' learning experiences.

In addition to technical skills, digital fluency requires critical thinking and adaptability. Educators must learn how to select appropriate tools for specific instructional objectives, evaluate their effectiveness, and adjust strategies based on student feedback and performance. This adaptability is crucial in blended learning environments, where flexibility and innovation are key to student engagement (Dumbuya, 2023).

The diverse needs of today's learners are also driving the demand for adaptive teaching methods. Students now expect more personalized and interactive learning experiences. They are accustomed to digital platforms that provide instant feedback, gamified content, and collaborative tools. Educators who lack the skills to design such experiences risk losing student interest and reducing overall teaching effectiveness.

The COVID-19 pandemic has further highlighted the importance of digital readiness. While educators already familiar with online tools were able to adapt more quickly to remote learning, others faced significant challenges in transitioning their classrooms (Perifanou et al., 2021). This experience has underscored the need for ongoing professional development to equip educators with the skills to navigate unforeseen disruptions and create resilient, technology-enabled learning environments.

Personalized professional development provides a path to building these critical skills. By tailoring learning experiences to educators' starting points, PPD ensures digital skills develop incrementally, fostering competence and confidence. It also introduces educators to adaptive teaching strategies that blend traditional methods with innovative practices to create engaging, inclusive, and future-proof classrooms.

3. AI AS A MENTOR: CORE CAPABILITIES

Artificial intelligence (AI)'s role in education is no longer limited to enhancing student learning. It's now becoming a mentor for educators, guiding their professional growth (Fitria, 2023). Through adaptive platforms, data-driven insights, and intelligent support systems, AI can help teachers improve their skills, enhance their teaching practices, and effectively manage their responsibilities (Jiménez, 2024). The following sections will explain the core capabilities of AI that make it a reliable partner for personalized professional development.

3.1. Adaptive Learning Platforms for Skill Development

Adaptive learning platforms are one of the most powerful ways AI can empower educators. These platforms analyze individual learning patterns and customize professional development paths. For example, educators looking to enhance their digital teaching can access carefully curated courses, tutorials, and assessments tailored to their current skill level and desired goals (Akavova et al., 2023).

These platforms continuously assess users' learning progress. When teachers quickly master a topic, the platform gradually advances to more complex content. If teachers struggle, the platform provides easier resources or additional practice. This ensures a balanced learning pace—neither too fast nor too slow—which reduces frustration and encourages steady student progress.

Another advantage is flexibility. Educators can access these platforms at any time, which is particularly useful for those who need to balance teaching schedules with administrative work. They can set aside small amounts of time daily or weekly for skill-building activities.

For institutions, these platforms also generate progress reports. Administrators can identify common skills gaps and plan targeted group courses. For example, if many faculty members need to learn blended instructional methods, the institution can organize targeted workshops while allowing each faculty member to continue their own independent learning.

By customizing the learning process, adaptive platforms make professional development more meaningful and efficient. Faculty can learn what they need, when they need it, without being overwhelmed by irrelevant material.

3.2. AI-Driven Feedback on Teaching Practices

Feedback is a crucial component of professional growth, but in traditional settings, it's often irregular and subjective. Artificial intelligence (AI) is changing this by providing continuous, data-driven feedback on teaching methods.

Modern classroom tools, such as AI-integrated learning management systems and classroom observation apps, can record lectures, analyze interactions, and assess engagement. For example, they can detect whether students are losing focus during a particular part of the class or whether certain topics are consistently confusing (Strielkowski et al., 2025).

AI-powered feedback highlights specific strengths and areas for improvement. Rather than offering general comments, it suggests concrete steps (Makwana, 2025). For example, if an educator spends too much time lecturing and too little time on interactive activities, the system can suggest group discussions or digital quizzes to increase engagement.

These systems also provide unbiased evaluations. While human feedback can sometimes be biased by personal opinion, AI focuses on measurable patterns, such as student response rates, question accuracy, or completion rates of digital assignments.

Furthermore, feedback is immediate. Educators no longer need to wait for annual performance reviews to identify issues. Instead, they can review weekly or monthly reports and adjust strategies in real time, improving teaching effectiveness faster.

By using AI for feedback, teachers gain access to a mentor who continuously observes, analyzes, and provides suggestions, helping them refine their teaching methods and create a better learning experience for their students.

3.3. Predictive Analytics to Identify Professional Growth Areas

Predictive analytics is another powerful AI capability that supports personalized development. It analyzes large amounts of data, such as teaching performance, student outcomes, and course evaluations, to anticipate future needs and development opportunities (Sajja et al., 2025).

For example, if student feedback indicates that learners are struggling with advanced computer science topics, predictive tools can analyze educators' teaching patterns. This might highlight issues with explaining complex concepts. Based on this insight, the platform can recommend targeted courses or training programs to strengthen learning in these areas.

Predictive analytics can also aid career planning. Educators interested in leadership positions or research opportunities can receive recommendations on the skills needed to succeed in those roles. If the system detects a global trend toward digital assessment tools, it could prompt educators to obtain certification in digital assessment methods to ensure they remain competitive and relevant (Kilag & Sasan, 2023).

Another advantage of predictive systems is their ability to identify potential challenges early. If data shows a decline in student engagement over time, the platform can alert educators before the problem impacts learning outcomes. This early warning allows teachers to take swift corrective action and avoid larger issues in the future.

By combining historical data with real-time analytics, predictive systems act like a career coach, helping educators make informed decisions throughout their careers.

3.4. Virtual AI Assistants for Time and Resource Management

Educators often juggle multiple responsibilities—preparing lessons, grading, mentoring students, attending meetings, and completing administrative tasks. This overwhelming workload leaves little time for personal development. Virtual AI assistants can help manage these tasks more efficiently, freeing up time for growth and reflection (Sajja et al., 2025).

These assistants can schedule meetings, set deadlines, and organize digital files. For example, if a teacher has multiple grading tasks to complete in a week, the assistant can prioritize them and send timely reminders.

They can also aid lesson planning by quickly accessing relevant teaching materials, the latest research, or interactive content ideas. Instead of spending hours searching, educators can simply request an assistant to generate a summary of the latest research or a compilation of useful resources on a specific topic.

For institutions, AI assistants can assist with resource allocation. If multiple faculty members request similar training, the system can suggest group sessions to optimize cost and time.

Another practical feature is language support. Educators teaching in multilingual classrooms can use AI assistants for quick translation or to create teaching materials tailored to diverse learners.

By handling repetitive tasks, virtual assistants can reduce teacher stress, allowing them to focus more on improving their teaching quality and professional skills. As reliable partners, they ensure educators can manage their time effectively and maintain a healthy balance between work and personal growth.

AI as a tutor isn't meant to replace human expertise, but rather to augment it. Adaptive learning platforms develop skills in a personalized way. AI-driven feedback provides timely, actionable insights. Predictive analytics guide educators to appropriate growth opportunities. Virtual assistants simplify routine tasks and create space for reflection and learning. Together, these features form a support system that helps educators thrive in the ever-evolving academic landscape. By embracing AI as a tutor, institutions can foster a culture of continuous, personalized professional development. This approach not only improves the quality of instruction but also enhances student outcomes, ensuring that education keeps pace with the demands of our dynamic, technology-driven world.

4. APPLICATIONS IN FACULTY GROWTH

Artificial intelligence is transforming how educators develop skills, manage workloads, and engage in research. From identifying areas for improvement to providing real-time classroom insights, AI empowers teachers to grow in flexible and personalized ways. The following applications highlight how AI supports skill development, continuous learning, classroom improvement, and research contributions.

4.1 Skill Assessment and Gap Analysis

Understanding one's strengths and weaknesses is the first step in any growth journey. AI-powered assessment platforms help educators track their professional competence in a structured manner. These platforms collect data from multiple sources, including student evaluations, peer reviews, and self-assessments (Kanthimathi et al., 2025). By analyzing this data, AI can generate a clear picture of skill gaps, helping teachers focus on those that require attention.

For example, educators may discover that their digital content creation skills are weaker than their classroom teaching skills. Based on this insight, the platform can recommend resources such as targeted workshops or online tutorials. This approach reduces guesswork and ensures that every step taken is aligned with measurable improvement.

As educators complete new training programs or earn certifications, the skills assessment tool updates in real time. This dynamic analysis helps teachers stay on track and continuously measure learning progress. Educators can see clear growth patterns over time, motivating them and building confidence. Institutions also benefit by gaining a deeper understanding of collective skills gaps, enabling them to design practical and cost-effective collective training programs (Maki & Kuh, 2023).

4.2 Personalized Learning Paths

One of AI's greatest advantages in teacher development is its ability to create customized learning paths. Unlike traditional training courses, which deliver the same content to every participant, AI analyzes individual needs and constructs customized microlearning modules. This makes learning both relevant and effective.

For example, an educator struggling to incorporate digital simulations into their instruction could be directed to a specific course on interactive tools. Another educator looking to explore blended instruction could take a course that includes case studies, simulations, and a certification program in blended learning technologies.

Micro-learning modules help teachers improve their skills while managing their teaching duties. These are short and focused lessons that can be completed during small breaks, such as between classes or free periods. This approach allows teachers to learn in small steps without feeling overwhelmed or neglecting their classroom work. Certified courses offered through AI-based platforms are often updated automatically to include the latest teaching methods and technology. This means teachers always have access to current information without spending time searching for resources (Shamir-Inbal & Blau, 2022). These learning tools make professional growth easier and encourage teachers to keep learning throughout their careers.

Institutions can also incorporate these learning paths into performance evaluations and promotions. When personal growth is documented and validated through certification, faculty can use it as evidence of their commitment to personal development during the evaluation or certification process.

4.3 Real-Time Feedback Systems

Feedback is one of the most powerful tools for student growth, and AI enhances this process by providing real-time insights into classroom performance. AI classroom analytics tools capture data during class via audio, video, or digital interactive platforms. This data is then analyzed to identify student strengths and areas for improvement.

For example, the system can track student engagement by analyzing how often students participate in discussions or access online course materials. It can also detect patterns, such as frequent dips in attention during specific parts of a class. Instructors can use this feedback to adjust their teaching style, improve content clarity, or implement new engagement strategies.

Real-time feedback also reduces the delay between action and improvement. Educators can make improvements immediately without waiting for end-of-term evaluations and see the effects in subsequent courses. Over time, this creates a continuous improvement cycle that steadily improves teaching quality.

Furthermore, these systems can generate visual dashboards that simplify data interpretation. Instead of dealing with complex reports, educators can see clear indicators such as "Student Engagement Score," "Clarity Index," or "Interactive Lesson Success Rate." This user-friendly approach enables teachers to easily make data-driven decisions without requiring technical expertise.

4.4 Research and Publication Support

Research is a critical component of faculty growth and institutional reputation. However, many educators struggle to keep up with the rapid pace of scholarly publishing. AI tools streamline this process by providing comprehensive support at every stage of research and publication (Khalifa & Albadawy, 2024).

4.4.1. Literature Review

Artificial intelligence platforms can scan thousands of journals and research papers in seconds and create a curated list of relevant sources. This saves significant time and ensures that teachers are using the latest and most reliable information. Some tools can even summarize the key points of each source, making it easier to identify gaps in the literature (Dergaa, 2023).

4.4.2. Data Analysis

Another area where AI's value lies is in processing large datasets. Machine learning-based tools can analyze complex data sets, identify patterns, and generate visualizations. This lowers the barrier to entry for educators who may lack a statistical background but need to draw meaningful conclusions from their research (Sarker, 2021).

4.4.3. Drafting and Editing

AI can help researchers draft and revise manuscripts more effectively. These tools can suggest improvements to the structure, ensure the manuscript follows specific journal formats, and make the writing clearer and more organized. They can also check grammar, improve readability, and detect unintentional plagiarism. This support helps authors produce high-quality manuscripts while saving time and reducing the chances of rejection (Carobene et al., 2024). By handling routine tasks, AI allows researchers to focus more on developing their ideas and improving the core content of their work.

4.4.4. Publication Strategy

Some platforms offer guidance on selecting the journal with the highest probability of acceptance based on the paper's topic and scope (Gupta et al., 2022). They also track submission deadlines and help manage revisions, thereby reducing the stress of the publishing process.

These tools reduce the time and effort required for research, allowing educators to focus on the creative and critical aspects of their work, such as formulating hypotheses and interpreting results. Over time, this will increase the impact of their research and lead to greater contributions to the academic community (Aithal & Aithal, 2023).

4.5 Institutional Benefits

The direct impact of AI applications is not only evident for individual educators, but also for institutions. With skills assessment data, management can more effectively allocate resources and invest in areas where faculty development is most needed. Personalized learning paths ensure that training budgets are used effectively, while real-time feedback systems help improve teaching outcomes and positively influence student evaluations and certification reviews.

Research support tools can improve the quality and quantity of an institution's publications, thereby strengthening its reputation in the academic community. These shared benefits create a virtuous cycle: a stronger faculty fosters institutional growth, which in turn attracts better talent and more research opportunities.

4.6 Practical Implementation Tips

To maximize the benefits of these AI applications, organizations should adopt a structured implementation approach:

1. **Start Small**

Begin by introducing one or two tools, such as a skills assessment platform or a research assistant, before moving on to more complex systems. Starting small allows teachers to become comfortable with new technology without feeling overwhelmed. This approach also makes it easier to address any issues early and gather feedback for improvement. Gradually expanding to more advanced tools ensures smoother adoption and more effective integration into teaching and research activities.

2. **Training and Support**

Provide onboarding training so that teachers clearly understand how to use these tools effectively. Without proper initial support, adoption rates may be low. Training should include step-by-step guidance, practical demonstrations, and access to ongoing help. For example, schools can organize short workshops where teachers practice using the tools in real classroom scenarios. This hands-on experience, combined with access to video tutorials or a support helpdesk, helps teachers build confidence and ensures they are more likely to use these tools regularly in their teaching.

3. **Feedback Loops**

Encourage teachers to share their experiences and suggestions for improving the system. This collaborative approach helps identify challenges and opportunities for improvement, increasing teacher engagement and participation. Regular feedback sessions, surveys, or discussion forums can provide valuable insights and ensure the tools meet teachers' needs. Involving teachers in the improvement process also creates a sense of ownership, making them more likely to use and support the system.

4. **Data Privacy and Ethics**

Develop clear guidelines for how data will be collected, stored, and used to build trust among teachers and ensure compliance with regulations. These guidelines should explain what data is collected, why it is needed, and how it will be protected. Providing transparency helps address concerns about privacy and encourages the responsible use of tools. Regular reviews of these guidelines can ensure they stay up to date with changing laws and ethical standards.

5. **Integration with Existing Systems**

Ensure that AI tools work smoothly with existing platforms, such as learning management systems or institutional databases, to avoid duplication of effort. Proper integration saves time and makes it easier for teachers to use the tools without switching between multiple systems. This can be achieved through compatibility testing and close coordination with IT teams. When tools are well integrated, they enhance workflow efficiency and provide a more cohesive experience for both teachers and students.

4.7 Future Prospects

As AI technology develops, its role in teacher development will continue to expand. Future systems may incorporate augmented reality to provide immersive training experiences or integrate predictive models to anticipate future skill needs based on industry trends. This proactive approach will keep educators ahead of the curve, ensuring their teaching and research remain relevant and effective.

Furthermore, inter-institutional collaboration can lead to shared AI platforms, reducing costs and creating larger data sets that yield more accurate insights. This joint effort can drive innovation and ensure that faculty development remains a priority across academia.

5. CASE STUDIES AND BEST PRACTICES

5.1. Examples of Institutions Integrating AI for Faculty Up skilling

Many institutions worldwide are already using AI to enhance teacher development and support continuous professional growth. For example, a leading university in Singapore implemented an adaptive learning platform for educators. This system analyzes individual teaching styles and recommends targeted training modules, resulting in over 70% of teachers reporting increased confidence in using digital tools for blended learning within a year (Kem, 2022). In India, a prominent management school uses AI-powered analytics to assess classroom interactions, providing faculty with insights to improve instruction and student engagement. Based on these insights, faculty members receive personalized training videos and peer learning suggestions tailored to their needs. In the United States, a medical school has adopted AI tools to support faculty in research writing. The platform assists with literature reviews, statistical analysis, and formatting, leading to a 25% increase in research publications. These examples highlight how AI can transform professional development across diverse educational contexts.

5.2. Measurable Improvements in Teaching Quality and Student Outcomes

The application of AI has significantly improved teacher performance and student success. In Singapore, overall student achievement improved by 15% due to more coordinated teaching strategies (Wang, 2021). Indian colleges report increased student engagement and higher teacher feedback ratings.

AI-powered real-time classroom analytics help educators identify gaps in content delivery and adjust lessons on the fly. As a result, students receive more personalized support, improving comprehension and retention. In research-focused programs, AI support reduces the time it takes faculty to publish papers, allowing them to focus more on innovative teaching and mentoring (Manoj et al., 2024).

5.3. Lessons Learned and Strategies for Effective Adoption

Successfully integrating AI into teacher development depends on strategic planning and a gradual implementation process. Institutions that begin with small-scale pilot projects and then gradually scale them up will have a smoother transition. A key lesson learned is that providing teachers with practical training to familiarize themselves with AI tools is crucial. Otherwise, adoption rates will remain low.

Another best practice is to ensure that AI platforms are tailored to the specific needs of the institution. Customization allows the system to recommend relevant content and development programs. Regular feedback sessions with faculty can also help improve the usability of these platforms. Leadership support is crucial. When management actively supports and participates in AI-driven initiatives, faculty are more likely to participate. Furthermore, combining AI insights with peer mentoring programs can create a balanced approach to professional development.

Finally, data privacy and ethical considerations must be addressed from the beginning. Institutions that clearly explain how data is collected, stored, and used can build trust among educators and encourage the adoption of new tools. Transparent policies and regular communication about data practices help reduce concerns and ensure compliance with regulations. This creates a safe and ethical environment where teachers feel confident using technology in their work.

The experiences of these institutions highlight the transformative potential of AI in teacher development. By providing customized learning paths, real-time feedback, and research-based support, AI empowers educators to enhance their skills while improving student outcomes. The key to success lies in careful planning, ongoing support, and a personalized approach to meet the unique needs of each educator.

6. ETHICAL AND PRACTICAL CONSIDERATIONS

The growing role of artificial intelligence (AI) in education and teacher development presents numerous opportunities, but also significant ethical and practical challenges. These challenges require careful consideration to ensure that AI tools are applied responsibly and fairly, while also enhancing human judgment and creativity. The following sections explore these challenges in detail across three key areas: ensuring data privacy and the ethical use of AI; avoiding overreliance on technology; and balancing automation with human input (Akgun & Greenhow, 2022).

6.1. Ensuring Data Privacy and Ethical AI Usage

Data is the foundation of AI systems. In the context of faculty development, this data often contains sensitive information, such as teaching performance metrics, class engagement data, research findings, and even personal preferences or learning styles. Ensuring the privacy, security, and ethical use of this data is one of the most important responsibilities of institutions (Khan, 2024)

First, a robust data protection policy must be in place. Institutions should adopt industry-standard encryption methods and secure storage protocols to prevent data leaks or unauthorized access. Furthermore, faculty and staff must be informed about what data is collected, how it is used, and who has access to it. This transparency builds trust and makes faculty and staff more comfortable using AI platforms.

Another key issue is adhering to legal and ethical frameworks. Many regions are implementing strict regulations, such as Europe's General Data Protection Regulation (GDPR) or similar regulations in other countries. Non-compliance can lead to legal action, reputational damage, and loss of faculty and staff trust. Therefore, educational institutions must work closely with legal and technical teams to ensure compliance at every stage of data processing (Cervi, 2022).

AI systems must also be designed to minimize bias and promote fairness. Algorithms trained on incomplete or biased datasets can inadvertently discriminate, for example by undervaluing faculty from certain departments or employing different teaching methods. Regular audits, bias detection tools, and diverse training datasets are essential to ensure fairness and equity.

Finally, ethics training and awareness-raising programs should be provided to administrators and faculty. By understanding the principles of ethical use of AI, educators can actively participate in shaping how AI tools are implemented and monitored. Ethical AI is not just about compliance; it's about fostering a culture where technology is used to empower educators, not to control or harm them.

6.2. Avoiding Over-Reliance on Technology

Artificial intelligence tools are designed to streamline processes, provide deep insights, and reduce repetitive tasks. However, there is a real risk that educators and institutions will become overly reliant on these systems. When this happens, human skills such as critical thinking, creativity, and professional judgment may begin to erode.

Overreliance can manifest in several ways. For example, if teachers rely solely on AI to evaluate their teaching effectiveness, they may overlook the importance of peer feedback or personal reflection. Similarly, if teachers blindly follow AI-generated professional development recommendations, they may miss opportunities to critically reflect on the approaches that best suit their circumstances or the unique needs of their students.

To mitigate this, institutions must promote a balanced approach. AI should be viewed as a support system, not a decision-maker. Hybrid models that combine human judgment with AI-driven insights can help maintain this balance. For example, AI can highlight trends in student engagement, but interpreting these trends and incorporating them into instructional design should still be the responsibility of educators.

Regular faculty development programs should also emphasize the importance of human input. By encouraging peer collaboration, group discussions, and workshops, institutions can foster an environment where technology complements, rather than replaces, human expertise. This approach emphasizes that while AI provides powerful tools, it is the knowledge and experience of educators that truly drives meaningful outcomes.

Another important step is to encourage critical evaluation of AI findings. Faculty should be trained to question, validate, and apply AI-generated insights, rather than simply accepting them at face value. This habit ensures that decisions are always grounded in context and aligned with institutional goals and values.

6.3. Balancing Automation with Human Judgment and Creativity

Automation is one of AI's most powerful capabilities. It can handle repetitive tasks, such as grading assignments, tracking student performance, or writing progress reports. However, while these efficiencies save educators valuable time, they also carry the risk of over-automation, where technology dominates processes, leaving little room for creativity or human judgment.

Finding the right balance starts with identifying which processes should be automated and which should be managed by humans. For example, generating a student performance dashboard can be automated, but helping struggling students should be managed by humans. This approach ensures that technology augments decision-making, rather than replacing it.

Creativity is another area where human input is irreplaceable. While AI can provide suggestions for curriculum planning or research directions, it lacks the nuanced cultural, social, and emotional understanding that educators possess. Teachers should leverage AI tools to enhance creativity—using them to brainstorm or explore new approaches—while applying their expertise to design innovative and practical solutions.

Furthermore, a balance between automation and human input enables personalization and adaptability. Every classroom, faculty member, and institution has unique needs. Human judgment ensures that AI-driven recommendations are appropriately tailored, ensuring professional development strategies remain relevant and impactful.

Institutions should also encourage collaborative environments where faculty can share their experiences using AI tools and discuss what works and what doesn't. This exchange of ideas can foster innovation and ensure that AI applications are grounded in practical applications rather than merely theoretical ones.

Finally, the ethical dimension of balancing automation with human judgment cannot be ignored. Teachers must always retain the right to override AI recommendations when they conflict with their professional experience or ethical considerations. This principle emphasizes that AI is an assistive tool, not a command system.

Ethical and practical considerations are crucial for responsibly integrating AI into teacher development. Protecting data privacy and ensuring the ethical use of AI builds trust and upholds the rights of educators. Avoiding overreliance on technology ensures that teachers maintain critical thinking skills and autonomy in their professional development. Balancing automation with human judgment and creativity allows institutions to reap the benefits of AI without losing the human qualities that make education meaningful. When these principles are carefully applied, AI becomes a powerful ally, not a controlling force. It supports teachers in their continuous improvement, empowers them to make informed decisions, and improves the overall quality of education. By combining technological efficiency with human wisdom, institutions can create a future where AI-driven innovation merges with ethical integrity and professional growth.

7. FUTURE DIRECTIONS

Artificial intelligence (AI) is reshaping how educators learn, teach, and develop their careers. As AI technologies mature, they are expected to play an even greater role in supporting faculty development and improving institutional outcomes. Future developments will focus on creating more collaborative environments, anticipating future skills needs, and redefining the role of educators in an AI-driven world. The following chapters explore three key areas: AI-enabled mentorship communities, predictive models for future skills needs, and the evolving role of educators in an AI-enhanced ecosystem.

7.1. AI-Powered Mentorship Communities for Peer Collaboration

Teacher development thrives in an environment that encourages collaboration and knowledge sharing. In the future, AI-powered mentoring communities will provide structured platforms for educators to connect, share expertise, and tackle challenges together.

AI systems can analyze teachers' profiles, skill sets, and interests and recommend personalized peer matches for mentoring or collaboration. For example, a teacher working on improving digital pedagogy could be connected with an experienced colleague or an expert in technology-assisted learning. This targeted matching ensures more productive and meaningful professional relationships.

AI can also facilitate group discussions, forums, and collaborative projects by recommending topics based on emerging trends or institutional needs. Intelligent assistants can help moderate conversations, summarize key points, and highlight actionable insights, making discussions more efficient and effective.

Another promising application is AI-driven knowledge hubs. These repositories can aggregate best practices, lesson plans, and research resources, curated by both humans and algorithms. Teachers can quickly access relevant information, saving time and fostering innovative teaching strategies.

Furthermore, such platforms can encourage cross-institutional collaboration. By connecting educators across regions or disciplines, AI can create a global community of mentors sharing diverse perspectives. This not only fosters individual growth but also promotes collective innovation in teaching and research practices.

The result is a more dynamic and connected academic ecosystem where instruction is continuous, data-driven, and accessible, ensuring educators are never isolated in their growth.

7.2. Predictive Modeling for Future Skill Requirements

As technology and societal demands continue to evolve, the skills educators will need will also evolve. AI-powered predictive models will play a key role in anticipating these skill needs, helping institutions prepare teachers for the future of education.

By analyzing data from labor market trends, industry reports, curriculum changes, and student feedback, AI models can identify emerging competencies that educators need to develop. For example, if data shows a growing demand for data analytics in engineering education, a predictive system can flag this need and recommend targeted training programs.

These insights will enable institutions to design proactive professional development programs rather than reacting to skills gaps after they emerge. Faculty will benefit from early access to customized resources, workshops, and microlearning modules, allowing them to stay ahead of the curve.

Predictive models can also assist with institutional planning. Administrators can use AI-generated reports to effectively allocate resources, prioritize training programs, and set long-term goals for teacher skills development. This ensures that teaching practices remain current and aligned with global trends.

Furthermore, predictive tools can help educators personalize their development paths. For example, an AI system might recommend advanced certifications in AI ethics or educational virtual reality based on predicted trends in digital education. By staying aligned with future needs, educators can remain relevant and adaptable in a rapidly changing academic landscape.

Ultimately, predictive models will serve as a strategic compass, guiding institutions and individuals to anticipate change rather than simply react to it. This proactive approach ensures that teachers' skills continue to align with the demands of the evolving education landscape.

7.3. The Evolving Role of Educators in an AI-Augmented Learning Ecosystem

As AI becomes more integrated with the academic ecosystem, the role of educators will shift from traditional knowledge disseminators to guides, mentors, and innovators. AI doesn't replace educators; it empowers them, allowing them to focus more on people-centered teaching, which technology can't replace.

In the classroom, AI will handle routine and time-consuming tasks such as grading, scheduling, and administrative reporting. This automation will free up teachers to spend more time on more meaningful interactions with students, such as mentoring, guiding research, or providing emotional and academic support.

Furthermore, educators will increasingly be required to interpret and act on insights generated by AI. For example, when predictive analytics identifies students at risk for learning difficulties, teachers will lead the development of personalized intervention strategies. This synergy between human judgment and AI data ensures that students receive balanced, compassionate, and effective support.

This evolving role also requires educators to actively learn. To thrive in an AI-driven ecosystem, teachers must develop digital literacy, data interpretation, and the ethical use of AI. Institutions will play a crucial role by providing training programs and fostering a culture of adaptability and innovation.

In research, AI will assist with literature reviews, data analysis, and even drafting publications, allowing teachers to focus on critical thinking and creativity. Educators can not only use AI tools but also refine these systems by providing valuable feedback based on real classroom experience.

Importantly, the human dimensions of education—empathy, ethics, and contextual understanding—will remain irreplaceable. Students will continue to rely on educators for guidance, motivation, and mentoring, reinforcing the idea that AI is a partner, not a replacement.

This shift also opens the door to new roles and opportunities. Educators can take on roles such as AI learning strategists, digital education experts, or interdisciplinary researchers, expanding their impact beyond traditional teaching roles.

Thus, the classroom of the future will no longer be AI-led but AI-augmented, with technology augmenting human expertise to provide a more personalized, engaging, and effective learning experience.

8. CONCLUSION

The use of AI in teacher professional development is changing how educators learn, adapt, and grow. AI is no longer just a tool; it acts as a guide and partner, helping teachers improve through personalized learning paths, real-time feedback, and by identifying skill gaps. This support helps teachers enhance their teaching methods and encourages innovation and research.

For AI to be effective, it must be used ethically and responsibly. Protecting data privacy, being transparent, and avoiding complete dependence on automated systems are key to building trust. AI should support, not replace, the human creativity, empathy, and judgment that are vital in education.

Looking ahead, institutions need to create AI-driven mentoring communities, use predictive tools to understand future skill needs, and redefine the educator's role in AI-supported learning environments. These steps will help teachers stay relevant and adaptable in a fast-changing education system.

In short, AI can make professional development more adaptive, personalized, and meaningful. By combining innovation with strong ethical values, institutions can prepare educators not only for the future but also to lead it.

REFERENCES

Aithal, P. S., & Aithal, S. (2023). Application of ChatGPT in higher education and research–A futuristic analysis. [IJAEML]. *International Journal of Applied Engineering and Management Letters*, *7*(3), 168–194.

Ajani, O. A. (2024). Enhancing pre-service teacher education: Crafting a technology-responsive curriculum for modern classrooms and adaptive learners. *Research in Educational Policy and Management*, *6*(2), 209–229.

Akavova, A., Temirkhanova, Z., & Lorsanova, Z. (2023). Adaptive learning and artificial intelligence in the educational space. In *E3S Web of Conferences* (Vol. 451, p. 06011). EDP Sciences.

Akgun, S., & Greenhow, C. (2022). Artificial intelligence in education: Addressing ethical challenges in K-12 settings. *AI and Ethics*, *2*(3), 431–440. PMID: 34790956

Ang, K. C., Afzal, F., & Crawford, L. H. (2021). Transitioning from passive to active learning: Preparing future project leaders. *Project Leadership and Society*, *2*, 100016.

Bartlett, K. A., & Camba, J. D. (2024). Generative artificial intelligence in product design education: Navigating concerns of originality and ethics.

Bitalo, J. U. (2024). The evolution of teacher professional development: Integrating digital and traditional approaches.

Blyznyuk, O., Kachak, T., Blyznyuk, T., & Nazaruk, S. K. (2025). Quality education in the digital age: Adapting to 21st century primary school learners. *Journal of Vasyl Stefanyk Precarpathian National University*, *12*(1), 58–68.

Brennan, A., & Gorman, A. (2023). Leading transformative professional learning for inclusion across the teacher education continuum: Lessons from online and on-site learning communities. *Professional Development in Education*, *49*(6), 1117–1130.

Carobene, A., Padoan, A., Cabitza, F., Banfi, G., & Plebani, M. (2024). Rising adoption of artificial intelligence in scientific publishing: Evaluating the role, risks, and ethical implications in paper drafting and review process. [CCLM]. *Clinical Chemistry and Laboratory Medicine*, *62*(5), 835–843. PMID: 38019961

Cervi, G. V. (2022). Why and how does the EU rule global digital policy: An empirical analysis of EU regulatory influence in data protection laws. *Digital Society : Ethics, Socio-Legal and Governance of Digital Technology*, *1*(2), 18.

Das, S., Mutsuddi, I., & Ray, N. (2025). Artificial intelligence in adaptive education: A transformative approach. In *Advancing adaptive education: Technological innovations for disability support* (pp. 21–50). IGI Global Scientific Publishing.

Dergaa, I. (2023). Artificial intelligence and promoting open access in academic publishing. *La Tunisie Medicale*, *101*(6), 533–536. PMID: 38372545

. Dumbuya, E. (2023). Developing a framework for revising the curriculum to incorporate future skills such as digital literacy, critical thinking, and adaptability.

Dumont, H., & Ready, D. D. (2023). On the promise of personalized learning for educational equity. *NPJ Science of Learning*, *8*(1), 26. PMID: 37542046

Ellerbee, K. D. (2025). Barriers to the implementation of learner-centered instruction in the Northeastern United States (Doctoral dissertation, Walden University).

Fairman, J. C., Smith, D. J., Pullen, P. C., & Lebel, S. J. (2022). The challenge of keeping teacher professional development relevant. In *Leadership for professional learning* (pp. 251–263). Routledge.

Fitria, T. N. (2023). The use of artificial intelligence in education (AIED): Can AI replace the teacher's role? *Epigram*, *20*(2), 165–187.

Gupta, S., Modgil, S., Bhattacharyya, S., & Bose, I. (2022). Artificial intelligence for decision support systems in the field of operations research: Review and future scope of research. *Annals of Operations Research*, *308*(1), 215–274.

Idowu, E. (2024). Personalized learning: Tailoring instruction to individual student needs.

Jegede, O. O. (2024). Artificial intelligence and English language learning: Exploring the roles of AI-driven tools in personalizing learning and providing instant feedback. *Universal Library of Languages and Literatures, 1*(2).

Jiménez, A. F. (2024). Integration of AI helping teachers in traditional teaching roles. *European Public & Social Innovation Review*, *9*, 1–17.

Kanthimathi, S., Nanda, P., Venkatraman, S., Renganayagan, V., & Eswaran, S. (2025). Transforming education through AI-powered personalized assessment models. In *Adopting Artificial Intelligence Tools in Higher Education* (pp. 136–154). CRC Press.

Kem, D. (2022). Personalised and adaptive learning: Emerging learning platforms in the era of digital and smart learning. *International Journal of Social Science and Human Research*, *5*(2), 385–391.

Khalifa, M., & Albadawy, M. (2024). Using artificial intelligence in academic writing and research: An essential productivity tool. *Computer Methods and Programs in Biomedicine Update*, *5*, 100145.

Khan, W. N. (2024). Ethical challenges of AI in education: Balancing innovation with data privacy. *AI EDIFY Journal*, *1*(1), 1–13.

Kilag, O. K. T., & Sasan, J. M. (2023). Unpacking the role of instructional leadership in teacher professional development. *Advanced Qualitative Research*, *1*(1), 63–73.

Maki, P. L., & Kuh, G. D. (2023). *Real-time student assessment: Meeting the imperative for improved time to degree, closing the opportunity gap, and assuring student competencies for 21st-century needs*. Routledge.

Makwana, V. (2025). A comparative analysis of AI-powered and teacher-led feedback: Investigating student perceptions and writing performance. *Journal of English Language Teaching*, *67*(1), 3–12.

Manoj, D., Dutt, A., & Saratha, B. (2024). AI-powered adaptive learning systems: Revolutionizing classroom education. *Advancing Knowledge from Multidisciplinary Perspective Engineering, Technology and Management*, 101.

Nisperos, J. N. S. (2025). Emerging needs of teacher education instructors in today's rapidly evolving educational landscape. *Balkan & Near Eastern Journal of Social Sciences (BNEJSS)*, *11*(1).

Okumu, J. B., & Opio, G. (2023). Continuous professional development and teachers improved pedagogical skills in secondary schools in Gulu City.

Opitz, I., & Walles, T. (2021). How to prepare for academic leadership: Scientific training curriculum. *Journal of Thoracic Disease*, *13*(3), 2068. PMID: 33841996

Orgaer, B. (2024). Designing for change: Implementing teacher-centric professional development.

Perifanou, M. A., Economides, A. A., & Tzafilkou, K. (2021). Teachers' digital skills readiness during COVID-19 pandemic. [iJET]. *International Journal of Emerging Technologies in Learning*.

Sajja, R., Sermet, Y., Cwiertny, D., & Demir, I. (2025). Integrating AI and learning analytics for data-driven pedagogical decisions and personalized interventions in education. *Technology, Knowledge and Learning*, 1-31.

Sarker, I. H. (2021). Machine learning: Algorithms, real-world applications and research directions. *SN Computer Science*, *2*(3), 160. PMID: 33778771

Selvaraj, V. (2025). Future of education in the artificial intelligence era: Redefining the roles of teachers in artificial intelligence enhanced education. In *Conference Monograph*.

Shamir-Inbal, T., & Blau, I. (2022). Micro-learning in designing professional development for ICT teacher leaders: The role of self-regulation and perceived learning. *Professional Development in Education*, *48*(5), 734–750.

Singun, A. J. (2025). Unveiling the barriers to digital transformation in higher education institutions: A systematic literature review. *Discover Education*, *4*(1), 37.

Strielkowski, W., Grebennikova, V., Lisovskiy, A., Rakhimova, G., & Vasileva, T. (2025). AI-driven adaptive learning for sustainable educational transformation. *Sustainable Development*, *33*(2), 1921–1947.

Wang, L. Y. (2021). Levelling up academically low-performing students in student-centric education in Singapore: Global trend, local policies and future directions. *Educational Review*, *73*(3), 374–390.

Chapter 9
Co-Creating the Future: Collaborative Strategies for Integrating AI Into Faculty Development Initiatives

Pritesh Pradeep Somani
https://orcid.org/0000-0002-0039-0358
Balaji Institute of International Business, Sri Balaji University, Pune, India

Prachi Wani
https://orcid.org/0000-0003-1274-9660
Balaji Institute of Management and Human Resource Development, Sri Balaji University, Pune, India

Vishwanathan Hariharan Iyer
https://orcid.org/0009-0007-1469-2369
Balaji Institute of International Business, Sri Balaji University, Pune, India

Ushmita Gupta
https://orcid.org/0000-0002-6442-1248
Balaji Institute of International Business, Sri Balaji University, Pune, India

ABSTRACT

This chapter explores the collaborative integration of Artificial Intelligence (AI) into faculty development programs across higher education. Grounded in a conceptual framework supported by six interconnected variables—including technological readiness, pedagogical alignment, and institutional support—it highlights how AI can transform teaching, research, and learning environments when implemented through co-creative strategies. The chapter presents qualitative literature reviews and verified global and Indian case studies, demonstrating how institutions have

DOI: 10.4018/979-8-3373-4129-3.ch009

effectively empowered educators to adopt AI tools in ways that are contextually relevant, ethical, and pedagogically sound. Emphasizing the importance of faculty-technologist collaboration, leadership engagement, and continuous learning ecosystems, this study contributes to both academic discourse and institutional practice. It holds relevance for policymakers, educators, and administrators seeking sustainable AI adoption in academia, with the broader goal of creating a digitally competent and innovative set-up ahead.

Background of the Study

Artificial intelligence (A.I.) is no longer an experimental part of university life; it is becoming the core manner through which information is created, shared, and experienced across the entire academic domain. A few studies across the domain have demonstrated that the depth and quality of research work on use of A.I. in education has grown exponentially since 2020. This means that higher education has entered a time of faster, data-driven innovation (Crompton & Burke, 2023). A.I. tools are currently used for everything right from preparing lectures to even generating full-fledged reports. These techniques range from adaptive content engines to large-language-model (L.L.M.) tutors. It must be understood that technology alone cannot change learning environments; it will require the support of every member of the academic community who plan, teach, and change the curriculum to match the requirement of industry thereby helping the growth and betterment of ultimate stakeholders i.e. the students at large.

The COVID-19 pandemic proved a 360 degree change forcing the educators to take entire learning online thereby offering a sudden shift towards teaching learning process, showcasing knowledge of faculty members to understand and effectively implement usage of technology as there was no face-to-face classroom contact and everything went online. When the teaching fraternity across the globe had to teach from home, they showcased that their digital competence, trust in their teaching methods, and willingness to try out new tools varied widely (Bond et al., 2021). The best of the academic institutions, schools, colleges, university across the globe were the ones that combined quick-response professional development programs with the rollout of new technology. This proved to be a good example stating investments on faculty skills upgradation is essential for any effective implementation of technology across any part of the globe.

In order to implement effective usage of AI across teaching domain came up with new set of problems which the regular set of training offered may not be able to solve. Modern A.I. systems are self-learning based, probabilistic, and often hard to understand, which is different from old outdated technology. So, faculty members need not only have access to operational fluency i.e., how to give effective prompt, fine-tune, and evaluate outputs but also interpretive power in other words the ability to investigate underlying data sets, find possible biases, and make sure that algorithmic recommendations are in line with disciplinary ethics. International policy analyses have started to see this wider range of skills as part of a bigger "responsible A.I." agenda. This agenda requires universities to promote collaboration between different groups and open design procedures (OECD, 2023). Co-creation has come up as a possible solution. This definition of co-creation includes faculty members, technology specialist, students, and administrators working together in a systematic way to design, test, and improve different A.I. based applications. This changes the role of teachers from passive delivery instructor to an actual trainer leading towards building digital transformation. In a study at a UK based university, teachers who helped design a generative-AI writing assistant said they were better at teaching, had students think more critically about the model's limitations, and saw measurable improvements in student learning compared to teachers who used off-the-shelf solutions (Webster et al., 2024). These results support the work of organisational theorists who say that participatory innovation increases both individual buy-in and institutional resilience (Katsamakas et al., 2024).

Still, strategic leadership has a big and key role to play is important. A study based on AI initiatives at different colleges and universities found that they failed when faculty feedback was sought too late or when there were not enough resources for redesigning the methodology (Khairullah et al., 2025). On the other hand, projects that were based on explicit governance frameworks spelt out data-ethics principles, protections for workloads, and reward schemes for pedagogical experimentation were the most likely to persist and grow.

Co-creation further has the ability to reduce the chances of getting unfair deals. Large language models that are mostly trained on English-language data may not work as well in multilingual classrooms. Predictive-analytics dashboards can show how biassed graduation rates have been in the past. Design teams can find contextual differences that generic vendor solutions miss by including a variety of faculty viewpoints, especially from fields and areas that are not well represented. Research on systems thinking backs this up by saying that include more people in the process makes the interventions stronger (Katsamakas et al., 2024).

The role of faculty members across universities is witnessing a massive change thereby not keeping the role restricted to only teaching based assignments. At the same time roles like "Prompt engineers," "AI-ethics stewards," and "learning-data translators" are some of the new job names in professional development catalogues. The available literature in the domain emphasised that academicians who use AI to make simulations, practical concepts-based teaching or peer review-based assessment tend to rethink how they teach instead of just automating the job which they are already doing (Mollick & Mollick, 2024). Co-creation frameworks want to make this kind of creative work a part of the system. Still, there are different problems faced like well documented incentive system, uneven infrastructure, and a lack of time towards executing new academic projects (Bond et al., 2021). In addition, the rapid paced commercialisation of AI has made it even hard to use "shiny" solutions without enough testing. To deal with these problems, we need to move from one-time workshops to cyclical, research-based growth pathways. These routes combine hands-on experimentation with organised reflection and evidence collection.

In short, the future of A.I. in higher education will depend more on the academic communities that use it than on new technologies. A research-based approach to faculty development that involves everyone working together to improve skills, taking it as a moral responsibility, and teaching methods is the best way to move forward. The present chapter is an attempt to look at how to think about, put into action, and assess this kind of approach to make sure that AI is a force for good, high-quality learning for everyone instead as a source for coming up with challenges towards working.

INTRODUCTION

Artificial Intelligence (AI) is changing the way academicians are delivering their lectures, the way colleges and universities are operating and the whole learning experience in higher education. Adaptive learning systems, intelligent tutoring, and predictive analytics are all apt examples of A.I. technology that has made education more personalised, keeping students more interested, and to top it all allowing the educational institutions run more smoothly. However, for AI to be successfully used in higher education, faculty members must be ready, have the right ideas about it, and be actively involved. They are the ones who will be making these new technologies work in an effective manner.

Recent research article has showcased the importance of viewpoints kept forward by academicians to integrate AI into teaching and learning in a meaningful way. Mah and Groß (2024) undertook an study of 122 faculty members to find out how confident they were in their AI skills, what they thought were the pros and cons of AI, and what they needed to do to improve their careers. The results showed that faculty members see the potential of AI to improve teaching efficiency and promote educational equity, but they also have worries about ethics, data protection, and their own lack of technical competence. The survey found four different types of faculty members: optimistic, critical, critically reflective, and neutral. This shows that there are a wide range of opinions about using AI in higher education.

It is also clear that academics need extensive professional development programs that are suited to their needs. Gašević et al. (2023) stress that teachers need to have the right knowledge and abilities to use AI technologies for them to be effectively integrated into the curriculum. Professional development programs should include not only technical training but also discussions of ethical issues, teaching methods, and ways to use AI tools to get students more involved.

The rapid progress of AI technology, as seen in the rise of generative AI tools like ChatGPT, has made it even more important for academicians to be involved and flexible. McDonald et al. (2024) looked at the policies of 116 U.S. universities and found that while many colleges are encouraging the use of generative AI, there is a strong need for clear rules and support systems to help teachers use these tools in their classrooms. The study also raises questions about the moral use of AI and the extra work it may need of teachers to keep changing how they teach as technology changes. Co-creation looks like a good way to help AI be used in higher education in a responsible and useful way. Co-creation makes sure that AI tools are pedagogically sound, ethically responsible, and meet the needs of the educational community by involving academics, students, administrators, and other stakeholders in the design and deployment of these tools. These kinds of interactive methods not only make AI applications more useful and relevant, but they also encourage a culture of shared accountability and constant progress.

Even while co-creation has known benefits, it is still not widely used in colleges and universities. Faculty members cannot take part in co-creative processes because of things like not having enough time, not getting enough support from their institutions, and not having enough training chances. To deal with these problems, we need strategic leadership, money for professional development, and enabling infrastructures that give teachers the power to take part in the co-creation of AI-enhanced teaching methods.

The current study is an attempt to investigate the role of faculty as they play such an important role in integrating AI technology and co-creation could help with this process. The study makes an attempt to address the research question towards coming up with the future course of action.

What are the best ways to use co-creation approaches to help teachers use AI technologies in higher education teaching and learning?

Objectives of the Study

1. To understand the role of educators in effective implementation of Artificial intelligence across teaching purpose.
2. To understand and implement different A.I. initiatives as game changers for betterment of student community.

REVIEW OF LITERATURE

Artificial Intelligence (AI) has brought about big changes in several areas, including higher education. AI technology like machine learning algorithms, natural language processing, and predictive analytics give teachers and students new ways to improve how they teach and learn respectively, as well as make administrative tasks easier. To ensure successful implementation of AI into higher education, several things need to happen, such as faculty preparedness, institutional support, professional development, and co-creation processes. The present section of Review of literature explores deep into these factors and look out for more details to figure out how they work together to make it appropriate for AI to be used in teaching and learning.

Technological Readiness and AI Infrastructure (TRAI)

Technological readiness—a concept rooted in innovation diffusion theory—encompasses not only physical infrastructure but also governance, workforce capability, and organizational strategy, which together support effective AI integration in faculty development. In higher education, TRAI comprises essential components such as hardware, software, robust network connectivity, reliable IT support systems, secure data environments, and aligned institutional policies.

Educause & AWS (2025), in their detailed work on "Generative AI Readiness Assessment" identifies three strategic pillars—technology/infrastructure leadership/governance, and academic innovation—that influence an institution's ability to deploy AI-driven faculty tools such as chatbots, analytics dashboards, or automated tutoring systems (Educause & AWS, 2025) Yet, Inside Higher Ed. reported that only 9% of U.S. university CTOs consider their institutions truly prepared for AI, citing fragmented policy frameworks and insufficient strategic direction as primary obstacles (Inside Higher Ed., 2024) . Research in the domain also signals the significance of having full-fledged familiarity with the tools and techniques among faculty members in the higher education domain. Salman et al. (2025) utilized the Technology Readiness Index 2.0 to show that, while awareness of AI tools was high, only approximately 52% of academic staff were actively using them, largely due to concerns about data privacy, intellectual property rights, and ethical use (Salman et al., 2025) A parallel Q-methodology study in Qatar similarly found that faculty readiness reflects a complex mix of technical aptitude and ethical orientation based on local cultural factors (Qatar Q-study, 2024) .

Infrastructure disparities persist globally. A study based on review of universities in Northern Nigeria highlighted major deficits in computing resources, data systems, and broadband access that severely limit AI adoption in faculty programs (Nigeria

Review, 2024) Addressing this digital divide demands targeted investment in hardware, connectivity, and dedicated training platforms.

Institutional leadership and governance frameworks are equally critical. Educause reinforces that mature governance covering data ethics, usage guidelines, and accountability enables institutions to leverage public cloud services and partner effectively with industry while maintaining transparency and trust. Barriers include heightened concerns about data privacy and security, which hamper deployment despite tool availability (Salman et al., 2025). Meanwhile, skill gaps in AI, such as prompt engineering and workflow automation, constrains with the IT departments. Nevertheless, cloud-based partnerships—especially with platforms like AWS—offer scalable and secure infrastructure solutions for institutions lacking in-house capacity (Educause & AWS, 2025). To cite an example from King Faisal University in Saudi Arabia, where a study with over 460 faculty participants demonstrated that access to AI tools, familiarity with digital platforms, and infrastructural readiness were significant predictors of readiness to implement AI-based teaching and learning innovations (King Faisal University, 2024).

In summary, TRAI is a multifaceted construct involving not just physical and digital assets but also organizational strategy, human capacity, and ethical governance. Institutions must build entire ecosystems—not just provision hardware—to enable sustainable, equitable, and strategically aligned integration of AI within faculty development initiatives.

Faculty Attitude and AI Self-Efficacy (FASE)

Faculty attitude toward AI, combined with their self-efficacy the belief in one's own ability to use AI tools emerges as a pivotal determinant in whether AI-enhanced faculty development efforts succeed. Drawing from both Technology Acceptance Model (TAM) and Social Cognitive Theory, this variable examined internal cognitive drivers such as perceived usefulness, ease of use, trust, and confidence, along with external social reinforcements that shape faculty motivation and behaviour. Rooted in Bandura's (1977) Social Cognitive Theory, self-efficacy refers to one's confidence in performing a task. In the AI context, it captures faculty's belief in their capacity to enact generative AI tools effectively in teaching, assessment, and development activities. Mah and Groß's (2024) study of 122 higher-ed faculty in Europe identified four profiles—"optimistic," "critical," "critically-reflected," and "neutral"—and showed that self-efficacy significantly predicted AI use among the optimistic cohort (Mah & Groß, 2024). Similarly, research on teachers of English L2 in primary schools indicated that professional development fostering mastery experiences significantly improved self-efficacy in AI integration (Wahyuningsih & Afandi, 2024). Intrinsic motivation personal interest and professional autonomy mediates the relationship between attitude and self-efficacy (Alper Aytaç et al., 2024) Teachers with high intrinsic motivation view AI tools as aligned with their growth and professional goals. However, even confident faculty might resist AI without seeing clear alignment with pedagogical practices or institutional goals, reinforcing the importance of both instrumental and intrinsic value. The role of faculty is a towards successful and effective implementation of such initiatives as it will help in making Faculty Development Program (FDP) successful. Once faculty members are able to implement these set of strategies in effective manner the training will be successful and it will make the role of trainers i.e. the faculty more clear and effective.

Institutional Support & Policy Alignment (ISPA)

Institutional support and policy alignment represent a critical organizational context for effective AI integration in faculty development. Comprising governance structures, resourcing, strategic vision, guidelines, and dedicated units, ISPA ensures that individual and technological capacities are effectively channelled into sustainable institutional practices. Institution-wide governance is essential for coherent AI integration. Educause's 2024 Action Plan recommends establishing dedicated AI oversight committees—beyond IT—to monitor usage, audit compliance, and ensure ethical governancE. Complementing this, McDonald et al. (2024) found that over 60% of U.S. universities encourage GenAI use through formal guidance, and 50% provide detailed curriculum resources aligned with academic integrity. These structures signal a proactive stance toward aligning AI initiatives with institutional goals and risk management. Sutedjo et al. (2025) analysed 15 universities and found that 30% of AI resource efforts in teaching and ethics were managed by Provost Offices, and 27% by CTLs. Additionally, policy frameworks for tenure, promotion, and evaluation were identified as tools for legitimizing AI engagement. This alignment embeds AI into faculty reward structures and institutional culture. High-quality policy frameworks are essential, especially to manage academic integrity concerns. McDonald et al. (2024) and Jin et al. (2024) show that 40–50% of institutions provide policies guiding ethical AI use and designing assessments resistant to misuse, such frameworks help faculty design AI-renewed assessments while mitigating risks related to cheating or bias. Ghimire & Edwards (2024) highlight persistent policy gaps, particularly regarding privacy, fairness, and accessibility. Equity considerations are another critical ISPA dimension. Educause advises that AI access and training must be distributed equitably across departments, preventing exacerbation of resource disparities. Jin et al. (2024) recommend multi-institutional policy frameworks to support lower-resourced institutions and facilitate broader standardization. A concerted policy environment across institutions can create economies of scale and shared best practices.

Collaborative Learning Ecosystems (CLE)

Collaborative learning ecosystems (CLE) are central to co-creating AI-infused faculty development. Rooted in theories of social constructivism, distributed cognition, and participatory design, CLEs encompass the networks, practices, and structures enabling faculty to collaboratively engage with AI, share knowledge, and generate new pedagogical insights through co-design and peer learning. Co-creation involves collaborative innovation toward shared goals, emphasizing reciprocity and mutual contribution among faculty, students, and AI tools (Campbell-Rogers, 2024). A conceptual review of co-creation in higher education positions dialogue, positioning, voice, and agency as core to these practices. Dialogue acts as the engine of co-creation: faculty and stakeholders negotiate roles and co-develop curriculum, policy, and pedagogies through sustained interaction loops. CLEs extend beyond human collaboration to include AI agents as active participants. The "CLAIS" model—designed for pre-service teachers—demonstrates how humans and AI speakers can collaboratively construct knowledge via jigsaw activities, significantly strengthening pedagogical knowledge. More broadly, Wong and colleagues (2021) adopted a distributed cognition perspective to analyse "student–AI–teacher" systems, positioning AI as a peer agent within a triadic learning ecosystem.

Pedagogical Alignment and Relevance (PAR)

The successful integration of AI into faculty development hinges on its pedagogical alignment, ensuring the technology supports desired learning objectives, instructional design models, and domain-specific practices. Aligning AI with pedagogy activates faculty agency and enriches teaching relevance. The Constructive Alignment model (Biggs, 1996) calls for harmony between learning outcomes, teaching methods, and assessment tools. AI tools, when thoughtfully integrated, can reinforce this framework. The AI-led consortium guidelines argue that aligning AI with core learning outcomes, and designing assessments that are AI-aware, enables curricular coherence and critical thinking enhancement. AI's generative capabilities offer opportunities to scaffold learners' higher-order thinking. AI can facilitate critical evaluation of sources, support problem-solving, and encourage reflective practice. For instance, the development of AI-resistant assessments—a processes-focused approach—allows faculty to integrate generative AI without compromising academic integrity.

Change Management & Leadership Engagement (CMLE)

Effective integration of AI into faculty development depends heavily on strategic leadership and the management of organizational change. CMLE guides the transformation process, shapes institutional attitudes toward AI, addresses resistance, and steers cultural, moral, technical, and resource alignment.

CONCEPTUAL FRAMEWORK

Figure 1. Conceptual framework

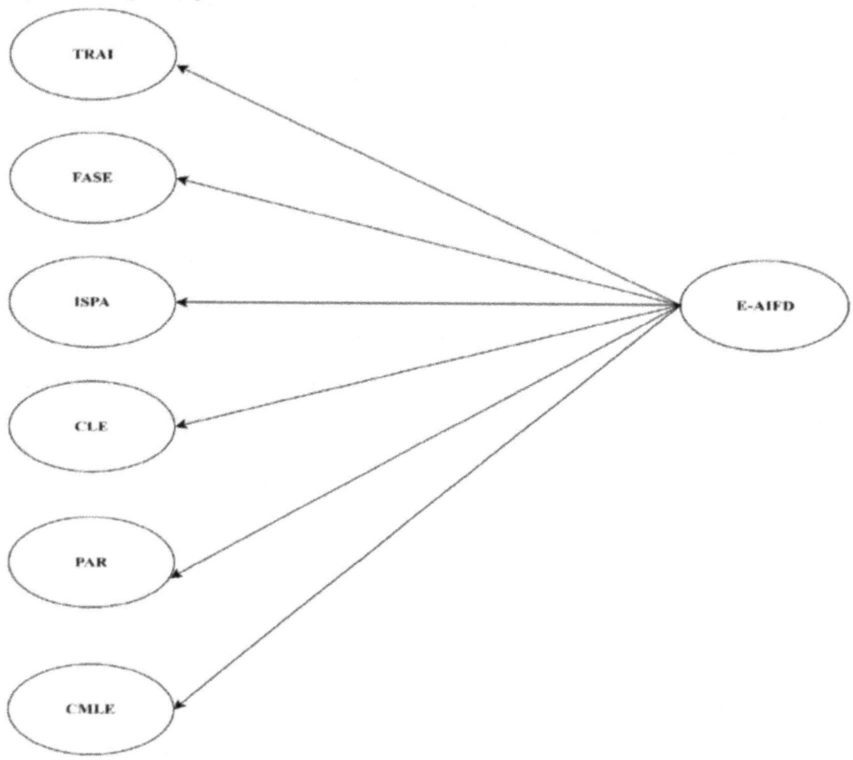

The conceptual model drafted in the form of Figure 1 tries to present integration of Artificial Intelligence into faculty development through six key interconnected factors. At the heart of the model is the dependent variable the Effectiveness of AI-Integrated Faculty Development (E-AIFD). This outcome is shaped by different independent variables namely Technological Readiness for AI (TRAI), which reflects the availability of necessary digital infrastructure. Faculty Attitude and AI Self-Efficacy (FASE), referring to the confidence and openness of educators to adopt AI. Institutional Support and Policy Alignment (ISPA), highlighting the role of policies, ethical standards, and administrative support in driving AI adoption. Collaborative Learning Ecosystems (CLE), which emphasize the importance of peer learning, co-creation, and shared innovation among faculty members. Pedagogical Alignment and Relevance (PAR), ensuring that AI tools are meaningfully tied to teaching goals, disciplinary contexts, and assessment standards. Change Management and Leadership Engagement (CMLE), which underscores the critical role of leadership in guiding, resourcing, and sustaining change efforts while addressing resistance. The arrows in the model demonstrate that these variables do not operate in isolation but interact dynamically to influence AI adoption outcomes. Leadership (CMLE) serves as an overarching driver that impacts every stage of the process, from technology implementation to faculty mindsets and policy alignment. Together, these interconnected elements form a comprehensive, human-centred framework that emphasizes readiness, collaboration, and purpose-driven use of AI in higher education—ensuring that technology serves pedagogy, not the other way around. The said independent variables are working as a key contributors in making the role of AI integrated Faculty development effective and full proof thereby making life of teachers simple and also allowing them to train the students in the best possible manner towards making the use of AI as a support catalyst for students and not just as a prompt replying machine.

CASE STUDIES AROUND THE WORLD

1. Georgia State University – "Pounce" AI Chatbot for Student and Faculty Support

Summary of the Case

In 2016, Georgia State University (GSU) was the first to use "Pounce," an AI-powered chatbot made in conjunction with Admit Hub (now Mainstay). The goal was to reduce "summer melt" among new students. "Summer melt" is when students are accepted to college and plan to go, but don't end up going because of problems that come up, like not knowing how to enrol or having queries that aren't answered. Pounce employs natural language processing (NLP) to provide automated solutions to students' questions about financial aid, registration, accommodation, orientation, and more via SMS.

The results were significant and were backed up by a randomised controlled experiment. Compared to the control group, GSU found that students who interacted with Pounce had 21.4% less summer melt and 3.9% more fall enrolment. In addition to enrolment, GSU made the chatbot useful for getting students involved in major undergraduate gateway courses. In a study of an introductory political science class, students who used the chatbot were 16% more likely to get a B or above. First-generation students made the biggest progress, with their average grades going up by 11 points (Georgia State University, 2022).

The faculty played a big part in this success. Instead, then only using AI for administrative tasks, GSU encouraged teachers and technologists to work together to create the chatbot's messaging bank, find the right interventions, and make sure that it was ethical. Faculty watched what the chatbot said and gave feedback to make it more accurate, appropriate, and useful for teaching. Also, the iterative training approach incorporated input from professors to change the content in real time based on how students acted and how schoolwork changes with the seasons. This method is an example of a faculty-involved co-creation technique that not only makes the institution more efficient but also improves student assistance and learning results through AI augmentation.

Pounce led to a 21.4% drop in summer melt and a roughly 4% rise in enrolment. When used in school, it helped 16% more students get a B or better (Georgia State University, 2022). Faculty members were very important in helping to build chatbots and keep an eye on their responses. This was a real cooperation with technologists.

2. University of Toronto Rotman School – "All Day TA" AI Teaching Assistant

Summary of the Case

The Rotman School of Management at the University of Toronto debuted "All Day TA" in 2025. This generative AI-powered teaching assistant was made to help teachers deal with the huge number of questions students ask in big classrooms. Professors Joshua Gans and Kevin Bryan directed the project, which involved 300 students in a core business analytics course over a 12-week pilot. The system, which was based on a big language model called GPT, answered more than 12,000 questions from students on things like clarifying lectures, due dates for assignments, and policy explanations.

The teaching assistant wasn't just put in the course without any background. Instead, it was built using a co-creation paradigm, in which faculty worked directly with AI developers to create prompt structures, answer criteria, course-specific training datasets, and usage regulations. The goal was to make sure that AI would improve, not hurt, the integrity of teaching. The faculty also worked closely with teaching assistants to check answers and point out any problems. The project leaders said that the assistant helped cut down on the number of emails teachers had to deal with and gave students almost quick help, which made the learning atmosphere much better.

The fact that this idea was so cheap made it stand out. The pilot cost less than $2 per student and showed that it could be used in a lot of different fields. Within a few months of its first testing, the model was used by more than 100 institutions throughout the world. Many of these institutions changed the technology to work with their own faculty-led training datasets. Rotman's example shows how AI teaching assistants may be an important part of faculty development plans. They don't replace teachers; instead, they provide them more time to mentor, grade, and come up with new ideas for the curriculum. The "All Day TA" trial answered more than 12,000 student questions and cut down on the number of emails teachers had to deal with by a lot. Over 100 schools have used it since it is cheap and can be scaled up. Faculty worked together to set ethical limits and design AI prompts.

3. Rishi Bankim Sardar College, Sundarbans (College Under Calcutta University) – AI Chatbots for Learning Enhancement (2025)

Summary of the Case

Facing a shortage of instructors for mandatory non-major subjects—such as English, Bengali, Environmental Science, and Indian Constitution—Rishi Bankim Sardar College in the Sundarbans region implemented AI-driven chatbots in February 2025 to support undergraduate students. The chatbots were customized to align with Calcutta University syllabi and were integrated into Android-based learning apps. These bots provided targeted content delivery, mock tests, doubt-clearing support, and question-pattern familiarization to first- and third-semester students (Roy, 2025). Designed and deployed by a multidisciplinary team of faculty and IT experts, the chatbots were iteratively refined based on student usage data. Feedback from students—such as "takes very less time to get a detailed overview" and helps "clear doubts and get question patterns"—underscored both faculty-led design and pedagogical alignment (Roy, 2025). This initiative provided equitable, scalable support in an underserved rural context without extensive classroom infrastructure, demonstrating effective co-creation (CLE), pedagogical relevance (PAR), and institutional responsiveness (ISPA) (Roy, 2025).

Rishi Bankim Sardar College launched AI chatbots for foundational subjects in February 2025, enabling syllabus-aligned content, mock tests, and doubt resolution via Android apps—designed collaboratively by faculty and IT teams—and reported strong student engagement (Roy, 2025).

ROLE OF FACULTY MEMBERS ACROSS THE SCALAR CHAIN

The success of AI integration into faculty development initiatives depends majorly on the active engagement and strategic involvement of a broad network of educational stakeholders—most notably, **educational developers,** who serve as the architects of pedagogical innovation and catalysts for digital transformation in higher education. Their role is foundational in ensuring that faculty are not merely consumers of AI tools but become co-creators in their pedagogical application.

Educational developers including instructional designers, teaching and learning specialists, and faculty development coordinators—act as the bridge between technology and pedagogy. They help translate AI capabilities into meaningful, curriculum-aligned practices. This involves curating AI tools suitable for different disciplines, facilitating training sessions, developing best practice guidelines, and co-designing AI-supported assessments and learning activities. These professionals also collaborate closely with faculty to ensure ethical considerations, inclusivity, and accessibility are maintained while integrating AI into teaching and research. Furthermore, they play a crucial role in building collaborative learning communities where knowledge about AI use is continuously shared and evolved.

Senior Faculty Members often act as champions or mentors in these initiatives. They bring domain expertise and institutional credibility that is vital for legitimizing and normalizing the use of AI in academic practice. Their experience allows them to guide junior faculty in aligning AI tools with discipline-specific learning outcomes, while also contributing to the development of institutional policies regarding AI use in teaching, research, and student engagement.

Mid-career Faculty Members, who are often balancing research, teaching, and administrative responsibilities, serve as the backbone of AI implementation. Their willingness to experiment, document outcomes, and iterate on practices is crucial for refining AI applications. Many mid-career educators become local change agents—leading departmental initiatives, contributing to internal training, and co-authoring scholarly work on AI-based pedagogy.

Early-career Faculty and Teaching Assistants (TAs) often act as early adopters and creative experimenters. Their familiarity with digital tools and openness to innovation allows them to test, adapt, and integrate AI tools into micro-teaching contexts such as tutorial sessions, lab environments, and formative assessments. TAs, in particular, play an essential role in managing AI-based interfaces, interpreting feedback mechanisms, and assisting students in engaging with AI tools meaningfully.

Academic Leaders and Administrators comprising of Deans, Directors of Centres for Teaching and Learning, and Vice-Chancellors, are responsible for aligning AI integration with institutional vision and educational policy. Their role involves allocating resources for faculty development programs, facilitating partnerships with AI technology providers, and ensuring that ethical frameworks, data privacy norms, and intellectual property concerns are addressed. Their leadership sets the tone for a culture of innovation and continuous professional learning.

External Experts and Technology Partners also play a collaborative role by working closely with educational developers and academic staff to customize AI tools, train faculty, and provide ongoing technical support. These collaborations can evolve into long-term partnerships where technology is not imposed but adapted to meet the pedagogical needs of faculty and students.

RECOMMENDATION TO STAKEHOLDERS

This study is important for Society because it helps ensure that the education system keeps up with rapid technological changes like Artificial Intelligence (AI). When faculty members are better trained and confident in using AI, they can prepare students more effectively for future jobs, innovations, and real-world problem-solving. An education system that evolves with technology creates a society that is more informed, adaptable, and capable of addressing new-age challenges.

For Academicians, this study offers a framework and practical guidance on how to use AI not just as a teaching tool but to enhance their own professional development. It encourages collaborative learning, continuous upskilling, and ethical AI use ensuring that educators remain relevant, impactful, and empowered in an ever-evolving academic landscape. It also opens opportunities for research, curriculum design, and interdisciplinary innovation.

For Students, the benefit lies in receiving a more engaging, responsive, and personalized learning experience. When faculty are trained to use A.I. tools well, students gain access to faster feedback, smarter learning resources, and better academic support. This creates a classroom environment where students feel more supported and motivated, and where learning can happen at their own pace and style.

From the government perspective, the study supports national goals related to digital education, skill development, and inclusive growth. A strong AI-ready teaching force contributes to building a future-ready workforce. This study helps align educational policies with real institutional practices, making sure that public investments in AI and education produce meaningful, long-term benefits for the country.

CONCLUSION

As the higher education landscape evolves, the integration of Artificial Intelligence into faculty development is no longer a futuristic vision but a present-day necessity. This chapter underscores that successful AI integration is not about technology alone, but about co-creating meaningful ecosystems where faculty, institutions, and policy stakeholders work in tandem. The conceptual model presented highlights six critical enablers—ranging from technological readiness and pedagogical alignment to leadership engagement and institutional policy support—all of which must work together for sustainable transformation. Through global and Indian case studies, we see how collaborative strategies lead to increased confidence among educators, improved student outcomes, and alignment with national education goals. Ultimately, equipping faculty with AI knowledge and tools builds not only smarter classrooms but a future-ready society capable of innovation, inclusiveness, and resilience in the age of intelligent education.

REFERENCES

Alper Aytaç, M., Alemdar, M., Akay, Y. E., & Avcu, Y. E. (2024). Fostering tech integration: Teachers' attitudes mediating lifelong learning and technology integration self-efficacy. Participatory Educational Research, 112–133.

Biggs, J. (1996). Enhancing teaching through constructive alignment. *Higher Education, 32*(3), 347–364.

Bond, M., Bedenlier, S., Marín, V. I., & Händel, M. (2021). Emergency remote teaching in higher education: Mapping the first global online semester. *International Journal of Educational Technology in Higher Education, 18*(1), 50. PMID: 34778537

Campbell-Rogers, A. (2024). Design affordances and user perception: Investigating the relationship between space design and pedagogical possibility in an innovative learning environment.

Crompton, H., & Burke, D. (2023). Artificial intelligence in higher education: The state of the field. *International Journal of Educational Technology in Higher Education, 20*, 22.

Educause & AWS. (2025, March 10). Higher Education Generative AI Readiness Assessment. Educause.

Gašević, D., Dawson, S., & Siemens, G. (2023). Perspectives of academic staff on artificial intelligence in higher education: Exploring areas of relevance. *Frontiers in Education, 8*, 1484904.

Inside Higher Ed. (2024). Most campus tech leaders say higher ed is unprepared for AI. Inside Higher Ed.

Katsamakas, E., Pavlov, O. V., & Saklad, R. (2024). Artificial intelligence and the transformation of higher education institutions: A systems approach. *Sustainability, 16*(14), 6118.

Khairullah, S. A., Harris, S., Hadi, H. J., Sandhu, R. A., Ahmad, N., & Alshara, M. A. (2025). Implementing artificial intelligence in academic and administrative processes through responsible strategic leadership in higher education institutions. *Frontiers in Education, 10*, 1548104.

King Faisal University. (2024). Factors affecting faculty members' readiness to integrate AI in teaching practices. *International Journal of Educational Technology in Higher Education, 21*(3), 45–62.

Mah, D.-K., & Groß, N. (2024). Artificial intelligence in higher education: Exploring faculty use, self-efficacy, distinct profiles, and professional development needs. *International Journal of Educational Technology in Higher Education, 21*, 58.

McDonald, N., Johri, A., Ali, A., & Hingle, A. (2024). Generative artificial intelligence in higher education: Evidence from an analysis of institutional policies and guidelines. arXiv preprint arXiv:2402.01659.

Mollick, E. R., & Mollick, L. (2024). Instructors as innovators: A future-focused approach to new AI learning opportunities, with prompts. The Wharton School Research Paper.

OECD. (2023). Multi-stakeholder collaboration and co-creation: Towards responsible application of AI in education. In *OECD Digital Education Outlook 2023*. OECD Publishing.

Qatar, Q Study. (2024). Understanding researchers' AI readiness in a higher education context: A Q method approach. *Middle East Journal of Educational Innovation, 8*(1), 24–41.

Review, N. (2024). A review of artificial intelligence readiness in higher education in Northern Nigeria. *Journal of African Higher Education Studies, 12*(2), 99–120.

Roy, S. (2025). AI Adoption and Central Banks in Emerging Markets: Challenges and Strategies. *Available at SSRN* 5121231.

Salman, H.. (2025). Technology readiness for generative AI among academic researchers: An index-based assessment. *Journal of Digital Learning and Innovation, 17*(1), 10–29.

Webster, R., Griffin, S. M., Chatterjee, I., Kuriakose, A., & Nguyen, H. (2024). A co-creation approach to using generative AI for enhanced learning gain. Journal of Learning Development in Higher Education, (32).

KEY TERMS AND DEFINITIONS

Artificial Intelligence (AI): AI is when machines are made to think, learn, and make decisions like people do. In higher education, AI encompasses tools like generative text models, intelligent tutoring systems, and predictive analytics that help with teaching, learning, and running a school.

Co-Creation: A procedure in which a number of people (faculty, students, administrators, and developers) work together to come up with solutions or learning spaces. In this chapter, co-creation means working together to come up with ways to help teachers grow that use AI.

Collaborative Learning Ecosystem: A changing space where different people, such teachers, students, technologists, and politicians, work together and share information to keep improving how digital tools are used in the classroom.

Educational Developers: People who help teachers come up with, put into action, and evaluate effective ways to teach. They help teachers figure out how to use AI tools in the classroom by showing them how to do it in the best way possible.

Ethical AI Use in Education: Practices that ensure the use of AI in learning environments upholds principles of fairness, transparency, privacy, inclusivity, and academic integrity.

Faculty Development: A planned way to help teachers in higher education improve their professional skills, teaching methods, and research skills. This includes workshops for training, mentorship, digital skills training, and instruction that makes you think.

Generative AI: A kind of AI that can make new things, such text, pictures, or code, based on cues. ChatGPT is an apt example of tools in this group that are being used more and more in schools.

Institutional Support: Refers to the rules, monetary support, leadership support, and administrative support needed to encourage new ideas and long-term success in faculty development programs, especially those that use cutting-edge technologies like AI.

Pedagogical Alignment: The process of making sure that the ways of teaching, the activities for learning, and the ways of testing are all in line with the desired learning outcomes and are backed up by the right technology, such as AI systems.

Technology Readiness: It simply means How ready people or organisations are to accept and use new technology well. It involves things like technical infrastructure, digital literacy, support from institutions, and a willingness to change in culture.

Chapter 10
Radical Transparency as an Antidote to Unclear Expectations for Generative AI Use

Jennifer C. Friberg-Fort
https://orcid.org/0009-0006-0342-2120
Illinois State University, USA

David Giovagnoli
Illinois State University, USA

ABSTRACT

This chapter shares our experiences as academic developers at a large, public, midwestern university as generative artificial intelligence (GenAI) exploded into the public consciousness in December of 2022. Needing to respond quickly to the issues that became evident with student and faculty use of GenAI, we looked at what we knew about evidence-informed pedagogy to develop resources and supports for our campus stakeholders – all focused on an adaptation of a popular pedagogical model: the Transparency in Learning and Teaching (TILT) framework. The chapter will present an adapted TILT framework for use in the age of GenAI and will share a model framework for how usage expectations can be clearly and consistently communicated to students across a course or a program of study. A case study will be presented to model the use of these models in an undergraduate writing course.

DOI: 10.4018/979-8-3373-4129-3.ch010

INTRODUCTION

This chapter shares our experiences as academic developers at a large, public, midwestern university as generative artificial intelligence (GenAI) exploded into the public consciousness in December of 2022. Needing to respond quickly to the issues that became evident with student and faculty use of GenAI, we looked at what we knew about evidence-informed pedagogy to develop resources and supports for our campus stakeholders – all focused on an adaptation of a popular pedagogical model: the Transparency in Learning and Teaching (TILT) framework. The chapter will present an adapted TILT framework for use in the age of GenAI and will share a model framework for how usage expectations can be clearly and consistently communicated to students across a course or a program of study. A case study will be presented to model the use of these models in an undergraduate writing course.

CENTERING TRANSPARENCY IN OUR RESPONSE TO GENAI

When generative artificial intelligence (GenAI) burst into public consciousness in late 2022, our work at the teaching and learning center shifted almost overnight. Until then, much of our energy had been focused on what we thought of as "business as usual:" helping instructors strengthen their courses with evidence-informed strategies, building programs to support engaged learning, and cultivating communities of practice around effective teaching. We were accustomed to scanning the higher education landscape for new ideas and innovations, but nothing prepared us for the urgency with which course instructors — and even campus administrators — turned to us for guidance once GenAI entered the spaces where teaching and learning happens. Questions about academic integrity, learning outcomes, and professional ethics abounded, and we found ourselves needing to move quickly, not just to respond but to help frame the conversation in ways that were constructive, rigorous, and grounded in research.

In the midst of that work, we held onto an important guiding principle about pedagogy: evidence matters most when uncertainty is highest. Rather than advocating that instructors and students should or should not use GenAI, we leaned into our long-standing commitment to evidence-informed teaching and learning. This meant carefully curating resources and creating them when there were none to be found. We spent a great deal of time developing workshops and designing faculty development programs that encouraged thoughtful experimentation while also providing guardrails grounded in pedagogy and scholarship. We sought to help colleagues ask the right questions, weigh the affordances and limitations of GenAI use, and integrate emerging tools in ways that would enhance—not erode—the integrity of teaching and learning. What began as a moment of disruption ultimately became an opportunity to reaffirm our own professional priorities: to support faculty in navigating change by anchoring their decisions in practices that are research-based, student-centered, and future-focused.

In our work together as academic developers, we have found that we have very similar philosophies about building a positive and supportive classroom culture. Specifically, we have centered the importance of transparent communication with students in most of our work. We have long understood that clear communication with students can foster belongingness, student success, student engagement, and the development of trust (Felten & Lambert, 2020), all things that enhance the climate of a learning context and support student (and arguably, faculty) success. As was the case with others in similar professional roles, GenAI led us to urgent, new work as academic developers: supporting instructors, whether they chose to allow students to use GenAI or not. In this work, we chose to use transparent communication as a unifying theme and focus.

ADVOCATING FOR RADICAL TRANSPARENCY

While the idea of transparency in teaching is well established through the TILT framework, the notion of radical transparency draws on a broader set of pedagogical and philosophical traditions. At its core, radical transparency extends the principles of clarity and openness by deliberately revealing the reasoning, evidence, and values behind instructional decisions. Rather than treating transparency as a matter of simply explaining assignments or grading criteria, radical transparency invites students into the "backstage" of teaching (Brookfield, 1995). This approach aligns with long-standing calls in the scholarship of teaching and learning (SoTL) for faculty to make their decision-making processes visible to cultivate trust and foster more equitable learning environments (Hutchings, 2000; Felten & Lambert, 2020).

Radical transparency also resonates with the literature on trust-building in higher education. Felten and Lambert (2020) highlight that authentic relationships between students and faculty are grounded in reliability, care, and openness. Similarly, Lang (2021) argues that students' sense of fairness and trust is enhanced when instructors not only state their expectations but explain the pedagogical rationales behind them. Radical transparency builds on these insights by positioning clarity not just as a cognitive support but as a relational move that signals respect and partnership in the learning process.

In addition, radical transparency shares affinities with traditions of critical pedagogy. Freire's (1970; 2000) call for education as a practice of freedom emphasizes dialogue, shared inquiry, and the co-construction of knowledge. By revealing the purposes and constraints that shape assignments, policies, and even institutional norms, radical transparency invites students to critically examine the structures of education rather than passively accept them. Giroux (2014) similarly underscored the importance of educators resisting opaqueness in the face of political and technological pressures, arguing for open conversations about power, equity, and democracy in education. In this sense, radical transparency is not only a teaching practice but also an ethical stance: it challenges the hidden curriculum by making explicit the values and assumptions that underlie academic work.

In the age of GenAI, radical transparency becomes especially important. Students and faculty alike face uncertainty about what constitutes appropriate or ethical use of new technologies (Trust, 2023). Without explicit guidance, students may misinterpret or unintentionally violate expectations. Radical transparency addresses this ambiguity by clarifying not only what the rules are but why they exist, situating expectations within disciplinary norms and broader educational values. In doing so, it fosters a culture of openness and dialogue in which emerging tools can be engaged thoughtfully rather than with suspicion or fear.

FROM RADICAL TRANSPARENCY TO TILT

Thinking about this notion of radical transparency led us to consider the well-known (to most academic developers, at least) Transparency in Learning and Teaching (TILT) framework, first developed by Winkelmes and colleagues (2016). The original TILT project sought to address a long-standing issue in college teaching: many students, especially those from historically underserved populations, often struggled not because they lacked ability, but because they lacked access to the "hidden curriculum" of higher education (Winkelmes et al., 2016). By making explicit the requirements and evaluation structure of academic work, TILT aimed to demystify faculty expectations, increase equity, and provide all students with a clearer roadmap for success.

Since its inception, research on TILT has consistently demonstrated its benefits. Studies have shown that transparent assignment design not only improves academic performance overall but has particularly strong positive effects for first-generation, low-income, and underrepresented students (Winkelmes et al., 2016). These findings have positioned TILT as both a pedagogical strategy and an equity initiative, linking transparent teaching practices to larger institutional goals of closing achievement gaps and fostering inclusive excellence.

Beyond equity, TILT has also been associated with gains in student motivation, confidence, and metacognitive awareness. By understanding why they are completing an assignment, how to approach it, and what success looks like, students report greater clarity about their learning process and stronger belief in their ability to succeed (Winkelmes, 2019). This connection between transparency and belonging aligns closely with broader work in higher education on the importance of relationship-rich learning environments (Felten & Lambert, 2020). TILT thus serves as both a practical tool for course and assignment design and a broader philosophy of student-centered, inclusive pedagogy.

The adaptability of TILT has also contributed to its widespread uptake. Faculty across disciplines, from STEM to the humanities to professional programs, have used TILT to reframe assignments and assessments in ways that better communicate expectations to students (Winkelmes, 2023). Moreover, academic developers and teaching centers have adopted TILT as a core framework for faculty development, institutional initiatives, and large-scale efforts to promote student success. In this sense, TILT represents not just a classroom practice but a field-defining model for transparency and equity in higher education.

Looking more specifically at the process of implementing TILT in the design of learning experiences, one can see that there is a standard approach to sharing requirements and expectations with students, using three standard components (purpose, tasks, and criteria for success) that are shared by instructors for each assignment or learning experience that they assign:

- **Purpose of activity**: what students will gain from doing the activity and why it matters. For instance, if a student was given an assignment to write a reflection paper about how a course reading connected to their own life, the purpose statement might read as follows: *The purpose of this reflection paper is to help you make personal and meaningful connections between course content and your own lived experiences. By relating the assigned reading to your life, you will deepen your understanding of key ideas and see how they apply beyond the classroom. This activity is designed to strengthen your ability to think critically about course material, practice self-reflection, and communicate your ideas clearly. Making these connections can also support long-term retention of the material and help you recognize its relevance to your future academic, professional, and personal contexts.*
- **Tasks involved**: step-by-step instructions for how students can successfully complete the activity. For that same reflection paper, an example of how required tasks might be completed is as follows:

    1. Carefully read the assigned text.
    2. Identify at least two themes, ideas, or arguments in the reading that connect to your own experiences, values, or observations.
    3. Write a 2–3 page reflection paper (double-spaced) in which you:

a. Briefly summarize the main idea(s) from the reading you are engaging with.
b. Explain how each selected idea connects to your own life, providing specific examples.
c. Reflect on how making these connections helps you better understand the reading and its broader relevance.

4. Conclude with a short paragraph that considers how this exercise might influence your future learning or perspectives.

- **Criteria for success**: specific information about how the activity will be graded. For the reflection paper reference in the purpose and task sections above, criteria for success might look like this: *Your reflection will be considered successful if it:*

1. Clearly identifies and accurately summarizes at least two ideas from the reading.
2. Provides thoughtful, specific, and relevant connections to your own life.
3. Demonstrates critical thinking by explaining why these connections matter and how they deepen your understanding.
4. Communicates ideas in a clear, organized, and coherent manner (grammar and mechanics matter).
5. Meets the length requirement (2–3 pages, double-spaced).

From these examples, you can see that the components of the TILT framework provide students with the opportunity to understand what they're doing, how it's connected to course content/their learning, what they need to do, and what is required to be successful. This structured transparency framework has been shown to significantly improve academic outcomes for students, especially for first-generation, low-income, and underrepresented students (Winkelmes 2023). Beyond those outcomes, the TILT framework has been shown to foster student confidence, metacognitive awareness, and a stronger sense of belonging (Winkelmes, 2023). TILT is adaptable across disciplines and learning environments, making it a practical process for use in encouraging transparency in teaching and learning across higher education contexts.

Despite its widespread use, the TILT framework didn't specifically speak to the need to be transparent about GenAI use for the simple reason that GenAI was not a variable in the teaching and learning environment until well after TILT's initial development in 2016. For that reason, as it was originally created, the TILT framework was not a total match for our goal of radical transparency in the age of GenAI, but we were confident that it could be adapted for that purpose.

ADAPTING TILT TO ACCOUNT FOR GENAI USE

We realized that any adaptation of TILT needed to extend the TILT framework by adding a fourth element specifically allowing for communication about what GenAI tools students could use: *GenAI Use*. This new component guides instructors in explicitly stating how, when, and to what extent students may (or may not) use GenAI tools in an assignment or course activity.

By clearly articulating expectations around GenAI use—whether it's permitted for brainstorming, drafting, editing, or prohibited entirely—this adaptation maintains the spirit of TILT: reducing ambiguity, fostering equitable access to learning, and helping all students make informed, ethical decisions about their work (Winkelmes, 2016). Like the original elements of Purpose, Task, and Criteria, the addition of GenAI Use as a standard TILT criterion helps students understand not just what to do, but how to navigate emerging technologies responsibly and in alignment with course goals.

Building on the example in the section above for the reflection paper that was used to demonstrate what each area of the TILT could look like for such an assignment, a possible AI Use statement might read as follows: *You may use GenAI tools to support your personal efficiency (e.g., summarizing your notes or clarifying parts of the reading), but the reflection paper itself must be written entirely in your own words. GenAI may not be used to generate drafts, outlines, or paragraphs for this assignment because you need to present your own unique and individual perspective to demonstrate your thinking and learning.*

CONSISTENCY ACROSS THE GENAI USAGE EXPECTATION MESSAGES

Next, to help course instructors be consistent and transparent in how they used the fourth element of our adapted TILT framework, we wanted to help develop a way for instructors and students to have access to an objective, clear, and consistent way of thinking about how GenAI might be used or mitigated in a variety of teaching and learning situations when using TILT for an individual assignment or even beyond that, for use to designate expectations for a whole course or program of study. From this desire came the creation of the "GenAI Usage Expectation Levels" system to assign a value to instructor expectations around GenAI use by students (Friberg & Giovagnoli, 2024). These levels offer one path towards clarity for instructors and students that can be used across a single learning experience, an individual course, a larger program, or an entire institution. In our mind we say a clear tie between the creation of this leveled system for use with the TILT framework, for just as TILT makes explicit the purpose, task, and criteria of learning activities, the GenAI Usage Expectation Levels make explicit the boundaries and rationale for AI use. Both, used together, brought us further toward our goal of radical transparency.

Our GenAI usage guidance includes seven distinct levels, ranging from absolutely no use of GenAI (Level 0) to unrestricted, unattributed use (Level 6). These levels are intentionally flexible so they can be adapted to the needs of different courses or disciplines. At the same time, what is most important is consistency within a given course or program. Our strong belief is that students should not be left to guess about instructor expectations. Clear and stable guidance ensures that students understand when and how GenAI may or may not be used as a learning tool. Instructors can assign levels in ways that align with course or program learning objectives, their own pedagogical preferences, and student learning needs, while maintaining internal consistency. Table 1 provides an overview of each level in the system.

Table 1. GenAI Usage Expectation Levels

	Level descriptor:	What this looks like in practice:
Level 0	**no use of GenAI**	Students will create their own, original work without the use of GenAI for any aspect of this course/learning experience.
Level 1	**organizational use of GenAI**	Students will create their own, original work without the use of GenAI for any aspect of this course/learning experience; however, the use of GenAI for personal efficiency (i.e., summarizing notes/readings, clarifying content) is acceptable.
Level 2	**use of GenAI for brainstorming or idea generation**	Students can consult GenAI as a tool for brainstorming or idea generation, but are expected to create their own, original work without the use of GenAI for all aspects of this course/learning experience.
Level 3	**use of GenAI for feedback**	Students are able to create their own work, then use GenAI as a tool to provide feedback on their work for any aspect of this course/learning experience. Students are expected to use feedback from GenAI to conduct their own revisions of their own work, so any work submitted should be GenAI-supported, not Gen-AI created.
Level 4	**use of GenAI to co-create and revise work**	Students can use GenAI to develop drafts/outlines of their work in this course/learning experience but are expected to carefully edit and revise GenAI-created content as appropriate for the learner and the learning context. It is expected that any use of GenAI-created content in this course/learning experience is properly disclosed and attributed.
Level 5	**unrestricted, attributed use of GenAI**	Students can freely use GenAI for any aspect of this course/learning experience if the use of any GenAI-created content is properly disclosed and attributed.
Level 6	**unrestricted, unattributed use of GenAI**	Students can freely use GenAI for any aspect of this course/learning experience in any form. Attribution is not necessary.

Applied consistently, we designed these levels to provide clear, transparent information to students regarding GenAI use for entire courses or individual learning experiences.

Individual Learning Experiences: Learning experiences can include individual assignments, projects, assessments, or other course activities completed by students. In courses where expectations for GenAI use may vary across these experiences, instructors can assign a specific GenAI Usage Expectation Level to each one. This approach ensures that students understand when and how GenAI may be used for a particular activity. Assigning levels at the level of individual learning experiences also opens space for dialogue between instructors and students about why GenAI might support learning in some situations but not in others, helping students see the pedagogical reasoning behind these decisions.

Entire Course/Program: If all learning experiences in a course share the same GenAI Usage Expectation Level, the course itself can be designated as a "Level X" course. Framing courses in this way creates opportunities for open dialogue between instructors and students about how consistent use—or non-use—of GenAI aligns with and supports the achievement of course learning outcomes. On a broader scale, an entire program, or even multiple programs within an institution, could be designated as a "Level X" program. In this model, expectations for GenAI use remain consistent across all courses in the program, providing students with a coherent and predictable framework for navigating AI use in their academic work.

STUDENT-CREATED ATTESTATION STATEMENT FOR GENAI USE

While we were pleased with the outcome of adapting the TILT framework and developing the GenAI Usage Expectation Levels, we recognized that students also needed to be actively engaged in the implementation of these models in real time. Providing clear and transparent information is essential, but transparency alone is not enough; instructors also need a way to understand whether students have followed the guidance provided. Without such mechanisms, transparency risks becoming a one-way directive rather than a shared process of accountability and responsibility.

Some might advocate for the use of AI checkers to verify compliance. However, the significant flaws of these tools (such as misidentifying human writing as AI-generated or falsely clearing AI-assisted work) raise concerns about fairness, bias, and due process, rendering their use problematic in most academic settings. As a more ethical and educational alternative, we proposed that each project, assignment, or learning experience conclude with a *student attestation statement*. This statement would require students either to confirm that they did not use GenAI to complete the task, or to describe how they used GenAI and reflect on its impact on their learning. In this way, attestation not only ensures accountability but also encourages students to critically consider their own choices, cultivating habits of reflection and ethical judgment they can carry forward into their professional lives. To support this practice, we developed suggested language for instructors to adapt in their courses:

- *AI Use statement: If you did NOT use GenAI to complete this assignment, provide an attestation to share that. If you used GenAI to complete your work, please report the following:*
    - o *What platform(s) you used (e.g., ChatGPT, CoPilot, Claude)*
    - o *What prompts did you use to ask your chosen AI platform(s) for information?*
    - o *What is your overall sense of how AI helped or hindered your work on this assignment?*

Information gathered from student attestation statements can serve many purposes beyond simply verifying GenAI use. When students are permitted to use GenAI and accurately report their practices, instructors gain valuable insights that can be used to guide and enhance future learning. For example, an instructor might recommend alternative GenAI platforms that align more closely with the objectives of the learning experience, or they might help students reflect on the quality of their prompt engineering and suggest strategies for refining their approaches. Attestation can also open conversations about the strengths and limitations of GenAI tools, encouraging students to evaluate when human judgment is more reliable than algorithmic output. In this way, attestation functions not only as a mechanism of accountability but also as a springboard for student growth—supporting learners in developing more intentional, ethical, and effective approaches to using GenAI as part of their academic and professional skill set.

In sum, student attestation statements offer a practical and ethical mechanism for reinforcing transparency and accountability in GenAI use. By shifting responsibility from external policing to student self-reflection and self-reporting, student attestations not only clarify whether guidelines have been followed but also encourage learners to examine how their choices with GenAI shape their own development. In short, these attestations close the transparency loop. Instructors use transparent practices to make clear their expectations and students then use transparent statements to illustrate how they met those expectations. This approach underscores that transparent teaching is not merely about setting boundaries, but about fostering shared responsibility and cultivating ethical habits that extend beyond the classroom.

IMPLEMENTATION OF OUR MODEL

We piloted our vision for radical transparency in an undergraduate writing course for communication sciences and disorders majors at our institution. The course included 13 separate assignments, each designed and communicated using the adapted TILT framework and paired with an appropriate GenAI Usage Expectation Level. This consistent application ensured that students not only understood the purpose, task, and criteria for their work but also had clear guidance about whether and how GenAI could be used in each case. By embedding both frameworks across the full set of assignments, we sought to create a learning environment in which transparency and accountability were seamlessly integrated into the student experience. An example assignment from this class is presented in Appendix A. Importantly, this pilot served as a proof of concept, showing how radical transparency can be put into practice to support both clarity and dialogue around GenAI, with implications for application across programs and disciplines.

FUTURE DIRECTIONS

Our work adapting the TILT framework and developing the GenAI Usage Expectation Levels is a first step in addressing the uncertainties that GenAI has introduced into higher education. Yet, as with any pedagogical innovation, the real test of its impact lies in sustained use, continued study, and iterative refinement. Looking forward, we see several avenues for future development and research.

Research Opportunities

Systematic research is needed to evaluate the effects of radical transparency in the context of GenAI. While existing studies demonstrate that transparency improves student achievement and equity outcomes (Winkelmes et al., 2016; Winkelmes, 2023), it is not yet clear how the addition of GenAI-specific guidance influences student learning, motivation, or ethical decision-making. Future studies might investigate whether students in courses with explicit GenAI Usage Expectation Levels report lower anxiety, greater confidence in their use of AI tools, or stronger adherence to ethical practices. Similarly, faculty perspectives warrant exploration: Do instructors who adopt radical transparency report greater clarity, reduced conflict, or improved student trust? Longitudinal studies could also examine whether students carry these habits of reflection and accountability into later courses or professional contexts.

Programmatic and Institutional Expansion

Our pilot was situated in a single undergraduate course, but the potential for broader adoption is significant. Future efforts should explore how GenAI Usage Expectation Levels might be scaled across programs or entire institutions. For instance, professional programs such as nursing, teacher education, or engineering could adopt shared levels of GenAI usage to provide students with consistent expectations across multiple courses. At the institutional level, integrating radical transparency into faculty development initiatives could establish a common language for discussing GenAI, reducing confusion and fostering alignment. Such expansion would not only support students in navigating complex academic landscapes but could also prepare institutions to meet external expectations for accountability, accreditation, and ethical leadership in the digital age.

Evolving Technologies and Pedagogies

Finally, the rapid pace of GenAI development ensures that today's guidance will need continual revision. Tools available now will be replaced or augmented by others with new capabilities and risks. Future work must remain agile, ensuring that transparency frameworks are updated to reflect emerging technologies without overwhelming faculty or students. This will require sustained collaboration among academic developers, disciplinary experts, and students themselves. Equally important is the integration of radical transparency with other pedagogical priorities, such as inclusive teaching, assessment for learning, and relationship-rich education (Felten & Lambert, 2020). In this way, radical transparency will not exist as a standalone response to GenAI, but as part of a larger ecosystem of evidence-informed, equity-driven teaching practices.

CONCLUSION

As GenAI reshapes the higher education landscape, the need for clarity, consistency, and shared responsibility in course and learning design has never been greater. Our adaptation of the TILT framework, paired with the GenAI Usage Expectation Levels and student attestation practices, offers one pathway toward radical transparency in teaching. By integrating these tools, instructors move beyond reactive responses to GenAI and instead provide students with structured, evidence-informed guidance that fosters agency, accountability, and ethical engagement with potentially disruptive technologies.

Importantly, this approach positions transparency not as a static disclosure but as a dynamic, relational practice. When instructors articulate their reasoning for GenAI policies and invite students to reflect on their own choices, our teaching and learning spaces have the potential to become spaces of trust and dialogue rather than suspicion and surveillance. Students have the chance to learn boundaries and rationales for AI use not as arbitrary restrictions but as purposeful decisions tied to learning goals and professional development standards. In turn, instructors can gain valuable insights into how students engage with these tools, creating opportunities to refine teaching practices and support deeper learning.

While our model is not a definitive solution, it represents a step toward cultivating classrooms that are resilient in the face of technological change. Radical transparency allows both students and instructors to navigate uncertainty with integrity, grounded in shared values and evidence-based pedagogy. As GenAI tools continue to evolve, we believe that approaches like this—anchored in clarity, trust, and reflective practice—will be essential for preparing students not only to succeed academically but also to act responsibly in their professional and civic lives.

REFERENCES

Brookfield, S. D. (1995). *Becoming a critically reflective teacher.* Jossey-Bass.

Felten, P., & Lambert, L. M. (2020). *Relationship rich education: How human connections drive success in college.* Johns Hopkins Press.

Freire, P. (2000). *Pedagogy of the oppressed* (30th anniversary ed.; M. B. Ramos, Trans.). Continuum. (Original work published 1970)

Friberg, J. C., & Giovagnoli, D. (2024, July 25). GenAI usage expectation levels: A path towards increased transparency in teaching and learning. *The SoTL Advocate* [weblog]. https://illinoisstateuniversitysotl.wordpress.com/2024/07/25/genai-usage-expectation-levels-a-path-towards-increased-transparency-in-teaching-and-learning/

Giroux, H. A. (2014). *Neoliberalism's war on higher education.* Haymarket Books.

Hutchings, P. (2000). *Opening lines: Approaches to the scholarship of teaching and learning.* Carnegie Foundation for the Advancement of Teaching.

Lang, J. M. (2021). *Distracted: Why students can't focus and what you can do about it.* Basic Books.

Trust, T. (2023). Navigating generative AI in higher education: Ethical considerations and teaching strategies. *Computers and Education: Artificial Intelligence, 4,* 100145. DOI: 10.1016/j.caeai.2023.100145

Winkelmes, M.-A. (2019). Transparent design in higher education teaching and leadership. In Miller, M. T., & Nadler, D. V. (Eds.), *Student engagement and retention: High-impact strategies to enhance student success* (pp. 89–103). Emerald Publishing.

Winkelmes, M-A. (2023). Introduction to transparency in teaching and learning. *Perspectives in Learning, 20*(1).

Winkelmes, M.-A., Bernacki, M., Butler, J., Zochowski, M., Golanics, J., & Weavil, K. H. (2016). A teaching intervention that increases underserved college students' success. *Peer Review : Emerging Trends and Key Debates in Undergraduate Education, 18*(1/2).

APPENDIX: SAMPLE ASSIGNMENT

Assignment 8: Define a Disorder

This assignment is worth 20 points and should take 1-2 hours to complete.

Purpose: The purpose of this assignment is to practice producing written materials that explore how professionals share information about specific communication disorders in an efficient and effective manner. You will create a "disorder brief" to outline one communication disorder, then provide an overview of how that disorder is assessed and treated. You will have a template (attached below) to help you format your work. You could imagine this assignment as a "one page" resource in a clinic for clients and families.

AI Use: This is a Level 2 assignment. The use of generative AI is acceptable for completion of this assignment, so long as YOU do the actual writing about the disorder. You can use AI to brainstorm and ask questions about your disorder, but since AI can get things wrong, make sure that you check facts and correct any inconsistencies between disciplinary sources and generative AI.

Task: Using the template available below, create a "one pager" that briefly explores a disorder of your choice that impacts communication. This can be a medical condition that isn't primarily a communication disorder (i.e., Parkinson's disease, autism) or can be a primary communication disorder (i.e., stuttering, hearing loss). Your job is to create a brief resource that outlines the basic aspects of this disorder and its connection to a human's ability to communicate. To complete this assignment, please do the following:

- Download the assignment template and look at what content categories you'll be required to write about.
- Identify a communication disorder or a disorder where communication is impacted that you'd like to focus on.
- Use time prior to class on March 3rd to draft a 1-2 page, at least 1.5 spaced, description of your disorder, following guidance in the template.
- Append an attestation statement to the end of your assignment that explores how you used AI to complete this work OR states that you didn't use AI to complete the assignment. If you did use AI, answer the following three questions (note your AI attestation statement can exceed the max page length, if needed):
  - what GenAI platform(s) did you use (e.g., ChatGPT, CoPilot)?
  - what prompts did you use to ask your chosen GenAI platform(s) for information?

    - what is your overall sense of how GenAI helped or hindered your work on this assignment?
- Bring two printed copies of your assignment to class on March 3rd for peer review.

Criteria for Success: This assignment will be graded for content as well as grammar and spelling. In terms of content, you'll be expected to accurately convey information about your disorder in a clear and effective manner that a layperson would be able to understand. Points for this assignment will be assigned as follows:

- 5 points for clarity
- 5 points for accuracy
- 5 points for speaking appropriately to your audience
- 5 points for grammar and spelling

Chapter 11
The Role of Educational Developers in AI Integration at Scale

R. N. Ravikumar
https://orcid.org/0009-0009-3705-1681
Marwadi University, Rajkot, India

S. Aarthi
https://orcid.org/0009-0006-9064-2091
Marwadi University, Rajkot, India

ABSTRACT

This chapter highlights how AI is reshaping higher education, with educational developers playing a key role in guiding this transition. As AI transforms curriculum design and teaching methods, developers support faculty in adopting tools like personalized learning paths, intelligent tutoring, and automated assessments while ensuring alignment with learning outcomes. They bridge pedagogy and technology, lead institutional AI strategies, and promote inclusive, ethical practices. Developers also assist in shaping policies that address bias, privacy, and transparency in AI use. Through collaboration and innovation, they help institutions implement scalable, responsible AI solutions. This chapter showcases real-world examples and strategies for fostering resilient, AI-integrated education systems that empower both educators and students.

DOI: 10.4018/979-8-3373-4129-3.ch011

1. INTRODUCTION

Artificial Intelligence (AI) is being introduced swiftly in universities and changing the ways classes are taught, programs are run, and plans are made for the future. Since AI is used in education, educational developers are gaining even greater importance. At this stage, educational developers can offer proper guidance to both academic leaders and teachers as teaching, technology, and changes at the institution merge. New methods of teaching are possible for educators while still upholding academic standards and caring about students. This chapter points out how educational developers can help promote the use of AI in various institutions. Apart from assisting single professors, they arrange professional training events, recommend rules and policies, and join projects that protect the institution's mission. They also ensure that mainly data privacy, fair programs, and students' freedom to decide are the main points of AI work. When developers use educational theories, it helps schools change permanently, encourages more student engagement, and improves the organization's strength. With the changes in universities, they help promote ethical and significant use of AI (Çela et al., 2024).

1.1 Overview of AI's Transformative Role in Higher Education

AI is changing the field of higher education by making personalized learning, using technology for teaching, and making data-based decisions easier. AI, adaptive learning software, virtual supporters, automated marking tools, and analytic systems, learning becomes more efficient and captures students' attention. With these handy tools, instructors can deliver material suited to each student and spend more time interacting with them. Besides, institutions are starting to include AI in their logistics by using it for student support and enrolment forecasting. Even though AI proves invaluable to businesses and individuals, it still raises questions of ethics, privacy, and equity. A narrowly defined range of strategic potential risks of such an approach might reinforce negative biases and distract from people-centeredness in education (Dias et al., 2025). Wisely, AI's educational, social, and managerial changes remain relevant. Every organization needs to articulate how AI augments their educational mission and how it humanizes education to people. Many environments emphasize organizational strategies that promote responsibility and nurture the creative capabilities of individuals. It is essential that AI is used in such a manner that the systemic barriers to quality and equity in education are lifted. Undoubtedly, the influence of AI on the education that is offered, the pedagogy used, forms of assessment, and students is increasing (Sholeh, 2025). Figure 1 demonstrates the transformative change AI has made in higher education around personalized learning, instructional technology, data-driven decision making, and student support. Table

1 brings together diverse AI applications in higher education, such as engagement, assessment, and instruction, with their relevant AI tools like adaptive learning systems, virtual assistants, and automated grading.

Figure 1. Role of AI in Higher Education

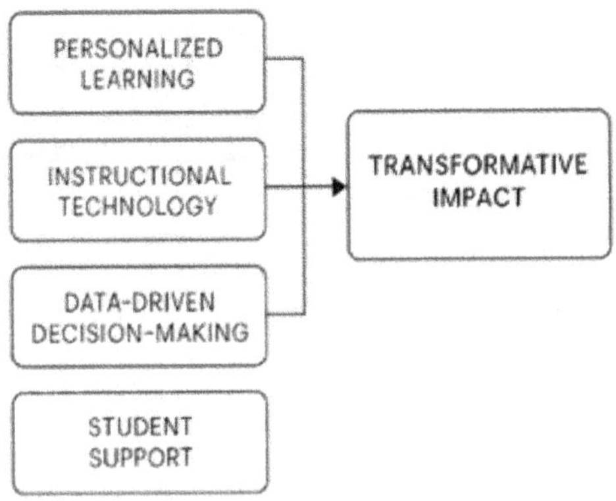

Table 1 AI Tools and Their Educational Applications

AI Tool	Educational Application	Benefit
Adaptive Learning System	Personalized Content Delivery	Improved engagement and outcomes
Virtual Assistants	Student Support Services	24/7 Help and Reduced Response Time
Automated Grading Tools	Assessment Automation	Faster Feedback and Reduced Workload

Figure 2. Impact of AI Tools in Higher Education

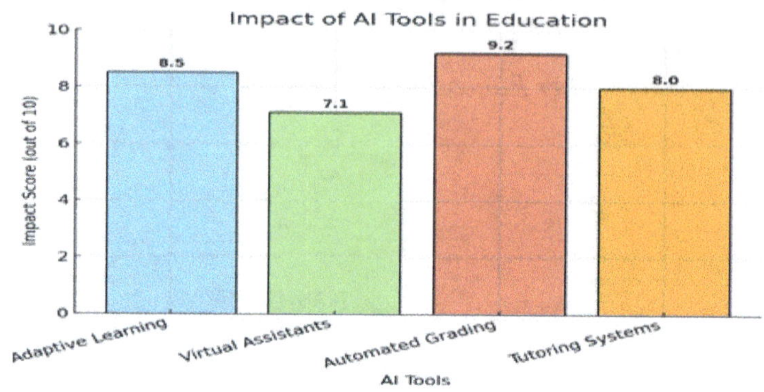

The Figure 2 illustrates the comparative impact of different AI tools Adaptive Learning, Virtual Assistants, Automated Grading, and Tutoring Systems on educational practices. Each tool is rated on a 10-point scale based on its effectiveness in enhancing learning, teaching efficiency, and student support. The graph provides a quick visual overview of which AI tools are perceived to have the highest influence in academic environments.

1.2 Importance of Educational Developers in Guiding AI Adoption

More and more, educational developers are helping colleges use AI responsibly and successfully. Since they are familiar with both educational theory and instructional technology, they act as a link between different groups in an institution. The main reason for their success is that AI is chosen for tasks that improve educational methods and match student targets. With the help of educational developers, professors understand the use and structure of AI and how to apply it in their teaching (Amani Mohammad et al., 2024). Such courses are created by using AI technology such as smart platforms and tutoring programs, all while ensuring the materials remain challenging and accessible to everyone. Moreover, they design workshops, training programs, and privacy communities for teachers, so they can learn and try innovative educational technologies. Apart from classroom work, educational developers participate in making institutional rules, promoting safe use of AI, diversity, and proper management of data. They ensure that the way AI is used at the university fits the university's mission and promotes both creativity and teamwork. With AI playing a bigger role in education today, educational developers guide others to shape this process carefully and equally (Dubey & Crevar, 2025).

2. EDUCATIONAL DEVELOPERS AS CATALYSTS FOR AI INTEGRATION

The presence of the institution's educational developers facilitates the integration of AI at the college and university level. their understanding of the curriculum, pedagogy and the needs of teachers puts them in the best position to integrate technology into the classroom. While tools of AI are becoming more commonplace in education, as educational developers, their' responsibility is to assist in the integration of AI in a way that enhances teaching and does not replace the instructor. They are expected to aid in the use of AI tools and the design of new instructional and evaluative frameworks. Developers create and provide professional development opportunities for instructors so they use platforms like adaptive learning and Intelligent Tutoring Systems (ITS) together with automated grading software. Educators are prompted by these guidelines to consider ethics, social issues, and culture in the use of AI. When departments collaborate, developers set up teams that are able to look for and scale AI solutions. Their strategic guidance, AI activities are incorporated into the main line of the institution's development plans. Since they are involved in transforming education, educational developers help staff confidently handle changes in AI-based pedagogy (George & Wooden, 2023).

2.1 Conceptual Framework of AI Adoption in Higher Education

In the context of the above paper, the integration of AI in education can be analyzed in relation to three 'levels' of consideration: the individual student, the individual educator, and the institution. From the student perspective, AI fosters personalized learning, increases agency, and promotes equitable resource access. From the educator perspective, AI encourages professional advancement, improves teaching designs and streamlines teaching workloads, enhancing the ability to perform more meaningful pedagogical activities. From an institution perspective, the use of AI supports the fulfillment of the institution's strategic objectives, the governance model, and the integration of functional silos which promotes cross-discipline AI use in a sustainable and ethically responsible manner. Educational developers are the primary professionals who conceptualize the connections between the aforementioned levels, ensuring integration of technology with pedagogy, ethics, and the mission of the institution. This model illustrates the need to consider the nexus of personalized student learning, faculty advancement, and institutional strategy in the deployment of meaningful AI." The Figure 3 showing how AI adoption interacts across students, faculty, and institutions, with educational developers positioned as mediators ensuring ethical and pedagogically sound implementation.

Figure 3. Conceptual Framework of AI Adoption in Higher Education

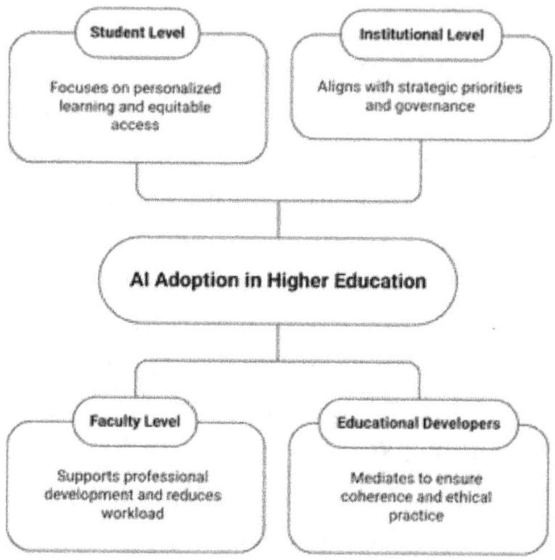

2.2 Unique Positioning of Developers to Bridge Pedagogy and Technology

In higher education, educational developers act as specialists who know about teaching theories as well as tech-related changes. Because of this dual skill, they can grasp how AI works with good teaching approaches. Even though faculty know their subjects well and technologists develop software, the educational developer makes sure technology is used effectively and fairly in education. Having learned about curriculum development, teaching others, and educational theories, developers can decide how different AI tools can support students' learning (Alexander et al., 2025). They assist in finding suitable times and methods to bring AI into classes, grading, and communication with students. When educational developers use new technologies in lessons, they make it easier for faculty to get used to them (Henshaw, 2025). They set up a well-structured process and encourage people from different fields to talk, making certain technology is used wisely and effectively. With this role, people help make sure AI isn't used wrongly or depended on too heavily, enabling teachers and schools to adopt technology that supports students (Rienties et al., 2020). The Figure 4 represents the core components of faculty development in the context of AI integration. Educational developers support faculty through workshops, learning communities, and individual consultations, equipping them with the skills, confidence, and collaborative environment needed to effectively implement AI tools in teaching and assessment practices. Each pathway ensures personalized support while fostering institutional AI readiness (Pedró, 2020).

Figure 4. Faculty Development for AI Adoption

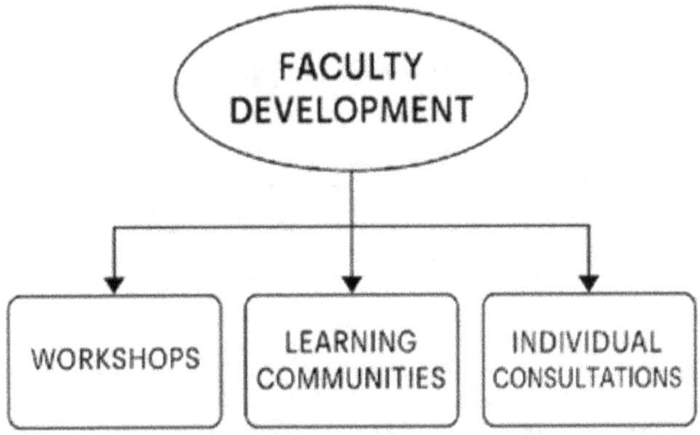

2.3 Supporting Faculty in Adopting AI-Enhanced Teaching Practices

A major part of educational developers' roles is to continually assist faculty members as they try out and adopt AI-powered teaching tools. Some educators may have a hard time figuring out the best way to bring AI tools into their lessons. To help seamlessly move to remote education, educational developers hold hands-on workshops, provide selected resources, build learning communities, and offer personal consultations for every faculty member's needs. Support for faculty goes down to helping them link AI with their course learning aims, ways of testing knowledge, and increasing students' interest. For example, developers could aid in altering a course so that learning materials are provided in a flexible manner based on students' results. They could also show educators how to make use of AI, so that formative assessments are graded automatically and more time is spent on helping students. Educational developers make sure that people reflect on how they learn. It encourages faculty to look at whether the AI tool matches their teaching objectives. What unfair ideas or biases could exist in the algorithm? Do all students have a fair chance to learn with this approach? These programs, developers help make a group of educators who know how to use AI and also care about its ethical and educational use (Wang et al., 2025). The table 2 Summarizes the types of support provided by educational developers to faculty for AI adoption, such as workshops, learning communities, and personalized consultations, along with their impact on teaching practices.

Table 2 Faculty Support Mechanisms for AI Adoption

Support Type	Description	Impact on Faculty
Workshops	Hands-on AI integration training	Increased confidence in using AI
Learning Communities	Peer-led discussions and sharing	Collaborative problem-solving
Individual Consultations	Custom guidance for specific courses	Tailored implementation strategies

3. FACULTY DEVELOPMENT AND CAPACITY BUILDING

Because AI is now widely used in higher education, faculty members are expected to know how to use these tools inside their classrooms. Transforming education largely depends on educational developers designing and leading workshops that help faculty get familiar with AI, use technology creatively, and focus on ethics. Some of these efforts are workshops, certification courses, web learning modules, and support groups that cover AI concepts, related platforms, and classroom uses. It is important that capacity building also helps people to think critically, experiment, and keep learning continuously. Learning developers' direct professors in finding new ways to teach with the use of AI-guided technology such as adaptive learning, smart tutoring, automated assessments, and analyzing learning data (Sanasintani, 2023). These new ideas allow students to learn in their own way and get better guidance, boosting their achievements. Furthermore, developers make it possible for faculty development to be available and open to people from many backgrounds and levels of experience. Training becomes easier to continue in the future when it is directed by the institutions and faculty's needs and goals. They argue that everyone should pay attention to ethics on the internet, the privacy of their data, and the way AI is used in learning. When strategic help is given, educational developers inspire faculty to be involved in how AI impacts education (Nurjanah et al., 2024).

3.1 Creation of Specialized Programs for Upskilling Educators in AI

Teachers are being offered special opportunities in AI by educational developers to help more students gain from this technology in education. With such programs, instructors are told about the benefits of AI and what is necessary to ensure learning is high quality and honourable. Programs of this type are regularly presented as workshops, fast online lessons called micro-credentials, AI fellowships, or learning groups for teachers. The topics discussed in the content are usually AI literacy, ethics in the use of AI, using data to guide teaching, Intelligent Tutoring Systems, systems for adaptive learning, and automated feedback. Skills development tools are adjusted according to a person's experience and job area, making them more useful and simpler to grasp. In addition, these programs work on other valuable skills as well. Such learning opportunities help teachers evaluate if and how using AI is useful in their teaching. People involved are taught to coordinate AI techniques with what the course is meant to achieve, what students need, and how to assess their progress. These measures, faculty members learn how to use and develop AI-supported learning tools, strengthening the ability of the institution to keep progressing and introducing new ideas into higher education (Popenici & Kerr, 2017). The table 3 Details different formats of upskilling programs designed by educational developers, including micro-credentials, AI fellowships, and online modules, and their core focus areas. From 2018 to 2024, faculty members adopting AI has taken a great stride, as shown in Figure 5 The added AI training devised by educational developers has contributed to the success of faculty development initiatives, due to the soaring percentage increase in AI adoption. The curve reflects the perceptibly rising assurance and skill of the educators in employing AI in teaching.

Table 3 Specialized Programs for Upskilling Educators in AI

Program Type	Delivery Format	Key Focus Areas
Micro-Credentials	Online Modules	AI Literacy, Ethics
AI Fellowships	Cohort-Based	Adaptive Learning, Algorithm Fairness
Webinars/Workshops	Synchronous/Hybrid	Tool Usage, Data Privacy

Figure 5. Faculty Adoption Trend of AI Tools (2018–2024)

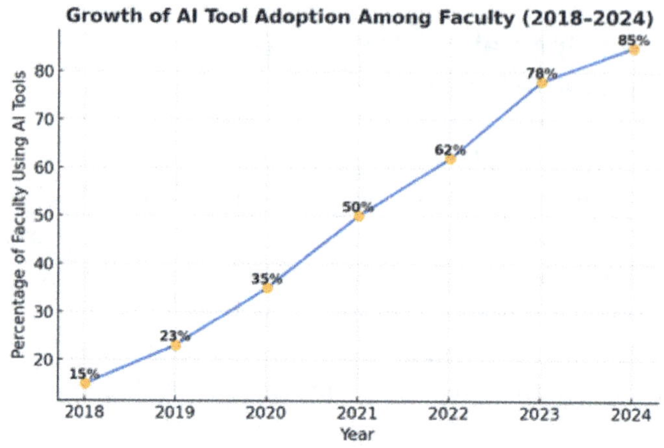

3.2 Emphasis on Instructional Design Innovations

The use of AI has significantly shifted how instruction in higher education works. These systems are shifting to tutoring aids, automated assessments in the classroom, and most of all, teaching instruction pathways. Education instruction, assessment, and assistance are all shifting in tandem. Learners on tailored pathways have flexible paces at which they progress, learning materials are optimized for the preferred learning styles of the students. They use guided instruction which the students greatly appreciate because they are talked to in a friendly manner as they are taken through all the stages of learning difficult topics. Automated marking systems dramatically reduces the turnaround time for assessments which means faster feedback for learners, and additional time for facilitators to prioritize the topics that require deeper explanations (Khan et al., 2024). These innovations, students' learning improves and faculty find it easier and more practical to shape how they instruct. It is the role of educational developers to help professors design and use these teaching methods with the right pedagogical approach and according to the expected outcomes of the institution. The table 4 Compares key instructional design strategies enhanced by AI personalized learning paths, Intelligent Tutoring Systems, and automated assessments with associated benefits and implementation challenges.

Table 4 Instructional Design Innovations Using AI

Innovation	Benefits	Challenges
Personalized Learning Paths	Learner-centered pacing	Data privacy and algorithmic bias
Intelligent Tutoring Systems (ITS)	Real-time adaptive support	High development cost and training
Automated Assessments	Fast, scalable feedback	Risk of over-reliance on automation

3.2.1 Personalized Learning Paths

Using AI to make personal learning paths is one of the top achievements in education. Learners are offered different content depending on their understanding, choices, and the pace they use. Unlike old-fashioned, identical programs, personalized learning platforms make lessons, activities, and tests adjust to each person on the spot. If a student encounters trouble with a basic concept, the system could give more details on the topic or simplify the next lesson. It is also possible for advanced students to quickly move forward by excluding redundant lessons. Personalization in teaching allows early responses to learning gaps, boosts students' attention, and encourages self-study. Developing courses that make use of adaptive technologies is one of the key duties for educational developers. They support instructors in matching individual learning plans with course requirements, so that flexibility remains combined with challenging tasks. Developers also focus on using data in an ethical way and support clear guidelines for how such data should be protected. If institutions personalize students' learning tracks carefully, they can make sure their education program is inclusive and supportive of everyone. With these innovations, attention is placed on student learning, so classes are more efficient and useful (Mahmoud & Sørensen, 2024). From the point of view of the students, AI-based can greatly improve the students' ownership of learning, especially, through personalized learning pathways and AI-tutoring systems.

AI also increases engagement among students who self-identify learning deficits, especially, if there is some form of automated real time feedback. It is also noted that some students are apprehensive about the amount of automated feedback provided, especially, if that feedback is provided in place of that provided by the teachers. AI should not only improve productivity of the institutions and the instructors but also increase student agency, motivation, and resource suggest equity use through the efficient use of learning resources. The Figure 6 illustrates the sequential application of AI in instructional design, highlighting three major innovations: Personalized Learning Paths, Intelligent Tutoring Systems, and Automated Assessments. These components represent how AI enhances student-centered learning, provides adaptive feedback, and streamlines evaluation. The progression shows how technology builds a robust learning ecosystem that supports tailored instruction and efficient performance tracking.

Figure 6. Instructional Design Innovations Using AI

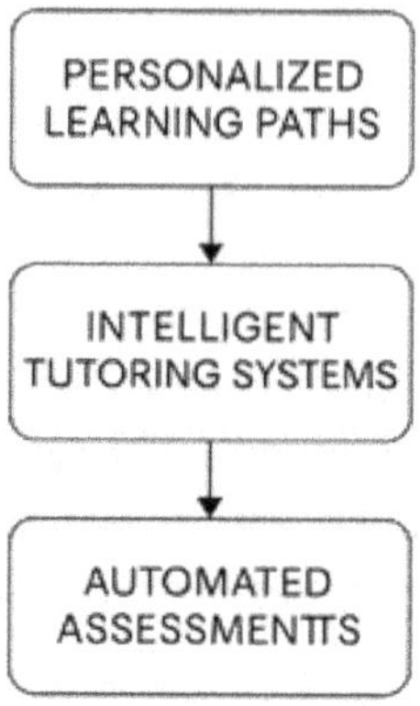

3.2.2 Intelligent Tutoring Systems

An ITS program provides learners with the same level of support as a classroom tutor thanks to AI integration. Achievement data models guide virtual tutors as they monitor student performance in real time by providing tailored suggestions, direction, and custom help. An ITS understands how both the student and the knowledge being learned are processed, which enables caregivers to use tailored intervention strategies to each individual. Instructional designers ensure that ITS is being utilized by aligning its features with intended instructional use. Professor evaluation data indicated that outside the classroom students are given further course objectives and self-management support as appropriate feedback is given. Topics like basic math, programming, and language courses have shown a prominent learning impact. It is not only intended to optimize learning; a teacher too gets the opportunity to attend to numerous students' individual concerns without being overwhelmed. Trainers help educators appreciate that ITS does not operate in a vacuum; the absence of real-world data sets increases the level of abstraction they have to work with (Aarthi et al., 2025). The use of an AI-driven ITS has been shown to increase equity for its users, and provide more foundational support to students with a absent human tutor.

These experts use techniques that allows even AI and machines to work morally and inclusively, engaging at the human level for the sake of optimum results.

3.2.3 Automated Assessments

The feedback systems which track students' responses also evaluate students' answers automatically, which saves them the effort of assigning grades to these assessments. These systems document students' assessments and do not require manual grading. Hybrid systems of assessment, ranging from automated multiple-choice and short-answer coding questions, to even automated essay evaluation through Machine Learning (ML), are available. Timely feedback, grading less, and gaining visibility into student performance are some of the main benefits. When instructors set up automated assessments that are maintained educationally and still aligned to learning objectives, educational developers assist them. Educational developers aid instructors in formulating robust systems such as question banks, grading frameworks, feedback and feedback data policies, and diverse learning resources. Developers maintain equity while accommodating different learning needs. This enables students to become independent, and instructors to make purposeful changes in their teaching strategies, based on the rich data available over time. Developers are cautioned not to depend on AI for critical thinking and essay writing. Embedding assessments in the educational context results in enhanced efficiency while sustaining educational standards. They also help faculty implement AI in teaching and ensure the outputs are aligned to students' needs and standards (Ravikumar et al., 2025).

4. SUPPORTING PEDAGOGICAL INTEGRITY

We must make sure the educational quality is not compromised as AI technology is brought into the classroom. Part of an educational developer's role is to ensure AI is used with good practice, upholds the main educational standards, and emphasizes important learning. It is better for developers to focus on the results rather than simply using new technologies. Developers offer assistance to faculty regarding when and how AI may be used without going against teaching values. To illustrate, although AI-generated feedback can help speed up the process, it must also provide advice that is both constructive and relates to every student's needs. Just like AI in admissions, AI should not influence what is taught in courses or reduce instructor decision-making. Notably, developers suggest that students need to stay engaged as they go through the learning process. AI should boost the connection between educators and students, instead of substituting it. Educational developers make certain the assessment process is fair, the course focuses on the main objectives, and it fulfill inclusivity goals. Developers in education support higher education's core values by encouraging students and teachers to adopt AI in a proper manner (Ayyoub et al., 2025).

4.1 Ensuring Alignment Between AI Tools, Learning Outcomes, and Assessment

To succeed in education, AI should be planned and matched with specific learning goals and suitable ways to measure students' progress. Educational developers make certain that AI tools serve a purpose in learning and are not only used casually. In other words, schools ought to use AI solutions that enhance the abilities teachers seek to develop in students. For this reason, if the outcome is meant to develop critical thinking, an AI tool that grades only multiple-choice questions may fail. On the other hand, developers could give faculty AI tools that give open-ended questions, review students' written arguments with natural language processing, and give formative feedback. Analytics based on AI should provide teachers with data on students' progress with learning, not just with their results. Personnel in educational development guide teachers in clarifying how each AI tool is matched with the kind of outcome expected at a cognitive level, whether this is recall, application, analysis, or synthesis. They make sure each assessment is legitimate, in line with set rules, and treats everyone fairly. If this does not happen, there is a chance that technology may push the course of instruction and not truly serve the goals of teaching (Black et al., 2024). Action taken by educational developers enables AI to support teaching instead of standing apart as a separate change.

4.2 Maintaining Student Agency and Engagement Through Ethical Use of AI

While AI gains a bigger role in schools, making certain students keep control of their learning is extremely important. Developers of education stress that, though AI personalizes lessons and performs certain tasks, it should never limit the student's independence, creativity, or voice. AI usage that is morally right must help students, not make them less powerful. Such AI systems as intelligent feedback engines and adaptive learning platforms need to show their users how they operate. It is important for students to know how their data is handled, how paths for them are built, and how recommendations are provided. Educational developers support faculty in choosing AI applications that support privacy, have open opt-in choices, and make it possible for learners to review AI guidance. Furthermore, engagement is focused on real interaction, more than just using advanced technology. With the help of developers, the learning environments use AI to promote investigative, conversational, and reasoning skills. Chatbots should be used to spark interest and virtual simulations to let learners learn and practice their skills hands-on. Making students aware of ethics, educational developers guarantee that AI adds to their learning experience by remaining active. They support spread of practices that emphasize open collaboration, fairness, and encourage all voices, ensuring that education is still centered on people in a world full of technology (Dulundu, 2024).

5. INSTITUTIONAL COLLABORATION AND CHANGE MANAGEMENT

AI is more likely to succeed in higher education when there is collaboration and good change management among different institutions. Often, adopting AI in education works best when administrators, faculty, IT, developers in schools, and external agencies join forces. Working as a team leads to a common goal and makes it easier to combine resources and abilities. Organizations have to create groups made up of different professionals to manage AI initiatives, so that using technology matches the main education and institution goals. Handling resistance and leading smooth changes are both important roles of managing change. It means being open with information, working with others, and always developing new skills. It is important for leaders in schools to be flexible and encourages an environment where feedback can be gathered to study outcomes and potential problems. Having policies that are clear and projects marked as 'test bed' or 'working example' can inspire others to join in with confidence. Furthermore, organizations should implement agile methods that help them carry out, check, and improve their AI tools step by step. If AI skills are taught to everyone, all team members are able to play a significant part in new projects. When AI is implemented with the help of both collaboration and proper change management, it remains sustainable and focused on the main goals of education (Kuhail et al., 2023). The Figure 7 representing an organization or initiative focused on AI development, research, and ethical oversight. The minimalist design suggests a professional or academic context. The table 5 Lists collaborative structures (e.g., AI task forces, innovation labs) that support AI integration, highlighting the roles of educational developers and the intended outcomes.

Figure 7. AI Task Force Logo

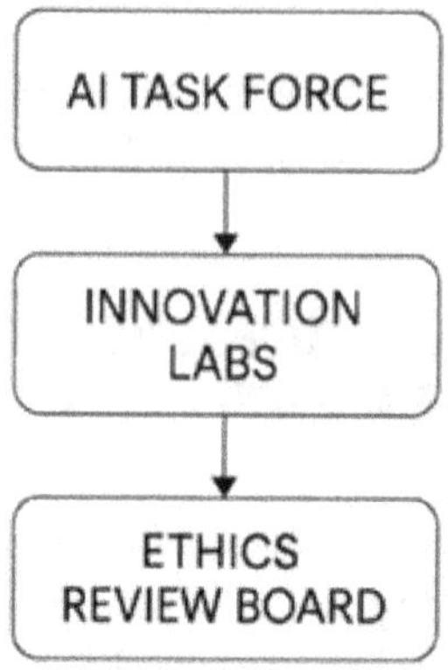

Table 5 Institutional Collaboration Frameworks for AI Integration

Structure Type	Participants Involved	Role of Developers	Desired Outcome
AI Task Force	Faculty, Admin, IT	Strategy Alignment	Responsible AI Implementation
Innovation Labs	Developers, Students, Educators	Co-design AI Tools	Pedagogically Sound Solutions
Ethics Review Board	Policy Makers, Developers	Bias and Privacy Review	Trustworthy and Fair AI Systems

5.1 EDUCATIONAL DEVELOPERS' ROLES

Assisting as Colleges implement AI technology, they work in various ways. In this case, they shape educational practice, policy, pedagogy, and technology integration, and therefore, they are key players in promoting the responsible, sustainable, and meaningful integration of AI in education. Their primary role is to implement the institution's vision by illustrating how AI helps enhance teaching and learning scenarios. They facilitate interfaces between educators and educational technologists to ensure that AI development is sufficiently pedagogically grounded. They also assist in enhancing faculty confidence and professional skills by a strategic design of AI-centered programs, workshops, and learning resources that offer academic responsibly and progress. Also, policy makers are instrumental in formulating AI policies of educational institutions which, in particular, are concerned with data ethics, equity and inclusion, the privacy of learners, and accountably open algorithms. They help create responsible rules and see to it that they are followed in school. Also, they help organize the process for change, foster cooperation among departments, collect feedback, and back up continual improvement. Educational developers promote using AI by encouraging reflection, fairness, and new approaches based on the mission (Doğan et al., 2025).

5.1.1 Shaping Campus-Wide AI Strategies

It is the job of educational developers to ensure that AI technology on campus supports and promotes the principles and goals of the institution. They involve educational methods in the planning process, so AI is introduced only when it will help with teaching, learning, and supporting students' achievements. Developers partner with senior employees to find out what the company wants to concentrate on and locate opportunities where AI can play a role. They urge for designing schools to put students first and encourage responsible applications of AI everywhere in schools. It also requires being part of strategic papers, special committees, and digital change plans. Having them part of the process means that projects will think about future success, make education easy for teachers, and look for ways to measure the benefit of AI. They also make sure that different departments work with a consistent approach, so nothing is fragmented. They point to success stories and help make them work in different institutions. In the end, educational developers turn AI into a platform that drives new ideas and matches the institution's goals for outstanding education. To ensure AI is used consistently and properly throughout the company, the contribution of key individuals is necessary (Mah & Groß, 2024).

5.1.2 Leading Cross-Functional Teams

AI is usually introduced in higher education by working together with IT, academics, research, libraries, and student support. The reason educational developers can lead such teams is their clear grasp of how teaching works as well as organizational behaviors. They encourage people with different goals to work together through forming shared purposes and terms. For instance, IT usually looks after performance and security of information whereas faculty determines if the system suits their teaching goals and is easy for students to use. Educational developers help to close the gap and make sure AI projects deliver on both technology and education needs. As part of their leadership, developers arrange trial activities, assess if the tools are effective, get feedback from different stages, and encourage improvement using what happens in the classroom. They show teams how to act ethically in making decisions, always provide clear explanations for AI advice, and handle data correctly. Also, they assist in forming a culture that supports new ideas and teamwork, so departments can generate ways to address challenges together. Such an approach helps professionals develop greater trust, want to use the technology, and end up with better context-aware AI systems (Salih, 2024). Managing teams from different areas, educational developers make it certain that AI work is done collaboratively and is anchored on common principles.

5.1.3 Aligning AI Initiatives with Institutional Missions

For AI usage to be effective and last, it has to be consistent with the institution's mission, vision, and values. Educational developers bring technological chances and educational objectives together by interpreting and linking them. They make sure that the use of AI does not violate the basic principles of the institution. Should a university appreciate inclusive education, developers would look at if AI tools are able to meet the needs of varied students, help learners from various backgrounds, or limit bias in evaluating students. When innovation is key, developers search for tools that give professors the ability to revise their classes or improve the way students interact (Oh & Sanfilippo, 2024). Developers of education also see that using AI in schools advances the main education goals and assists departments in setting goals and assessing the results. They suggest AI should not step in for human interaction, creative thinking, and guidance in education. By taking part in discussions about governance and strategic planning, educational developers add AI efforts to the university's growth, assessments for accreditation, and procedures for evaluating staff members (Yeralan & Lee, 2023). When the goals are aligned, there is clear and reliable practice, which also increases how strong and important the institution is seen. All in all, educational developers link AI work to the university's identity to make sure higher education is changed in line with its mission.

6. ETHICAL FRAMEWORKS AND RESPONSIBLE AI USE

Higher education should include ethical rules when using AI. Since AI has an impact on making choices, personal learning ways, and evaluation, firms should set up policies that center on being clear, fair, private, and responsible. Ethical frameworks serve as the basis for considering AI tools by their results and their effects on students' rights, data privacy, and fairness in education. Nowadays, to use AI effectively in the classroom, it is important that students and teachers see how the system operates. AI systems should be carefully monitored by institutions to ensure they are not unfair to certain groups based on race, gender, or where they come from financially. People involved in education development and making policies should team up to ensure that all students' information is respected and protected. Also, responsible AI focuses on making sure human supervision is a priority. Teachers should be the ones making the major choices, so AI does not take over their responsibilities (Karimi & Khawaja, 2023). Giving faculty and students knowledge about AI will create users who are aware of its strengths and weaknesses. After all, ethical use of AI helps maintain the standards of academics and encourages trust in all educational changes. Such efforts resonate with the philosophical underpinnings of the Recommendation on the Ethics of Artificial Intelligence (2021) by UNESCO, which stresses the importance of clarity, inclusion, human oversight, and control over data. Correspondingly, the OECD's AI in Education Guidelines (2023) stresses the importance of risk and innovation equilibrium, alongside the protection of privacy, inequity, and academic dishonesty. An institution's strategy on the thoughtful and responsible implementation of Artificial Intelligence in higher education will become more relevant and well-governed with internationally accepted and recognized frameworks.

6.1 Addressing Bias, Privacy, and Transparency in AI-Based Learning

Even though AI-based learning systems may bring major changes to education, they raise important issues about bias, privacy, and how transparent they are. Sometimes, AI outcomes are not fair to students because the training data is biased. If historical data lacks representation of some groups, an AI tutor could choose the students from those groups more often. One should use several kinds of input data and incorporate algorithms that ensure fairness to limit this problem. Having regular checks and all-inclusive tests during the development process can help detect and solve any biases before launching the system. Many people are concerned about privacy, since AI gathers plenty of information about students, including their outcomes and daily behaviors. Without proper protection, private data may fall into wrong hands or be taken through breaches. The main rules you should follow are GDPR, FERPA, and protect information by encryption and anonymization. School staff and students should manage their personal data and determine whether to opt out whenever they want. Showing your work allows (Hannan & Liu, 2021)people to clarify and describe how AI made a decision. It is difficult to understand how certain conclusions are reached in deep learning because these models are a "black box". Tools have to present the basics for everyone who uses AI in education. With open-source frameworks and full descriptions about them, trust can be improved.

Making sure that AI-based learning is fair, private, and transparent allows it to deliver results and follow good practices.

6.2 Promoting Digital Ethics and Inclusive Design Principles

It ensures that technology in education respects people's rights, treats everyone equally, and does not cause any damage. Discrimination should not occur in algorithms, people's agreement should be sought for using their data, and those who use AI must be accountable. All developers involved in AI work should obey ethical standards to ensure that everyone using AI is safe. AI-powered tools can be used by all learners when helping is included in their design. With text-to-speech, different languages, and flexible interfaces, accessibility problems can be tackled. When AI tools are co-designed with the help of marginalized groups, they receive what they require. Also, giving educators and students digital literacy helps them interact with AI in a thoughtful way. The content of training should deal with ethical aspects of AI, privacy issues when handling data, and learning to see biases. If we make sure that digital ethics and inclusivity are part of AI design, we can develop learning spaces that treat all people alike and support their growth (Bing & Leong, 2025).

7. CASE STUDIES AND BEST PRACTICES

This part looks at how AI has been successfully used in education by highlighting the main contribution of educational developers. In an instance study, a university introduced AI in learning, asking educational developers to prepare teachers to adapt materials according to each student's test results. The usage of AI alongside sustaining the guidance of teachers, shows increased learning and engagement which is why it is tailor-made for instructor-led scenarios. Another instance is of an institution that opted for the implementation of AI powered chatbots to guide the students. To ensure that the chatbots provided academic support by answering queries within the shortest possible time, the Faculty, IT unit and educational developers worked collaboratively. The cashpoints emphasizes the need for the automation and compassion convergence that the world as technology specialists and educators must come to. Some of the best methods learned are Training workshops set up for educators that show them how to include AI without swaying the academic integrity. These guidelines for AI were made with input from educational developers to fight bias and protect information privacy in the use of AI. Advisors and coaches are involved in the process as feedback is gathered to improve it (Krishna Pasupuleti, 2024). These illustrations show that in order to use AI well, educational developers should align technology with the institution's values and help it improve learning. The Figure 8 highlights the University of Michigan's "Adaptive STEM Courses," emphasizing innovation in science and technology education. It showcases a focus on "Improved Student Outcomes," suggesting data-driven advancements in learning effectiveness. The clean, text-based design reflects an academic or promotional context, likely for a program, report, or presentation.

Figure 8. University of Michigan STEM Initiative

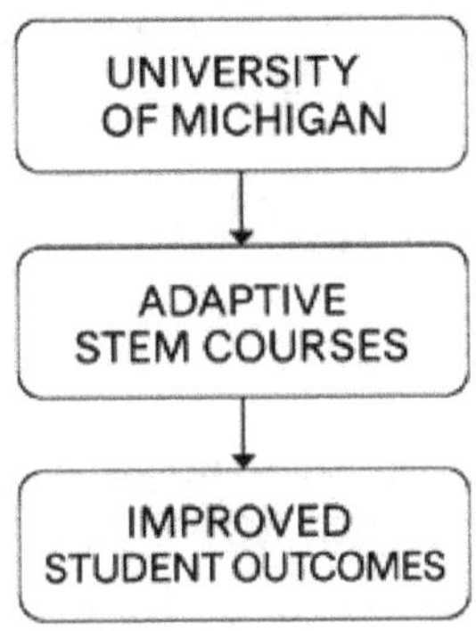

7.1 Real-World AI: Developer Innovations

A major advancement of AI in education, teaching and learning, has seen to the efforts of all the members of the team involved in the advancement of education 'AI in education, teaching and learning' the members of the team involved in the advancement of education. In cooperated to provide AI driven adaptive learning for STEM subjects. Along with the students themselves, the trainers participated in the workshops which were aimed to help trainers custom the AI strategies to suit the individual needs of each student. With the adoption of these policies, course completions increased by 20%, which indicates the effectiveness of the faculty in implementing AI in the teaching process. Chatbot systems aimed at advising students constitute just one of many examples of this collaboration. Along with the educators, the developers ensured that the automation of the Chatbot system was in compliance with the policies which govern human council in order to avoid conflict between the automated council and the humans (Slimi & Carballido, 2023). There was an initial 30% reduction in the volume of routine inquiries directed to the advisers, enabling them to focus more of their efforts on the student's more serious concerns. Analysts and developmental staff helped faculty consider the data and came up with helpful measures that improved retention by 15%. They show that when developers lead AI projects, their results can definitely help education. The table 6 Showcases the quantitative and qualitative outcomes from real-world case studies (e.g., University of Michigan, Arizona State University) where educational developers guided AI adoption in courses.

Table 6 Outcomes of Developer-Led AI Integration Initiatives

Institution	AI Initiative	Outcome Metrics
University of Michigan	Adaptive STEM Courses	+22% exam scores, -35% DFW rate
Arizona State University	AI Writing Assistant	+40% revision rate, 8-10 hours saved/week

7.1.1 Example 1: Adaptive Learning Platform in STEM Courses (University of Michigan)

Educational developers at the University of Michigan partnered with faculty to implement an AI-powered adaptive learning system in introductory STEM courses. The developers:

- Conducted workshops to train instructors on personalizing AI-generated content.
- Integrated real-time analytics dashboards to track student progress.
- Established feedback loops to refine algorithms based on pedagogical needs.

Results:

- 22% improvement in exam scores compared to traditional courses.
- 35% reduction in DFW (D, F, Withdrawal) rates.
- Faculty reported better ability to identify and support struggling students. This case demonstrates how developer-led training and iterative design can make AI integration pedagogically effective. The Figure 9 compares the percentage change in exam scores and DFW (D, F, Withdrawal) rates between traditional and AI-adaptive STEM courses. It shows a 22% improvement in exam scores and a 35% reduction in DFW rates with AI integration at the University of Michigan.

Figure 9. Impact of AI-Powered Adaptive Learning in STEM Courses

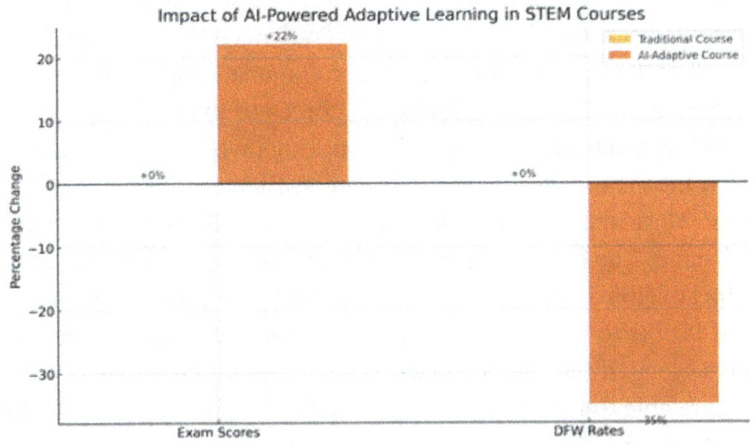

7.1.2 Example 2: AI Writing Assistant Rollout (Arizona State University)

ASU's educational technology team developed a phased implementation of an AI writing feedback tool across composition courses. Developers:

- Created discipline-specific rubric alignments for different writing assignments.
- Ran faculty "sandbox" sessions to test and customize feedback parameters.
- Developed student-facing tutorials on interpreting AI suggestions critically.

Results:

- 40% increase in student writing revisions submitted.
- Faculty saved 8-10 hours/week on initial feedback cycles.
- No significant decrease in instructor-student writing conferences. This example shows how careful scaffolding by developers can lead to AI augmenting rather than replacing human instruction. Both cases highlight the crucial mediating role of educational developers in ensuring AI tools are Pedagogically aligned, Faculty-supported, Implemented with appropriate training structures, and Continuously improved through feedback mechanisms.

7.1.3 Global Case Studies Beyond the U.S.

The strategies on new approaches and innovative ways, including the use of context-sensitive approaches on the aim of AI within education particularly, coming from the U. S. is the central aim of the other countries approaches as well. Understanding the nuances of the world when it comes to the policies and pedagogical strategies and regional differences in its workings would further help understand its impact on the AI use in educational sectors. Elements of AI is an open-access course by the University of Helsinki in Finland focused on advocating AI literacy on a global scale. The course is a part of larger EU initiative to aid in the use and understanding of ethically guided technology. With over 300,000 participants around the globe AI is able to foster democratic education. It is through specialized public engagements blended through scholarship of the teaching and accessible designs; universities are able to facilitate public understanding of AI systems. The NUS has established AI powered systems to gauge students engagement on a mental, emotional and social level. NUS pays special attention to the policies regarding student data and centers them in the work including governance regarding the artificial intelligence systems. On the African continent, the University of South Africa (UNISA) has begun experimenting with AI-driven tutoring chatbots for distance education. Due to the sheer size and diversity of the student population, UNISA has to utilize AI systems to respond to more routine queries, allowing human tutors to offer more complex academic assistance. This example shows how AI can help overcome gaps in higher education hyper constrained systems and the relatively common resource-poor faculty to student ratios. All of these international examples together show that the adoption of AI is not synonymous with advanced economies. Quite the opposite, these international case studies show that context, equity, and governance in transcendent factors influence the ways in which each region will approach AI in the transformation of higher education. The below table 7 compares international initiatives demonstrating diverse approaches to AI adoption in higher education across regions.

Table 7. Global Case Studies of AI in Higher Education

Region	Institution	AI Initiative	Key Outcomes	Distinctive Features
Europe	University of Helsinki (Finland)	Elements of AI open-access course	300,000+ learners worldwide; improved AI literacy	Scalable, democratized AI education; aligns with EU ethics and digital literacy policies
Asia	National University of Singapore (NUS)	AI-powered student analytics	Enhanced tracking of engagement and well-being; data-informed interventions	Strong data governance; linked to Singapore's national AI strategy
Africa	University of South Africa (UNISA)	AI tutoring chatbots for distance learning	Improved response time to routine queries; better academic support in large cohorts	Cost-effective solution for high student–faculty ratios; supports remote learners
North America (for comparison)	University of Michigan & Arizona State University (U.S.)	Adaptive STEM courses; AI writing assistant	Higher exam scores, reduced DFW rates; increased revision rates, faculty time savings	Strong faculty–developer collaboration; structured scaling models

7.2 Highlighting Organizational Structures That Support Sustainable Change

Successful AI integration requires institutional frameworks that encourage innovation while maintaining pedagogical integrity. Key structures include:

- AI Task Forces – Cross-functional teams (faculty, developers, IT, and administrators) that guide AI strategy and policy.
- Faculty Learning Communities – Peer-led groups where educators share AI best practices and troubleshoot challenges.
- Pilot Programs with Scalability in Mind – Small-scale AI trials that incorporate feedback before wider rollout.

For example, one university established an AI Innovation Lab, where educational developers, instructors, and students co-design AI tools. This collaborative approach ensures that solutions are pedagogically sound and aligned with institutional goals. Another institution implemented AI ethics review boards to evaluate tools for bias, privacy, and transparency before adoption. These examples demonstrate that when educational developers lead AI integration within supportive organizational structures, institutions can achieve sustainable, scalable, and ethical advancements in teaching and learning (Suresh et al., 2024). The Figure 10 chart visualizes the influence of AI writing assistants on key educational outcomes. It highlights a 40%

increase in student writing revisions and 8-10 hours of faculty time saved weekly, while showing no significant change in instructor-student conferences demonstrating AI's ability to augment rather than replace human interaction.

Figure 10. Impact of AI Writing Assistant at Arizona State University

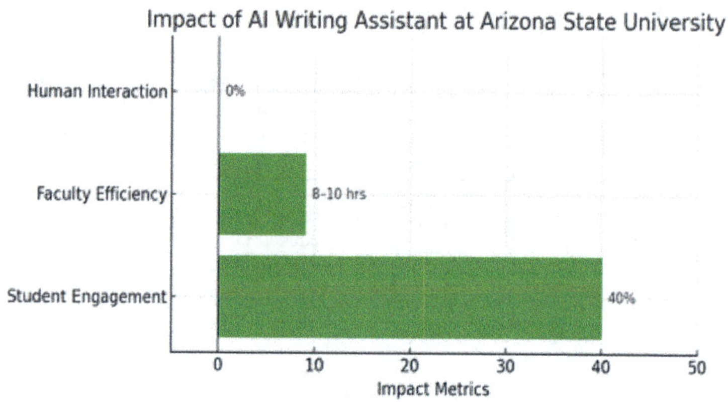

7.3 The Central Role of Educational Developers

Educational developers bridge the gap between technological innovation and pedagogical practice. Their expertise allows them to translate AI's potential into tangible benefits for teaching and learning while mitigating risks such as bias, privacy concerns, and loss of human agency. Key responsibilities include:

- Faculty Empowerment: Through workshops, learning communities, and one-on-one support, they equip educators with the skills to integrate AI tools like adaptive learning platforms, Intelligent Tutoring Systems, and automated assessments effectively.
- Curriculum Alignment: They ensure AI tools enhance rather than disrupt learning outcomes by aligning technology with instructional goals and assessment strategies.
- Ethical Leadership: By advocating for transparency, inclusivity, and data privacy, they help institutions navigate the ethical complexities of AI adoption. Case studies from the University of Michigan and Arizona State University

demonstrate how developer-led initiatives such as adaptive STEM courses and AI writing assistants yield measurable improvements in student performance, engagement, and faculty efficiency (Ogunsakin, 2024). These successes hinge on structured training, iterative feedback, and collaborative design, all facilitated by educational developers.

7.4 Sustainable Change Through Institutional Collaboration

For AI integration to endure, it must be embedded within supportive organizational structures. Educational developers drive this process by:

- Leading Cross-Functional Teams: They unite faculty, IT, administrators, and students to co-design solutions that balance technological capabilities with educational values.
- Shaping Policy: By contributing to AI task forces and ethics review boards, they institutionalize best practices for fairness, accountability, and accessibility.
- Piloting Scalable Models: Small-scale AI projects, refined through feedback, allow institutions to test and adapt tools before full deployment. Examples like AI Innovation Labs and faculty learning communities illustrate how these structures foster cultures of experimentation and continuous improvement. When institutions invest in such frameworks, AI integration becomes a strategic priority rather than an isolated initiative.

7.5 The Future of AI in Higher Education

As AI evolves, educational developers will remain essential in addressing emerging challenges and opportunities. Future priorities include:

- Expanding Digital Ethics: Ensuring AI tools are audited for bias, transparent in decision-making, and respectful of student autonomy.
- Promoting Inclusive Design: Collaborating with diverse stakeholders to create AI systems that serve all learners equitably.
- Balancing Automation and Human Touch: Preserving the irreplaceable role of educator-student interactions while leveraging AI for efficiency.

The effective use of AI in colleges and universities depends mostly on thinking about people and their needs, rather than technology alone. The vision falls under the care of educational developers to make sure AI does not challenge the key values of education. It proves that AI should be handled deliberately and cannot solve issues by itself. Since they are knowledgeable about teaching and technology, educational developers are best able to use AI safely and effectively. When they invest in faculty growth, ethical foundations, and working side by side, they allow universities to deal with the challenges of digitalization (Selvam & González Vallejo, 2025). Because higher education is always adapting, the leadership will guide it so that AI helps address equity, improves thinking, and supports student achievements. As education moves toward using AI, developers will guide institutions and ensure they experience change confidently and clearly.

8. CONCLUSION

There is a big change in how schools operate and change when AI is adopted within higher education. Improvements in technology prove that educational developers have become very important. Since they are in the midst of education, technology, and policy, educational developers make sure AI is handled wisely and appropriately. They take part in various roles, for example, assisting professors with development, organizing AI with the purpose of education, preventing fraud, and encouraging the use of ethics in AI. Educational developers play an important part in explaining AI to teachers so they are not confused. When faculty take part in designed lessons, practical work, and continuous learning, they find out how to use AI like the latest smart tutors, adaptive tools, and automated testing. Working through these tools improves teaching methods and encourages students to take part in their studies. By helping AI be used in classrooms, educational developers make sure it supports and improves teachers' work. Besides training, educational developers play an important part in preserving the pedagogical quality of any program. They state that AI should add value, but not completely control how teaching is done. They need to make sure that AI tools suit the expected learning outcomes, promote inclusiveness in education, and care about students' freedom and confidentiality.

The field of AI encourages people to develop algorithms that are fair and easy to explain. To maintain the focus on people at the heart of higher education, this monitoring is very important. It is also important to cooperate when using AI, and education experts are great at heading groups that involve teachers, technicians, administrators, and students. They help everyone involved share their ideas, use technology to meet needs in education, and test AI solutions for wide use. These groups play a vital role in bringing AI into the institution's strategy and plan for the future. AI is embedded into digital transformation plans by developers so that major digital transformation goals are always met. Applying AI in real applications highlights the usefulness of AI developed by developers. According to the University of Michigan and Arizona State University, the use of adaptive learning systems and feedback tools made possible by AI, together with educational developer advice, improves academic results, helps students remember information, and makes faculty work more productive. This shows that AI projects benefit most from structured support, repeating development, and a solid educational base. In the future, educational developers will play an even more important part. As AI continues to improve, the problems involving ethics, inclusive design, and the relationship between machines and people will grow as well. Because of their background, educational developers can lead the way to making sure that AI benefits education and doesn't cause any problems. Thanks to their knowledge of education and technology, the way AI is used in education can stay true to its main purpose. All in all, educational developers do not just help with changes they take responsibility for new ideas.

REFERENCES

Aarthi, S., Ravikumar, R. N., Khudayberganov, S., Ismailov, A., & Khujaniyozova, O. (2025). Using Intelligent Tutoring Systems to enhance student engagement. In *Advances in Computational Intelligence and Robotics* (pp. 155–188). IGI Global., DOI: 10.4018/979-8-3373-1827-1.ch008

Alexander, L. M., Bowser, J., Caruthers, K., Sekhon, L., Statler, M., Straker, H., Rizzolo, D., De La Rosa, H., & Simeon, D. T. (2025). Fear factor: Faculty perceptions of artificial intelligence in physician associate education. *The Journal of Physician Assistant Education : the Official Journal of the Physician Assistant Education Association*, *36*(3), e288–e294. DOI: 10.1097/JPA.0000000000000667 PMID: 40168397

Amani Mohammad, H., Abeer, B. H., Aya, A., Ghadi, B., & Farah, A. (2024). "impact of artificial intelligence on faculty's teaching development: A quantitative research in Saudi private universities." Communications of International Proceedings. https://doi.org/DOI: 10.5171/2024.4342624

Ayyoub, A. M., Khlaif, Z. N., Shamali, M., Abu Eideh, B., Assali, A., Hattab, M. K., Barham, K. A., & Bsharat, T. R. K. (2025). Advancing higher education with GenAI: Factors influencing educator AI literacy. *Frontiers in Education, 10*. Advance online publication. DOI: 10.3389/feduc.2025.1530721

Bing, Z. J., & Leong, W. Y. (2025). Ethical design of AI for education and learning systems. *ASM Science Journal, 20*(1), 1–9. DOI: 10.32802/asmscj.2025.1917

Black, N. B., George, S., Eguchi, A., Dempsey, J. C., Langran, E., Fraga, L., Brunvand, S., & Howard, N. (2024). A framework for approaching AI education in Educator Preparation Programs. Proceedings of the ... AAAI Conference on Artificial Intelligence. AAAI Conference on Artificial Intelligence, 38(21), 23069–23077. https://doi.org/DOI: 10.1609/aaai.v38i21.30351

Çela, E., Fonkam, M. M., Vajjhala, N. R., & Vedishchev, A. (2024). Artificial intelligence in education. In *Advances in Educational Technologies and Instructional Design* (pp. 1–20). IGI Global., DOI: 10.4018/979-8-3693-7220-3.ch001

Dias, J. T., Santos, A., & Mamede, H. S. (2025). From data to action. In *Advances in Computational Intelligence and Robotics* (pp. 229–252). IGI Global., DOI: 10.4018/979-8-3693-7195-4.ch010

Doğan, M., Celik, A., & Arslan, H. (2025). AI in higher education: Risks and opportunities from the academician perspective. *European Journal of Education, 60*(1). Advance online publication. DOI: 10.1111/ejed.12863

Dubey, P. K., & Crevar, A. R. (2025). Integrating Artificial Intelligence in higher education. In *Advances in Educational Technologies and Instructional Design* (pp. 181–208). IGI Global., DOI: 10.4018/979-8-3373-0502-8.ch008

Dulundu, A. (2024). AI in education: Benefits and concerns. *Next Generation Journal for The Young Researchers*, *8*(1), 81. DOI: 10.62802/3fr4f412

George, B., & Wooden, O. (2023). Managing the strategic transformation of higher education through artificial intelligence. *Administrative Sciences*, *13*(9), 196. DOI: 10.3390/admsci13090196

Hannan, E., & Liu, S. (2021). AI: new source of competitiveness in higher education. Competitiveness Review Journal, ahead-of-print(ahead-of-print). https://doi .org/DOI: 10.1108/cr-03-2021-0045

Henshaw, C. A. (2025). Multimedia learning and UDL in UK higher education. *Journal of Advanced Research in Education*, *4*(2), 27–33. DOI: 10.56397/jare.2025.03.03

Karimi, H., & Khawaja, S. (2023). The impact of artificial intelligence on higher education in England. *Creative Education*, *14*(12), 2405–2415. DOI: 10.4236/ce.2023.1412154

Khan, M. J., Lajber, M., Bilal, N., & Khan, S., Zarrin `Siddiqi, & Ahmad, A. (2024). The barriers and solution to artificial Intelligence adoption in Medical Education: A qualitative study. Journal of Saidu Medical College. *Swat*, *14*(4), 341–347. DOI: 10.52206/jsmc.2024.14.4.957

Krishna Pasupuleti, M. (2024). AI-Powered Learning: Transformative innovations in Smart Education Technology. In Advanced AI-Driven EdTech: Transformative Innovations in Smart Learning (pp. 292–310). National Education Services. https://doi.org/DOI: 10.62311/nesx/802874

Kuhail, M. A., Alturki, N., Alramlawi, S., & Alhejori, K. (2023). Interacting with educational chatbots: A systematic review. *Education and Information Technologies*, *28*(1), 973–1018. DOI: 10.1007/s10639-022-11177-3

Mah, D.-K., & Groß, N. (2024). Artificial intelligence in higher education: Exploring faculty use, self-efficacy, distinct profiles, and professional development needs. *International Journal of Educational Technology in Higher Education*, *21*(1). Advance online publication. DOI: 10.1186/s41239-024-00490-1

Mahmoud, C. F., & Sørensen, J. T. (2024). Artificial Intelligence in personalized learning with a focus on current developments and future prospects. *Research and Advances in Education*, *3*(8), 25–31. DOI: 10.56397/rae.2024.08.04

Nurjanah, A., Salsabila, I. N., Azzahra, A., Rahayu, R., & Marlina, N. (2024). Artificial intelligence (AI) usage in today's teaching and learning process: A review. *Syntax Idea*, *6*(3), 1517–1523. DOI: 10.46799/syntax-idea.v6i3.3126

Ogunsakin, I. (2024). Unlocking the potential of artificial intellignce. *International Journal of Research in STEM Education*, *6*(2), 37–49. DOI: 10.33830/ijrse.v6i2.1698

Oh, S. H., & Sanfilippo, M. (2024). University governance for responsible AI. *Proceedings of the ALISE Annual Conference*. https://doi.org/DOI: 10.21900/j.alise.2024.1706

Pedró, F. (2020). Applications of Artificial Intelligence to higher education: Possibilities, evidence, and challenges. *IUL Research*, *1*(1), 61–76. DOI: 10.57568/iulres.v1i1.43

Popenici, S. A. D., & Kerr, S. (2017). Exploring the impact of artificial intelligence on teaching and learning in higher education. *Research and Practice in Technology Enhanced Learning*, *12*(1), 22. DOI: 10.1186/s41039-017-0062-8 PMID: 30595727

Ravikumar, R. N., Aarthi, S., Ruzimova, F., & Mamadiyarov, Z. (2025). Training and development in AI-driven education scaling solutions. In *Advances in Computational Intelligence and Robotics* (pp. 267–298). IGI Global Scientific Publishing., DOI: 10.4018/979-8-3373-2185-1.ch010

Rienties, B., Køhler Simonsen, H., & Herodotou, C. (2020). Defining the boundaries between artificial intelligence in education, computer-supported collaborative learning, educational data mining, and learning analytics: A need for coherence. *Frontiers in Education*, *5*. Advance online publication. DOI: 10.3389/feduc.2020.00128

Salih, S. M. (2024). Perceptions of faculty and students about use of artificial intelligence in medical education: A qualitative study. *Cureus*, *16*(4), e57605. DOI: 10.7759/cureus.57605 PMID: 38707183

Sanasintani, S. (2023). Revitalizing the higher education curriculum through an artificial intelligence approach: An overview. *Journal of Social Science Utilizing Technology*, *1*(4), 239–248. DOI: 10.55849/jssut.v1i4.670

Selvam, M., & González Vallejo, R. (2025). Ethical and privacy considerations in AI-driven language learning. *LatIA*, *3*, 328. DOI: 10.62486/latia2025328

Sholeh, M. I. (2025). Educational transformation through artificial intelligence. In *Advances in Computational Intelligence and Robotics* (pp. 25–40). IGI Global., DOI: 10.4018/979-8-3693-7260-9.ch002

Slimi, Z., & Carballido, B. V. (2023). Systematic review: AI's impact on higher education - learning, teaching, and career opportunities. TEM Journal, 1627–1637. https://doi.org/DOI: 10.18421/tem123-44

Suresh, C., Ali, S. M., & Devaki, V. (2024). Perception about usage of GAI tools in teaching and research by teachers and students in higher education institutions. In *Advances in Educational Technologies and Instructional Design* (pp. 381–412). IGI Global., DOI: 10.4018/979-8-3693-8191-5.ch015

Wang, J., Hussain, Y., & Mao, C. (2025). Artificial intelligence-driven personalized learning: Psychological implications and educational outcomes. International Journal of Education. *Humanities and Social Sciences*, *2*(1), 24–39. DOI: 10.70088/3wnrs278

Yeralan, S., & Lee, L. A. (2023). Generative AI: Challenges to higher education. *Sustainable Engineering and Innovation*, *5*(2), 107–116. DOI: 10.37868/sei.v5i2.id196

KEY TERMS AND DEFINITIONS

Adaptive Learning Systems: AI-powered platforms that deliver personalized content and adjust learning paths based on a student's performance, pace, and preferences.

AI Task Forces: Cross-disciplinary institutional groups formed to align AI adoption with educational missions and policies while addressing risks and opportunities.

Artificial Intelligence (AI) in Education: The use of intelligent algorithms and systems such as adaptive learning, tutoring platforms, and automated assessments to enhance teaching, learning, and institutional processes.

Automated Grading Tools: AI applications that evaluate assignments, quizzes, or essays, providing quick feedback and reducing faculty workload while maintaining academic standards.

Bias in AI: Systematic unfairness that arises when AI algorithms reflect or amplify pre-existing inequalities in the data, potentially disadvantaging certain student groups.

Case Studies in AI Adoption: Real-world examples (e.g., University of Michigan's adaptive STEM courses, Arizona State University's AI writing assistant) demonstrating successful developer-led AI integration.

Change Management: Strategic processes employed by institutions to ensure smooth adoption of AI, including stakeholder engagement, feedback loops, and scalable implementation.

Digital Ethics: Principles ensuring that AI-driven technologies respect user rights, promote equity, and prevent misuse of learner data in education.

Educational Developers: Specialists who bridge pedagogy and technology, guiding faculty and institutions in the responsible integration of AI into higher education while ensuring ethical and pedagogical integrity.

Ethical AI Use: The responsible deployment of AI in education that prioritizes fairness, transparency, data privacy, inclusivity, and human oversight.

Faculty Development: Structured training, workshops, and communities designed to equip educators with the knowledge and skills to adopt and apply AI in teaching.

Inclusive Design: Designing AI systems in education to be accessible and equitable for all learners, including marginalized groups, through features such as multilingual support and adaptive interfaces.

Innovation Labs: Collaborative spaces where developers, faculty, and students co-design and test AI tools to ensure pedagogical relevance and inclusivity.

Institutional Collaboration: Cross-functional teamwork among faculty, IT, administrators, developers, and policymakers to integrate AI in alignment with an institution's mission and goals.

Intelligent Tutoring Systems (ITS): AI-based systems that mimic human tutors by providing real-time, adaptive feedback and support tailored to individual learners.

Personalized Learning Paths: Customized educational journeys created by AI systems, allowing learners to progress at their own pace with content adapted to their needs and abilities.

Virtual Assistants: AI-driven tools that provide student support services such as answering queries, scheduling, and enrollment assistance, often available 24/7.

Chapter 12

Scaling Faculty AI Literacy:

Strategic Models for Institutional Transformation and Sustainable Adoption

Ramadevi Vitthal Salunkhe
https://orcid.org/0009-0005-0247-0115
G.H. Raisoni College of Engineering, Nagpur, India

Roshan Ramesh Kolte
https://orcid.org/0009-0005-1861-8399
K.D.K. College of Engineering, Nagpur, India

Chetan Arun Raut
St. Vincent Pallotti College of Engineering and Technology, Nagpur, India

Piyush K. Ingole
https://orcid.org/0000-0002-2257-1053
Yeshwantrao Chavan College of Engineering, Nagpur, India

Gunjan Chimote
Ramdeobaba University, Nagpur, India

Annaji Kuthe
https://orcid.org/0000-0003-0720-8421
K.D.K. College of Engineering, Nagpur, India

Shruti Sarwate
Jain University, India

ABSTRACT

The accelerating integration of artificial intelligence (AI) in higher education is reshaping faculty roles and institutional strategies. Beyond basic tool use, faculty now require multidimensional competencies that include technical proficiency, pedagogical integration, ethical reasoning, and continuous professional growth. This chapter investigates how institutions can scale AI literacy effectively by addressing barriers such as lack of training, time constraints, infrastructural gaps, and policy

DOI: 10.4018/979-8-3373-4129-3.ch012

ambiguity. Drawing on surveys, interviews, and policy analysis, it proposes sustainable models including progressive immersion, peer mentorship, and policy-driven innovation. International case studies demonstrate best practices in tiered learning, ethics integration, and community engagement. The chapter concludes with a phased roadmap and actionable recommendations for administrators, policymakers, and educators to foster systemic, equitable, and responsible AI literacy adoption.

1. INTRODUCTION

The integration of artificial intelligence (AI) into higher education is no longer a theoretical consideration—it is a present and accelerating reality that is reshaping academic landscapes worldwide. Institutions are increasingly expected to prepare faculty not only to adopt emerging AI tools but also to critically evaluate their implications for pedagogy, ethics, and policy. This transformation requires more than isolated professional development workshops; it demands a strategic, institution-wide approach that connects faculty skill-building to broader goals of innovation, equity, and sustainability. The introduction that follows sets the stage for understanding why AI literacy has become a cornerstone of institutional transformation, outlining the rationale for this study, the problems it seeks to address, its scope, and its significance in shaping the future of faculty development.

Figure 1. The Rising Urgency of AI Literacy in Higher Education

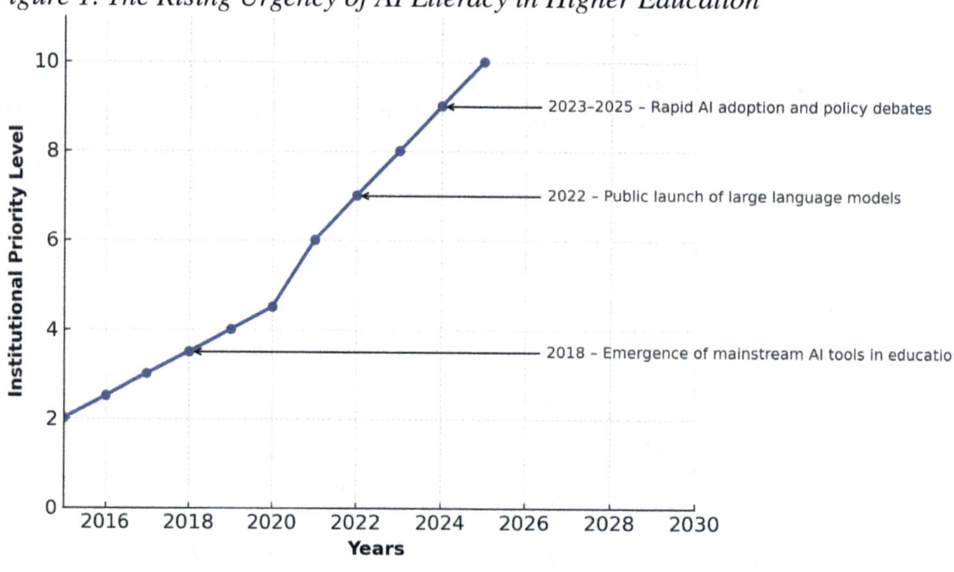

This Fig.1 illustrates the growing urgency for AI literacy in higher education, showing a gradual increase in institutional priority between 2015 and 2019, followed by a sharp escalation after the release of advanced generative AI systems in the early 2020s.

1.1 Context and Rationale

Artificial intelligence (AI) has emerged as one of the most disruptive forces in contemporary higher education. From generative AI tools such as ChatGPT and DALL·E to predictive analytics dashboards, adaptive learning systems, and AI-driven assessment platforms, universities are facing a technological shift that is faster and more complex than previous digital transitions. The pace of AI's development—measured in months rather than decades—means that institutions must respond urgently to avoid skill gaps and uneven adoption.

In this new reality, **faculty AI literacy** is no longer an optional competency (Laupichler et al., 2022; Zawacki-Richter et al., 2019). It is a multi-dimensional skillset that includes:

1. **Technical Proficiency** – Understanding AI fundamentals, machine learning concepts, and prompt engineering techniques.
2. **Pedagogical Application** – Designing AI-enhanced lessons, assessments, and research projects.
3. **Critical Evaluation** – Identifying bias, inaccuracies, and ethical issues in AI outputs.
4. **Ethical and Policy Awareness** – Navigating data privacy, intellectual property, and institutional compliance frameworks.
5. **Continuous Learning** – Updating skills as AI technologies evolve.

These competencies do not exist in isolation. They are interconnected and require **institutional support** to ensure sustainable adoption.

Figure 2. Core Components of Faculty AI Literacy

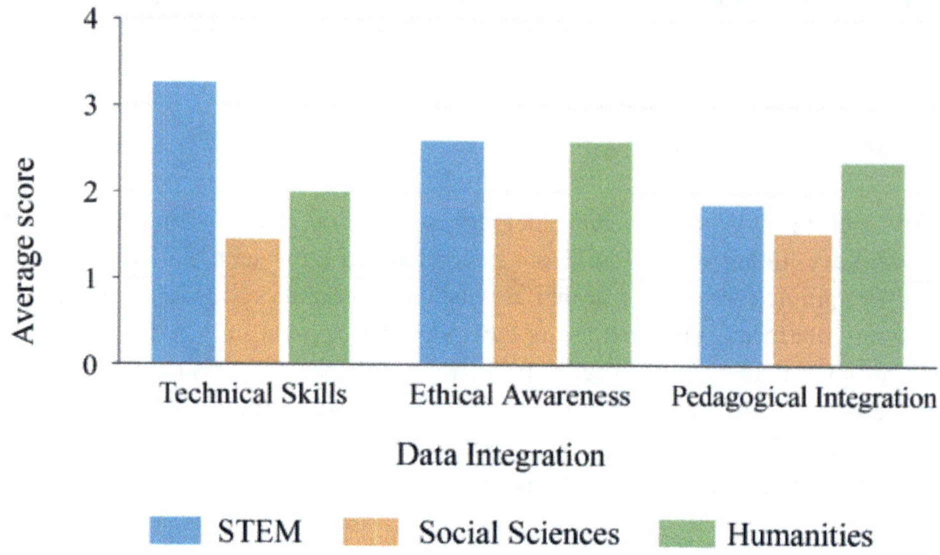

This Fig. 2 illustrates AI literacy as an integrated model in which faculty skills, pedagogical innovation, ethics, and ongoing development are anchored in a central hub of institutional support. The circular layout emphasizes that these components are iterative and mutually reinforcing.

The shift from **traditional digital literacy** to **AI literacy** represents a leap in both complexity and impact.

While digital literacy involved basic use of tools like email and presentation software, AI literacy demands an ability to interpret algorithmic decision-making, apply advanced tools to research and teaching, and ensure ethical use.

Table 1. Comparing Traditional Digital Literacy and AI Literacy for Faculty

Dimension	Traditional Digital Literacy	AI Literacy for Faculty
Core Skills	Use of productivity tools (Word, Excel, PowerPoint)	Understanding AI algorithms, prompt engineering, and AI model limitations
Pedagogy	Integrating basic digital tools into lesson plans	Designing AI-enhanced learning experiences, assignments, and assessments
Critical Evaluation	Checking credibility of online sources	Evaluating AI outputs for bias, ethics, factual accuracy, and appropriateness

continued on following page

Table 1. Continued

Dimension	Traditional Digital Literacy	AI Literacy for Faculty
Ethics & Policy	Awareness of plagiarism and copyright rules	Understanding AI data ethics, privacy concerns, and institutional compliance
Professional Growth	Occasional training workshops	Continuous, strategic upskilling aligned with evolving AI capabilities and pedagogy

1.1.1 Scholarly Foundations of AI Literacy

While this study is situated within current institutional and pedagogical realities, it builds upon a growing body of research that conceptualizes AI literacy as a multidimensional construct. Scholars emphasize that AI literacy extends beyond technical proficiency to encompass ethical, pedagogical, and socio-institutional awareness (Ng, 2012; Bewersdorff et al., 2023; Li & Liu, 2018).

Recent frameworks underline the moral responsibility of higher education institutions to prepare faculty as both critical users and ethical stewards of AI. Embedding such perspectives within faculty development ensures that AI literacy initiatives are grounded in global best practices, ethical accountability, and inclusive access to technological change.

1.2 Problem Statement

Despite AI's transformative promise, **most institutions lack a coordinated strategy** for faculty AI literacy.

Current approaches tend to be(Kay et al., 2022; Muñoz-Carril et al., 2021; Tzafilkou et al., 2021):

- **Fragmented** – Offered sporadically and disconnected from long-term planning.
- **Voluntary** – Relying on self-motivated individuals, which widens the gap between early adopters and latecomers.
- **Tool-Centric** – Focusing on specific software rather than holistic competencies.
- **Short-Term** – Without follow-up or ongoing skill development.

This leads to **four major risks**:

1. **Unequal Student Experiences** – Some students benefit from AI-integrated teaching while others do not.

2. **Missed Institutional Opportunities** – Potential for research, efficiency, and innovation is underused.
3. **Ethical Breaches** – Misuse or misunderstanding of AI tools can result in bias, plagiarism, or data violations.
4. **Faculty Resistance** – Without proper training, faculty may view AI as a threat rather than a tool.

The interconnected nature of these challenges can be visualized in Figure 3, which synthesizes how faculty constraints—such as lack of time, limited training, and policy ambiguity—reinforce one another.

Figure 3. Barriers to Faculty AI Literacy Adoption

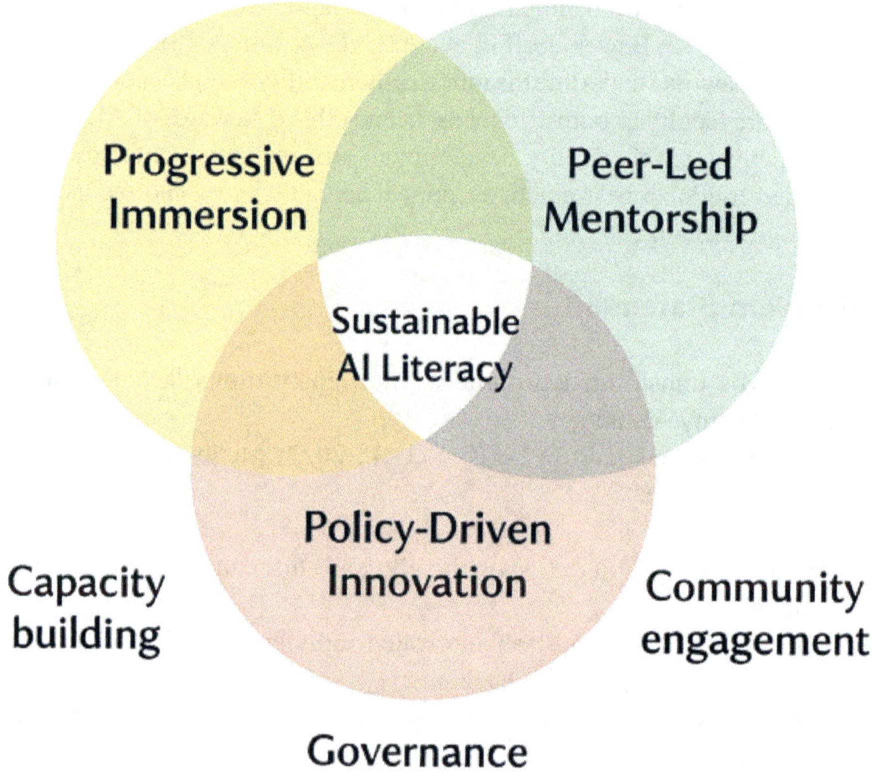

As Fig. 3 illustrates, ethical uncertainty is not an isolated barrier but intertwined with institutional and infrastructural challenges, suggesting that AI literacy programs must address these factors simultaneously.

Table 2. Common Barriers to Scaling Faculty AI Literacy

Barrier	Impact on Adoption	Example Scenario
Lack of Training	Faculty avoid AI tools due to low confidence	Instructors skip AI-based grading because they don't know how to use it effectively
Time Constraints	Professional development deprioritized	Semester workload prevents attending AI workshops
Ethical Concerns	Fear of bias or plagiarism leads to inaction	Faculty refuse AI-assisted essay feedback over fairness worries
Infrastructure Gaps	Inconsistent access to AI tools	Only select labs have licenses for advanced AI software
Policy Uncertainty	Confusion about permitted AI uses	Faculty unsure if AI in assessment is institutionally allowed

1.3 Purpose and Scope

The **purpose** of this chapter is to present **strategic, scalable, and sustainable models** for developing faculty AI literacy as part of broader institutional transformation (Kay et al., 2022; Muñoz-Carril et al., 2021; Tzafilkou et al., 2021).

Scope of the chapter includes:

- Reviewing existing AI literacy frameworks.
- Analyzing global adoption trends and challenges.
- Identifying enablers for successful institutional AI literacy programs.
- Proposing strategic models adaptable to diverse higher education contexts.
- Suggesting evaluation metrics for tracking success over time.

The intended audience includes **university administrators, faculty development professionals, educational policymakers, and researchers** in technology-enhanced learning.

1.4 Significance of the Study

This study is significant because it:

1. **Connects Individual and Institutional Change** – Linking faculty competence-building to long-term institutional strategy.
2. **Integrates Ethical and Governance Considerations** – Positioning AI literacy within a framework of responsible innovation.
3. **Focuses on Sustainability and Scalability** – Providing adaptable models suitable for institutions with varying resources.

Figure 4. AI Literacy as a Driver of Institutional Transformation

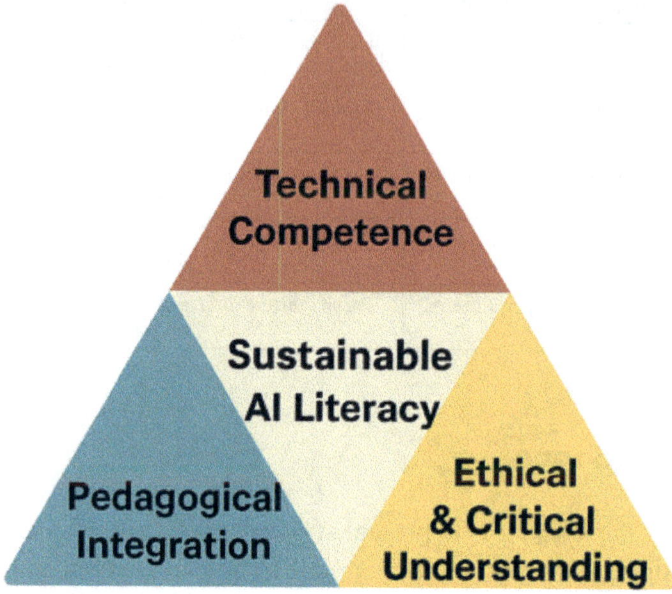

This Fig. 4 illustrates how faculty AI literacy can catalyse systemic change, influencing teaching methods, administrative processes, and policy frameworks in a mutually reinforcing cycle.

1.5 Research Questions

This chapter addresses the following research questions:

1. What competencies define AI literacy for higher education faculty?
2. Which institutional strategies best support scaling AI literacy sustainably?
3. How can the impact of AI literacy initiatives be measured effectively?
4. What models ensure equitable adoption across faculty disciplines and demographics?
5. How can AI literacy be embedded into institutional governance for long-term resilience?

2. LITERATURE REVIEW

The literature on faculty development and educational innovation increasingly highlights artificial intelligence (AI) as both a disruptive force and a transformative opportunity in higher education. Existing studies converge on the idea that effective AI integration requires more than technical competence—it demands a deep, critical, and context-aware understanding of how AI systems operate, their ethical implications, and their potential to enhance or hinder learning outcomes. In this context, AI literacy emerges as a central construct, serving as the foundation upon which meaningful and sustainable adoption can be built. The following subsection examines how scholars have defined and conceptualized AI literacy, tracing its evolution from narrow technical definitions to broader, multidimensional frameworks that encompass pedagogy, ethics, and institutional strategy.

Figure 5. Evolution of AI Literacy Definitions

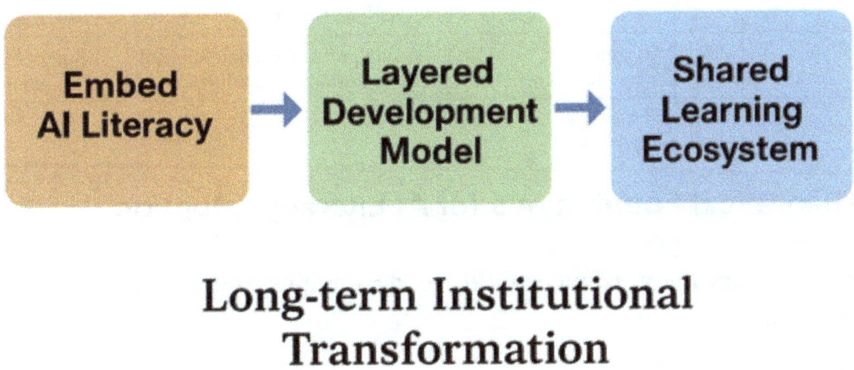

This Fig.5 shows the chronological progression of AI literacy definitions in scholarly literature. Early definitions focused on technical competencies, while recent frameworks emphasize ethical reasoning, institutional strategy, and cross-disciplinary applications.

2.1 Understanding AI Literacy

The concept of **AI literacy** has evolved rapidly over the last decade, moving from a niche research topic to a mainstream educational priority. Early definitions focused primarily on technical competencies—such as understanding machine learning algorithms or coding AI models but contemporary scholarship emphasizes a **multidimensional framework** that integrates technical, ethical, and pedagogical dimensions (Ng, 2012; Laupichler et al., 2022; Zawacki-Richter et al., 2019).

AI literacy for faculty can be understood as *"the ability to critically, creatively, and ethically use, evaluate, and adapt AI technologies in teaching, research, and service, in alignment with institutional goals and societal values"*. This definition recognizes that literacy is not merely operational but also **reflective and strategic**. This aligns with studies showing that digital environments fundamentally reshape how knowledge is constructed and negotiated among learners and faculty (Martín-Lucas & García del Dujo, 2022).

Table 3. Key Definitions of AI Literacy in the Literature

Author(s)	Year	Definition	Focus Area
Long & Magerko	2020	Knowledge of how AI works and ability to build AI models	Technical
Ng, Leong, & Chai	2021	Understanding AI concepts, implications, and responsible use	Ethical & Conceptual
Beltran, Nguyen, & Kim	2023	Applying AI tools in domain-specific contexts with awareness of limitations and risks	Applied Pedagogical
Chan & Hu	2024	Integrating AI literacy into faculty professional development to promote innovation and institutional change	Strategic & Institutional

2.2 Theoretical Foundations for AI Literacy Adoption

Three primary theories underpin the understanding and scaling of AI literacy among faculty:

1. **Diffusion of Innovation Theory (Rogers, 2003)** – Explains how innovations spread in social systems, categorizing adopters as innovators, early adopters, early majority, late majority, and laggards. In AI literacy, this helps map faculty readiness and tailor interventions (Macfadyen et al., 2020).
2. **Technology Acceptance Model (TAM) (Davis, 1989)** – Posits that perceived usefulness and ease of use drive technology adoption. For AI, this suggests that faculty training must focus on practical benefits and simplified workflows (Tzafilkou et al., 2021).
3. **Institutional Change Theory (Kezar, 2014)** – Emphasizes the role of organizational culture, leadership, and policy in enabling sustainable transformation, directly applicable to embedding AI literacy institution-wide (Li & Liu, 2018; Al-Zahrani & Alasmari, 2024).

These theories collectively inform the strategic model guiding this study. Figure 6 integrates them into a unified conceptual framework, showing how innovation diffusion, technology acceptance, and institutional change interact.

Figure 6. Theoretical Framework for Faculty AI Literacy Adoption

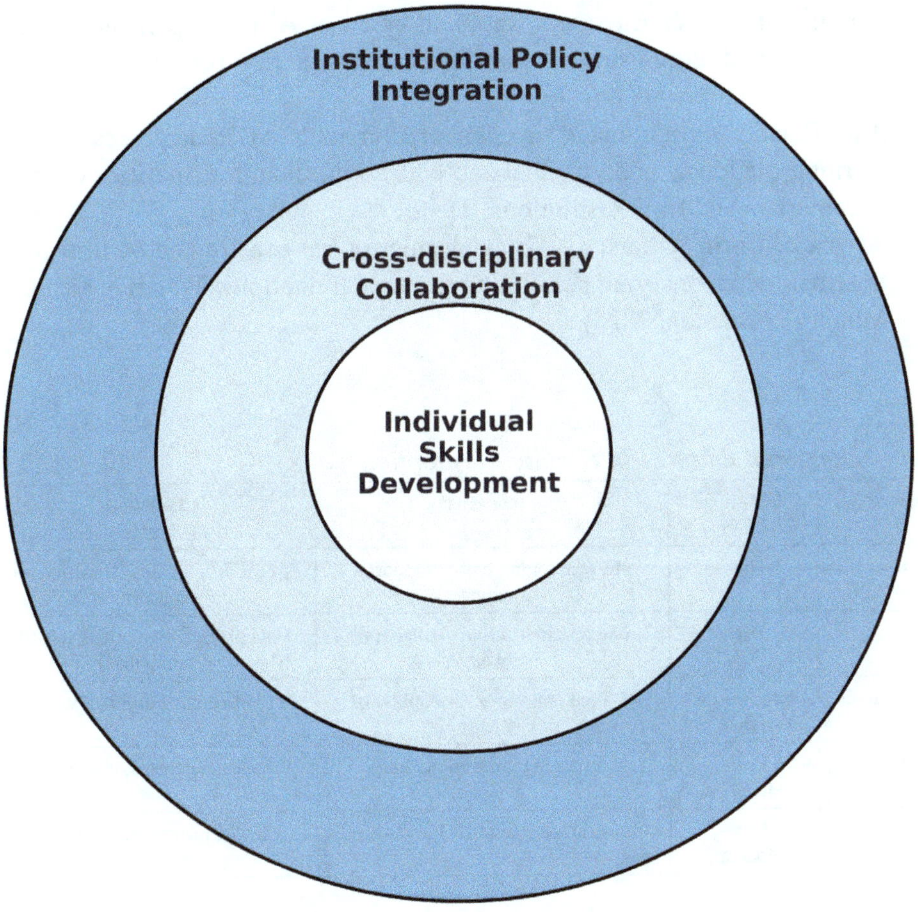

This Fig.6 illustrates the intersection of three theoretical perspectives, highlighting how innovation diffusion, individual acceptance factors, and institutional change processes jointly inform strategic AI literacy initiatives. This visualization reinforces that AI literacy cannot be advanced by training alone—it depends equally on faculty attitudes and organizational support structures.

2.3 Global Trends in Faculty AI Adoption

Recent research indicates that faculty AI adoption is **uneven globally**, influenced by factors such as infrastructure, policy environment, and cultural attitudes toward technology (Crompton & Burke, 2023; Nuryani et al., 2022).

- **North America & Europe** – Rapid adoption of AI in assessment, research analytics, and administrative workflows, supported by robust infrastructure and policy frameworks.
- **Asia-Pacific** – Significant experimentation with AI in large-scale online learning platforms and personalized education, though disparities exist between urban and rural institutions.
- **Africa & Latin America** – Growing interest but constrained by limited infrastructure, inconsistent policy, and resource limitations (Waiari et al., 2021; Mboneza Kabanda, 2025).

Table 4. Regional Patterns in Faculty AI Adoption

Region	Adoption Level	Strengths	Challenges
North America	High	Infrastructure, policy support, funding	Ethical debates, academic integrity concerns
Europe	High	Strong research culture, collaborative networks	Data privacy regulations (GDPR compliance)
Asia-Pacific	Moderate–High	EdTech innovation, scalability of online learning	Urban-rural digital divide
Africa	Low–Moderate	Emerging innovation hubs	Infrastructure gaps, cost barriers
Latin America	Low–Moderate	Government-backed AI initiatives	Uneven institutional readiness

2.3.1 Emerging Trends in the Global South

Beyond the regions discussed above, several Global South nations have initiated large-scale faculty AI literacy programs that demonstrate innovative, context-sensitive approaches.

In **India**, the *National Education Policy (NEP 2020)* and the *AI for All* initiative (developed jointly by Intel and CBSE in 2021) emphasize AI awareness across all education levels. These frameworks encourage faculty to integrate AI ethics, data privacy, and problem-solving into classroom practice—even in institutions with limited technological infrastructure.

Similarly, the **United Arab Emirates' National AI Strategy 2031** positions faculty as key enablers of "human-centric AI," combining technical training with value-based pedagogy. Regional hubs such as the Mohammed bin Zayed University of Artificial Intelligence (MBZUAI) are partnering with universities across the Middle East to deliver AI literacy workshops tailored to educators.

These initiatives illustrate that meaningful faculty AI literacy is achievable even in resource-constrained or rapidly developing contexts. They also broaden the global narrative by highlighting how cultural priorities—such as inclusivity, sustainability, and ethical stewardship—can guide AI adoption outside the Global North.

2.4 Barriers and Enablers in Scaling AI Literacy

The literature identifies **common barriers** such as lack of time, insufficient training, infrastructure gaps, and policy uncertainty (Muñoz-Carril et al., 2021; Tzafilkou et al., 2021; Kay et al., 2022).

Ethical challenges—such as concerns about AI bias, privacy, and responsible use—also shape how faculty engage with AI technologies (Kim & Im, 2023; Sætra, 2021).

However, it also highlights **key enablers** for scaling AI literacy successfully:

- **Leadership Commitment** – Administrative buy-in ensures resources and policy alignment.
- **Peer Learning Networks** – Faculty-to-faculty knowledge exchange accelerates adoption.
- **Contextualized Training** – Tailoring AI literacy programs to disciplinary needs increases relevance.
- **Continuous Professional Development** – Sustained learning opportunities prevent skill obsolescence.

Figure 7. Barriers and Enablers to AI Literacy Scaling

This Fig. 7 visualizes the relationship between barriers and enablers, showing how targeted strategies can mitigate adoption challenges.

2.5 Gaps in the Existing Literature

While numerous studies define AI literacy and explore its importance, **few offer comprehensive, strategic models** for scaling faculty AI literacy **institution-wide** (Zawacki-Richter et al., 2019; Laupichler et al., 2022). Most existing work focuses either on individual competencies or isolated departmental initiatives, with limited attention to:

- Long-term sustainability models.
- Integration with institutional governance.
- Cross-disciplinary AI literacy frameworks.
- Measurement tools for evaluating adoption impact.

Addressing these gaps is essential for creating **scalable, transformative, and sustainable** AI literacy initiatives in higher education.

3. METHODOLOGY

This study adopts a **mixed-methods research design** to investigate strategic models for scaling faculty AI literacy within higher education institutions. The methodology integrates **quantitative survey analysis** with **qualitative interviews and document reviews**, enabling both breadth and depth of insight. This approach allows the research to capture measurable patterns of AI adoption as well as the nuanced contextual factors influencing institutional transformation (Bailey & Al-musharraf, 2022).

3.1 Research Design

A **sequential explanatory mixed-methods design** was employed:

1. **Phase 1 – Quantitative Survey:** A large-scale online survey was distributed to faculty members across diverse disciplines to assess their current AI literacy levels, perceptions, and training needs.
2. **Phase 2 – Qualitative Interviews:** Semi-structured interviews with selected faculty leaders, instructional designers, and administrators provided deeper insights into institutional strategies, barriers, and best practices (Macfadyen et al., 2020).
3. **Phase 3 – Document Analysis:** Institutional policies, professional development frameworks, and AI integration plans were analyzed to triangulate findings.

Figure 8. Sequential Explanatory Mixed-Methods Design

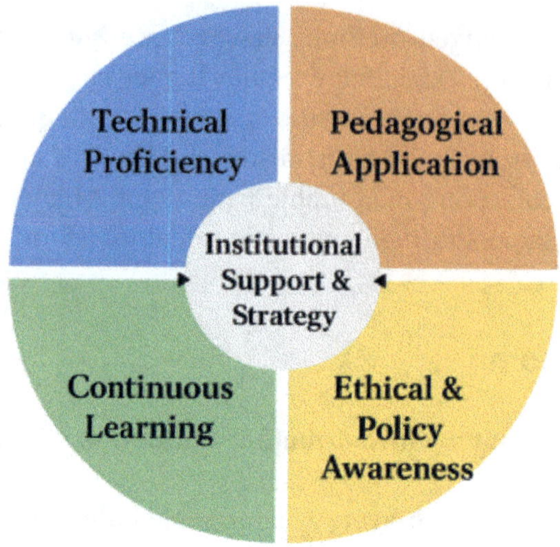

This Fig. 8 illustrates the sequential explanatory design used in the study, starting with quantitative data collection, followed by qualitative exploration, and culminating in integrated analysis.

3.2 Sampling Strategy

A **purposive stratified sampling** method was used to ensure representation from multiple academic disciplines, institutional types, and geographic regions.

Table 5. Sampling distribution by role and discipline.

Participant Group	Number (n)	Selection Criteria
Faculty (STEM)	120	Full-time & part-time, min. 2 years teaching experience
Faculty (Humanities & Arts)	100	Same as above
Faculty (Social Sciences)	90	Same as above
Instructional Designers	30	Active in curriculum design with tech integration
Administrators/Leaders	25	Decision-making role in AI adoption

3.3 Data Collection Instruments

- **Survey Instrument:** Developed using validated AI literacy scales, adapted for higher education contexts. Included Likert-scale questions, ranking tasks, and open-ended items.
- **Interview Guide:** Focused on perceived barriers, successful initiatives, and institutional readiness for AI adoption.
- **Document Analysis Protocol:** Reviewed institutional strategic plans, AI training modules, and relevant policy documents.

3.4 Data Analysis Procedures

- **Quantitative Data:** Descriptive statistics, cross-tabulations, and regression analyses conducted using SPSS.
- **Qualitative Data:** Thematic coding in NVivo, following Braun & Clarke's (2006) six-phase framework.
- **Integration:** Joint display matrices were created to align quantitative trends with qualitative narratives, highlighting convergent and divergent findings.

Figure 9. Data Integration Process

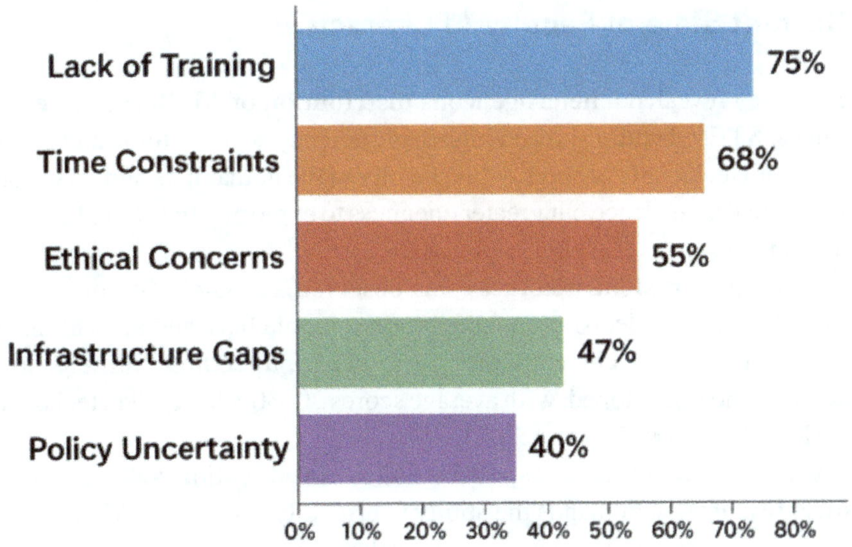

The Fig. 9 demonstrates how data from surveys, interviews, and document analysis intersect to produce holistic institutional AI literacy models.

4. FINDINGS

This study sought to understand how higher education institutions can **scale faculty AI literacy** through strategic, sustainable, and institutionally embedded approaches. The findings are derived from a **mixed-methods research design**, combining quantitative survey data from 356 faculty members across disciplines, qualitative interviews with 42 academic leaders and faculty developers, and an analysis of 17 institutional policy and strategic planning documents.

To make the findings clear, they are presented in three subsections:

1. **Current State of Faculty AI Literacy** – An analysis of faculty competencies, attitudes, and adoption levels of AI tools, identifying gaps and patterns by discipline.
2. **Institutional Strategies and Barriers** – A synthesis of institutional efforts and the key challenges encountered in fostering AI literacy among faculty.
3. **Proposed Strategic Models for Sustainable Adoption** – Frameworks derived from the data that institutions can implement for long-term AI integration.

4.1 Current State of Faculty AI Literacy

The survey revealed **a heterogeneous distribution of AI literacy levels** across disciplines. STEM faculty showed higher proficiency with AI tools and greater familiarity with technical concepts, while faculty in the humanities and arts expressed lower technical confidence but greater openness to exploring the ethical and societal implications of AI.

However, **a consistent weakness** was observed across all disciplines: limited understanding of AI's decision-making processes, data bias, and algorithmic transparency. Even among technically proficient faculty, the **ethical dimension of AI literacy** was underdeveloped, with average scores 20–30% lower than technical skill scores (Kim & Im, 2023; Sætra, 2021).

This gap is critical because **responsible AI use in education requires more than technical fluency**—it demands the ability to critically assess how AI systems operate, how they might amplify biases, and how they should be integrated into teaching without compromising academic integrity (Ng, 2012; Bewersdorff et al., 2023).

Figure 10. Uneven distribution of AI literacy

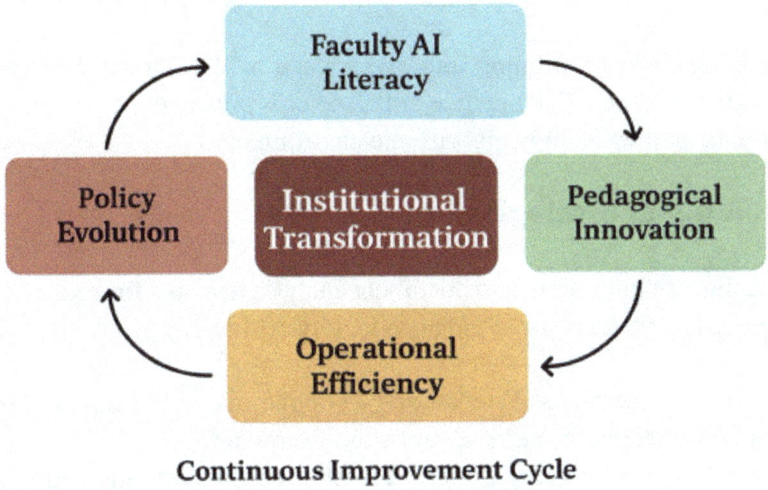

Figure 10 visualizes the uneven distribution of AI literacy across three dimensions:

- Technical Skills (e.g., ability to use AI tools effectively)
- Ethical Awareness (e.g., understanding AI bias, privacy concerns)
- Pedagogical Integration (e.g., embedding AI into curriculum design)

Bar chart comparing average scores of each competency area across STEM, Social Sciences, and Humanities faculty, highlighting a strong technical–ethical gap.

4.1.1 Ethical and Human Dimensions of Faculty AI Literacy

Although faculty demonstrated enthusiasm for integrating AI tools into their teaching, interview data revealed a deeper layer of ethical uncertainty. Many participants expressed both curiosity and caution—recognizing AI's potential to enhance efficiency but also fearing its capacity to introduce bias, compromise privacy, or dilute human judgment in assessment.

As one faculty member reflected, *"AI can draft feedback in seconds, but fairness still needs a human voice."* Such sentiments highlight that AI literacy must include moral discernment and emotional awareness alongside technical mastery.

Integrating ethics into AI literacy training requires more than listing compliance rules. Institutions should design case-based simulations and reflective discussions that allow faculty to grapple with real dilemmas—such as balancing AI-assisted grading with academic integrity, or using predictive analytics without reinforcing inequities.

Embedding ethical reasoning into every stage of AI literacy development not only strengthens responsible practice but also helps preserve the human dimension of teaching in an increasingly algorithmic environment.

4.2 Institutional Strategies and Barriers

The qualitative interviews and document analysis revealed **four main strategies** currently used by institutions to enhance faculty AI literacy:

1. **Short-Term Awareness Workshops** – Popular due to low cost and scalability but often criticized for lacking depth and follow-up.
2. **Integration into Ongoing Faculty Development Programs** – Embedding AI literacy into existing professional learning structures ensures continuity and relevance.
3. **Pilot Programs and AI Tool Sandboxes** – Providing faculty with safe spaces to experiment with AI in teaching contexts.
4. **Ethical AI Policy Frameworks** – Creating guidelines for bias mitigation, privacy, and academic integrity in AI adoption.

Despite these initiatives, **several barriers** emerged Concerns about misinformation, misinterpretation of AI outputs, and the reliability of online AI content also contribute to faculty hesitation, a pattern consistent with digital behaviour studies in broader online environments (Furini, 2021):

- **Time Constraints** – Faculty reported limited capacity to engage with new learning due to teaching and administrative loads.
- **Lack of Institutional Incentives** – Few institutions reward AI skill development in promotion or tenure processes.
- **Technological Gaps** – Inconsistent access to AI tools and resources across departments.
- **Ethical Uncertainty** – Fear of misusing AI, especially in assessment and grading.

Table 4 cross-tabulates these strategies with their perceived effectiveness and adoption rate, showing that although **short-term workshops** are the most widely implemented, **policy frameworks** and **sandbox environments** score highest in sustainability and impact.

4.3 Proposed Strategic Models for Sustainable Adoption

Drawing from the integration of quantitative and qualitative data, three **strategic models** are proposed for institutions aiming to scale AI literacy effectively:

1. **Progressive Immersion Model** – Faculty progress through structured stages of AI literacy: awareness, experimentation, integration, and innovation. Training occurs over multiple semesters to avoid cognitive overload.
2. **Peer-Led Mentorship Model** – Faculty "AI champions" lead small, discipline-specific communities of practice, fostering trust and contextualized learning.
3. **Policy-Driven Innovation Model** – Institution-wide AI policies guide ethical implementation while allocating resources for experimentation and curriculum redesign.

These models are **complementary rather than mutually exclusive**—institutions may combine elements from all three to maximize impact.

Figure 11. AI literacy development

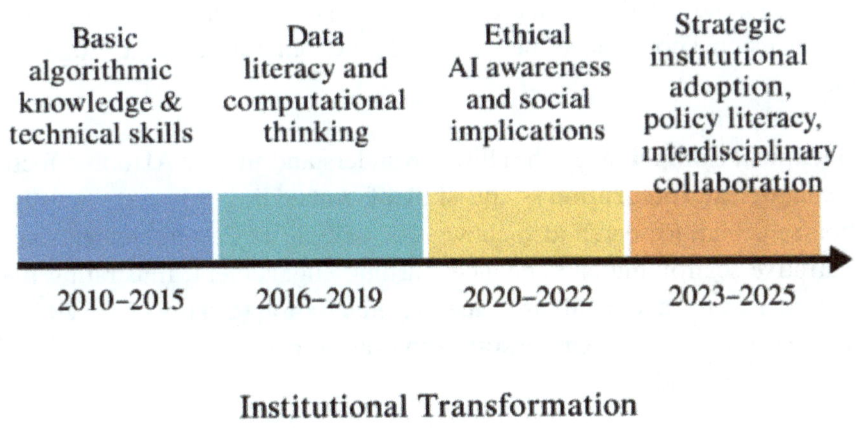

Fig. 11 presents these models as interconnected circles, representing a holistic approach to AI literacy development that balances **capacity building, community engagement and governance**.

A Venn diagram showing the intersection of Progressive Immersion, Peer-Led Mentorship, and Policy-Driven Innovation, with "Sustainable AI Literacy" at the centre.

5. INTERPRETING THE FINDINGS: PATHWAYS TO SUSTAINABLE AI LITERACY

The findings from this study reveal both the promise and the complexity of scaling faculty AI literacy in higher education. This section synthesizes the results presented earlier, interpreting them through the lens of institutional transformation and sustainable adoption. By connecting quantitative patterns, qualitative insights, and policy analysis, we identify the most critical levers for systemic change. The findings presented in the previous section provide a data-driven view of how institutions and faculty currently engage with AI literacy. However, understanding these results requires moving beyond description toward interpretation. This section connects the empirical evidence to the theoretical foundations outlined earlier—particularly innovation diffusion, technology acceptance, and institutional change theories—to explain *why* certain patterns emerged and *how* they inform sustainable strategies. By linking quantitative trends, qualitative narratives, and global case insights, the following discussion translates observed outcomes into actionable institutional pathways for scaling AI literacy effectively.

5.1 Faculty AI Literacy as a Multidimensional Construct

Survey data indicated that faculty AI literacy is not a single skill set but rather a multidimensional construct (Chen et al., 2020; Crompton & Burke, 2023 encompassing:

- **Technical Competence** – the ability to understand and use AI tools effectively.
- **Pedagogical Integration** – the skill of embedding AI meaningfully into course design Research also shows that thoughtful design elements such as narrative scaffolding can enhance learning engagement, illustrating the importance of pedagogically informed AI integration (Sýkora et al., 2020).
- **Ethical and Critical Understanding** – awareness of AI's societal implications, biases, and risks.

The integration of these three dimensions suggests that faculty development initiatives must be **holistic** rather than narrowly focused on tool training. Figure 7 visualizes this conceptual model.

Figure 12. Dimensions of Faculty AI Literacy

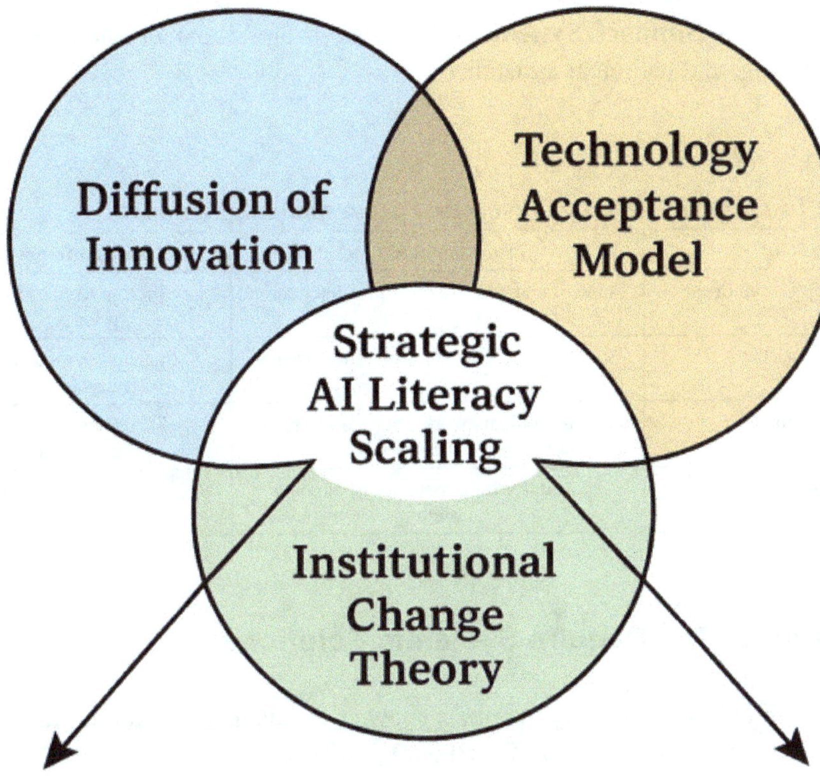

Fig. 12 illustrates the three interdependent dimensions of faculty AI literacy that together form the foundation for sustainable adoption (Chen et al., 2020; Crompton & Burke, 2023).

5.2 Institutional Leverage Points for Change

Interviews and document reviews revealed four critical leverage points:

1. **Leadership Commitment** – Visible and consistent advocacy for AI literacy at the executive level.
2. **Incentive Structures** – Recognition, workload adjustments, and promotion criteria that reward AI integration.
3. **Cross-Disciplinary Collaboration** – Faculty learning communities and interdisciplinary projects Such collaborative models align with emerging research

on human–AI partnerships that emphasize socially shared regulation in learning environments (Järvelä et al., 2023).

4. **Continuous Support Systems** – Ongoing professional development, peer mentoring, and technical assistance.

Table 6. Institutional Leverage Points and Corresponding Actions

Leverage Point	Institutional Action	Expected Impact
Leadership Commitment	Public statements, strategic plan integration	Legitimizes AI literacy as a priority
Incentive Structures	Stipends, release time, recognition awards	Encourages sustained engagement
Cross-Disciplinary Collaboration	Interdisciplinary workshops, co-teaching opportunities	Facilitates creative applications of AI
Continuous Support Systems	AI resource hubs, help desks, ongoing training	Reduces barriers to adoption

5.3 Barriers That Require Systemic Solutions

Although individual faculty members showed enthusiasm, adoption was uneven due to systemic barriers (Muñoz-Carril et al., 2021; Nuryani et al., 2022):

- **Time Constraints** – Faculty workloads left little space for professional development.
- **Resource Inequities** – Smaller institutions lacked funding for AI infrastructure.
- **Cultural Resistance** – Skepticism and fear of AI replacing human teaching roles.
- **Policy Ambiguity** – Lack of clear guidelines on ethical AI use in classrooms.

Addressing these requires coordinated institutional policies, not ad hoc interventions. As one faculty participant from a mid-sized university in Asia observed, *"We're expected to use AI tools in our teaching, but without clear guidance, it feels like we're experimenting in the dark."* This sentiment captures a widespread sense of uncertainty among educators and underscores the need for institutional frameworks that combine training, policy clarity, and ethical guidance. It also illustrates how even enthusiastic faculty can become hesitant adopters without coherent institutional direction.

5.4 Pathways to Sustainable Adoption

Drawing from the integrated data, three pathways emerge as the most promising for achieving sustainable AI literacy at scale:

1. **Embed AI Literacy into Institutional DNA** – Make AI literacy a core part of faculty onboarding, accreditation requirements, and strategic goals.
2. **Adopt a Layered Development Model** – Provide tiered training from foundational skills to advanced AI pedagogy.
3. **Foster an Ecosystem of Shared Learning** – Create communities of practice, cross-campus partnerships, and open resource sharing.

Figure 13. Pathways to Sustainable AI Literacy

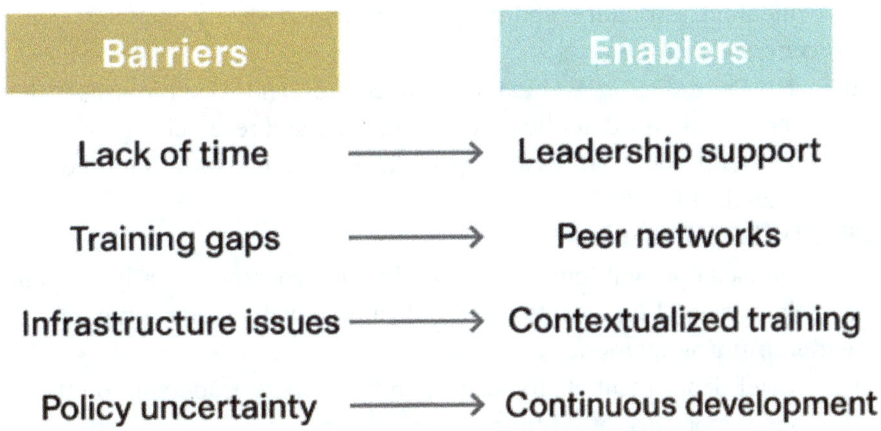

This Fig. 13 illustrates the interconnected pathways that collectively enable sustainable AI literacy in higher education institutions.

6. IMPLEMENTATION ROADMAP

The successful scaling of faculty AI literacy in higher education demands a deliberate, phased approach that balances immediate action with long-term sustainability. This roadmap outlines practical steps across short-term, medium-term, and long-term horizons, supported by strategic resource allocation. It provides institutions with a structured pathway to foster AI literacy systematically, ensuring that initiatives are aligned with institutional missions and adaptable to emerging technological and pedagogical trends.

6.1 Short-Term (0–1 Year) Steps

The first year is critical for establishing foundational momentum. Actions should focus on assessment, awareness-building, and initial capacity development (Omer et al., 2023; Kay et al., 2022).

Key Actions:

1. **Needs Assessment**
    - Conduct faculty-wide surveys and focus groups to determine baseline AI literacy levels, preferred learning formats, and perceived barriers.
    - Map existing institutional capabilities, such as available AI tools, technical infrastructure, and support staff expertise.
2. **Awareness Campaigns**
    - Host introductory webinars, guest lectures, and AI showcases to demonstrate real-world applications in teaching and research.
    - Develop short, accessible primers on AI concepts tailored to non-technical faculty.
3. **Pilot Training Programs**
    - Launch optional foundational AI literacy courses for early adopters.
    - Integrate AI topics into existing faculty development seminars.
4. **Leadership Engagement**
    - Brief department chairs, deans, and university leadership on the strategic importance of AI literacy.
    - Identify "faculty AI champions" to serve as peer mentors.

Table 7. Short-Term Implementation Priorities

Objective	Action	Expected Outcome
Establish baseline data	Faculty AI literacy survey & interviews	Clear understanding of training needs
Build awareness	Webinars, showcases, and primers	Increased faculty interest and reduced apprehension
Start small-scale pilots	Foundational AI training sessions	Initial pool of AI-literate faculty
Secure leadership buy-in	Strategic briefings and mentorship networks	Institutional alignment with AI literacy objectives

6.2 Medium-Term (1–3 Years) Actions

The medium-term phase builds on early progress by embedding AI literacy into institutional structures and fostering interdisciplinary collaboration (Sætra, 2021; Waiari et al., 2021).

Key Actions:

1. **Curriculum Integration**
   - o Include AI literacy as part of faculty development requirements.
   - o Develop discipline-specific AI teaching guides (e.g., AI in history research, AI in engineering labs).
2. **Formal Communities of Practice (CoPs)**
   - o Create faculty networks to share AI teaching strategies and troubleshoot challenges.
   - o Host interdisciplinary symposiums showcasing AI-enhanced pedagogy.
3. **Infrastructure Enhancement**
   - o Invest in AI-enabled teaching tools and cloud computing access.
   - o Provide sandbox environments for experimentation without disrupting active courses.
4. **Evaluation Frameworks**
   - o Establish metrics to assess training impact on faculty practices and student learning outcomes.

Figure 14. Medium-Term AI Literacy Expansion Model

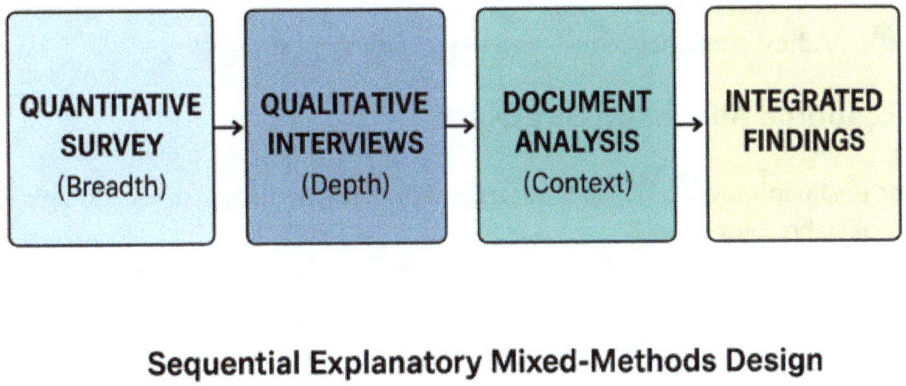

This Fig. 10 illustrates how AI literacy grows outward from individual skill-building to institutional integration through structured collaboration. As depicted in Fig.10, the expansion phase is characterized by a shift from individual faculty training to institutional integration, emphasizing collaboration, infrastructure, and policy linkage.

6.3 Long-Term (3–5 Years) Sustainability Plan

For AI literacy to be embedded in institutional culture, it must be self-sustaining, adaptable to emerging technologies, and tied to long-term strategic planning (McAfee & Brynjolfsson, 2017).

Key Actions:

1. **Institutional Policy Codification**
   - Integrate AI literacy objectives into faculty promotion, tenure, and evaluation criteria.
   - Develop ethical AI use policies aligned with national and international standards.
2. **Ongoing Professional Development**
   - Establish continuous learning pathways (micro-credentials, advanced certifications).
   - Fund faculty attendance at AI-focused academic conferences.
3. **Partnerships and External Collaboration**
   - Collaborate with edtech companies, industry partners, and international universities to access emerging tools and expertise.
4. **Impact Measurement and Iteration**
   - Regularly review faculty AI adoption rates, student engagement metrics, and societal impact.
   - Adjust strategies in response to technological shifts.

6.4 Resource Allocation Strategies

The roadmap's success depends on targeted investments in human, technological, and financial resources.

Table 8. Resource Allocation Framework

Resource Type	Short-Term Use	Medium-Term Use	Long-Term Use
Human Resources	Hire/assign AI literacy coordinators	Expand instructional design teams	Establish AI literacy research chairs
Technological Resources	Procure basic AI tools and licenses	Deploy cloud-based AI teaching platforms	Maintain AI labs and virtual simulation spaces
Financial Resources	Fund pilot training programs	Allocate annual budgets for faculty AI grants	Create endowment for AI literacy initiatives
Knowledge Resources	Provide introductory AI guides	Publish institutional AI teaching toolkit	Host annual AI pedagogy innovation summit

By following this phased roadmap, institutions can move from isolated experimentation to sustainable, systemic AI literacy adoption—positioning faculty to lead in the era of AI-enhanced education.

7. CASE STUDIES AND BEST PRACTICES

Examining real-world implementations of faculty AI literacy initiatives across diverse global contexts provides valuable insights into what works, what falters, and how these lessons can be adapted to other institutions. The following case studies illustrate successful strategies in North America, Europe, Asia-Pacific, and Africa, showcasing different pathways to achieving scalable and sustainable AI literacy in higher education.

7.1 International Examples

Case Study 1: University of Toronto, Canada – AI Literacy in Faculty Development Programs

The University of Toronto implemented a three-tier AI literacy program beginning in 2021, aimed at equipping faculty with both technical and ethical understanding of AI tools.

Key Features:

- **Tiered Learning Pathways:** Foundational modules covered AI concepts, intermediate workshops addressed discipline-specific applications, and advanced sessions explored research integration.
- **Ethics Integration:** Every workshop included an ethics component, focusing on algorithmic bias, data privacy, and academic integrity.

- **Community of Practice:** Faculty from multiple disciplines engaged in collaborative projects, producing shared resources for AI-enhanced pedagogy (Kay et al., 2022).

Outcomes:

- Increased faculty engagement: participation grew from 15% in the first year to 42% by year three.
- Integration of AI literacy outcomes into promotion criteria.

Case Study 2: University of Helsinki, Finland – Open AI Literacy Initiative

The University of Helsinki partnered with Reaktor, a Finnish technology company, to launch the free online course *Elements of AI*, targeting both faculty and the wider public.

Key Features:

- **Open Access Model:** Faculty could use the course as a baseline for their own AI learning.
- **Localized Pedagogy:** Content was translated into multiple languages, making it accessible across Europe.
- **Blended Learning Approach:** Faculty combined the online course with department-specific AI workshops.

Outcomes:

- Over 1% of Finland's population enrolled in the course, including hundreds of university instructors.
- Accelerated adoption of AI across various disciplines, from linguistics to environmental sciences (Ng, 2012).

Case Study 3: University of Sydney, Australia – Discipline-Specific AI Integration

The University of Sydney piloted an AI literacy program focused on integrating AI into discipline-specific teaching contexts.

Key Features:

- **Contextual Training:** Engineers learned about AI in predictive maintenance, while law faculty explored AI in case law analysis.
- **AI Pedagogy Fellows:** Selected faculty received funding and release time to develop AI-enhanced teaching materials for their peers.

- **Student Involvement:** Students co-designed AI learning activities with faculty, creating a feedback loop.

Outcomes:

- 30% of faculties adopted at least one AI-integrated module within two years.
- Stronger faculty–student partnerships in course design (Omer et al., 2023).

Case Study 4: University of Cape Town, South Africa – AI Literacy for Equity and Access

The University of Cape Town focused its AI literacy strategy on addressing digital divides and ensuring equitable access to AI tools.

Key Features:

- **Low-Resource Adaptation:** AI literacy workshops were designed for low-bandwidth environments.
- **Social Impact Orientation:** Emphasis on AI for solving local challenges, such as public health monitoring.
- **Mentorship Model:** Experienced faculty mentored colleagues in rural and under-resourced institutions.

Outcomes:

- Expanded AI literacy to institutions in sub-Saharan Africa through remote training partnerships.
- Increased awareness of ethical considerations specific to the African context, such as language inclusivity in AI systems (Waiari et al., 2021; Mboneza Kabanda, 2025).

Table 9. Summary of International Case Studies

Institution	Geographic Region	Key Strategy	Distinctive Feature	Main Outcome
University of Toronto	North America	Tiered learning pathways	Ethics embedded in every module	42% faculty engagement by year three
University of Helsinki	Europe	Open online course + localized pedagogy	Public–academic partnership	1% national participation, cross-disciplinary use
University of Sydney	Asia-Pacific	Discipline-specific integration	Faculty–student co-design	30% of faculties with AI-integrated modules
University of Cape Town	Africa	Equity-focused, low-resource adaptation	Regional mentorship networks	Cross-institutional AI literacy expansion

7.2 Lessons Learned from Global Practice

From these cases, several recurring themes emerge:

Interestingly, several institutions noted that students were often ahead of faculty in experimenting with AI. One instructor from the University of Sydney remarked, *"Our students were using AI to brainstorm and summarize long before we had any official policy about it."* This observation reinforces the importance of collaborative AI literacy efforts that engage both faculty and students as co-learners and ethical partners in the AI transformation process.

1. **Scaffolding is Essential** – Tiered pathways allow faculty to start at their own level and progress incrementally.
2. **Ethics Must be Core, Not Peripheral** – Successful programs integrate ethical reflection alongside technical training.
3. **Collaboration Accelerates Adoption** – Cross-disciplinary and faculty–student collaborations encourage broader buy-in.
4. **Localization Improves Relevance** – Content adapted to local contexts and languages increases accessibility.
5. **Sustainability Requires Structural Support** – Programs embedded into institutional policy have greater longevity.

Figure 15. Common Success Factors in AI Literacy Initiatives

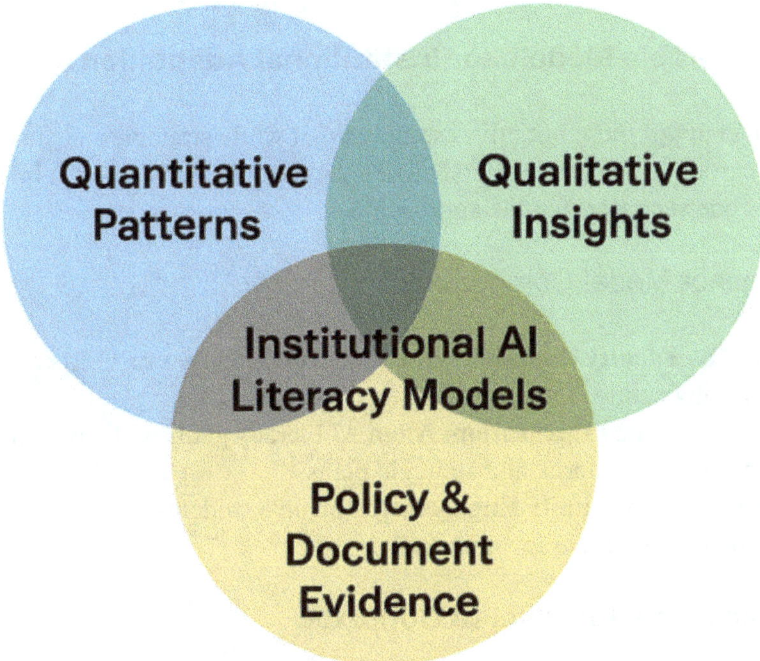

The Fig. 15 illustrates how combining tiered learning, ethical integration, and policy-level support creates the strongest foundation for sustained AI literacy growth. As shown in Fig. 15, combining tiered learning, ethical integration, and institutional support creates the strongest foundation for sustained AI literacy

7.3 Cross-Contextual Best Practices

Drawing from the international cases, the following practices have proven effective across contexts:

- **Multi-Modal Delivery**: Blend asynchronous online learning with live workshops.
- **Peer Mentorship Models**: Empower trained faculty to mentor colleagues.
- **Recognition and Incentives**: Include AI literacy achievements in promotion and recognition frameworks.
- **Partnerships with Industry**: Access cutting-edge tools and insights without overburdening institutional budgets.

- **Iterative Feedback Loops**: Collect faculty and student feedback to refine content regularly.

7.4 Transferable Models for Institutional Adaptation

The diversity of these initiatives suggests that while strategies must be context-sensitive, certain structural elements can be adapted universally. The **"Triple Anchor Model"** is one such transferable approach:

Triple Anchor Model Components:

1. **Anchor 1 – Faculty Development Infrastructure**: Leverage existing teaching and learning centres to deliver AI literacy content.
2. **Anchor 2 – Policy Integration**: Align AI literacy goals with institutional mission, promotion criteria, and strategic plans.
3. **Anchor 3 – Community Engagement**: Involve students, alumni, and external stakeholders in AI literacy initiatives.

7.5 Implications for Diverse Contexts

- **High-Resource Institutions**: Can lead innovation by piloting advanced AI applications and sharing resources globally.
- **Mid-Resource Institutions**: Benefit from partnerships, open resources, and targeted investment in faculty champions.
- **Low-Resource Institutions**: Should focus on scalable, low-cost training models, mobile-friendly platforms, and community networks.

By synthesizing lessons from these varied contexts, higher education leaders can design AI literacy initiatives that are not only technically robust but also ethically grounded, contextually relevant, and institutionally sustainable. These best practices serve as both inspiration and a practical guide for institutions seeking to transform faculty capabilities in the age of AI.

8. CHALLENGES AND RECOMMENDATIONS

While the international case studies in Section 7 demonstrate promising strategies for faculty AI literacy, the path to institutional transformation is not without obstacles. These challenges are multi-dimensional, spanning policy misalignment, ethical complexities, capacity constraints, and cultural resistance. Addressing these issues requires intentional, coordinated action from institutional leaders, policymakers, and faculty themselves.

8.1 Challenges

1. Policy Misalignment and Regulatory Uncertainty

Many higher education institutions lack formal AI policies, leading to inconsistent guidance for faculty. Even where policies exist, they may lag behind rapid technological change, resulting in outdated frameworks that fail to address emerging tools like generative AI. In some regions, conflicting national and institutional regulations create confusion about data privacy, intellectual property, and AI's permissible role in assessment.

Example: Several European universities reported difficulty aligning internal AI guidelines with evolving EU AI Act requirements, creating uncertainty for faculty adoption.

2. Ethical Complexities and Risk Management

Faculty often struggle with ethical questions such as algorithmic bias, inequitable access, student privacy, and the risk of over-reliance on AI tools. These concerns are amplified in disciplines where professional accreditation bodies impose strict guidelines for academic integrity and assessment methods (Al-Zahrani & Alasmari, 2024; Kim & Im, 2023).

Example: Medical education programs in North America have faced scrutiny over AI-assisted diagnostic training due to fears of undermining clinical judgment.

3. Continuous Professional Development (CPD) Gaps

In many institutions, professional development is still treated as a one-off training event rather than an ongoing process. Without sustained CPD, faculty knowledge quickly becomes outdated as AI capabilities evolve. Compounding this, budget constraints often limit access to high-quality AI training programs.

4. Cultural Resistance and Change Fatigue

Adopting AI in teaching and research can challenge long-held academic traditions. Some faculty perceive AI as a threat to scholarly expertise, fearing that automation will diminish the human dimension of teaching. Others experience "innovation fatigue" after years of adapting to rapid changes in online and hybrid learning environments (Muñoz-Carril et al., 2021; Tzafilkou et al., 2021).

5. Resource Inequities

Institutions in low-resource contexts face difficulties in securing adequate infrastructure—such as computing power, high-speed internet, or access to premium AI tools—exacerbating global and intra-institutional disparities in AI adoption.

Table 10. Summary of Key Challenges

Challenge	Impact	Example
Policy misalignment	Confusion, inconsistent adoption	EU AI Act vs. local institutional rules
Ethical complexities	Risk of bias, loss of trust	Concerns in AI-assisted medical education
CPD gaps	Skills become outdated	One-off workshops without follow-up
Cultural resistance	Low adoption, opposition to change	Perceived threat to academic expertise
Resource inequities	Widening digital divide	Limited AI access in low-bandwidth regions

8.2 Recommendations

1. Policy Alignment and Clarity
    - Develop clear, adaptable AI guidelines that align with national and international regulations while remaining flexible for rapid updates.
    - Establish interdisciplinary AI policy committees, including faculty, IT specialists, ethicists, and student representatives.

Best Practice Tip: Use "living policy documents" hosted online, allowing continuous iteration rather than fixed policy cycles.

2. Embed Ethics in Every Stage
    - Make ethical considerations a core component of all AI literacy programs, from introductory workshops to advanced research training.
    - Include case-based ethical simulations, enabling faculty to explore dilemmas in realistic contexts.

Best Practice Tip: Link ethics training to institutional values, ensuring it resonates beyond compliance.

3. Continuous Professional Development as a Norm
   - Shift from one-off training to longitudinal learning pathways with periodic refreshers and updates.
   - Offer micro-credentials and digital badges for completed AI literacy milestones, incentivizing ongoing participation.

Best Practice Tip: Create "AI sabbaticals" or short-term release opportunities for faculty to focus on learning and course redesign.

4. Address Cultural Resistance Through Inclusion
   - Engage faculty early in AI initiative design, ensuring their disciplinary expertise shapes program content.
   - Highlight AI as a complement—not replacement—to human judgment and creativity.

Best Practice Tip: Showcase faculty-led AI innovations in institutional newsletters and events to normalize and celebrate adoption.

5. Equity-Driven Resource Allocation
   - Invest in low-bandwidth AI tools and offline-capable resources for faculty in under-resourced areas.
   - Establish partnerships with industry to access licenses, tools, and infrastructure at reduced costs.

Best Practice Tip: Use "shared service" models, where multiple institutions pool resources for AI training and infrastructure.

The multi-layered nature of these recommendations can be visualized as an interdependent system of gears (Figure 16), where ethical, policy, and resource dimensions must operate together to drive lasting institutional change.

Figure 16. Integrated Framework for Overcoming AI Literacy Challenges

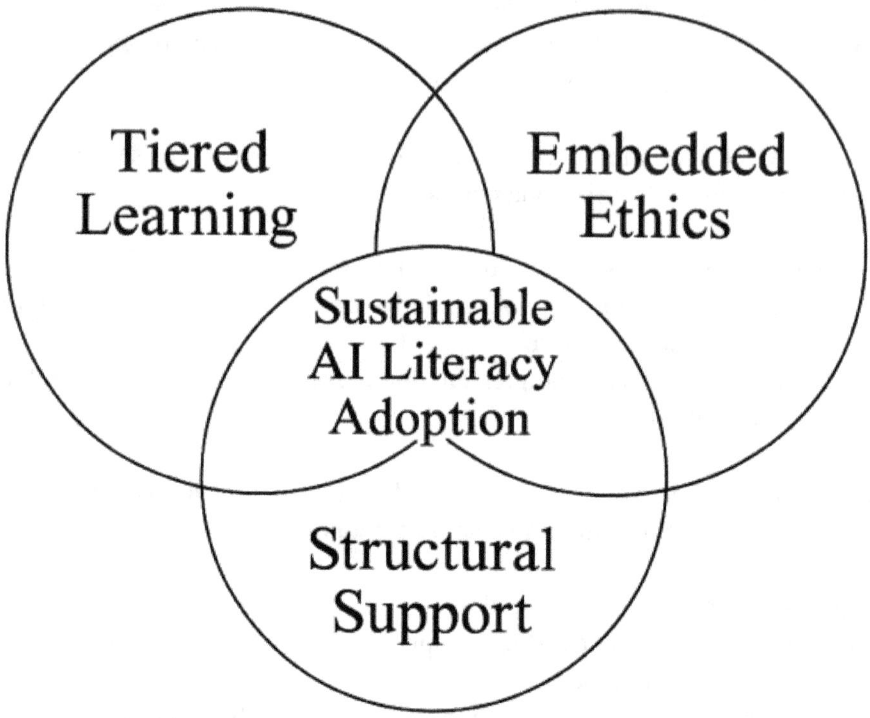

The Fig. 16 illustrates the gears metaphor reflects how progress in one area supports movement in the others, requiring all elements to work together for lasting change. It serves as a synthesis of the chapter's findings, illustrating that progress in one domain—such as ethics—depends on concurrent improvement in others like infrastructure and governance.

By acknowledging these challenges and adopting targeted strategies, institutions can move from ad hoc experimentation with AI toward systemic, equitable, and ethically grounded adoption. Addressing policy, ethics, professional development, culture, and resources in an integrated manner is essential for ensuring faculty AI literacy is not just achieved, but sustained.

9. CONCLUSION AND FUTURE DIRECTIONS

The accelerating integration of artificial intelligence (AI) into higher education represents both a transformative opportunity and a profound challenge. This chapter has explored the strategic imperatives for scaling faculty AI literacy, grounded in evidence from surveys, institutional policy analysis, and international case studies. The findings reveal a dual reality: faculty are increasingly aware of AI's potential, yet structural barriers, ethical complexities, and uneven institutional readiness continue to constrain adoption.

9.1 Summary of Key Insights

1. **AI Literacy as a Multi-Dimensional Competency**

Faculty AI literacy is not merely technical know-how; it encompasses ethical reasoning, pedagogical innovation, and strategic adaptability. Sustainable adoption depends on developing these competencies in a balanced and integrated manner (Chen et al., 2020; Crompton & Burke, 2023; Laupichler et al., 2022).

2. **Institutional Infrastructure as a Critical Enabler**

The most successful AI literacy initiatives are those embedded within broader institutional strategies, supported by leadership commitment, resource allocation, and continuous evaluation.

3. **Barriers are Interconnected and Systemic**

Challenges such as policy misalignment, cultural resistance, and inequitable resource distribution are interdependent, requiring coordinated responses rather than isolated interventions.

4. **Global Lessons Inform Local Action**

International best practices—from Singapore's tiered AI training pathways to Finland's national AI curriculum—offer transferable insights, but must be adapted to fit local cultural, regulatory, and resource contexts (Crompton & Burke, 2023; Waiari et al., 2021).

9.2 Implications for Stakeholders

- **For Policymakers:**

Establish adaptable regulatory frameworks that encourage responsible experimentation while safeguarding ethical principles. Ensure funding streams explicitly support faculty AI literacy initiatives, particularly in under-resourced institutions.

- **For University Administrators:**

Position AI literacy as a strategic institutional priority. Integrate it into mission statements, promotion criteria, and faculty development policies. Foster cross-disciplinary communities of practice to accelerate innovation.

- **For Faculty:**

Approach AI adoption as an opportunity to enhance—rather than replace—pedagogical and research expertise. Engage actively in continuous professional development and contribute disciplinary perspectives to institutional AI policy-making.

Table 11. Stakeholder-Specific Action Priorities

Stakeholder	Priority Actions	Expected Outcomes
Policymakers	Fund and regulate AI literacy programs	Equitable access and ethical compliance
Administrators	Embed AI literacy in strategic planning and incentives	Institution-wide adoption and innovation
Faculty	Pursue ongoing AI training and ethical integration	Enhanced teaching, research, and student engagement

9.3 Future Research Directions

While this chapter synthesizes current knowledge and practical strategies, several areas remain underexplored:

1. **Longitudinal Impact Studies**

More research is needed to track the effects of faculty AI literacy over time, particularly its influence on student outcomes and institutional innovation.

2. **Disciplinary Nuances**

   Investigations into how AI adoption varies between disciplines could inform more tailored literacy programs.

3. **Equity-Focused Research**

Studies examining how AI literacy initiatives can reduce—not reinforce—existing inequalities in higher education are crucial.

4. **AI Policy Implementation Studies**

There is limited empirical evidence on how institutional AI policies are enacted in practice, and how policy clarity impacts faculty engagement.

9.3.1 Integrating Ethics and Human Agency

The findings of this chapter reaffirm that AI literacy is not only a technical or pedagogical concern but a profoundly ethical and human one. As faculty navigate an increasingly AI-mediated academic environment, their capacity for moral judgment, empathy, and critical thinking becomes as essential as their technical skill.

Institutions must therefore treat ethical reasoning and human-centered decision-making as core competencies within AI literacy frameworks—not as optional add-ons. This involves embedding discussions of fairness, bias, privacy, and accountability into faculty training at every stage.

Ultimately, fostering faculty AI literacy means empowering educators to act as ethical interpreters of technology—professionals who can question, adapt, and humanize AI for learning contexts. When AI literacy development protects both *technical confidence* and *moral consciousness*, it aligns educational innovation with its deeper purpose: advancing human understanding and social good.

9.4 Closing Reflection

The journey toward institutional AI literacy is not a single project with a fixed endpoint; it is an ongoing, adaptive process requiring sustained commitment. The models and strategies discussed in this chapter highlight that meaningful transformation is achieved when technical skills, ethical reasoning, and institutional vision evolve together.

As AI continues to reshape the academic landscape, the role of faculty as critical interpreters, ethical stewards, and pedagogical innovators becomes even more vital. Institutions that invest in comprehensive, equitable, and sustainable AI literacy frameworks will not only future-proof their operations but also empower educators to lead in shaping AI's role in society.

In this sense, scaling faculty AI literacy is not simply a matter of institutional competitiveness—it is an act of educational responsibility, ensuring that higher education remains a space where technology serves human learning, rather than the other way around.

REFERENCES

Al-Zahrani, A. M., & Alasmari, T. M. (2024). Exploring the impact of artificial intelligence on higher education: The dynamics of ethical, social, and educational implications. *Humanities & Social Sciences Communications, 11*(1). Advance online publication. DOI: 10.1057/s41599-024-03432-4

Bailey, D. R., & Almusharraf, N. (2022). A structural equation model of second language writing strategies and their influence on anxiety, proficiency, and perceived benefits with online writing. *Education and Information Technologies, 27*. Advance online publication. DOI: 10.1007/s10639-022-11045-0 PMID: 35464111

Bewersdorff, , A., Zhai, X., Roberts, J., & Nerdel, C. (2023). Myths, mis- and preconceptions of artificial intelligence: A review of the literature. *Computers and Education: Artificial Intelligence, 4*(100143). Advance online publication. DOI: 10.1016/j.caeai.2023.100143

Chen, L., Chen, P., & Lin, Z. (2020). Artificial Intelligence in Education: A Review. *IEEE Access : Practical Innovations, Open Solutions, 8*(8), 75264–75278. DOI: 10.1109/ACCESS.2020.2988510

Crompton, H., & Burke, D. (2023). Artificial intelligence in higher education: The state of the field. *International Journal of Educational Technology in Higher Education, 20*(22), 1–22. DOI: 10.1186/s41239-023-00392-8

Furini, M. (2021). Identifying the features of ProVax and NoVax groups from social media conversations. *Computers in Human Behavior, 120*, 106751. DOI: 10.1016/j.chb.2021.106751

Järvelä, S., Nguyen, A., & Hadwin, A. (2023). Human and artificial intelligence collaboration for socially shared regulation in learning. *British Journal of Educational Technology, 54*(5). Advance online publication. DOI: 10.1111/bjet.13325

Kabanda, M. (2025). Literature Review Artificial Intelligence Integration in Higher Education: Enhancing Academic Processes and Leadership Dynamics. *EIKI Journal of Effective Teaching Methods, 3*(1), 169–191. DOI: 10.59652/jetm.v3i1.404

Kay, J., Bartimote, K., Kitto, K., Kummerfeld, B., Liu, D., & Reimann, P. (2022). Enhancing learning by Open Learner Model (OLM) driven data design. *Computers and Education: Artificial Intelligence, 3*, 100069. DOI: 10.1016/j.caeai.2022.100069

Kim, J., & Im, I. (2023). Anthropomorphic response: Understanding interactions between humans and artificial intelligence agents. *Computers in Human Behavior, 139*, 107512. DOI: 10.1016/j.chb.2022.107512

Laupichler, M. C., Aster, A., Schirch, J., & Raupach, T. (2022). Artificial Intelligence Literacy in Higher and Adult education: A Scoping Literature Review. *Computers and Education: Artificial Intelligence, 3*, 100101. DOI: 10.1016/j.caeai.2022.100101

Li, S., & Liu, B. (2018). Joseph E. Aoun: Robot-proof: higher education in the age of artificial intelligence. *Higher Education, 77*(4), 757–759. DOI: 10.1007/s10734-018-0289-3

Macfadyen, L. P., Lockyer, L., & Rienties, B. (2020). Learning Design and Learning Analytics: Snapshot 2020. *Journal of Learning Analytics, 7*(3), 6–12. DOI: 10.18608/jla.2020.73.2

Martín-Lucas, J., & García del Dujo, Á. (2022). Knowledge-building in an environment mediated by digital technology: A case study in higher education. *Education and Information Technologies, 28.* Advance online publication. DOI: 10.1007/s10639-022-11304-0 PMID: 36119125

McAfee, A., & Brynjolfsson, E. (2017). *Machine, platform, crowd: Harnessing our digital future.* Wwnorton.com. https://wwnorton.com/books/Machine-Platform-Crowd/

Muñoz-Carril, P.-C., Hernández-Sellés, N., Fuentes-Abeledo, E.-J., & González-Sanmamed, M. (2021). Factors influencing students' perceived impact of learning and satisfaction in Computer Supported Collaborative Learning. *Computers & Education, 174*, 104310. DOI: 10.1016/j.compedu.2021.104310

Ng, W. (2012). Can we teach digital natives digital literacy? *Computers & Education, 59*(3), 1065–1078. DOI: 10.1016/j.compedu.2012.04.016

Nuryani, S. A., Arnyana, I. P., Parwati, N., Dantes, G., & Juanamasta, Ig. (2022). Development of blended learning model integrated nursing leadership training using web-based in Indonesia. *Journal of Education and Health Promotion, 11*(1), 222. DOI: 10.4103/jehp.jehp_1170_21 PMID: 36177429

Omer, M., & Amairi, A., & Mohammed Muneerali Thottoli. (2023). Surfing the technology wave: An international perspective on enhancing teaching and learning in accounting. *Computers and Education: Artificial Intelligence, 4*, 100144. DOI: 10.1016/j.caeai.2023.100144

Sætra, H. S. (2021). Using Padlet to Enable Online Collaborative Mediation and Scaffolding in a Statistics Course. *Education Sciences, 11*(5), 219. DOI: 10.3390/educsci11050219

Sýkora, T., Stárková, T., & Brom, C. (2020). Can narrative cutscenes improve home learning from a math game? An experimental study with children. *British Journal of Educational Technology*, *52*(1). Advance online publication. DOI: 10.1111/bjet.12939

Tzafilkou, K., Perifanou, M. A., & Economides, A. A. (2021). Teachers' trainers' intention and motivation to transfer ICT training: The role of ICT individual factors, gender, and ICT self-efficacy. *Education and Information Technologies*, *26*(5), 5563–5589. DOI: 10.1007/s10639-021-10541-z

Waiari, D. A. K., Lim, W. T., Thomson-Baker, A. P., Freestone, M. K., Thompson, S., Manuela, S., & Mayeda, D., Purdy (Te Rarawa, Ngai Takoto), S., & Le Grice (Ngāpuhi, Te Rarawa), J. (2021). Stoking the Fires for Māori & Pacific Student Success in Psychology. *Higher Education Research & Development*, *40*(1), 117–131. DOI: 10.1080/07294360.2020.1852186

Zawacki-Richter, O., Marín, V. I., Bond, M., & Gouverneur, F. (2019). Systematic review of research on artificial intelligence applications in higher education – where are the educators? *International Journal of Educational Technology in Higher Education*, *16*(1), 1–27. DOI: 10.1186/s41239-019-0171-0

KEY TERMS AND DEFINITIONS

Artificial Intelligence (AI): The simulation of human intelligence processes by machines, especially computer systems, which may include learning, reasoning, problem-solving, perception, and natural language understanding.

AI Literacy: A composite competency that encompasses the knowledge, skills, and ethical awareness required to understand, evaluate, and effectively use artificial intelligence tools and concepts in personal, academic, and professional contexts.

Faculty Development: Planned activities, programs, and resources designed to enhance faculty members' professional knowledge, pedagogical skills, and technological proficiency, enabling them to integrate innovative teaching strategies, including AI, into their practice.

Institutional Transformation: A structured process through which a higher education institution fundamentally changes its strategies, culture, policies, and operational models to adapt to evolving technological, social, and economic environments.

Sustainable Adoption: The long-term and continuous integration of new practices, tools, or technologies into an institution's operations in a manner that is resource-efficient, adaptable to change, and capable of enduring beyond initial implementation phases.

Generative AI: A subset of artificial intelligence that creates new content—such as text, images, code, or audio—based on patterns learned from existing data, often using large-scale machine learning models.

Pedagogical Integration: The deliberate incorporation of technological tools and AI applications into teaching strategies, curriculum design, and assessment methods to improve student engagement, learning outcomes, and skill development.

Ethical AI Use: The application of artificial intelligence in ways that uphold fairness, transparency, accountability, privacy, and respect for human rights, while avoiding bias, discrimination, or harm.

Communities of Practice (CoP): Groups of faculty or practitioners who share a common interest in AI in education and engage in regular interaction to exchange knowledge, solve problems, and co-develop innovations.

Digital Competence Framework: A structured model outlining the essential digital knowledge, skills, and attitudes required by educators and learners, often serving as a reference for AI literacy training.

Capacity Building: Efforts aimed at improving the abilities, resources, and institutional readiness of faculty and organizations to effectively implement and sustain AI-related initiatives.

Change Management: A systematic approach to guiding individuals, teams, and institutions through the process of adopting and adapting to technological or organizational change, minimizing resistance and maximizing engagement.

Compilation of References

Aarthi, S., Ravikumar, R. N., Khudayberganov, S., Ismailov, A., & Khujaniyozova, O. (2025). Using Intelligent Tutoring Systems to enhance student engagement. In *Advances in Computational Intelligence and Robotics* (pp. 155–188). IGI Global., DOI: 10.4018/979-8-3373-1827-1.ch008

Acosta-Vargas, P., Acosta-Vargas, G., Salvador-Acosta, B., & Jadán-Guerrero, J. (2024). Addressing web accessibility challenges with generative artificial intelligence tools for inclusive education. In *2024 Tenth International Conference on eDemocracy & eGovernment (ICEDEG)* (1-7). IEEE. https://doi.org/DOI: 10.1109/ICEDEG61611.2024.10702085

Adami, C. (2021). A brief history of artificial intelligence research. *Artificial Life, 27*(2), 131–147. DOI: 10.1162/artl_a_00349

Adesiji, T. T. (2024). Integrating Artificial Intelligence in Nigerian University Curricula: Challenges, Opportunities, and Future Prospects. *In 2024 IEEE 5th International Conference on Electro-Computing Technologies for Humanity (NIGERCON)* (1-7). IEEE. https://doi.org/DOI: 10.1109/NIGERCON62786.2024.10927366

Aithal, P. S., & Maiya, A. K. (2023). Innovations in higher education industry–Shaping the future. [IJCSBE]. *International Journal of Case Studies in Business, IT, and Education, 7*(4), 283–311.

Akintayo, O. T., Eden, C. A., Ayeni, O. O., & Onyebuchi, N. C. (2024). Integrating AI with emotional and social learning in primary education: Developing a holistic adaptive learning ecosystem. *Computer Science & IT Research Journal, 5*(5), 1076–1089. DOI: 10.53022/oarjms.2024.7.2.0025

Alakoum, A., Nica, E., & Abiad, M. (2024). Revolutionizing faculty performance evaluation: The future role of AI in higher education. *Journal of Self-Governance and Management Economics, 12*(1), 25–49.

Alenezi, A. (2023). Teacher perspectives on AI-driven gamification: Impact on student motivation, engagement, and learning outcomes. *Information Technologies and Learning Tools*, *97*(5), 138–148. DOI: 10.33407/itlt.v97i5.5437

Aleven, V., McLaughlin, E. A., Glenn, R., & Koedinger, K. R. (2016). Instruction based on adaptive learning technologies. In Sawyer, R. K. (Ed.), *The Cambridge handbook of the learning sciences* (2nd ed., pp. 522–549). Cambridge University Press.

Alexander, L. M., Bowser, J., Caruthers, K., Sekhon, L., Statler, M., Straker, H., Rizzolo, D., De La Rosa, H., & Simeon, D. T. (2025). Fear factor: Faculty perceptions of artificial intelligence in physician associate education. *The Journal of Physician Assistant Education : the Official Journal of the Physician Assistant Education Association*, *36*(3), e288–e294. DOI: 10.1097/JPA.0000000000000667 PMID: 40168397

Alfarra, A. H., Amhan, L. F., Mosa, M. J., Alajrami, M. A., El Kahlout, F., Abu-Nasser, B. S., & Abu-Naser, S. S. (2024). AI-driven learning: Advances and challenges in intelligent tutoring systems.

Alhawiti, K. M. (2014). Natural language processing and its use in education. *International Journal of Advanced Computer Science and Applications*, *5*(12), 72–76.

Al-Mughairi, H., & Bhaskar, P. (2024). Exploring the factors affecting the adoption AI techniques in higher education: insights from teachers' perspectives on ChatGPT. *Journal of Research in Innovative Teaching & Learning*.

Alper Aytaç, M., Alemdar, M., Akay, Y. E., & Avcu, Y. E. (2024). Fostering tech integration: Teachers' attitudes mediating lifelong learning and technology integration self-efficacy. Participatory Educational Research, 112–133.

Al-Zahrani, A. M., & Alasmari, T. M. (2024). Exploring the impact of artificial intelligence on higher education: The dynamics of ethical, social, and educational implications. *Humanities & Social Sciences Communications*, *11*(1). Advance online publication. DOI: 10.1057/s41599-024-03432-4

Amani Mohammad, H., Abeer, B. H., Aya, A., Ghadi, B., & Farah, A. (2024). "impact of artificial intelligence on faculty's teaching development: A quantitative research in Saudi private universities." Communications of International Proceedings. https://doi.org/DOI: 10.5171/2024.4342624

Anvari, R., Moradi, F., & Shirvani, A. (2024). Digital learning ecosystem at educational institutions: a 4-university perspective. *Professional studies: theory and practice*, 28(1), 100-110.

Arnold, K. E., & Pistilli, M. D. (2012). Course signals at Purdue: Using learning analytics to increase student success. *Proceedings of the 2nd International Conference on Learning Analytics and Knowledge*, 267–270.

Awasthi, R., & Tiwari, A. (2024). Role of Data Mining in Redesigning the Existing Curriculum: A Survey Based Literature Review. *Journal of Computational Analysis and Applications*, *33*(7).

Ayyoub, A. M., Khlaif, Z. N., Shamali, M., Abu Eideh, B., Assali, A., Hattab, M. K., Barham, K. A., & Bsharat, T. R. K. (2025). Advancing higher education with GenAI: Factors influencing educator AI literacy. *Frontiers in Education*, *10*. Advance online publication. DOI: 10.3389/feduc.2025.1530721

Azahar, M. Z. A. B., & Ghauth, K. I. B. (2022). A hybrid automated essay scoring using NLP and random forest regression. In *International Conference on Computer, Information Technology and Intelligent Computing (CITIC 2022)* (448-457). Atlantis Press.

Bailey, D. R., & Almusharraf, N. (2022). A structural equation model of second language writing strategies and their influence on anxiety, proficiency, and perceived benefits with online writing. *Education and Information Technologies*, *27*. Advance online publication. DOI: 10.1007/s10639-022-11045-0 PMID: 35464111

Bai, X., & Wang, S. (2022). Faculty development for AI integration in higher education: Strategies and challenges. *Journal of Educational Technology*, *43*(2), 123–138. DOI: 10.1016/j.jedt.2022.01.004

Baker, R. S., Hawn, A., Ritter, S., Corbett, A. T., Aleven, V., & Fancsali, S. (2020). Algorithmic bias in education. *Harvard Educational Review*, *90*(2), 1–28.

Baker, R. S., & Inventado, P. S. (2014). Educational data mining and learning analytics. In Larusson, J. A., & White, B. (Eds.), *Learning analytics* (pp. 61–75). Springer.

Bayne, S. (2015). What's the matter with "technology-enhanced learning"? *Learning, Media and Technology*, *40*(1), 5–20.

Beck, J., Stern, M., & Haugsjaa, E. (1996). Applications of AI in Education. *XRDS: Crossroads. The ACM Magazine for Students*, *3*(1), 11–15.

Belshaw, D. (2023, March 18). *AI literacy*. Doug Belshaw's blog. https://dougbelshaw.com/blog/2023/03/18/ai-literacy/

Belshaw, D. (2012). *The essential elements of digital literacies*. CreateSpace Independent Publishing.

Bender, E. M., Gebru, T., McMillan-Major, A., & Shmitchell, S. (2021). On the dangers of stochastic parrots: Can language models be too big? *Proceedings of the 2021 ACM Conference on Fairness, Accountability, and Transparency,* 610-623. https://doi.org/DOI: 10.1145/3442188.3445922

Berger, P. L., & Luckmann, T. (1966). *The social construction of reality: A treatise in the sociology of knowledge*. Anchor Books.

Bewersdorff, , A., Zhai, X., Roberts, J., & Nerdel, C. (2023). Myths, mis- and preconceptions of artificial intelligence: A review of the literature. *Computers and Education: Artificial Intelligence*, *4*(100143). Advance online publication. DOI: 10.1016/j.caeai.2023.100143

Biggs, J. (1996). Enhancing teaching through constructive alignment. *Higher Education*, *32*(3), 347–364.

Bilquise, G., & Shaalan, K. (2022). AI-based academic advising framework: A knowledge management perspective. *International Journal of Advanced Computer Science and Applications*, *13*(8).

Bing, Z. J., & Leong, W. Y. (2025). Ethical design of AI for education and learning systems. *ASM Science Journal*, *20*(1), 1–9. DOI: 10.32802/asmscj.2025.1917

Black, N. B., George, S., Eguchi, A., Dempsey, J. C., Langran, E., Fraga, L., Brunvand, S., & Howard, N. (2024). A framework for approaching AI education in Educator Preparation Programs. Proceedings of the ... AAAI Conference on Artificial Intelligence. AAAI Conference on Artificial Intelligence, 38(21), 23069–23077. https://doi.org/DOI: 10.1609/aaai.v38i21.30351

Bloom, B. S. (Ed.). (1956). *Taxonomy of educational objectives: The classification of educational goals. Handbook I: Cognitive domain*. Longmans, Green.

Boateng, O., & Boateng, B. (2025). Algorithmic bias in educational systems: Examining the impact of AI-driven decision making in modern education. *World Journal of Advanced Research and Reviews*, *25*(1), 2012–2017. DOI: 10.30574/wjarr.2025.25.1.0253

Bodily, R., & Verbert, K. (2017). Review of research on student-facing learning analytics dashboards and educational recommender systems. *IEEE Transactions on Learning Technologies*, *10*(4), 405–418.

Boller, S., & Fletcher, L. (2020). *Design thinking for training and development: Creating learning journeys that get results*. Association for Talent Development.

Bond, M., Bedenlier, S., Marín, V. I., & Händel, M. (2021). Emergency remote teaching in higher education: Mapping the first global online semester. *International Journal of Educational Technology in Higher Education, 18*(1), 50. PMID: 34778537

Boud, D., & Molloy, E. (2013). *Feedback in higher and professional education: Understanding it and doing it well.* Routledge.

Brookfield, S. (2017). *Becoming a critically reflective teacher* (2nd ed.). Jossey-Bass.

Brown, J. S., Collins, A., & Duguid, P. (1989). Situated cognition and the culture of learning. *Educational Researcher, 18*(1), 32–42.

Brown, M. (2020). *Education and technology: Critical perspectives, possible futures*. Routledge.

Burrell, J. (2016). How the machine "thinks": Understanding opacity in machine learning algorithms. *Big Data & Society, 3*(1), 1–12. DOI: 10.1177/2053951715622512

Campbell-Rogers, A. (2024). Design affordances and user perception: Investigating the relationship between space design and pedagogical possibility in an innovative learning environment.

Çela, E., Fonkam, M. M., Vajjhala, N. R., & Vedishchev, A. (2024). Artificial intelligence in education. In *Advances in Educational Technologies and Instructional Design* (pp. 1–20). IGI Global., DOI: 10.4018/979-8-3693-7220-3.ch001

Çelik, I. (2023). Towards Intelligent-TPACK: An empirical study on teachers' professional knowledge to ethically integrate artificial intelligence (AI)-based tools into education. *Computers in Human Behavior, 138*, 107468. DOI: 10.1016/j.chb.2022.107468

Cetina, K. K. (2007). Culture in global knowledge societies: Knowledge cultures and epistemic cultures. *Interdisciplinary Science Reviews, 32*(4), 361–375. DOI: 10.1179/030801807X163571

Chakraborty, N., Mishra, Y., Bhattacharya, R., & Bhattacharya, B. (2023). Artificial Intelligence: The road ahead for the accessibility of persons with Disability. *Materials Today: Proceedings, 80*, 3757–3761. DOI: 10.1016/j.matpr.2021.07.374

Chanyi, L., Mokhtar, M. M., & Ayub, A. F. M. (2025). The 5P Funnel Framework: An AI-Integrated Instructional Design for Enhancing Teacher Professional Development. *Journal of Public Administration and Governance, 14*(2), 78–96. DOI: 10.5296/jpag.v14i2S.22590

Chatterjee, S., & Bhattacharjee, K. K. (2020). Adoption of artificial intelligence in higher education: A quantitative analysis using structural equation modelling. *Education and Information Technologies, 25*(5), 3443–3463. DOI: 10.69557/ujrra.v3i4.124

Chemnad, K., & Othman, A. (2024). Digital accessibility in the era of artificial intelligence—Bibliometric analysis and systematic review. *Frontiers in Artificial Intelligence, 7*. Advance online publication. DOI: 10.3389/frai.2024.1349668

Chen, L., Chen, P., & Lin, Z. (2020). Artificial Intelligence in Education: A Review. *IEEE Access : Practical Innovations, Open Solutions, 8*(8), 75264–75278. DOI: 10.1109/ACCESS.2020.2988510

Chen, N. S., Smyrnova-Trybulska, E., Morze, N., Ślósarz, A., Glushkova, T., Przybyła-Kasperek, M., & Gubo, Š. (2024). Education in the Era of AI, Enhancing Skills, Challenges and Perspectives–International Context and National Experience. *International Journal of Research in E-learning, 10*(2), 1–30.

Chen, X., Xie, H., & Yang, L. (2020). AI in education: Content creation and curation. *Journal of Educational Technology, 14*(3), 45–60.

Chen, X., Xie, H., Zou, D., & Hwang, G. J. (2020). Application and theory gaps during the rise of artificial intelligence in education. *Computers and Education: Artificial Intelligence, 1*, 100002. DOI: 10.1016/j.caeai.2020.100002

Chu, T. S., & Ashraf, M. (2025). Artificial Intelligence in Curriculum Design: A Data-Driven Approach to Higher Education Innovation. *Knowledge (Beverly Hills, Calif.), 5*(3), 14.

Collins, H. (2018). Why artificial intelligence needs sociology of knowledge. *Social Studies of Science, 48*(6), 813–831.

Collins, J., & Blot, R. K. (2003). *Literacy and literacies: Texts, power, and identity*. Cambridge University Press.

Copur-Gencturk, Y., Li, J., & Atabas, S. (2024). Improving teaching at scale: Can AI be incorporated into professional development to create interactive, personalized learning for teachers? *American Educational Research Journal, 61*(4), 767–802.

Crawford, K. (2021). *Atlas of AI: Power, politics, and the planetary costs of artificial intelligence*. Yale University Press.

Crompton, H., & Burke, D. (2023). Artificial intelligence in higher education: The state of the field. *International Journal of Educational Technology in Higher Education, 20*, 22.

Cummings, C., & Ferris, M. (2021). Data privacy in AI-powered education systems. *Journal of Learning Analytics*, *8*(2), 33–49.

Dahal, P., Nugroho, S., Schmidt, C., & Sänger, V. (2025). AI-Based Learning Recommendations: Use in Higher Education. *Future Internet*, *17*(7), 285. DOI: 10.3390/fi17070285

Darling-Hammond, L., Hyler, M. E., & Gardner, M. (2017). Effective teacher professional development. Learning Policy Institute. https://learningpolicyinstitute.org/product/effective-teacher-professional-development-report

Dede, C. (2014). *The role of digital technologies in deeper learning. Students at the Center: Deeper Learning Research Series*. Jobs for the Future.

Deri, M. N., Zaazie, P., & Singh, A. (2024). Digital Future of the Hospitality Industry and Hospitality Education Globally. In Sharma, A. (Ed.), *International Handbook of Skill, Education, Learning, and Research Development in Tourism and Hospitality. Springer International Handbooks of Education*. Springer., DOI: 10.1007/978-981-97-4318-6_14

Dewey, J. (1981). *The later works, 1925-1953* (Vol. 3). SIU Press.

Digital Education Council. (2024). *Digital Education Council AI literacy framework*. https://www.digitaleducationcouncil.com/post/digital-education-council-ai-literacy-framework

Digital Promise. (2024). *AI literacy: A framework to understand, evaluate, and use emerging technology*. https://digitalpromise.org/2024/06/18/ai-literacy-a-framework-to-understand-evaluate-and-use-emerging-technology/

Doğan, M., Celik, A., & Arslan, H. (2025). AI in higher education: Risks and opportunities from the academician perspective. *European Journal of Education*, *60*(1). Advance online publication. DOI: 10.1111/ejed.12863

Dulundu, A. (2024). AI in education: Benefits and concerns. *Next Generation Journal for The Young Researchers*, *8*(1), 81. DOI: 10.62802/3fr4f412

Eden, C. A., Chisom, O. N., & Adeniyi, I. S. (2024). Integrating AI in education: Opportunities, challenges, and ethical considerations. *Magna Scientia Advanced Research and Reviews, 10*(2), 006-013.

Educause & AWS. (2025, March 10). Higher Education Generative AI Readiness Assessment. Educause.

Elkins, S., Kochmar, E., Cheung, J. C., & Serban, I. (2024). How teachers can use large language models and bloom's taxonomy to create educational quizzes. *Proceedings of the AAAI Conference on Artificial Intelligence, 38*(21), 23084–23091. DOI: 10.1609/aaai.v38i21.30353

Ersozlu, Z., Taheri, S., & Koch, I. (2024). A review of machine learning methods used for educational data. *Education and Information Technologies, 29*(16), 22125–22145.

European Commission. (2020). Ethics guidelines for trustworthy AI. https://digital-strategy.ec.europa.eu/en/library/ethics-guidelines-trustworthy-ai

Fakhar, H., Lamrabet, M., Echantoufi, N., & Ajana, L. (2024). Towards a New Artificial Intelligence-based Framework for Teachers' Online Continuous Professional Development Programs: Systematic Review. *International Journal of Advanced Computer Science and Applications, 15*(4).

Felten, P. (2013). Principles of good practice in SoTL. *Teaching & Learning Inquiry, 1*(1), 121–125.

Felten, P., & Lambert, L. M. (2020). *Relationship rich education: How human connections drive success in college*. Johns Hopkins Press.

Ferguson, R., Clow, D., & Macfadyen, L. (2021). Interdisciplinary approaches to AI in education: Challenges and opportunities. *International Journal of Artificial Intelligence in Education, 31*(4), 567–586. DOI: 10.1007/s40593-020-00226-2

Flores-Chacón, E., Pacheco, A., Gonzales-Ortiz, Y., Moreno-Vega, L., del-Castillo-Palacios, F., & Perez-Rojas, E. (2023). Educational innovation: The architecture of digital technologies as a catalyst for change in university teacher training. *Scientific Reports, 13*(1), 20991. PMID: 38017148

Floridi, L., Cowls, J., Beltrametti, M., Chatila, R., Chazerand, P., Dignum, V., & Vayena, E. (2018). AI4People—An ethical framework for a good AI society. *Science and Engineering Ethics, 24*(1), 103–130. DOI: 10.1007/s11948-017-9901-2 PMID: 30930541

Freire, P. (2000). *Pedagogy of the oppressed* (30th anniversary ed.; M. B. Ramos, Trans.). Continuum. (Original work published 1970)

Friberg, J. C., & Giovagnoli, D. (2024, July 25). GenAI usage expectation levels: A path towards increased transparency in teaching and learning. *The SoTL Advocate* [weblog]. https://illinoisstateuniversitysotl.wordpress.com/2024/07/25/genai-usage-expectation-levels-a-path-towards-increased-transparency-in-teaching-and-learning/

Furini, M. (2021). Identifying the features of ProVax and NoVax groups from social media conversations. *Computers in Human Behavior, 120*, 106751. DOI: 10.1016/j.chb.2021.106751

Gabriel, I. (2020). Artificial Intelligence, Values, and Alignment. *Minds and Machines, 30*, 411–437.

Garg, A., Singh, A., & Yanan, J. (2024). Exploring the Impact of Digital Detoxification on Higher Education Students' Learning. In Grima, S., Chaudhary, S., Sood, K., & Kumar, S. (Eds.), *Business Drivers in Promoting Digital Detoxification* (pp. 111–126). IGI Global Scientific Publishing., DOI: 10.4018/979-8-3693-1107-3.ch008

Gašević, D., Dawson, S., & Siemens, G. (2023). Perspectives of academic staff on artificial intelligence in higher education: Exploring areas of relevance. *Frontiers in Education, 8*, 1484904.

Gee, J. P. (1999). The new literacy studies and the "social turn." [ERIC document]. https://files.eric.ed.gov/fulltext/ED442118.pdf

Gee, J. P. (1989). Literacy, discourse, and linguistics: Introduction. *Journal of Education, 171*(1), 5–17. DOI: 10.1177/002205748917100101

George, B., & Wooden, O. (2023). Managing the strategic transformation of higher education through artificial intelligence. *Administrative Sciences, 13*(9), 196. DOI: 10.3390/admsci13090196

Ge, Z., & Hu, Y. (2020, April). Innovative application of artificial intelligence (AI) in the management of higher education and teaching. [). IOP Publishing.]. *Journal of Physics: Conference Series, 1533*(3), 032089.

Gikandi, J. W., Morrow, D., & Davis, N. E. (2011). Online formative assessment in higher education: A review of the literature. *Computers & Education, 57*(4), 2333–2351.

Gillespie, T. (2014). The relevance of algorithms. In Gillespie, T., Boczkowski, P., & Foot, K. (Eds.), *Media technologies: Essays on communication, materiality, and society* (pp. 167–193). MIT Press.

Giroux, H. A. (2014). *Neoliberalism's war on higher education*. Haymarket Books.

Goel, A., & Polepeddi, L. (2016). Jill Watson: A virtual teaching assistant for online education. Georgia Tech Technical Report.

Guan, C., Mou, J., & Jiang, Z. (2020). Artificial intelligence innovation in education: A twenty-year data-driven historical analysis. *International Journal of Innovation Studies, 4*(4), 134–147.

Guan, J., Zhang, J., & Zhang, X. (2023). The Influence of Generative Artificial Intelligence on High School Students' Academic Planning–ChatGPT. *Lecture Notes in Education Psychology and Public Media, 24*(1), 205–210. DOI: 10.54254/2753-7048/24/20230705

Gunder, A. (2021). *The open turn: Portraits, practices, and perspectives on the remix of open educational resources* [Doctoral dissertation, The University of Arizona]. http://hdl.handle.net/10150/663131

Gunder, A., Herron, J., Weber, N., Chelf, C., & Birdwell, S. (2024). *Dimensions of AI literacies*. Opened Culture. https://openedculture.com/projects/dimensions-of-ai-literacies/

Gunder, A. (2024). *Constellating AI literacies: Illuminating the sociocultural and pluralistic dimensions of AI in education*. Opened Culture.

Hacking, I. (1999). *The social construction of what?* Harvard University Press.

Hammond, Z. (2015). *Culturally responsive teaching and the brain: Promoting authentic engagement and rigor among culturally and linguistically diverse students*. Corwin.

Hannan, E., & Liu, S. (2021). AI: new source of competitiveness in higher education. Competitiveness Review Journal, ahead-of-print(ahead-of-print). https://doi.org/DOI: 10.1108/cr-03-2021-0045

Harry, A. (2023). Role of AI in education. *Interdiciplinary Journal & Hummanity (INJURITY), 2*(3).

Heath, C., & Heath, D. (2017). *The power of moments: Why certain experiences have extraordinary impact*. Simon & Schuster.

Henshaw, C. A. (2025). Multimedia learning and UDL in UK higher education. *Journal of Advanced Research in Education, 4*(2), 27–33. DOI: 10.56397/jare.2025.03.03

He, R., Cao, J., & Tan, T. (2025). Generative artificial intelligence: A historical perspective. *National Science Review, 12*(5). Advance online publication. DOI: 10.1093/nsr/nwaf050

Herodotou, C., Rienties, B., Verdin, B., & Boroowa, A. (2019). Predictive learning analytics 'at scale': Guidelines to successful implementation in Higher Education based on the case of the Open University UK. *Journal of Learning Analytics, 6*(1), 85–95. DOI: 10.18608/jla.2019.61.5

Herrington, J., & Oliver, R. (2000). An instructional design framework for authentic learning environments. *Educational Technology Research and Development, 48*(3), 23–48.

Herrington, J., Reeves, T. C., & Oliver, R. (2010). *A guide to authentic e-learning*. Routledge.

Herrington, J., Reeves, T. C., & Oliver, R. (2014). Authentic learning environments. In Spector, J. M., Merrill, M. D., Elen, J., & Bishop, M. J. (Eds.), *Handbook of research on educational communications and technology* (pp. 401–412). Springer.

Hibbert, M., Altman, E., Shippen, T., & Wright, M. (2024, June 3). *A framework for AI literacy*. In EDUCAUSE Review. EDUCAUSE. https://er.educause.edu/articles/2024/6/a-framework-for-ai-literacy

Higher Education Policy Institute. (2025, February 26). Student generative AI survey 2025. https://www.hepi.ac.uk/2025/02/26/student-generative-ai-survey-2025/

Hmelo-Silver, C. E., Duncan, R. G., & Chinn, C. A. (2007). Scaffolding and achievement in problem-based and inquiry learning: A response to Kirschner, Sweller, and Clark (2006). *Educational Psychologist, 42*(2), 99–107.

Hochstetter-Diez, J., Negrier-Seguel, M., Diéguez-Rebolledo, M., Candia-Garrido, E., & Vidal, E. (2025). From Mapping to Action: SmartRubrics, an AI Tool for Competency-Based Assessment in Engineering Education. *Sustainability, 17*(13), 6098. DOI: 10.3390/su17136098

Holmes, W., Bialik, M., & Fadel, C. (2019). *Artificial intelligence in education promises and implications for teaching and learning*. Center for Curriculum Redesign.

Holmes, W., Bialik, M., & Fadel, C. (2021). *Artificial intelligence in education: Promises and implications for teaching and learning*. Center for Curriculum Redesign.

Holmes, W., Bialik, M., & Fadel, C. (2021). *Artificial Intelligence in Education: Promises and Implications for Teaching and Learning*. Center for Curriculum Redesign.

Holmes, W., & Tuomi, I. (2022). State of the art and practice in AI in education. *European Journal of Education, 57*(4), 542–570.

Holstein, K., McLaren, B. M., & Aleven, V. (2019). Intelligent tutors as teachers' aides: AI systems to support classroom instruction. *ACM Transactions on Computer-Human Interaction, 26*(6), 1–28. DOI: 10.1145/3359183

Hooda, M., Rana, C., Dahiya, O., Rizwan, A., & Hossain, M. S. (2022). Artificial intelligence for assessment and feedback to enhance student success in higher education. *Mathematical Problems in Engineering, 2022*(1). https://doi.org/DOI: 10.1155/2022/5215722

Hubballi, R. B., Selvakumar, P., Seenivasan, R., Dinesh, N., & Seelam, P. K. (2025). Overview of Current AI Technologies in Education. In *Transformative AI Practices for Personalized Learning Strategies* (pp. 1–26). IGI Global Scientific Publishing.

Hunt, T., Carter, R., Zhang, L., & Yang, S. (2020). Micro-credentials: The potential of personalized professional development. *Development and Learning in Organizations*, *34*(2), 33–35. DOI: 10.1108/DLO-09-2019-0215

Hutchings, P. (2000). *Opening lines: Approaches to the scholarship of teaching and learning*. Carnegie Foundation for the Advancement of Teaching.

Iatrellis, O., Samaras, N., Kokkinos, K., & Panagiotakopoulos, T. (2024). Leveraging generative AI for sustainable academic advising: Enhancing educational practices through AI-driven recommendations. *Sustainability*, *16*(17), 7829. DOI: 10.3390/su16177829

Inside Higher Ed. (2024). Most campus tech leaders say higher ed is unprepared for AI. Inside Higher Ed.

Ismail, O. S. (2024). Empowering the modern learning ecosystem: Integrative approaches for a holistic educational experience. In *Revitalizing the Learning Ecosystem for Modern Students* (pp. 145–167). IGI Global Scientific Publishing.

Järvelä, S., Nguyen, A., & Hadwin, A. (2023). Human and artificial intelligence collaboration for socially shared regulation in learning. *British Journal of Educational Technology*, *54*(5). Advance online publication. DOI: 10.1111/bjet.13325

Jisc. (2024, March 8). *Principles for the use of AI in FE colleges*. Jisc. https://nationalcentreforai.jiscinvolve.org/wp/2024/03/08/principles-for-the-use-of-ai-in-fe-colleges/

Jones, A., & Patel, R. (2021). Blending adaptive learning with traditional humanities education: A case study. *Journal of Higher Education Innovation*, *15*(3), 45–59.

Kabanda, M. (2025). Literature Review Artificial Intelligence Integration in Higher Education: Enhancing Academic Processes and Leadership Dynamics. *EIKI Journal of Effective Teaching Methods*, *3*(1), 169–191. DOI: 10.59652/jetm.v3i1.404

Kalaigian, M., Thompson, M. S., VanLone, J., & Nickel, R. (2024). *Using Generative AI to Implement UDL Principles in Traditional STEM Classrooms. In 2024 IEEE Frontiers in Education Conference (FIE) (1-9).* IEEE., DOI: 10.1109/FIE61694.2024.10893115

Kantayya, S. (Director). (2020). *Coded bias* [Film]. 7th Empire Media.

Karimi, H., & Khawaja, S. (2023). The impact of artificial intelligence on higher education in England. *Creative Education, 14*(12), 2405–2415. DOI: 10.4236/ce.2023.1412154

Kasztelnik, K. (2024). Artificial Intelligence-Assisted Curriculum Development: Innovations in Designing Educational Content for the 21st Century Learner. *Journal of Higher Education Theory and Practice, 24*(11), 51–59.

Katona, J., & Gyonyoru, K. I. K. (2025). AI-based Adaptive Programming Education for Socially Disadvantaged Students: Bridging the Digital Divide. *TechTrends, 69*, 925–942. DOI: 10.1007/s11528-025-01088-8

Katsamakas, E., Pavlov, O. V., & Saklad, R. (2024). Artificial intelligence and the transformation of higher education institutions: A systems approach. *Sustainability, 16*(14), 6118.

Kay, J., Bartimote, K., Kitto, K., Kummerfeld, B., Liu, D., & Reimann, P. (2022). Enhancing learning by Open Learner Model (OLM) driven data design. *Computers and Education: Artificial Intelligence, 3*, 100069. DOI: 10.1016/j.caeai.2022.100069

Kerly, A., Ellis, R., & Bull, S. (2007). CALMsystem: A conversational agent for learner modelling. *Knowledge-Based Systems, 20*(2), 139–148.

Kerres, M., & Buntins, K. (2020). Recommender in AI-enhanced learning: An assessment from the perspective of instructional design. *Open Education Studies, 2*(1), 101–111. DOI: 10.1515/edu-2020-0119

Kezar, A., & Eckel, P. D. (2002). Coming in from the margins: Faculty development's emerging organizational development role in institutional change. *The Journal of Higher Education, 73*(1), 26–48. DOI: 10.1080/00221546.2002.11777132

Khairullah, S. A., Harris, S., Hadi, H. J., Sandhu, R. A., Ahmad, N., & Alshara, M. A. (2025). Implementing artificial intelligence in academic and administrative processes through responsible strategic leadership in higher education institutions. *Frontiers in Education, 10*, 1548104.

Khajuria, R., Sharma, A., & Sharma, A. (2023). A detailed survey regarding the usage of different ICT technology modes adopted by higher education institutions. *Indonesian Journal of Electrical Engineering and Computer Science*, *29*(3), 1634–1641.

Khalid, U., Kashif, H., Alamdar, R., & Naseer, F. (2024). Redefining faculty roles in an AI-driven educational ecosystem with implications for teaching and curriculum development. *Journal of Media Horizons*, *5*(4), 127–139.

Khan, M. J., Lajber, M., Bilal, N., & Khan, S., Zarrin `Siddiqi, & Ahmad, A. (2024). The barriers and solution to artificial Intelligence adoption in Medical Education: A qualitative study. Journal of Saidu Medical College. *Swat*, *14*(4), 341–347. DOI: 10.52206/jsmc.2024.14.4.957

Kim, J., & Im, I. (2023). Anthropomorphic response: Understanding interactions between humans and artificial intelligence agents. *Computers in Human Behavior*, *139*, 107512. DOI: 10.1016/j.chb.2022.107512

King Faisal University. (2024). Factors affecting faculty members' readiness to integrate AI in teaching practices. *International Journal of Educational Technology in Higher Education*, *21*(3), 45–62.

Kohen-Vacs, D., Amzalag, M., Weigelt-Marom, H., Gal, L., Kahana, O., Raz-Fogel, N., & Usher, M. (2024). Towards a call for transformative practices in academia enhanced by generative AI. *European Journal of Open. Distance & E-Learning*, *26*(1), 35–50. DOI: 10.2478/eurodl-2024-0006

Kökver, Y., Pektaş, H. M., & Çelik, H. (2025). Artificial intelligence applications in education: Natural language processing in detecting misconceptions. *Education and Information Technologies*, *30*(3), 3035–3066. DOI: 10.1007/s10639-024-12919-1

Kozanitis, A., & Nenciovici, L. (2023). Effect of active learning versus traditional lecturing on learning achievement in the humanities and social sciences: A meta-analysis. *Higher Education*, *86*(6), 1377–1394.

Krathwohl, D. R. (2002). A revision of Bloom's taxonomy: An overview. *Theory into Practice*, *41*(4), 212–218. DOI: 10.1207/s15430421tip4104_2

Krishna Pasupuleti, M. (2024). AI-Powered Learning: Transformative innovations in Smart Education Technology. In Advanced AI-Driven EdTech: Transformative Innovations in Smart Learning (pp. 292–310). National Education Services. https://doi.org/DOI: 10.62311/nesx/802874

Krouska, A., Troussas, C., Voyiatzis, I., Mylonas, P., & Sgouropoulou, C. (2024, November). ChatGPT-based recommendations for personalized content creation and instructional design with a tailored prompt generator. In *2024 2nd International Conference on Foundation and Large Language Models (FLLM)* (295-299). IEEE. https://doi.org/DOI: 10.1109/FLLM63129.2024.10852487

Kuhail, M. A., Alturki, N., Alramlawi, S., & Alhejori, K. (2023). Interacting with educational chatbots: A systematic review. *Education and Information Technologies*, *28*(1), 973–1018. DOI: 10.1007/s10639-022-11177-3

Lai, J. W. (2024). Adapting self-regulated learning in an age of generative artificial intelligence chatbots. *Future Internet*, *16*(6), 218. DOI: 10.3390/fi16060218

Lakhe Shrestha, B. L., Dahal, N., Hasan, M. K., Paudel, S., & Kapar, H. (2025, June). Generative AI on professional development: a narrative inquiry using TPACK framework. In *Frontiers in Education* (Vol. 10). https://doi.org/DOI: 10.3389/feduc.2025.1550773

Lang, J. M. (2021). *Distracted: Why students can't focus and what you can do about it*. Basic Books.

Latour, B., & Woolgar, S. (1979). Laboratory life: The social construction of scientific facts. *Sage (Atlanta, Ga.)*.

Laupichler, M. C., Aster, A., Schirch, J., & Raupach, T. (2022). Artificial Intelligence Literacy in Higher and Adult education: A Scoping Literature Review. *Computers and Education: Artificial Intelligence*, *3*, 100101. DOI: 10.1016/j.caeai.2022.100101

Lave, J., & Wenger, E. (1991). *Situated learning: Legitimate peripheral participation*. Cambridge University Press.

Lawrence-Lightfoot, S., & Davis, J. H. (1997). *The art and science of portraiture*. Jossey-Bass.

Lee, A. V. Y. (2023). Supporting students' generation of feedback in large-scale online course with artificial intelligence-enabled evaluation. *Studies in Educational Evaluation*, *77*, 101250. DOI: 10.1016/j.stueduc.2023.101250

Le-Nguyen, H. T., & Tran, T. T. (2024). Generative AI in terms of its ethical problems for both teachers and learners: Striking a balance. In *Generative AI in teaching and learning* (pp. 144–173). IGI Global Scientific Publishing.

Lhakard, P. (2024). AI Catalyst: Revolutionizing Workforce Development-A Comprehensive Study of Intelligent Learning Systems. Asian Journal of Management. *Entrepreneurship and Social Science*, *4*(04), 331–346.

Liang, C., Zhang, B., Gong, X., Li, M., Guo, H., & Li, R. (2022). A Survey of Automated Essay Scoring System Based on Naive Bayes Classifier. In *Artificial Intelligence in Education and Teaching Assessment* (pp. 247–250). Springer Singapore., DOI: 10.1007/978-981-16-6502-8_21

Li, S., & Liu, B. (2018). Joseph E. Aoun: Robot-proof: higher education in the age of artificial intelligence. *Higher Education*, *77*(4), 757–759. DOI: 10.1007/s10734-018-0289-3

Liz-Domínguez, M., Caeiro-Rodríguez, M., Llamas-Nistal, M., & Mikic-Fonte, F. A. (2019). Systematic literature review of predictive analysis tools in higher education. *Applied Sciences (Basel, Switzerland)*, *9*(24), 5569. DOI: 10.3390/app9245569

Long, K. C., Gunder, A., Robinson, B., Davis, V. L., Barth, D., Adams, T., & Ross, O. (2024). *Leading the AI Revolution: The Crucial Role of HBCUs in Steering AI Leadership*. Online Learning Consortium.

Long, P., & Siemens, G. (2011). Penetrating the fog: Analytics in learning and education. *EDUCAUSE Review*, *46*(5), 31–40. https://er.educause.edu/articles/2011/9/penetrating-the-fog-analytics-in-learning-and-education

Loughran, J. (2002). Effective reflective practice: In search of meaning in learning about teaching. *Journal of Teacher Education*, *53*(1), 33–43. DOI: 10.1177/0022487102053001004

Luckin, R., Holmes, W., Griffiths, M., & Forcier, L. B. (2016). Intelligence unleashed: An argument for AI in education. Pearson Education. https://www.pearson.com/content/dam/corporate/global/pearson-dot-com/files/innovation/Intelligence-Unleashed-Publication.pdf

Luckin, R. (2018). *Machine Learning and Human Intelligence: The Future of Education for the 21st Century*. UCL Institute of Education Press.

Lytras, M. D., Serban, A. C., Alkhaldi, A., Aldosemani, T., & Malik, S. (2024). Digital transformation in higher education in times of artificial intelligence: Setting the emerging landscape. In *Digital Transformation in Higher Education, Part A* (pp. 1-22). Emerald Publishing Limited.

Macfadyen, L. P., Lockyer, L., & Rienties, B. (2020). Learning Design and Learning Analytics: Snapshot 2020. *Journal of Learning Analytics*, *7*(3), 6–12. DOI: 10.18608/jla.2020.73.2

Mahamuni, A. J., & Tonpe, S. S. (2024). Enhancing educational assessment with artificial intelligence: Challenges and opportunities. In *2024 International Conference on Knowledge Engineering and Communication Systems (ICKECS)* Vol. 1. (1-5). IEEE. https://doi.org/DOI: 10.1109/ICKECS61492.2024.10616620

Mah, D.-K., & Groß, N. (2024). Artificial intelligence in higher education: Exploring faculty use, self-efficacy, distinct profiles, and professional development needs. *International Journal of Educational Technology in Higher Education*, *21*, 58.

Mahmoud, C. F., & Sørensen, J. T. (2024). Artificial Intelligence in personalized learning with a focus on current developments and future prospects. *Research and Advances in Education*, *3*(8), 25–31. DOI: 10.56397/rae.2024.08.04

Malik, R. (2023). Impact of technology-based education on student learning outcomes and engagement. In 2023 *10th International Conference on Computing for Sustainable Global Development (INDIACom)* 784-788. IEEE. Electronic ISBN:978-93-80544-47-2

Mannheim, K. (1936). *Ideology and Utopia: An Introduction to the Sociology of Knowledge*. Harcourt, Brace & Company.

Martín-Lucas, J., & García del Dujo, Á. (2022). Knowledge-building in an environment mediated by digital technology: A case study in higher education. *Education and Information Technologies*, *28*. Advance online publication. DOI: 10.1007/s10639-022-11304-0 PMID: 36119125

McAfee, A., & Brynjolfsson, E. (2017). *Machine, platform, crowd: Harnessing our digital future*. Wwnorton.com. https://wwnorton.com/books/Machine-Platform-Crowd/

McDonald, N., Johri, A., Ali, A., & Hingle, A. (2024). Generative artificial intelligence in higher education: Evidence from an analysis of institutional policies and guidelines. arXiv preprint arXiv:2402.01659.

Memarian, B., & Doleck, T. (2023). *Fairness, accountability, transparency, and ethics (FATE) in artificial intelligence (AI) and higher education: A systematic review*. Computers & Education. *Artificial Intelligence*, *5*, 100152. DOI: 10.1016/j.caeai.2023.100152

Mills, K. A. (2010). A review of the "digital turn" in the new literacy studies. *Review of Educational Research*, *80*(2), 246–271. DOI: 10.3102/0034654310364401

Mishra, P., Warr, M., & Islam, R. (2023). TPACK in the age of ChatGPT and Generative AI. *Journal of Digital Learning in Teacher Education*, *39*(4), 235–251. DOI: 10.1080/21532974.2023.2247480

Mitrache, M. D., Spulbar, L. F., & Mitrache, L. A. (2024). The Influence of AI Technology in Stimulating Growth and Innovation in Business. *Revista de Stiinte Politice*, (81), 51–61.

Mollick, E. R., & Mollick, L. (2024). Instructors as innovators: A future-focused approach to new AI learning opportunities, with prompts. The Wharton School Research Paper.

Montebello, M. (2024). Learner Profiling and Pedagogical Customization. In *Encyclopedia of Educational Innovation* (pp. 1–5). Springer.

Morton, T. B. (2026). Enlightening Educators: Unlocking the Benefits of AI in Faculty Development. In *Harnessing AI's Potential to Support Student Success and Teaching Excellence* (pp. 109-128). IGI Global Scientific Publishing.

Mousa, M. (2025). AI-Supported Formative Assessments: Enhancing Student-Centered Learning and Teacher Perceptions. *Journal of Pedagogy and Education Science*, *4*(02), 127–141.

Muñoz-Carril, P.-C., Hernández-Sellés, N., Fuentes-Abeledo, E.-J., & González-Sanmamed, M. (2021). Factors influencing students' perceived impact of learning and satisfaction in Computer Supported Collaborative Learning. *Computers & Education*, *174*, 104310. DOI: 10.1016/j.compedu.2021.104310

Murgia, M. (2022). *Code dependent: Living in the shadow of AI*. Henry Holt & Company.

Mutambik, I. (2024). The use of AI-driven automation to enhance student learning experiences in the KSA: An alternative pathway to sustainable education. *Sustainability*, *16*(14), 5970.

Nafea, A. A., Alameri, S. A., Majeed, R. R., Khalaf, M. A., & Al-Ani, M. M. (2024). A short review on supervised machine learning and deep learning techniques in computer vision. *Babylonian Journal of Machine Learning*, *2024*, 48–55.

Newmann, F. M., Marks, H. M., & Gamoran, A. (1996). Authentic pedagogy and student performance. *American Journal of Education*, *104*(4), 280–312.

Ng, D. T. K., Leung, J. K. L., Chu, S. K. W., & Qiao, M. S. (2021). Conceptualizing AI literacy: An exploratory review. *Computers and Education: Artificial Intelligence*, *2*, 100041. DOI: 10.1016/j.caeai.2021.100041

Nguyen, L. T., & Tuamsuk, K. (2022). Digital learning ecosystem at educational institutions: A content analysis of scholarly discourse. *Cogent Education*, *9*(1), 2111033. DOI: 10.1080/2331186X.2022.2111033

Nguyen, N. D. (2023). Exploring the role of AI in education. *London Journal of Social Sciences*, (6), 84–95.

Ng, W. (2012). Can we teach digital natives digital literacy? *Computers & Education, 59*(3), 1065–1078. DOI: 10.1016/j.compedu.2012.04.016

Nicol, D. J., & Macfarlane-Dick, D. (2006). Formative assessment and self-regulated learning: A model and seven principles of good feedback practice. *Studies in Higher Education, 31*(2), 199–218.

Novita, R. (2025). AI in Lesson Planning: Improving Teacher Efficiency and Instructional Design. *Jurnal Riset Rumpun Ilmu Pendidikan, 4*(2), 192–202. DOI: 10.55606/jurripen.v4i2.5560

Nuong Deri, M., Singh, A., Zaazie, P., & Anandene, D. (2024). Leveraging Artificial Intelligence in Higher Educational Institutions: A Comprehensive Overview. *Education and Law Review*, (30). Advance online publication. DOI: 10.1344/REYD2024.30.45777

Nurjanah, A., Salsabila, I. N., Azzahra, A., Rahayu, R., & Marlina, N. (2024). Artificial intelligence (AI) usage in today's teaching and learning process: A review. *Syntax Idea, 6*(3), 1517–1523. DOI: 10.46799/syntax-idea.v6i3.3126

Nuryani, S. A., Arnyana, I. P., Parwati, N., Dantes, G., & Juanamasta, Ig. (2022). Development of blended learning model integrated nursing leadership training using web-based in Indonesia. *Journal of Education and Health Promotion, 11*(1), 222. DOI: 10.4103/jehp.jehp_1170_21 PMID: 36177429

OECD. (2021). *AI in Education: Challenges and Opportunities*. OECD Publishing.

OECD. (2023). Multi-stakeholder collaboration and co-creation: Towards responsible application of AI in education. In *OECD Digital Education Outlook 2023*. OECD Publishing.

Ogburn, W. F. (1922). *Social change with respect to culture and original nature*. B. W. Huebsch.

Ogunbodede, K. F., & Atchrim, I. A. (2025). Artificial Intelligence in Nigeria: A Catalyst for Economic Growth, Innovation, and Technological Advancement. *Faculty of Natural and Applied Sciences Journal of Computing and Applications, 2*(2), 111–116.

Ogunsakin, I. (2024). Unlocking the potential of artificial intellignce. *International Journal of Research in STEM Education, 6*(2), 37–49. DOI: 10.33830/ijrse.v6i2.1698

Oh, S. H., & Sanfilippo, M. (2024). University governance for responsible AI. *Proceedings of the ALISE Annual Conference*. https://doi.org/DOI: 10.21900/j.alise.2024.1706

Omer, M., & Amairi, A., & Mohammed Muneerali Thottoli. (2023). Surfing the technology wave: An international perspective on enhancing teaching and learning in accounting. *Computers and Education: Artificial Intelligence*, *4*, 100144. DOI: 10.1016/j.caeai.2023.100144

Orman, R., Şimşek, E., & Kozak Çakır, M. A. (2023). Micro-credentials and reflections on higher education. *Higher Education Evaluation and Development*, *17*(2), 96–112. DOI: 10.1108/HEED-08-2022-0028

Ozogul, G., Zheng, X., Min, W., Lee, S., Carpenter, D., & Lester, J. (2025). Towards AI-Enhanced Classroom Response System Eliciting Self-Explanations in Computer Science Courses. *The Journal of Applied Instructional Design*, *14*(2).

Paris, S. G., & Paris, A. H. (2001). Classroom applications of research on self-regulated learning. *Educational Psychologist*, *36*(2), 89–101.

Pedro, F., Subosa, M., Rivas, A., & Valverde, P. (2019). Artificial intelligence in education: Challenges and opportunities for sustainable development.

Pedró, F. (2020). Applications of Artificial Intelligence to higher education: Possibilities, evidence, and challenges. *IUL Research*, *1*(1), 61–76. DOI: 10.57568/iulres.v1i1.43

Piaget, J. (1954). *The construction of reality in the child*. Basic Books.

Pine, B. J., & Gilmore, J. H. (2019). *The experience economy: Competing for customer time, attention, and money* (Updated ed.). Harvard Business Review Press.

Popenici, S. A. D., & Kerr, S. (2017). Exploring the impact of artificial intelligence on teaching and learning in higher education. *Research and Practice in Technology Enhanced Learning*, *12*(1), 22. DOI: 10.1186/s41039-017-0062-8 PMID: 30595727

Punziano, G. (2025). Adaptive Epistemology: Embracing Generative AI as a Paradigm Shift in Social Science. *Societies (Basel, Switzerland)*, *15*(7), 205. DOI: 10.3390/soc15070205

Qatar, Q Study. (2024). Understanding researchers' AI readiness in a higher education context: A Q method approach. *Middle East Journal of Educational Innovation*, *8*(1), 24–41.

Qayyum, A., Rafique, Z., Shah, S. S. W. A., Ahmad, S., & Haider, Z. (2025). Artificial intelligence (AI)-driven curriculum development in early childhood education: Educators' insights, barriers, and policy pathways. *Research Journal of Psychology*, *3*(1), 713–733. DOI: 10.59075/rjs.v3i1.102

Radanliev, P. (2024). Artificial intelligence: Reflecting on the past and looking towards the next paradigm shift. *Journal of Experimental & Theoretical Artificial Intelligence*, •••, 1045–1062. DOI: 10.1080/0952813X.2024.2323042

Rahayu, S., & Bablu, T. A. (2023). AI-Augmented Learning and Development Platforms: Transforming Employee Training and Skill Enhancement. *Journal of Computing Innovations and Applications*, *1*(01), 19–38.

Ramos, R. F., De Angel, R. M., Ruetas, A. P., Lagman, A. C., Morano, J., Payongayong, R. T., & Enrile, J. C. (2024, August). Effective Lesson Planning and Assessment Design Using Leveraging Microsoft Copilot Implementation. In *2024 IEEE 15th Control and System Graduate Research Colloquium (ICSGRC)* (331-336). IEEE. https://doi.org/DOI: 10.1109/ICSGRC62081.2024.10691289

Reinitz, B. (2020). *Consider the Three Ds When Talking about Digital Transformation*. Retrieved from: https://er.educause.edu/blogs/2020/6/consider-the-three-ds-when-talking-about-digital-transformation

Review, N. (2024). A review of artificial intelligence readiness in higher education in Northern Nigeria. *Journal of African Higher Education Studies*, *12*(2), 99–120.

Rezaie, F., Asino, T. I., & Panwar, K. (2025). Leveraging Instructional Design Models for Corporate Training and Professional Development using Artificial Intelligence (AI). *The Journal of Applied Instructional Design*, *14*(2).

Rienties, B., Køhler Simonsen, H., & Herodotou, C. (2020). Defining the boundaries between artificial intelligence in education, computer-supported collaborative learning, educational data mining, and learning analytics: A need for coherence. *Frontiers in Education*, *5*. Advance online publication. DOI: 10.3389/feduc.2020.00128

Rossman, J. R., & Duerden, M. D. (2019). *Designing experiences*. Columbia Business School Publishing.

Rowsell, J. (2025, January 17). Academics fear students becoming too reliant on AI tools. *Times Higher Education*. https://www.timeshighereducation.com/news/academics-fear-students-becoming-too-reliant-ai-tools

Roy, S. (2025). AI Adoption and Central Banks in Emerging Markets: Challenges and Strategies. *Available at SSRN* 5121231.

Sætra, H. S. (2021). Using Padlet to Enable Online Collaborative Mediation and Scaffolding in a Statistics Course. *Education Sciences*, *11*(5), 219. DOI: 10.3390/educsci11050219

Salih, S. M. (2024). Perceptions of faculty and students about use of artificial intelligence in medical education: A qualitative study. *Cureus*, *16*(4), e57605. DOI: 10.7759/cureus.57605 PMID: 38707183

Salman, H.. (2025). Technology readiness for generative AI among academic researchers: An index-based assessment. *Journal of Digital Learning and Innovation*, *17*(1), 10–29.

Sanasintani, S. (2023). Revitalizing the higher education curriculum through an artificial intelligence approach: An overview. *Journal of Social Science Utilizing Technology*, *1*(4), 239–248. DOI: 10.55849/jssut.v1i4.670

Schiff, D. (2022). Education for AI, not AI for education: The role of education and ethics in national AI policy strategies. *International Journal of Artificial Intelligence in Education*, *32*(3), 527–563.

Schön, D. A. (1983). *The reflective practitioner: How professionals think in action.* Basic Books.

Seldon, A., & Abidoye, O. (2018). *The fourth education revolution: Will artificial intelligence liberate or infantilise humanity?* University of Buckingham Press.

Selvam, M., & González Vallejo, R. (2025). Ethical and privacy considerations in AI-driven language learning. *LatIA*, *3*, 328. DOI: 10.62486/latia2025328

Selwyn, N. (2019). Should robots replace teachers? AI and the future of education. *Polity*.

Selwyn, N. (2022). *Education and technology: Key issues and debates* (3rd ed.). Bloomsbury.

Selwyn, N. (2022). The future of AI and education: Some cautionary notes. *European Journal of Education*, *57*(4), 620–631.

Shah, S. S., & Asad, M. M. (2024). Impact of Critical Thinking Approach on Learners' Dependence on Innovative Transformation Through Artificial Intelligence. In *The Evolution of Artificial Intelligence in Higher Education: Challenges, Risks, and Ethical Considerations* (pp. 161–182). Emerald Publishing Limited.

Shamsudin, N. M., & Hoon, T. S. (2024). Exploring the Synergy of Learning Experience Platforms (LXP) with Artificial Intelligence for Enhanced Educational Outcomes. In *International Conference on Innovation & Entrepreneurship in Computing, Engineering & Science Education (InvENT 2024)* (pp. 30-40). Atlantis Press.

Sharma, R., & Singh, A. (2024). Use of Digital Technology in Improving Quality Education: A Global Perspectives and Trends. In Nadda, V., Tyagi, P., Moniz Vieira, R., & Tyagi, P. (Eds.), *Implementing Sustainable Development Goals in the Service Sector* (pp. 14–26). IGI Global., DOI: 10.4018/979-8-3693-2065-5.ch002

Shermis, M. D., & Burstein, J. (2013). *Handbook of automated essay evaluation: Current applications and new directions*. Routledge.

Siddiqui, M. T., Mansoori, M. V., Siddiqui, M. A., & Yadav, A. (2025). AI-enabled pedagogy: Advancing education through innovative teaching tools and the AI-TEACH model. *Journal of Informatics Education and Research, 5*(1), 2526–2539.

Singh, A. (2022). Conceptual framework on Smart Learning Environment- An Indian perspective. *Journal of Education and Law*, (25). Advance online publication. DOI: 10.1344/REYD2022.25.36706

Singh, A. (2024a). The Role of Digital Transformation and Its Effects on the Education Sector. In Chakraborty, S. (Ed.), *Challenges of Globalization and Inclusivity in Academic Research* (pp. 92–99). IGI Global Scientific Publishing., DOI: 10.4018/979-8-3693-1371-8.ch007

Singh, A. (2024b). Endorsing Gamification Pedagogy for Nurturing Employability Skills in Higher Education Institutions (HEI). In Membrive, V. (Ed.), *Practices and Implementation of Gamification in Higher Education* (pp. 172–183). IGI Global Scientific Publishing., DOI: 10.4018/979-8-3693-0716-8.ch008

Singh, A. (2024c). Impact of E-learning on Student Motivation in Higher Education Institutions: An Indian Perspective. *Journal of Education and Law*, (29). Advance online publication. DOI: 10.1344/REYD2024.29.43214

Singh, A. (2024c). Students Wellbeing and Performance in Higher Education Institutions. In Aloka, P. (Ed.), *Factors Impacting Student Well-Being and Coping Tactics* (pp. 1–12). IGI Global Scientific Publishing., DOI: 10.4018/979-8-3693-8860-0.ch001

Singh, A., & Kumar, P. (2024). E-Learning Ecosystem in Higher Education Institutions: Trends and Practices. In Al Husseiny, F., & Munna, A. (Eds.), *Preparing Students for the Future Educational Paradigm* (pp. 1–18). IGI Global Scientific Publishing., DOI: 10.4018/979-8-3693-1536-1.ch001

Singh, A., & Sihmar, P. (2025). Higher Education Institution Sustainability: Role of Green Human Resource Management. In Adu-Gyamfi, M., Boateng, F., & Atiku, S. (Eds.), *Green HRM Awareness and Training in Higher Education Institutions* (pp. 1–14). IGI Global Scientific Publishing., DOI: 10.4018/979-8-3693-2956-6.ch001

Singh, A., Singh, D., & Chhikara, S. (2024). Online Learning: Challenges and Suggestions to Enhance Student Engagement in Higher Education Institutions. In Naidoo, V., & Verma, R. (Eds.), *Reshaping Entrepreneurial Education Within an Industry 4.0 Context* (pp. 59–80). IGI Global Scientific Publishing., DOI: 10.4018/979-8-3693-0409-9.ch004

Slimi, Z., & Carballido, B. V. (2023). Systematic review: AI's impact on higher education - learning, teaching, and career opportunities. TEM Journal, 1627–1637. https://doi.org/DOI: 10.18421/tem123-44

Smith, T., Liu, M., & Ramirez, J. (2022). AI-enhanced collaborative learning in engineering education at Stanford University. *International Journal of Engineering Pedagogy*, *12*(1), 76–89.

Soomro, A. A., Khan, M. H., Umar, M., Khan, S., & Ali, O. (2025). AI-Driven Academic Advising in Higher Education: Leveraging Intelligent Systems to Personalize Student Support, Improve Retention, and Optimize Career Pathways. *The Critical Review of Social Sciences Studies*, *3*(2), 229–248. DOI: 10.59075/vy3v7k17

Stake, R. E. (1995). The art of case study research. *Sage (Atlanta, Ga.).*

Steinberg, M. P., & Sartain, L. (2015). Does teacher evaluation improve school performance? Experimental evidence from Chicago's Excellence in Teaching project. *Education Finance and Policy*, *10*(4), 535–572. DOI: 10.1162/EDFP_a_00173

Street, B. V. (1984). *Literacy in theory and practice*. Cambridge University Press.

Strielkowski, W., Grebennikova, V., Lisovskiy, A., Rakhimova, G., & Vasileva, T. (2025). AI-driven adaptive learning for sustainable educational transformation. *Sustainable Development*, *33*(2), 1921–1947.

Swallow, M. J., & Olofson, M. W. (2017). Contextual understandings in the TPACK framework. *Journal of Research on Technology in Education*, *49*(3-4), 228–244. DOI: 10.1080/15391523.2017.1347537

Sýkora, T., Stárková, T., & Brom, C. (2020). Can narrative cutscenes improve home learning from a math game? An experimental study with children. *British Journal of Educational Technology*, *52*(1). Advance online publication. DOI: 10.1111/bjet.12939

Tan, H., & Lee, K. (2023). Integrating ethical AI assessment tools in business education. *Journal of Business Ethics Education*, *20*(1), 101–118.

Tillmanns, T., Salomão Filho, A., Rudra, S., Weber, P., Dawitz, J., Wiersma, E., Dudenaite, D., & Reynolds, S. (2025). Mapping Tomorrow's Teaching and Learning Spaces: A Systematic Review on GenAI in Higher Education. *Trends in Higher Education*, *4*(1), 2. DOI: 10.3390/higheredu4010002

Trajkovski, G., & Hayes, H. (2025). AI-Assisted Formative Assessment and Feedback. In: AI-Assisted Assessment in Education. Digital Education and Learning. (283-312) Springer Nature Switzerland. Palgrave Macmillan, Cham. https://doi.org/ DOI: 10.1007/978-3-031-88252-4_7

Trilaksana, H., & Soelistiono, S. (2024). Campus Learning Based on AI: Implementation of ChatGPT in AILS and Its Implications for Curriculum Development in Indonesia. *Influence: international journal of science review, 6*(1), 63-72.

Trust, T. (2023). Navigating generative AI in higher education: Ethical considerations and teaching strategies. *Computers and Education: Artificial Intelligence*, *4*, 100145. DOI: 10.1016/j.caeai.2023.100145

Tzafilkou, K., Perifanou, M. A., & Economides, A. A. (2021). Teachers' trainers' intention and motivation to transfer ICT training: The role of ICT individual factors, gender, and ICT self-efficacy. *Education and Information Technologies*, *26*(5), 5563–5589. DOI: 10.1007/s10639-021-10541-z

Uhran, J. J., Batill, S. M., & Silliman, S. E. (2005, October). A curriculum renovation revisited. In *Proceedings Frontiers in Education 35th Annual Conference* (pp. F1D-10). IEEE.

UNESCO. (2021). AI and Education: Guidance for Policy-makers. Paris: UNESCO. https://unesdoc.unesco.org/ark:/48223/pf0000376709

UNESCO. (2024). *AI competency framework for teachers*. UNESCO Publishing., DOI: 10.54675/ZJTE2084

United Nations Educational, Scientific and Cultural Organization. (2023). *Guidance for generative AI in education and research*. UNESCO. https://unesdoc.unesco.org/ark:/48223/pf0000386693

Usher, M., Hershkovitz, A., & Forkosh-Baruch, A. (2021). From data to actions: Instructors' reflections about learners' data in online emergency remote teaching. *British Journal of Educational Technology*, *52*(4), 1338–1356. DOI: 10.1111/bjet.13108 van Niekerk, J., Delport, P. M. J., & Sutherland, I. (2025). Addressing the use of generative AI in academic writing. *Computers and Education: Artificial Intelligence*, *8*, 100342. DOI: 10.1016/j.caeai.2025.100342

VanLehn, K. (2011). The relative effectiveness of human tutoring, intelligent tutoring systems, and other tutoring systems. *Educational Psychologist*, *46*(4), 197–221.

Vega, J., Rodriguez, M., Check, E., Moran, H., & Loo, L. (2024, July). Duolingo evolution: From automation to artificial intelligence. In *IEEE Colombian Conference on Applications of Computational Intelligence* (pp. 54-71). Cham: Springer Nature Switzerland.

Veletsianos, G. (2020). *Learning online: The student experience*. Johns Hopkins University Press.

Villegas-Ch, W., Buenano-Fernandez, D., Navarro, A. M., & Mera-Navarrete, A. (2025). Adaptive intelligent tutoring systems for STEM education: Analysis of the learning impact and effectiveness of personalized feedback. *Smart Learning Environments*, *12*(1). Advance online publication. DOI: 10.1186/s40561-025-00389-y

Visscher, A. J. (2021). On the value of data-based decision making in education: The evidence from six intervention studies. *Studies in Educational Evaluation*, *69*. Advance online publication. DOI: 10.1016/j.stueduc.2020.100899

Voronov, V. V., Menshikov, V. V., & Ruza, O. P. (2023). Artificial intelligence: A catalyst for entrepreneurship education in the Baltics. *Baltic Region*, *15*(3), 45–65.

Vygotsky, L. S. (1978). *Mind in society: The development of higher psychological processes*. Harvard University Press.

Wacquant, L. (2015). For a sociology of flesh and blood. *Qualitative Sociology*, *38*(1), 1–11. DOI: 10.1007/s11133-014-9291-y

Wahyuningsih, T., Manongga, D., Sembiring, I., & Wijono, S. (2024). Comparison of effectiveness of logistic regression, naive bayes, and random forest algorithms in predicting student arguments. *Procedia Computer Science*, *234*, 349–356. DOI: 10.1016/j.procs.2024.03.014

Waiari, D. A. K., Lim, W. T., Thomson-Baker, A. P., Freestone, M. K., Thompson, S., Manuela, S., & Mayeda, D., Purdy (Te Rarawa, Ngai Takoto), S., & Le Grice (Ngāpuhi, Te Rarawa), J. (2021). Stoking the Fires for Māori & Pacific Student Success in Psychology. *Higher Education Research & Development*, *40*(1), 117–131. DOI: 10.1080/07294360.2020.1852186

Wang, D., Bian, C., & Chen, G. (2024). Using explainable AI to unravel classroom dialogue analysis: Effects of explanations on teachers' trust, technology acceptance and cognitive load. *British Journal of Educational Technology*, *55*(6), 2530–2556. DOI: 10.1111/bjet.13466

Wang, J., Hussain, Y., & Mao, C. (2025). Artificial intelligence-driven personalized learning: Psychological implications and educational outcomes. International Journal of Education. *Humanities and Social Sciences*, *2*(1), 24–39. DOI: 10.70088/3wnrs278

Wang, L. (2020, May). Artificial intelligence and career development of college teachers: Challenge and countermeasures. [). IOP Publishing.]. *Journal of Physics: Conference Series*, *1550*(2), 022030.

Webster, R., Griffin, S. M., Chatterjee, I., Kuriakose, A., & Nguyen, H. (2024). A co-creation approach to using generative AI for enhanced learning gain. Journal of Learning Development in Higher Education, (32).

Wei, Z., Zhang, G., Zhang, M., & Cui, W. (2025). The Symbiotic Integration of Cognitive-Enhanced Artificial Intelligence and University Education: Building the Future Intelligent Learning Ecosystem. In *Proceedings of the 2025 4th International Conference on Big Data, Information and Computer Network* (434-439). https://doi .org/DOI: 10.1145/3727353.3727424

Wenger, E. (1998). *Communities of practice: Learning, meaning, and identity*. Cambridge University Press.

Wenger, E., McDermott, R., & Snyder, W. (2002). *Cultivating communities of practice: A guide to managing knowledge*. Harvard Business Review Press.

Wiggins, G. P., & McTighe, J. (2005). *Understanding by design* (2nd ed.). Pearson.

Willard, J., & Hutson, J. (2024). Beyond Automation: AI as a Catalyst for New Job Creation in Software Development. International Journal Of Engineering Research And Development, 20(8).

Williamson, B. (2017). Big data in education. *Sage (Atlanta, Ga.)*.

Williamson, B., & Piattoeva, N. (2021). Education governance and datafication. *Learning, Media and Technology*, *46*(1), 1–8.

Williamson, B., & Piattoeva, N. (2022). Objectivity as standardization in data-scientific educational governance: Grasping the global through the local. *Learning, Media and Technology*, *47*(1), 1–15. DOI: 10.1080/17439884.2022.2032512

Winder, G., Bass, S., Schiele, D., & Buchner, J. (2024). Using large language models for content creation impacts online learning evaluation outcomes. In *International Journal on E-Learning* (305-318). Association for the Advancement of Computing in Education (AACE). https://doi.org/DOI: 10.70725/423664moqcrd

Winkelmes, M-A. (2023). Introduction to transparency in teaching and learning. *Perspectives in Learning, 20*(1).

Winkelmes, M.-A. (2019). Transparent design in higher education teaching and leadership. In Miller, M. T., & Nadler, D. V. (Eds.), *Student engagement and retention: High-impact strategies to enhance student success* (pp. 89–103). Emerald Publishing.

Winkelmes, M.-A., Bernacki, M., Butler, J., Zochowski, M., Golanics, J., & Weavil, K. H. (2016). A teaching intervention that increases underserved college students' success. *Peer Review : Emerging Trends and Key Debates in Undergraduate Education, 18*(1/2).

Winne, P. H., & Hadwin, A. F. (2013). *Metacognition in education: A focus on self-regulated learning*. Routledge.

Wood, D., Bruner, J. S., & Ross, G. (1976). The role of tutoring in problem solving. *Journal of Child Psychology and Psychiatry, and Allied Disciplines, 17*(2), 89–100. PMID: 932126

Woolf, B. P. (2010). *Building intelligent interactive tutors: Student-centered strategies for revolutionizing e-learning*. Morgan Kaufmann.

Yeralan, S., & Lee, L. A. (2023). Generative AI: Challenges to higher education. *Sustainable Engineering and Innovation, 5*(2), 107–116. DOI: 10.37868/sei.v5i2.id196

Yin, R. K. (2018). *Case study research and applications: Design and methods* (6th ed.). Sage.

Zawacki-Richter, O., Marín, V. I., Bond, M., & Gouverneur, F. (2019). Systematic review of research on artificial intelligence applications in higher education-where are the educators. *International Journal of Educational Technology in Higher Education, 16*(1), 39. DOI: 10.1186/s41239-019-0171-0

Zhai, X., Chu, X., Chai, C. S., Jong, M. S. Y., Istenic, A., Spector, M., & Li, Y. (2021). A Review of Artificial Intelligence (AI) in Education from 2010 to 2020. *Complexity, 2021*(1), 8812542.

Zhang, F., Wang, X., & Zhang, X. (2025). Applications of deep learning method of artificial intelligence in education. *Education and Information Technologies, 30*(2), 1563–1587.

Zhang, J. (2025). Generative AI in Higher Education: Challenges and Opportunities for Course Learning. [REMOVED HYPERLINK FIELD]. *Advances in Social Sciences Research Journal, 12*(01), 11–18. DOI: 10.14738/assrj.1201.18121

Zhang, J., Kizilcec, R. F., & Chen, B. (2021). Enhancing collaboration with AI-supported group formation in online learning. *Computers & Education, 165*, 104134. DOI: 10.1016/j.compedu.2021.104134

About the Contributors

Nathan Pritts is Global Campus Professor and Program Chair for First Year Writing at the University of Arizona Global Campus where he also serves as Faculty Fellow for AI Strategy. He leads initiatives at the intersection of pedagogy, design, and emerging technologies and has spearheaded efforts in the strategic implementation of online learning tools, faculty training, and scalable interventions that support both educators and students. With a background that bridges writing, general education, and educational technology, his work balances innovation with thoughtful pedagogy and student-centered design. His recent work focuses on bringing a humanistic lens to the integration of AI in higher education, developing practical frameworks for integrating AI into curriculum design and faculty development across diverse institutional settings. As author and researcher, Dr. Pritts has published widely on digital pedagogy, curriculum design, and the evolving role of AI in higher education. He is the author or co-author of twelve books, including *Decoherence* (Indiana University Press), *Film: From Watching to Seeing* (3e), *Research & Writing* (2e), and *Essentials of Academic Writing* (4e). He also served as editor for *Living Online: A Digital Fluency Handbook* and the forthcoming *Empowering Educational Development and Faculty Growth With AI.*

JoAnna Boudreaux is an Assistant Professor of Teaching Coordinator in the Department of Sociology at the University of Memphis. She teaches a variety of courses including Racial & Ethnic Minorities, Social Theory and Medical Sociology. Her current interests include AI in education, pedagogical innovation, and student-centered learning. She develops courses that encourage critical engagement, collaboration, and ethical reasoning, aiming to empower students as active participants in the production of knowledge.

Colette A. Chelf, Ed.D., is a strategist and researcher in digital learning and organizational transformation, with expertise in building collaborative networks, integrating educational systems, and designing learning ecosystems that expand access and student success. With over two decades of experience spanning higher education and cross-sector partnerships, she leads initiatives that strengthen institutional capacity, align digital learning infrastructures, and support inclusive and student-centered pedagogies. Her recent work focuses on the development of AI literacies, the sociocultural dimensions of technology and leadership in education, and collaborative approaches to open learning design.

Jennifer Friberg is the Director of Scholarly Teaching and Cross Endowed Chair in the Scholarship of Teaching and Learning for the Center for Integrated Development at Illinois State University. There, she also serves as a professor of communication sciences and disorders. She is the co-editor of three recent volumes: Scholarship of Teaching and Learning in Communication Sciences and Disorders (2024), Going Public Reconsidered: Engaging the World Beyond Academe Through the Scholarship of Teaching and Learning (2022), and Evidence-Based Education in the Classroom: Examples from Clinical Disciplines (2022). Friberg is a founding editorial board member of the peer reviewed journal Teaching and Learning in Communication Sciences & Disorders.

Angela Gunder is the Chief Executive Officer and founder of Opened Culture, a pioneering collaboratory that empowers educators and institutions to advance access to education through open collaboration, academic innovation, and community engagement. Through leading-edge research, professional development, and strategic guidance, she and her team support educational communities in guiding and sustaining cultures of openness to instantiate a more inclusive future of learning. Dr. Gunder also serves as an innovative pedagogy specialist for the University Center for Assessment, Teaching & Technology, and an online instructor for the College of Information Science, both at The University of Arizona.

Josh Herron is a digital learning practitioner, leader, and researcher. He has held dean, director, and faculty roles in digital learning across a variety of colleges and universities. His research interests include educational innovation, learning design, and digital media. He is a prolific contributor to publications and presentations on these topics. He holds a PhD in Communication and Information Design from Clemson University. He also completed Penn State University and the Online Learning Consortium's Institute for Emerging Leadership in Online Learning.

Vishwanathan Iyer is a dedicated researcher who is dedicated to exploring various academic fields such as finance, accounting, marketing, HR, and law to the best of his abilities. His research is based on primary data as well as secondary data. Being consistent at research and providing quality research work is the ultimate aim of Dr Iyer. Collaborating with authors across the spectrum is one of his strengths.

Publishing articles and writing chapters are motivating factors for Dr Iyer to pursue his dream of becoming a researcher to be reckoned with.

Roshan R. Kolte, is working as Assistant Professor of Department of IT at K.D.K College of Engineering, Nagpur, MS, India. He received a bachelor's degree in Computer Science & Engineering from RTMNU University and a master's degree in Computer Science & Engineering from RGPV University. He has more than 15 years of teaching experience at UG (B.E/B.Tech level) & 1 year of teaching experience at PG (MCA). He has published more than 25 papers to his credit in National & International Journals. He is a life member of ISTE, BANAE, AMIEE & GSTE. He has completed many online certification courses from upGrad, NPTEL, EduSkills. He is interested in research area includes Data science, Data warehousing & Mining, AI and Machine Learning.

Annaji Kuthe is pursuing PhD in CSE and has completed BE (CT), ME (WCC), M.Tech. in Computer Science & Engineering. He is working as an Assistant Professor in the department of Computer Science & Engineering at KDK College of Engineering Nagpur, India. He is a committed academic professional with a total experience of 22 Years, which includes Academic (21), Industrial (01). He has published more than 34 Research Papers in International Journals (Scopus/SCIE) and conferences. He has published book chapter in Springer LNN. He has Received 06 Patent and 01 copyright from government of India. He has reviewed IEEE Conference papers. He is presently active Member of Board of Study CSE/IT (RTMNU) Nagpur University. He has worked as Moderator and at University Level & Autonomous institute. Guided Project for UG Students. He has worked as Reviewer Judge in Project Exhibition. He works at different committee for NBA & NAAC Accreditation Processes. He is Life Member of ISTE, AMIEE & IAENG. His Research Areas include Wireless Networks, Ad-hoc networks Computer Communications, Databases, Data structure etc

K. Lalitha is an Assistant Professor in the Department of Computer Science and Engineering at Santhiram Engineering College, Nandyal, Andhra Pradesh, India. She received her Master of Technology in Computer Science and Engineering from Vaagdevi Institute of Technology & Science, Proddatur, Andhra Pradesh, India. Her research interests include machine learning, data mining, and healthcare informatics. She has published multiple research articles in reputed journals.

O. Bhaskaru is an Assistant Professor in the Department of Computer Science and Engineering at Vignan's Foundation for Science, Technology & Research, Guntur, Andhra Pradesh, India. He received his Ph.D. in Computer Science and Engineering from KL University, Vijayawada, Andhra Pradesh, India. His research interests include machine learning, data mining, and artificial intelligence. He has published several papers in national and international journals.

Ravikumar R. Natarajan is an experienced academician with over 12+ years of teaching and research expertise across institutions in India, the UAE, and the Maldives. He currently serves as an Assistant Professor at Marwadi University, Rajkot, specializing in Machine Learning, Recommender Systems, and AI-driven applications in healthcare and security. He holds a Ph.D. in Machine Learning and Recommender Systems from Amity University, Jaipur, a Master of Engineering in CSE from VMRF University, Salem, and a Bachelor of Engineering in CSE from Anna University. He also has a MiniMBA from the Swiss eLearning Institute. Dr. Ravikumar has authored more than 8+ multiple SCIE/Scopus-indexed journal articles, 23+ IEEE conference papers, and co-authored a book on Artificial Intelligence. He has also published 9 patents and contributed 10+ book chapters in emerging domains such as Federated Learning, Blockchain, and Digital Twins for IGI Global, Wiley and Springer publisher. He actively mentors students through initiatives like the Research Activities Club (RAC) and Student Research Internship Training (SRIT), promoting innovation and research culture.

Aarthi S is a dedicated Assistant Professor in Computer Science with over six years of teaching experience. She is currently pursuing her Ph.D. at Marwadi University, Gujarat, and holds an M.Phil. and MCA from Bharathiar University, Tamil Nadu. Throughout her academic career, Aarthi has specialized in programming languages such as C++, Java, and C, and contributed to research in recommender systems and AI-related data privacy. She has published journal articles, contributed to book chapters, and actively participated in technical workshops. Known for her student mentorship and engagement in academic events, Aarthi remains committed to fostering innovation and excellence in computer science education.

Ramadevi Vitthal Salunkhe is an Assistant Professor in the Department of Artificial Intelligence at G. H. Raisoni College of Engineering, Nagpur, India, and a Research Scholar pursuing her Ph.D. in Computer Science and Engineering at VNIT, Nagpur. She holds an M.Tech and B.E. in Computer Science and Engineering and has over 11 years of experience spanning academia, central and state government institutions, and the IT industry. Her research focuses on artificial intelligence, machine learning, big data analytics, and intelligent automation. She has authored and co-authored books, several IGI Global book chapters, and presented at international conferences, including ICMCER 2024 (Thailand) and ARET 2025 (India). She also serves in academic leadership roles, mentors student projects, organizes technical events, and is a member of the International Association of Engineers (IAENG).

Amrik Singh is working as Professor in the School of Hotel Management and Tourism at Lovely Professional University, Punjab, India. He obtained his Ph.D. degree in Hotel Management from Kurukshetra University, Kurukshetra. He started his academic career at Lovely Professional University, Punjab, India in the year 2007. He has published more than 40 research papers in UGC and peer-reviewed and Scopus/Web of Science) journals. He has published 12 patents and 01 patent has been granted in the inter-disciplinary domain. Dr. Amrik Singh participated and acted as a resource person in various national and international conferences, seminars, research workshops, and industry talks. His area of research interest is accommodation management, ergonomics, green practices, human resource management in hospitality, waste management, AR VR in hospitality, etc. He is currently guiding 8Ph.D. scholars and 2 Ph.D. scholars have been awarded Ph.D.

Mukesh Kumar Tripathi, Ph.D. in Computer Science and Engineering, is an accomplished academician with over 15 years of extensive experience in teaching, research, and administration.he specializes in Advanced Machine Learning, Theory of Computation, Compiler Design, and Python Programming. His research portfolio includes 31 international journal publications, 6 SCI-indexed papers, and a notable doctoral contribution on the development of a Neutrosophic Machine Learning Framework for Mango Fruit Quality Assessment and Grading. Dr. Tripathi has collaborated on patents, book chapters, and actively mentors both undergraduate and postgraduate students. As a peer reviewer for reputed journals like IEEE Access and Springer, he demonstrates a strong commitment to academic rigor and scholarly excellence. Beyond research, he has successfully secured grants, organized international conferences and faculty development programs, and contributed to academic leadership through curriculum innovation and quality assurance. Passionate about fostering research-driven learning, Dr. Tripathi continues to bridge the gap between academia and industry through innovative teaching and interdisciplinary collaboration.

Prachi Wani teaches postgraduate students various marketing courses and supervises their research projects on relevant and emerging topics. She also leverages practical and industry-oriented insights from her previous roles in sales at Taj Lands' End and Intercontinental Brands to enrich her teaching and research. She has published multiple papers in reputable journals and presented at international conferences. Additionally, Dr Prachi has served as an internal auditor for ISO 9001:2008, conducting quality audits in her previous educational institution. Her experience also includes guiding various colleges and universities in preparing for NAAC accreditation, focusing on quality assurance, documentation, and institutional improvement. Additionally, Dr Wani held the position of President of the Institution's Innovation Council (IIC), where she led initiatives to foster innovation and entrepreneurship among students and faculty. Dr. Prachi is proud to have pursued an entrepreneurial venture, which, despite failing, has strengthened her resilience, problem-solving skills, and business acumen.

Nicole Weber is an assistant professor in the Department of Educational Foundations at the University of Wisconsin-Whitewater where she also coordinates the Instructional Design and Learning Technology Master's Degree Program. She received her PhD in Urban Education, focusing on Social Foundations of Education and Learning Environment Design from the University of Wisconsin-Milwaukee. Her research and professional contributions center on emerging learning technologies and pedagogies, with a current focus on artificial intelligence and its implications for teaching and learning design.

Index

A

Adaptive Learning Systems 72, 74, 80, 88, 100, 101, 174, 224, 251, 256, 291, 316, 321, 325
AI-Enhanced Curriculum Development 123
AI-Enhanced Instructional Design 103, 110, 126, 130, 131
AI In Education 4, 22, 65, 67, 69, 76, 87, 89, 94, 95, 96, 97, 98, 99, 129, 130, 166, 168, 169, 171, 174, 200, 201, 251, 270, 293, 303, 304, 307, 309, 319, 322, 368
AI in Faculty Development 173, 198, 201, 218
AI in Higher Education 80, 82, 83, 90, 104, 108, 130, 139, 200, 256, 263, 286, 313, 315, 318
AI Integration 4, 18, 34, 48, 64, 65, 76, 83, 86, 87, 90, 91, 92, 93, 94, 97, 110, 111, 113, 115, 117, 131, 141, 166, 219, 220, 258, 259, 260, 266, 268, 289, 293, 295, 296, 300, 303, 304, 310, 313, 315, 321, 331, 337, 340, 344, 345, 352
AI Literacy 3, 7, 18, 21, 35, 38, 67, 68, 89, 94, 101, 108, 161, 165, 199, 203, 218, 220, 221, 297, 312, 313, 318, 323, 324, 325, 326, 327, 328, 329, 330, 331, 332, 333, 334, 335, 336, 337, 339, 340, 341, 342, 343, 344, 345, 346, 347, 348, 349, 350, 351, 352, 353, 354, 355, 356, 358, 359, 360, 361, 362, 363, 367, 368
AI Mindsets 68
AI Skillsets 69
AI Technology 2, 6, 222, 241, 257, 258, 267, 292, 301, 304, 305
Artificial Intelligence 2, 7, 13, 18, 20, 21, 22, 23, 24, 25, 26, 28, 33, 34, 71, 72, 98, 99, 100, 101, 103, 104, 105, 106, 108, 112, 122, 123, 125, 128, 130, 132, 133, 134, 135, 136, 137, 139, 141, 142, 151, 162, 166, 167, 170, 171, 173, 174, 176, 177, 178, 181, 182, 188, 190, 193, 195, 196, 198, 200, 201, 203, 204, 205, 210, 211, 212, 213, 215, 217, 221, 222, 223, 224, 227, 228, 229, 233, 234, 236, 238, 242, 243, 245, 249, 250, 251, 252, 253, 254, 256, 257, 258, 262, 267, 268, 269, 270, 273, 274, 286, 290, 307, 312, 318, 319, 320, 321, 323, 324, 325, 331, 335, 360, 365, 366, 367, 368
Artificial Intelligence in Education 98, 133, 134, 135, 170, 171, 174, 201, 210, 249, 250, 318, 320, 365
Authentic Learning 71, 72, 74, 75, 76, 77, 78, 79, 80, 82, 83, 84, 85, 86, 87, 88, 89, 90, 92, 93, 94, 95, 98, 101
Automation in Education 207

C

Constellating AI Literacies 34, 38, 67, 69
Curriculum Innovation 141, 142, 144, 146, 205

D

Digital Pedagogy 4, 176, 181, 183, 186, 224, 246
Dimensions of AI Literacies 33, 34, 36, 39, 58, 62, 63, 64, 65, 67

E

EdTech 153, 162, 165, 319, 334, 350
Educational Developers 34, 41, 47, 55, 56, 57, 58, 59, 60, 61, 62, 63, 64, 65, 266, 267, 271, 289, 290, 292, 293, 294, 295, 296, 297, 298, 299, 301, 302, 303, 304, 305, 306, 308, 310, 311, 313, 314, 315, 316, 317, 322
Educational Innovation 170, 220, 222, 270, 331, 363
Educational Technology 22, 97, 98, 100, 138, 204, 205, 220, 232, 269, 270,

311, 319, 365, 367
Ethical AI Use 53, 55, 56, 76, 86, 260, 267, 271, 322, 346, 350, 368

F

Faculty AI Literacy 323, 325, 327, 329, 330, 334, 335, 336, 337, 340, 341, 342, 344, 345, 347, 348, 351, 356, 360, 361, 362, 363
Faculty Development 41, 42, 44, 46, 48, 50, 52, 54, 56, 64, 68, 86, 94, 97, 173, 174, 176, 177, 178, 181, 182, 184, 185, 187, 193, 196, 198, 199, 201, 204, 205, 212, 213, 214, 218, 220, 224, 227, 229, 239, 241, 243, 244, 245, 253, 256, 258, 259, 260, 261, 262, 263, 265, 266, 268, 271, 274, 277, 284, 295, 296, 297, 322, 324, 327, 329, 331, 342, 344, 348, 349, 351, 356, 362, 367
Future Skills 245, 250

G

Generative AI 3, 4, 9, 10, 20, 21, 22, 26, 27, 40, 45, 47, 50, 54, 61, 62, 63, 95, 106, 116, 134, 135, 136, 139, 203, 257, 258, 259, 261, 264, 269, 270, 271, 273, 286, 287, 321, 325, 357, 368
Generative Artificial Intelligence 26, 132, 133, 135, 249, 270, 273, 274

H

Higher Education 3, 4, 12, 13, 17, 20, 21, 22, 23, 68, 71, 72, 73, 74, 75, 76, 77, 80, 81, 82, 83, 87, 90, 92, 94, 96, 97, 98, 99, 100, 103, 104, 105, 106, 107, 108, 109, 110, 118, 119, 120, 121, 122, 123, 126, 128, 130, 131, 133, 134, 135, 136, 137, 138, 139, 157, 162, 164, 169, 170, 173, 175, 176, 177, 179, 180, 181, 182, 188, 193, 194, 196, 199, 200, 201, 203, 204, 205, 211, 212, 219, 220, 222, 223, 224, 249, 250, 252, 253, 254, 256, 257, 258, 261, 263, 266, 268, 269, 270, 271, 274, 275, 276, 277, 278, 283, 284, 286, 289, 290, 291, 293, 294, 296, 297, 298, 302, 303, 305, 306, 307, 312, 313, 315, 316, 318, 319, 320, 321, 322, 323, 324, 325, 327, 329, 330, 331, 336, 337, 339, 340, 344, 347, 351, 356, 357, 360, 363, 364, 365, 366, 367

I

Institutional Transformation 323, 324, 329, 337, 344, 356, 367

L

Learning Analytics 89, 97, 108, 113, 114, 120, 121, 122, 124, 131, 134, 150, 151, 157, 158, 167, 170, 173, 174, 182, 184, 189, 190, 213, 251, 320, 366

N

Next-Generation Learning Ecosystems 103, 104, 105, 106, 119

O

Open Remix 33, 34, 36

P

Pedagogical Innovation 55, 109, 177, 188, 192, 199, 204, 212, 266, 283, 326, 361
Pedagogical Integration 108, 323, 341, 344, 368
Personalized Learning 73, 74, 76, 85, 95, 101, 105, 120, 124, 125, 127, 147, 152, 158, 162, 163, 165, 167, 170, 177, 180, 187, 188, 190, 192, 196, 199, 200, 207, 211, 212, 221, 224, 225, 237, 239, 248, 250, 267, 289, 290, 293, 298, 299, 319, 321, 322
Personalized Professional Growth 227
Personalized Professional Learning 173, 186

Professional Growth 87, 122, 173, 176, 180, 193, 199, 204, 205, 227, 228, 229, 230, 232, 233, 234, 237, 241, 245, 323, 327

S

Social Science 1, 21, 222, 250, 320
Sociology 2, 3, 5, 7, 10, 11, 15, 17, 18, 19, 20, 21, 22, 23, 24, 25, 27, 28, 30
Sustainable Adoption 323, 325, 331, 340, 343, 344, 345, 347, 361, 367
Syllabus 5, 6, 11, 23, 27, 46, 59, 144, 145, 147, 150, 151, 156, 158, 168, 265

T

TILT 273, 274, 275, 276, 277, 278, 279, 281, 283, 284
Transparent Teaching 276, 282

www.ingramcontent.com/pod-product-compliance
Lightning Source LLC
LaVergne TN
LVHW062323300926
849161LV00007B/1546